Frontiers in Sociology of Education

Frontiers in Sociology and Social Research

Volume 1

Series Editor:

Howard B. Kaplan

Texas A&M University, College Station, USA

Frontiers of Sociology and Sociological Research publishes a series of edited volumes that will focus on new directions in (sub)specialties of sociology as these are reflected in novel theoretical paradigms, innovative methodologies, and contemporary substantive findings that exemplify and anticipate trends in these field. The volumes will parallel and complement the volumes in the *Handbooks of the Sociology and Social Research* series. *Frontiers of Sociology and Sociological Research* series begins where the *Handbooks* leave off by looking to the future. The series is predicated on the observation that any field of knowledge in contemporary times is a dynamic, rapidly changing body of perspectives and understanding that continuously builds upon the foundation of extant scholarship.

For further volumes:
http://www.springer.com/series/8690

Maureen T. Hallinan
Editor

Frontiers in Sociology of Education

Springer

Editor
Maureen T. Hallinan
Department of Sociology
University of Notre Dame
Notre Dame, Indiana
USA
mhallina@nd.edu

ISBN 978-94-007-1575-2   e-ISBN 978-94-007-1576-9
DOI 10.1007/978-94-007-1576-9
Springer Dordrecht Heidelberg London New York

Library of Congress Control Number: 2011933228

© Springer Science+Business Media B.V. 2011
No part of this work may be reproduced, stored in a retrieval system, or transmitted in any form or by any means, electronic, mechanical, photocopying, microfilming, recording or otherwise, without written permission from the Publisher, with the exception of any material supplied specifically for the purpose of being entered and executed on a computer system, for exclusive use by the purchaser of the work.

Printed on acid-free paper

Springer is part of Springer Science+Business Media (www.springer.com)

To Warren Kubitschek

Accomplished Sociologist

Generous Collaborator

Trusted Mentor

Faithful Friend

Foreword

When unsuspecting high-school students read the new bowdlerized edition of *Huckleberry Finn*, in which the word "slave" replaces the word "nigger," they might not be aware that someone in an official capacity has exchanged their possible discomfort in confronting a noxious word for missing one of the major points of the novel. An educational "effect," of a curricular nature and of as yet unknown magnitude, will have occurred.

During an investigation of schooling in the Chicago area, Rebecca Barr and I discovered that students in one of the nine fourth-grade math classes we observed showed very substantial achievement gains, considerably better than the other fourth-grade math class in the same working-class multi-ethnic school whose class composition and text were the same, and better than results obtained in a far more affluent suburb. We asked the teacher how she designed her instruction. She said she starts the year in the middle of the textbook where fourth-grade-level math starts. The first half of the book, she remarked, reviews third-grade math; why go through that when third-grade math is already incorporated in the fourth-grade materials? All the other teachers we studied started fourth-grade math instruction in January; she started in September.

In another case, the superintendent of the moderately affluent suburb noted above appointed a new coordinator of elementary reading instruction in the belief that first-grade reading achievement levels were too low. Her task was to introduce a new instructional program and enforce it—a bureaucratic and unpopular mandate. She introduced a demanding, eclectic, wide-ranging basal series with a high ceiling, and also increased substantially the time allocated to reading instruction. Learning improved markedly. So did her popularity. Students in the low-reading groups did notably better than those in some of the comparable middle and high groups in other schools whose reading programs were not as well designed.

What we have here are cases of educational change (and, by implication, absence of change) based upon prevailing ideas and practices. They draw attention to the supply side of educational organization, to what the educational system, at each level from the state to the classroom, makes available for the process of schooling: administrative decisions, curricular materials, teachers' knowledge and practices, time allocations. The supply side is critical. Since the mid-1960s, sociologists have overwhelmingly—though not entirely—treated the educational process in schools as a demand-side problem: preoccupations with individual aspiration and achievement and with equality of opportunity being apposite cases in point. They have been expressed in a large survey methodology that ascribes the characteristics of collectivities, usually schools, to individual students in analyses that resemble status attainment research, where individual achievement is the final outcome. This approach, which relies mainly on very large overall samples of students with very small samples from within schools, entirely appropriate for status attainment problems, does not adequately investigate schooling events that transpire at the levels of classrooms, grades, subject matters, and grade sequences, because these aspects of educational organization are not appropriately represented in the samples.

The supply side pertains to the provision of education, to forms of government action at all levels—federal, state, township, municipal. It also includes considerations that are not explicitly educational, but pertain to education (e.g., taxation and the definition of political boundaries that define the distribution of school populations). It includes the design, production, and distribution of curricular materials as well as their employment in classrooms. At issue is students' exposure to knowledge—what version of American history will they read in Texas, or edition of *Huckleberry Finn*? The supply side also encompasses not just the preparation of teachers, but the state of knowledge underlying teachers' work, which is a property of the occupation of teaching. It also refers to the governance and management of school systems, from the level of districts to small instructional groups.

The legacy of the status attainment approach to educational effects is the presumption that individual achievement is the most important outcome of educational efforts no matter what their origin, no matter where those efforts occur. A case in point is studies that examine the intended effects of school segregation and desegregation, at district and cross-district levels, without considering the considerations (conditions and practices) that intervene between the definition of a district's racial and ethnic composition and individual learning. In addition to the status attainment legacy, there is the common assumption that the school as a unitary entity is the key unit educational activity, and that if we "improve" or "reform" the school, not only will individual achievement improve, but so will the nation's educational standing among other nations. But this subordinates the significant variation in educational conditions and practices both within schools and outside of them.

In short, each level and segment of an educational system establishes conditions according to which other levels and segments operate. Which ones have a direct impact on individual learning is an empirical question, not one to be begged. And which ones exert an impact on how other components of the system operate, but without a necessary direct effect on learning? Consider the case of teacher training. The American system of teacher education is as decentralized and uneven as the public school system itself and does not integrate the preparation of teachers with a national curriculum. This is far different from countries with ministerial educational systems. It is of more than passing interest to know, then, how occupational knowledge is created, transmitted, and, at the end of the line, employed in classroom. As John Meyer has persuasively argued, it is clearly the case that schools and schooling, based upon age-segregated, physically distinct classrooms; separated from the family; arranged in a yearly curricular sequence; and employing textbook-based knowledge, have become internationally institutionalized. Yet, given the high degree of institutional and structural commonality, national differences of substantial magnitude exist.

We tend, however, to fixate on differences expressed as aggregated individual achievement, flagellate ourselves about the shortcomings, and then propose "remedies" premised on bad metaphors. What is missing is proper attention to the supply side, to the structure and working of educational systems in different societies, the forces impinging on them, their internal components, and the connections among those components. Among the key issues is national differences in the occupational knowledge of teachers and others engaged in the educational enterprise, what that knowledge is, and how it is both developed and imparted in training institutions and in work experience.

The great strength of this volume rests in the great variety and depth of its explorations into the supply side of the educational enterprise. In this country, we are prone to proposing apoplectic remedies for what we construe to be educational deficiencies based on dubious cross-national comparisons: the United States vs. Shanghai?! I read the contributions to this volume as explorations into the nature and workings of educational organizations broadly considered, which is exactly where the emphasis should be. Matters pertaining to individual achievement, where most of the past attention has been directed, of course continue to be significant. But there needs to be a shift in emphasis toward what I have called the supply side. If constructive changes are to emerge, their viability will depend on how we understand the enterprise to operate.

Attending to the supply side needs to include thinking about the contributions of sociology, which in an oddly self-referential way is part of the supply side: a source of ideas that bear on the educational enterprise. Sociology has had far more to say about education than its sister social sciences. Neither psychology nor economics has contributed much to the organizational and institutional sides of education, and apart from some excellent exceptions, political science has been largely silent. Historians, of course, have made large and important contributions, but it is not clear how many think of themselves as social scientists. Sociologists, as well as members of other fields, however, are academics; they write mostly for each other, not primarily for an audience of educational practitioners. Many of the ideas they generate are highly relevant to educational practice, and to that extent they reside on the supply side. But that assertion, however, may be only a conceit in light of the often frosty relations between academics and educational practitioners.

The generation of educational knowledge, both for the understanding of education and for its practice, remains high on the agenda of outstanding problems. What this volume has to say addresses key issues on that agenda.

University of Chicago   Robert Dreeben

Preface

An edited series in Sociology, entitled *Handbook of Sociology and Social Research*, was launched by Kluwer Academic/Plenum Publishers in 2000. Professor Howard Kaplan agreed to serve as editor of the series. In 2005, the Social Science division of Kluwer Academic/Plenum Publishers was taken over by Springer publishers. To date, 20 volumes in the *Handbook* series have been published and others are in the planning stage.

Since more than a decade has passed since the *Handbook* series was initiated, Springer publishers is updating the volumes as each book reaches its decade mark. In addition, Springer is inaugurating a related series entitled *Frontiers in Sociology* with Professor Kaplan again serving as the series editor.

The *Handbook* and *Frontiers* series have different though related aims. *Handbook* authors survey and evaluate the extant research in various subfields of sociology and enrich the best of these studies with their own current research. *Frontiers* authors will identify ongoing and anticipated societal problems that face social institutions as they evolve over time. Based on their particular sociological perspectives, authors will propose theoretically grounded and empirically rigorous studies designed to help provide solutions to these approaching societal problems. Some of the *Frontiers* volumes will represent the same subdisciplines that appear in the *Handbook*. In this way, the *Handbook* provides a foundation on which to build the research described in *Frontiers in Sociology*.

Frontiers in Sociology of Education is the first volume of the new *Frontiers* series. The aim of this volume is to encourage sociologists to initiate research that will assist academics, practitioners, and policymakers in solving problems not yet facing schools. By anticipating these kinds of problems and beginning to study them now, sociologists of education will have research findings available when educators and policymakers need them to guide their practice and policy decisions. The volume will provide educators with new insights, ideas, and empirical research to inform the decisions they must make to improve educational outcomes.

Frontiers in Sociology of Education follows an innovative plan. The first part of the book contains nine chapters, written by sociologists of education. In each chapter, authors anticipate social or institutional changes that will affect schools in the future.

They then propose research that would help educators understand how these societal changes are likely to influence educational outcomes. By beginning the proposed research now, researchers will be ready to share results with educators and policymakers when they are called on to guide school reform.

Part II of *Frontiers in Sociology of Education* consists of thirteen essays written by academics and specialists whose areas of expertise are other than sociology of education. These persons are national figures noteworthy for their deep interest in and concern about education. They contribute short reflections on contemporary education as they view it from their academic perspectives, experience, and training, and suggest research that sociologists of education should conduct to demonstrate how future social changes will affect schooling. The essays cover considerable breadth and depth and provide an interesting counterpoint to the chapters in Part I of the volume. They are designed to increase the likelihood that the substantive chapters in Part I and research by other sociologists of education are well grounded in what is both important and realistic, in terms of providing critical guidance to educational decision makers of the future.

When sociologists conduct research designed to link social change to schooling outcomes, the time lag between initiating an empirical research project and providing findings is such that many studies are not available when major education decisions must be made. The research and essays in *Frontiers in Sociology of Education* represent an invitation to reflect on forthcoming societal factors that will affect schooling and to inaugurate studies now in order to have results available when educators and policymakers need them.

It is of note that academics are seldom invited to report research findings in public forums, such as Congressional hearings and teacher conferences. This is because the choice of research topics and the availability of research findings are out of sync with the needs of policymakers. For example, little rigorous sociological research on teacher quality was available when school administrators were charged with evaluating teacher performance, as mandated by No Child Left Behind. By the time rigorous studies on teacher quality were available, public attitudes had already been shaped and educational policy decisions were made. As a result, ill-informed and ultimately unsuccessful policies were implemented that did little to advance school reform. Sociologists of education might be more deeply involved in shaping educational policy if their research focused on education issues of wide public concern and was available when needed by the education community.

Many individuals deserve gratitude for their contributions to this volume. I am grateful to Teresa Krauss at Springer for supporting the idea of the *Frontiers* series with enthusiasm and encouragement. I also thank Esther Otten who took over the supervision of the volume when Springer called upon Teresa to assume responsibility for the publisher's new behavioral and mental health program. Working with both series managers has been smooth and pleasant and led to a firm bond of friendship among us. Howard Kaplan deserves credit for contributing to the field of sociology by overseeing both the *Handbook* and the *Frontiers* series, making them available as bedrock references for the discipline. A number of people insured the high quality of the chapters and essays in the *Frontiers in Sociology of Education* by reviewing the submissions. While their names must remain confidential, I applaud their contributions and hope they realize how important a service they performed.

My trusted editor, Cheryl Pauley, managed correspondence and manuscript submission for the volume. In addition, she carefully read and edited each manuscript as it was shepherded from initial submission to final paper. As always, Cheryl performed these important but tedious and time-consuming tasks with patience, grace, and humor. The volume would not exist were it not for Cheryl's impressive editing skills, good judgment, and endless encouragement. I hope she knows the depth of my gratitude for her contributions.

Finally, I take great pleasure in acknowledging Warren Kubitschek's tireless assistance in reviewing manuscripts for this volume and for his long-standing and ongoing help and support at all points in the process of preparing the volume for publication. For these, and numerous other reasons, I proudly dedicate the *Frontiers in Sociology of Education* to him.

Maureen T. Hallinan

Contents

1 Improving the Interaction Between Sociological Research and Educational Policy 1
Maureen T. Hallinan

Part I Research Articles: Theoretical and Empirical Analyses of Schooling

2 The Future of the Schooled Society: The Transforming Culture of Education in Postindustrial Society 11
David P. Baker

3 Frontiers in Comparative and International Sociology of Education: American Distinctiveness and Global Diversity 35
Claudia Buchmann

4 Toward a Theory of the Political Construction of Empty Spaces in Public Education 53
Pamela Barnhouse Walters

5 Methodological Transactionalism and the Sociology of Education 87
Daniel A. McFarland, David Diehl, and Craig Rawlings

6 Designing Instruction and Grouping Students to Enhance the Learning of All: New Hope or False Promise? 111
Adam Gamoran

7 Getting Ideas into Action: Building Networked Improvement Communities in Education 127
Anthony S. Bryk, Louis M. Gomez, and Alicia Grunow

8 Improving Teacher Quality: A Sociological Presage 163
Barbara Schneider, Erin Grogan, and Adam Maier

| 9 | Perfectionist Dreams and Hidden Stratification: Is Perfection the Enemy of the Good? | 181 |

James E. Rosenbaum, Janet E. Rosenbaum, and Jennifer L. Stephan

| 10 | Changing Family, Changing Education | 205 |

Laura Hamilton, Regina Werum, Lala Carr Steelman, and Brian Powell

Part II Essays by Social Scientists and Educators

| 11 | Creating Our Future: Some Challenges for American Precollegiate Education | 227 |

George W. Bohrnstedt

| 12 | Some Potential Contributions of Social Psychology to Public Education in the Face of the Current Disinvestment in Education | 235 |

Karen S. Cook

| 13 | From Data to Actionable Evidence: How Sociologists Can Drive School Reform | 241 |

Paul Goren and Emily Krone

| 14 | Grasping the Past to Inform the Present | 245 |

Patricia Albjerg Graham

| 15 | Reforming General Education and Diffusing Reform | 251 |

Daniel J. Myers

| 16 | The Rise and Fall of Civic Education in American Schools | 257 |

Sandra Day O'Connor

| 17 | Improving Grades: Urban Public Schools, Racial and Socioeconomic Segregation, and the Promise of Innovation | 265 |

James M. Quane and William Julius Wilson

| 18 | Policymaking and Research | 273 |

Diane Ravitch

| 19 | Sociology for the Future Historian | 277 |

William Reese

| 20 | How the Sociology of Education Can Help Us Better Understand Religion and Morality | 281 |

Christian Smith

| 21 | Thoughts on Reform and the Sociology of Education: Toward Active Engagement | 285 |

Marshall S. Smith

22	**How Would We Know If Public Colleges and Universities Are Productive?**..	297
	Teresa A. Sullivan	
23	**Hispanics and US Schools: Problems, Puzzles, and Possibilities**........	303
	Marta Tienda	

Index.. 311

Contributors

David P. Baker Penn State University, University Park, PA 16802-3203, USA

George W. Bohrnstedt American Institutes for Research, Washington, DC 20007, USA

Anthony S. Bryk Carnegie Foundation for the Advancement of Teaching, Stanford, CA 94305, USA

Claudia Buchmann Department of Sociology, The Ohio State University, Columbus, OH 43210, USA

Karen S. Cook Department of Sociology, Stanford University, Stanford, CA 94305-2047, USA

David Diehl School of Education, Stanford University, Stanford, CA 94305-3084, USA

Robert Dreeben Professor Emeritus, University of Chicago, Evanston, IL 60202-1317, USA

Adam Gamoran Department of Sociology, University of Wisconsin, Madison, WI 53706, USA

Louis M. Gomez School of Education, University of Pittsburgh, Pittsburgh, PA 15260, USA

Paul Goren Consortium on Chicago School Research, University of Chicago Urban Education Institute, Chicago, IL 60637, USA

Patricia Albjerg Graham Harvard Graduate School of Education, Harvard University, Cambridge, MA 02138, USA

Erin Grogan The New Teacher Project, Keene, NH 03431, USA

Alicia Grunow Carnegie Foundation for the Advancement of Teaching, Stanford, CA 94305, USA

Maureen T. Hallinan Department of Sociology, University of Notre Dame, Notre Dame, IN 46556, USA

Laura Hamilton School of Social Sciences, Humanities and Arts, University of California-Merced, Merced, CA 95343, USA

Emily Krone Consortium on Chicago School Research, University of Chicago Urban Education Institute, Chicago, IL 60637, USA

Adam Maier The New Teacher Project, Rochester Hills, MI 48307, USA

Daniel A. McFarland School of Education, Stanford University, Stanford, CA 94305-3084, USA

Daniel J. Myers Department of Sociology, University of Notre Dame, Notre Dame, IN 46556, USA

Sandra Day O'Connor Supreme Court of the United States, Washington, DC 20543, USA

Brian Powell Indiana University, Bloomington, IN 47405, USA

James M. Quane John F. Kennedy School of Government, Harvard University, Cambridge, MA 02138, USA

Diane Ravitch New York University, Southold, NY 11971, USA

Craig Rawlings School of Education, Stanford University, Stanford, CA 94305-3084, USA

William Reese History of Education, University of Wisconsin, Madison, WI 53706, USA

James E. Rosenbaum Institute for Policy Research, Northwestern University, Evanston, IL 60208, USA

Janet E. Rosenbaum University of Maryland Population Center, University of Maryland, College Park, MD 20742, USA

Barbara Schneider College of Education, Michigan State University, East Lansing, MI 48824, USA

Christian Smith Department of Sociology, University of Notre Dame, Notre Dame, IN 46556, USA

Marshall S. Smith Carnegie Foundation for the Advancement of Teaching, Stanford, CA 94305, USA

Lala Carr Steelman Department of Sociology, University of South Carolina, Columbia, SC 29208, USA

Jennifer L. Stephan Institute for Policy Research, Northwestern University, Evanston, IL 60208, USA

Teresa A. Sullivan University of Virginia, Charlottesville, VA 22904, USA

Marta Tienda Office of Population Research, Princeton University, Princeton, NJ 08544, USA

Pamela Barnhouse Walters Department of Sociology, Indiana University, Bloomington, IN 47405, USA

Regina Werum Department of Sociology, Emory University, Atlanta, GA 30322, USA

William Julius Wilson John F. Kennedy School of Government, Harvard University, Cambridge, MA 02138, USA

Author Biographies

David P. Baker is Professor of Education and Sociology at the Population Research Institute and the Center for the Study of Higher Education at the Pennsylvania State University, where he directs a research program on education's impact on globalization and international trends. He is a principal investigator of a National Science Foundation–funded multidisciplinary research project on understanding the effect of education on population health, including the HIV/AIDS pandemic in sub-Saharan Africa and the Peruvian highlands. His social science research has encompassed over 60 nations worldwide and has been reported in over 50 scientific journal articles, and his most recent book is *National Differences, Global Similarities: World Culture and the Future of Schooling* (Stanford University Press).

George W. Bohrnstedt is Senior Vice President for Research Emeritus at the American Institutes for Research (AIR), to which he brings a deep interest in education research and policy issues. Bohrnstedt currently chairs the National Center for Education Statistics' NAEP Validity Studies Panel, is principal investigator of the NCES-funded State NAEP (National Assessment of Educational Progress) contract, as well as the principal investigator of the evaluation of the Say Yes Foundation's reform effort in Syracuse City Public Schools. Formerly, Bohrnstedt was the principal investigator of a grant from the Bill and Melinda Gates Foundation to evaluate their initiative to create small, personalized high schools and the co-principal investigator of the evaluation of California's K-3 Class Size Reduction program. Bohrnstedt has been honored as a Belding Scholar at the Foundation for Child Development, an Inaugural Fellow in the American Education Research Association, and a Fellow at Stanford's Center for Advanced Studies in the Behavioral Sciences.

Anthony S. Bryk is the ninth President of the Carnegie Foundation for the Advancement of Teaching. He held the Spencer Chair in Organizational Studies in the School of Education and the Graduate School of Business at Stanford University from 2004 until assuming Carnegie's presidency in September 2008. Prior to Stanford, he held the Marshall Field IV Professor of Education post in the Sociology Department at the University of Chicago, where he founded the Center for Urban School Improvement which supports reform efforts in the Chicago Public Schools.

Bryk also founded the Consortium on Chicago School Research which has produced a range of studies to advance and assess urban school reform. In addition, he has made contributions to the development of new statistical methods in educational research. His major books include *Hierarchical Linear Models*, *Catholic Schools for the Common Good*, *Trust in Schools*, and *Organizing Schools for Improvement*.

Claudia Buchmann is a Professor in the Department of Sociology at the Ohio State University. After receiving her Ph.D. from Indiana University in 1996, Buchmann taught at Duke University before moving to Ohio State in 2004. She studies the topics of stratification and education in the United States and internationally. Buchmann's recent research has focused on gender, race, and class inequalities in education. Articles with Thomas A. DiPrete (Columbia University) in the *American Sociological Review*, *Demography*, and the *Annual Review of Sociology* examine the sources of the growing female advantage in college completion. In an article in *Social Forces*, she and coauthors investigated race and class inequalities in access to SAT test preparation and the impact of these inequalities on SAT scores and subsequent college admission. Professor Buchmann is deputy editor of the *American Sociological Review* and past chair of the Sociology of Education Section of the American Sociological Association.

Karen S. Cook is Ray Lyman Wilbur Professor of Sociology and Director of the Institute for Research in the Social Sciences (IRiSS) at Stanford. She conducts research on social interaction, social networks, and trust. She has edited a number of books in the Russell Sage Foundation Trust Series that she coedits with M. Levi and R. Hardin, including *Trust in Society* (2001); *Trust and Distrust in Organizations: Emerging Perspectives* (with R. Kramer, 2004); *eTrust: Forming Relations in the Online World* (with C. Snijders, V. Buskens, and Coye Cheshire, 2009); and *Whom Can You Trust?* (with M. Levi and R. Hardin, 2009). She is coauthor of *Cooperation without Trust?* (with R. Hardin and M. Levi, 2005), and she coedited *Sociological Perspectives on Social Psychology* (with Gary Alan Fine and James S. House, 1995). In 1996, she was elected to the American Academy of Arts and Sciences and, in 2007, to the National Academy of Sciences. In 2004, she received the ASA Social Psychology Section Cooley Mead Award for Career Contributions to Social Psychology.

David Diehl is a doctoral student in the Sociology of Education at Stanford University. His research focuses primarily on understanding the mechanisms through which actors and organizations collectively make meaning and order within heterogeneous social settings. Drawing primarily on organizational theory, social network analysis, and microinteraction, David tries to theoretically and empirically understand such social processes both in the immediate contexts of face-to-face interaction as well as within the longer-term processes of organizational change. His work has been published in the *American Journal of Sociology*.

Robert Dreeben is Professor Emeritus at the University of Chicago, former chair of the Department of Education, and chair of the Sociology of Education Section of the American Sociological Association (ASA). His work has focused on school organization and the processes of schooling, with emphasis on instruction, curriculum, and stratification; it has also treated the comparison of occupations and the nature of their work, with attention to teaching. Publications include *On What Is Learned in School* (1968); "American Schooling: Patterns and Processes of Stability and Change" (1971); "The School as a Workplace" (1973); *How Schools Work* (1983, coauthor Rebecca Barr); "The Sociology of Education: Its Development in the United States" (1994, received the Willard Waller Award from the ASA); and "Teaching and the Competence of Occupations" (2005).

Adam Gamoran is John D. MacArthur Professor of Sociology and Educational Policy Studies and Director of the Wisconsin Center for Education Research at the University of Wisconsin–Madison. His research focuses on inequality in education and school reform. Current studies include a large-scale randomized trial that examines the impact of a multifamily after-school intervention designed to promote social capital and child development in elementary schools in Phoenix, Arizona, and San Antonio, Texas. Among his recent publications are two edited volumes: *Standards-Based Reform and the Poverty Gap: Lessons for No Child Left Behind* (Brookings Institution Press, 2007) and, with Yossi Shavit and Richard Arum, *Stratification in Higher Education: A Comparative Study* (Stanford University Press, 2007).

Louis M. Gomez is Helen Faison Professor of Urban Education at The University of Pittsburgh, senior scientist at the Learning Research and Development Center (LRDC), and the first executive director of the University's Center for Urban Education. Professor Gomez is also currently serving as a senior partner at the Carnegie Foundation for the Advancement of Teaching. His scholarship focuses on understanding how to support organizational change in schools and other institutions. Along with his colleagues, Professor Gomez has been dedicated to collaborative research and development with urban communities to bring the current state of the art in instruction and support for community formation to traditionally underserved schools. Most recently, Professor Gomez has turned his attention to problem-solving research and development. This is R&D organized around high-leverage problems embedded in the day-to-day work of teaching and learning and the institutions in which these activities occur.

Paul Goren is Lewis-Sebring Director of the Consortium on Chicago School Research at the University of Chicago Urban Education Institute. Goren served as senior vice president of The Spencer Foundation from 2001 to 2010 and as executive director of the Spencer Forum, focusing on the dissemination of research to the policy and practice communities. Previously, Goren was the director of Child and Youth Development at the John D. and Catherine T. MacArthur Foundation and education director at the National Governors Association (NGA). A former middle-school teacher, he worked as executive director (assistant superintendent) for Policy and Strategic Services in the Minneapolis Public Schools from 1995 to 1998 and as a policy analyst and educational researcher in the San Diego City Schools in the mid-1980s. Goren has written on professional development and public engagement for the NGA, served as the chief accountability officer in the Minneapolis schools where he helped develop capacity for data-driven decision making, and led the Spencer

Foundation's efforts to disseminate studies and findings to multiple audiences. His writing includes commentaries for the National Society for the Study of Education yearbook on *Developing the Teacher Workforce,* and for *Education Week* on the relationship of foundations and philanthropy to school districts. He received the Ian Axford (New Zealand) fellowship in public policy through Fulbright New Zealand to study Maori education policy where he published "How Policy Travels: Making Sense of Ka-Hikitia-Managing Success, the Maori Education System 2008–2012.

Patricia Albjerg Graham is Charles Warren Professor of the History of Education Emerita at Harvard. She received her B.S. and M.S. from Purdue University and her Ph.D. from Columbia University. Graham has received a John Simon Guggenheim Foundation fellowship, a Woodrow Wilson fellowship, and a Radcliffe Institute fellowship. Her books include *Progressive Education: From Arcady to Academe; Community and Class in American Education; Women in Higher Education; S.O.S.: Sustain Our Schools*; and *Schooling America.* Formerly, she was director of the National Institute of Education (1977–1979), dean of the Harvard Graduate School of Education (1982–1991), and president of the Spencer Foundation (1991–2000).

Erin Grogan (Ph.D., Michigan State University) is a Senior Research Associate with The New Teacher Project. Broadly, her research focuses on teacher recruitment, selection, and retention, with particular interest in how teacher effectiveness is operationalized and measured at each of these phases. In her current role, she is involved in the development and implementation of a comprehensive evaluation system for early career teachers. Additional projects include an exploration of how measures collected during selection and preservice training relate to teacher effectiveness, as well as research regarding the antecedents of teacher self-evaluations of effectiveness at raising student achievement.

Alicia Grunow is Associate Partner at the Carnegie Foundation for the Advancement of Teaching. In that capacity, she leads efforts to explore and adapt the tools of improvement research to support practice improvement in education. She is playing a lead role in the Foundation's emergent program of work focused on the retention and support of effective early career teachers. Grunow's professional background has afforded her with an unusual combination of practical experience in the development of teachers and technical skills in statistical analysis. For the past 4 years, she has worked as an instructor in Stanford's Teacher Education Program (STEP), teaching classes on practices to support the academic achievement of English Language Learners. During that time, she also has worked on a variety of research projects, largely focused on the educational experiences of English Language Learners. Grunow currently is finishing her Master's in Economics and Doctorate in Administration and Policy Analysis at Stanford University. Before coming to Stanford, she taught for 7 years in Denver and New York City.

Maureen T. Hallinan is William P. and Hazel B. White Professor of Sociology in the Center for Research on Educational Opportunity, Institute for Educational Initiatives, at the University of Notre Dame. Her research interests include the effects of the formal and informal organization of schools on students' cognitive and social development. She presently is examining sector effects on student achievement. With over 120 articles in professional journals, Professor Hallinan is the author or editor of eight books and has chapters in several edited volumes. She is former editor of *Sociology of Education*, and is past president of the American Sociological Association and the Sociological Research Association and a vice president of the National Academy of Education. She is a recipient of the Willard Waller Award from the American Sociological Association, Notre Dame's Presidential Award, and the Award for Excellence in Research on Catholic Education.

Laura Hamilton is an assistant professor at the University of California-Merced. Her mixed-method dissertation asked whether or not parental investments during college translate into the educational and career gains predicted by sociologists. Her other work explores parental investments in adoptive youth (see Hamilton, Cheng, and Powell's "Adoptive parents, adaptive parents: Evaluating the importance of biological ties for parental investment" in *American Sociological Review*); the intersection of gender, class, sexuality, and school organization among college students (see Hamilton and Armstrong's "Gendered sexuality in young adulthood: Double binds and flawed options" in *Gender & Society*); and strategies for capturing contemporary gender attitudes (see Hamilton, Geist, and Powell's "Marital name change as a window into gender attitudes" in *Gender & Society*).

Emily Krone is Associate Director for Communications at the Consortium on Chicago School Research (CCSR) at the University of Chicago Urban Education Institute. She previously worked as senior education and immigration reporter at the *Daily Herald*, the third-largest daily newspaper in Illinois. She has written extensively on school accountability, charter schools, urban school reform, school finance, teacher evaluation, and civil rights issues in education. She received a Master's in Science and Journalism from Medill at Northwestern University and a B.A. in History from Princeton University.

Adam Maier is a former graduate student of Education Policy in the College of Education at Michigan State University. His research interests focus on the connection between education and work, with an emphasis on credentialing theory. In particular, his research has concentrated on teacher labor markets, including the role of teacher preparation programs, as well as the effects of the timing of teacher hiring on turnover. He currently teaches mathematics at University Liggett School in Grosse Pointe Woods, Michigan.

Daniel A. McFarland is Associate Professor in the School of Education at Stanford University and has courtesy appointments in Sociology and Organizational Behavior. His research focuses on social network theory and methods, and he applies those approaches to the study of educational settings such as classrooms, schools, universities, and scientific disciplines. In addition, he is involved in multiple NSF projects concerning social network dynamics and the study of scientific innovation. Dan has published in the *American Journal of Sociology, American Sociological Review, Sociology of Education, Social Psychology Quarterly, Social Science Research, Teachers College Record*, and a variety of computer science conference proceedings.

Daniel J. Myers is Professor of Sociology and Associate Dean for Research and the Social Sciences at the University of Notre Dame. His current research examines racial rioting in the 1960s and 1970s; deterministic and stochastic models of diffusion for collective violence; mathematical models of collective action; media coverage of protests, demonstrations, and riots; and game-theoretic analyses of small group negotiation. He currently is leading a comprehensive reassessment of US race-related rioting in the 1960s, funded by two grants from the National Science Foundation. He has published six books including *Toward a More Perfect Union: The Governance of Metropolitan America* (with Ralph Conant), *Social Psychology* (with John DeLamater), and *Identity Work in Social Movements* (with Jo Regger and Rachel Einwohner).

Sandra Day O'Connor (Retired), Associate Justice, was born in El Paso, Texas, March 26, 1930. She married John Jay O'Connor III in 1952 and has three sons—Scott, Brian, and Jay. She received her B.A. and LL.B. from Stanford University. She served as Deputy County Attorney of San Mateo County, California, from 1952 to 1953 and as a civilian attorney for Quartermaster Market Center, Frankfurt, Germany, from 1954 to 1957. From 1958 to 1960, she practiced law in Maryvale, Arizona, and served as Assistant Attorney General of Arizona from 1965 to 1969. She was appointed to the Arizona State Senate in 1969 and was subsequently reelected to two 2-year terms. In 1975, she was elected Judge of the Maricopa County Superior Court and served until 1979, when she was appointed to the Arizona Court of Appeals. President Reagan nominated her as an Associate Justice of the Supreme Court, and she took her seat September 25, 1981. Justice O'Connor retired from the Supreme Court on January 31, 2006.

Brian Powell is James H. Rudy Professor of Sociology at Indiana University. Recent work, which has appeared in *Social Forces*, *American Journal of Sociology*, and *American Sociological Review*, explores parental educational investments to children among several increasingly visible groups of atypical family forms—families with older parents, bi/multiracial families, and adoptive families. His book (coauthored with Catherine Bolzendahl, Claudia Geist, and Lala Carr Steelman), *Counted Out: Same-Sex Relations and Americans' Definitions of Family* (Russell Sage Foundation/American Sociological Association Rose Series, 2010), examines the boundaries that Americans draw between families and nonfamilies and how people are making sense of changes in living arrangements in the United States. He currently is investigating Americans' views regarding the value of a college degree and the roles that parents, students, and the government should assume in the funding of colleges.

James M. Quane is Associate Director of the Joblessness and Urban Poverty Research Program at Harvard University's John F. Kennedy School of Government. His main research interests include the study of concentrated poverty, especially as it relates to the impact on youth in disadvantaged neighborhoods. Recently, he participated in a longitudinal study of the impact of welfare reform on low-income families in three major US cities. His recent publications considered the impact of the reforms on the work and family lives of low-income caregivers, among other things. In earlier publications, Quane wrote about the effects of social and physical isolation on youth in high-poverty neighborhoods, as well as the role of after-school programs in contributing to the prosocial development of urban youth. His work has appeared in *Family Relations, Social Problems, Social Forces*, and *Social Services Review*, as well as in other professional journals and edited volumes.

Diane Ravitch is Research Professor of Education at New York University. She is a historian of education and the author of many books, including *The Great School Wars: New York City, 1805–1973* (1974); *The Troubled Crusade: American Education, 1945–1980* (1983); *Left Back: A Century of Battles Over School Reform* (2000); *The Language Police: How Pressure Groups Restrict What Students Learn* (2003); and *The Death and Life of the Great American School System: How Testing and Choice Are Undermining Education* (2010). She served as Assistant Secretary of Education in charge of the Office of Educational Research and Improvement from 1991 to 1993 and was a member of the National Assessment Governing Board from 1997 to 2004.

Craig Rawlings is a Postdoctoral Research Fellow at Stanford University's Center for Education Policy Analysis. He received his Ph.D. in Sociology from the University of California, Santa Barbara. He studies social networks in complex organizational environments, the causes and consequences of organizational differentiation, and issues concerning meaning and measurement.

William Reese is Carl F. Kaestle WARF Professor of Educational Policy Studies and History at the University of Wisconsin–Madison. He teaches courses at the undergraduate and graduate levels on the history of American education and the history of childhood and adolescence. Recent books include *America's Public Schools: From the Common School to 'No Child Left Behind'* (2005; expanded edition, 2011); *History, Education, and the Schools* (2007); and a coedited volume entitled *Rethinking the History of American Education* (2008). Former editor of the *History of Education Quarterly*, he is a member of the National Academy of Education and a Fellow of the American Educational Research Association.

James E. Rosenbaum is Professor of Sociology, Education, and Social Policy at Northwestern University. His books include *Crossing the Class and Color Lines* (University of Chicago Press, 2000) and *Beyond College for All* (Russell Sage Foundation, 2001), which was awarded the Waller Prize in Sociology. His book, *After Admission: From College Access to College Success*, was published in 2006, with coauthors Regina Deil-Amen and Ann Person. He is an advisor to *Education Week*; the National Assessment of Career and Technical Education; New Community College, CUNY; and CWICstats Advisory Council, NORC. His most recent research showed the positive impact of a college coach program in Chicago Public Schools, which led to expansion of the program.

Janet E. Rosenbaum is Assistant Professor at the University of Maryland School of Public Health. She studies the role of economic and educational factors in adolescent women's sexual decisions, health risk behaviors among community college students, and the accuracy of self-reported risk behavior. Her work has been published in *Pediatrics*, the *American Journal of Public Health*, the *American Journal of Epidemiology*, and the journal *Science*. She earned a Ph.D. in health policy and statistics, an M.A. in statistics, and a B.A. in physics, all from Harvard University, and completed a postdoctoral fellowship in sexually transmitted infections at the Johns Hopkins Bloomberg School of Public Health. Her dissertation studied adolescent survey report inconsistency and the role of religion and virginity pledges in adolescent sexual decision making, using causal inference models and matched sampling.

Barbara Schneider is John A. Hannah Distinguished Professor in the College of Education and Department of Sociology at Michigan State University. Author of multiple publications, Schneider's research focuses primarily on the social context of families and schools and their relationship to adolescent development. She currently directs a major study examining how public schools can assist low-income minority students access and persist in postsecondary education. Additionally, she is also a principal investigator of a policy study examining the impact of curricular change on student high-school graduation and college attendance. Two of her most recent books are *Estimating Causal Effects Using Experimental and Observational Designs* and *Being Together Working Apart: Dual Career Families and the Work-Life Balance*.

Christian Smith is William R. Kenan, Jr. Professor of Sociology at the University of Notre Dame, director of the Center for the Study of Religion and Society, director of the Notre Dame Center for Social Research, principal investigator of the National Study of Youth and Religion, and principal investigator of the Science of Generosity Initiative. Prior to working for Notre Dame, Smith worked at the University of North Carolina at Chapel Hill from 1994 to 2006, where he served as associate chair of the Department of Sociology from 2000 to 2005. Smith holds an M.A. (1987) and Ph.D. (1990) in Sociology from Harvard University. Smith's B.A. is in Sociology (1983), from Gordon College, Wenham, Massachusetts. Before moving to UNC Chapel Hill in 1994, Smith taught for 6 years at Gordon College. Smith is the author, coauthor, or editor of numerous journal articles and books, including *Souls in Transition: The Religious and Spiritual Lives of American Emerging Adults*. Smith's scholarly interests focus on adolescents and emerging adults, American religion, cultural sociology, generosity, and sociological theory.

Marshall S. Smith is retired and a Visiting Resident Scholar at the Carnegie Foundation for the Advancement of Teaching. His most recent full-time job was as the Senior Counselor to US Secretary of Education, Arne Duncan, and Director, Office of International Affairs, US Department of Education. Earlier, Dr. Smith was the Program Director for Education at The William and Flora Hewlett Foundation. In the Clinton administration, he was the Undersecretary and the Acting Deputy

Secretary of Education and, under President Carter, the Assistant Commissioner of Policy Studies in Education and the first Chief of Staff for the first Secretary of Education. Smith has been a Fellow at the Center for Advanced Study in the Behavioral Sciences and has been recognized for his contributions in several ways. He also has been an associate professor at Harvard, a professor and director of the Center on Education Research at the University of Wisconsin–Madison, and a professor and the dean of the School of Education at Stanford University. He has published over 100 books, articles, and chapters on educational issues of policy and practice, technology, social mobility, early childhood, evaluation, and methodology and currently serves as a consultant or board member for various organizations.

Lala Carr Steelman is Professor and Chair of the Sociology Department at the University of South Carolina, Columbia. She studies the link between the family and educational development and opportunities. Her research interests usually focus on the link between family and education. She began her career with publications on the impact of the sibling group on individual achievement, and this interest later expanded to include an emphasis on the types of resources children acquire from their family and eventual educational success. Her research also has focused on the usage and effect of early ability grouping for instruction on young children. Most recently, she coauthored the book *Counted Out: Same-Sex Relations and Americans' Definitions of Family*

Jennifer L. Stephan is a Postdoctoral Research Fellow in the Institute for Policy Research at Northwestern University, where she received her Ph.D. in Human Development and Social Policy. Her dissertation research, for which she received a dissertation fellowship from the Spencer Foundation, focused on college choice for low-income urban high-school students. Currently, she studies issues of college access and success for disadvantaged students. More broadly, she is interested in how schools, programs, and policies reduce or reinforce social stratification in postsecondary outcomes.

Teresa A. Sullivan is President of the University of Virginia, where she is also the George M. Kaufman Presidential Professor of Sociology. She previously served as Provost of the University of Michigan in Ann Arbor and before that, as Executive Vice Chancellor for Academic Affairs of the University of Texas System. Trained as a social demographer, she was for many years a member of the faculty of the Department of Sociology at The University of Texas at Austin. She is the chair of a panel of the National Research Council on measuring higher education productivity. She earned her Ph.D. in Sociology at the University of Chicago.

Marta Tienda is Maurice P. During '22 Professor of Demographic Studies and Professor of Sociology and Public Affairs at Princeton University. Her research addresses various aspects of racial and ethnic stratification, including poverty and immigration. She recently completed a decade-long study on equity and access to postsecondary education in Texas. Currently, she is spearheading a multination study of child migration and another on immigration of the elderly to the United States. She is coauthor or coeditor of numerous papers and several books, including

Africa on the Move: African Migration and Urbanisation in Comparative Perspective (Wits University Press, 2006); *Multiple Origins, Uncertain Destinies: Hispanics and the American Future* (National Academy Press, 2006); *Ethnicity and Causal Mechanisms* (Cambridge, 2005); *Youth in Cities* (Cambridge, 2002); *The Color of Opportunity* (Chicago, 2001); *The Hispanic Population of the United States* (Russell Sage, 1987); *Divided Opportunities* (Plenum, 1988); and *Hispanics and the U.S. Economy* (Academic, 1985).

Pamela Barnhouse Walters, James H. Rudy Professor of Sociology at Indiana University, Bloomington, has spent her career studying social inequality in American education. She particularly is interested in the tensions between the role of education as one of the most important forms of state social provision in modern societies—a social right, an entitlement that follows from citizenship—and the ways in which education reproduces and legitimates existing social inequalities. More specifically, in her current research she is studying the political processes that have created new forms of racial segregation and inequality in contemporary American education and the policy debates over the meaning of educational equality in post–Civil Rights America. She is the former editor of *Sociology of Education*, the recipient of numerous grants from the Spencer Foundation and the NSF, and the recipient of fellowships from the Spencer Foundation, the Guggenheim Foundation, the Rockefeller Foundation, and the Center for Advanced Study in the Behavioral Sciences.

Regina Werum is Associate Professor of Sociology at Emory University in Atlanta. She currently serves as program director for sociology at the National Science Foundation. Her main areas of interest focus on sociology of education, social stratification, political sociology, and social movements. Within these fields, she particularly is interested in longitudinal and cross-national trends. She has current and forthcoming publications in journals such as the *American Journal of Education* and *Mobilization* and in the book *After the Bell: Family Background and Educational Success* (Dalton Conley and Karen Albright, eds.).

William Julius Wilson is Lewis P. and Linda L. Geyser University Professor at Harvard University. His major areas of study are poverty, inner-city school to work transition, racial tensions in urban neighborhoods, and the effects of poor neighborhoods on the social outcomes of adolescents. His current research focuses on the increasing concentration of poverty in many large central cities. Recent studies he directed in Chicago examined this "new urban poverty" from a broad perspective that considers the causative role of macroeconomic conditions, culture, social welfare policy, and historical circumstances. His research also addresses the impact of inequality and poverty concentration on racial and ethnic relations, family structure, and joblessness, as well as the role of public policies in both alleviating and exacerbating these problems. Wilson's publications include *The Declining Significance of Race, The Truly Disadvantaged, When Work Disappears,* and *There Goes the Neighborhood.* His most recent book is *More than Just Race: Being Black and Poor in the Inner City.*

Chapter 1
Improving the Interaction Between Sociological Research and Educational Policy

Maureen T. Hallinan

Sociologists have conducted numerous scholarly analyses of education and its impact on society. Many early studies, especially those by sociologists of education, are models of insight into the dynamics of social institutions. These researchers (e.g., Bidwell 1965; Coleman 1961, 1988, 1990; Dreeben 1968; Durkheim 1961; Kerckhoff 1976, 1993; Meyer 1977; Weber 1978) formulated powerful middle-range theories which laid the foundation for current analyses of schools. What was absent from this early research was rigorous empirical tests of these theories.

Contemporary sociologists of education have available methods and statistics to test various conceptualizations of schooling (e.g., Bryk et al. 1993; Entwisle and Alexander 1994; Jencks and Phillips 1998). New methods of gathering observational and experimental data and advances in collecting large longitudinal surveys improve the quality of empirical data, while new statistical models enable rigorous analyses of these data.

Given this history, one might expect that contemporary research on schools would exhibit both theoretical strength and analytical rigor. Arguably, this is not the case. For various reasons, current school studies seem to be conceptually shallow and empirically incremental. Few recent studies have made a major contribution to our understanding of the role of today's schools in a rapidly changing global society. processes nor leads to policies that effectively promote student learning.

If future research in the sociology of education is to be more effective, a different, more enlightened, and practical approach to studying schools is required. Since US federal and state governments have become more proactive in mandating school reforms, sociologists of education need to provide the findings of theoretical and

M.T. Hallinan (✉)
Department of Sociology, University of Notre Dame,
Notre Dame, IN 46556, USA
e-mail: mhallina@nd.edu

empirical studies that will help educators make wise educational decisions. To attain this goal, sociologists of education must conduct theoretically rich research that identifies mechanisms that link exogenous and endogenous factors to student outcomes. Further, studies need to be empirically rigorous for educators to consider the results sufficiently valid to support widespread school reform efforts.

Frontiers in Sociology of Education calls for a bold new strategy for conducting research in the sociology of education. To insure that the field is making landmark contributions to the study of schools, researchers must initiate projects like those described in the chapters and essays in this volume. The authors and essayists take into account social, political, economic, and religious factors, that comprise the rapidly and radically cschools from their disciplinary perspectives, the essayists communicate a sense of urgency aimed at motivating sociologists of education to undertake research that will inform policymakers in the near future. Chapter authors identify macro- and micro-level societal changes that are occurring presently and whose impact on schools is expected to be felt in the next few years.

Understanding contemporary societal factors that are expected to affect schools in the future requires sociologists of education to develop an ongoing, systematic program of research that will inform educators and policymakers when they face decisions about ways to improve student learning. Anticipating the effects of these societal factors on schools allows researchers to select their research projects judiciously. Doing so can be expected to shrink the gap between the availability of research findings and educators' need for such findings.

Societal factors include the following:

- *Globalization*: A global perspective is critical to an understanding of the educational process. Current world events dramatically illustrate the interconnectedness of contemporary society. They allow us to see, for example, whether a country's characteristics, such as its professional and social networks, stratification system, or labor market, affect students' opportunities to learn. Awareness of the implications of globalization for education should lead to the formulation of new questions about the role of schools in fostering the cognitive, social, and behavioral dimensions of student learning and the preparation of students for participation in civic society. Global consciousness also underscores the heightened importance of cross-national research on schooling.

  In Chap. 2 of *Frontiers*, Baker describes the current state of education as an outcome of an education revolution. He points out that the evolution of the institution of education has radically changed all aspects of society, including the role of education. Theory and empirical studies lead him to believe that education is on the verge of dominating and transforming global society. For this reason, he argues that sociologists of education must work toward understanding the educational implications of this transformation.

- *Educational access and comparative studies*: Access to education is a transformative factor in globalization. In addition to the United States, other developed nations, such as England and Israel, have a high degree of educational access. The increased availability of schooling, from preschool through higher education, makes these nations more competitive in the global job market. Nevertheless, as educational access increases, class-based inequalities in a society seem to decrease (Boudon 1974; Mare 1981). Comparative analysis of developed nations is necessary to identify factors that affect inequalities in nations with expanded opportunities for schooling. Sociologists of education could make a significant contribution to the outcome of these processes by identifying the mechanisms that link access and opportunity. In doing so, they will contribute to the economic stability of individual countries and the world community.

In Chap. 3, Buchmann warns sociologists of education against a strictly nationalistic perspective in studying schools. Past studies of US schools have produced a body of useful information about how these schools operate and how we can improve educational outcomes. At the same time, this narrow focus constrains theoretical development, and precludes sharpening outcomes through comparison with the educational systems of other countries. Buchmann encourages sociologists to conduct more comparative studies to better identify the mechanisms that explain educational outcomes generated by greater access to education.

- *Political influences on education*: Most studies by sociologists of education are concerned with individual level determinants of educational achievement and attainment. Yet, one of the factors that explain schooling processes is the political context that leads to school characteristics and outcomes. In the past, little attention was given to the way politics affect school policy and practice. Obvious exceptions, of course, are studies of desegregation and more recently, charter schools, vouchers, and school prayer.

In Chap. 4, Walters challenges this limited perspective on schooling. She considers more basic issues about schools, such as why schools are structured the way they are, who chooses the curriculum and to what end, and why schools vary in the opportunities they provide for students. To answer these questions, she suggests that sociologists of education analyze education policy as an outcome of national or local political processes as revealed in legislative and judicial arguments throughout the country. While her focus is education policy development in the USA, her approach can be replicated easily and fruitfully in comparative analyses of cross-national studies.

- *Social networks*: Since Coleman's (1961) highly regarded study of the school as a social system, sociologists have been interested in the social networks of schools and classrooms. Early studies of classroom networks typically depicted the structure of students' relationships in a classroom. Based on these data, researchers inferred how the social structure of a classroom affects students' attitudes, values and behaviors. Granovetter (1995) conducted one of the few theoretically rich studies of network influences on organizations, presaging research on the effects of social capital on student outcomes. Remarkable progress in network analysis has been made since these earlier studies. New data collection methods and statistical models allow researchers to pursue previously unstudied questions about schooling. However, few new social network studies have been conducted, primarily because not many sociologists have acquired the skills to analyze network data. Sociologists of education should learn to use these new tools to obtain critical insights about schooling.

In Chap. 5, McFarland, Diehl, and Rawlings argue for the importance of social network analysis in the study of classroom interaction and status attainment. They develop a theoretical framework that supports the study of social interactions in networks by using streamed behavioral and transactional data. Given the importance of network studies to sociologists of education interested in classroom processes, McFarland and colleagues believe that researchers today have an unprecedented opportunity to collect and analyze data that are expected to shed new light on education processes and outcomes.

- *Classroom organization*: One of the most studied characteristics of classroom and school organization is the differentiation of students for instruction based on cognitive ability. Assigning students to classrooms or groups within classrooms by ability is popular among teachers since it facilitates instruction, but less so among parents and students who fear it confers lower status on children assigned to low-ability level groups while giving disproportionate attention and resources to students in high level groups. The issue has political overtones since assignment level correlates with student race and ethnicity. What would be ideal would be an assignment process that benefits all students regardless of their cognitive ability and one that matches students to teachers who can best meet their learning needs.

In Chap. 6, Gamoran discusses new research that examines and tests approaches for matching students to teachers for instruction. He cites studies being conducted in the USA in which students are assigned to instructional groups based on a computer algorithm. While he finds the goal attractive, he stresses the difficulty involved in implementing these kinds of techniques. Gamoran encourages sociologists of education to conduct new conceptual and empirical studies in this area, given the importance their findings could have in reducing social inequalities in schools.

- *Interaction between research and practice*: As argued repeatedly in this volume, a considerable gap exists between research and practice in education. Two tensions account for this gap. First, educational research and school practice follow different time frames. Research is a slow process that requires many steps. Conducting scholarly research may require writing a proposal to obtain funding for a study, securing approval by a university's Human Subjects Committee, obtaining permission for data collection from schools and parents, collecting and analyzing data, and disseminating results through peer-reviewed journals and elsewhere. While this process can take years, practitioners typically need results quickly to address pressing demands from administrators, teachers, unions, and parents for school improvement. By the time research findings are disseminated, schools have long since moved on to other school reform projects. The second tension stems from the perception of many school personnel that the results of educational research are neither valid nor relevant to their school situation.

Better communication between researchers and practitioners should reduce both of these tensions. Sociologists of education are well situated to improve communication between researchers and practitioners, particularly because they conduct applied as well as basic research. Consequently, they have some understanding of how and where to disseminate their findings in ways that are most useful to practitioners.

In Chap. 7, Bryk, Gomez, and Grunow provide an example of the social organization of a networked community that demonstrates a successful interaction between research and practice. They argue that to create such a community requires that researchers and practitioners work together on a daily basis to determine how variation in the design, engineering, and development of educational research can improve learning. Bryk et al. believe that when scholars and practitioners collaborate, researchers are more likely to produce studies that meet the needs of practitioners, while practitioners are more likely to understand how they can both influence and utilize educational research.

- *The teaching profession*: In the wake of the 2008 recession, economists, politicians, and educators have turned their attention to improving student learning in an effort to restore the US prominence in a highly competitive job market. Given the severe budgetary constraints imposed by the recession, they search for simple but cost effective ways to improve education. Many turn their attention to the teacher as the solution to educational reform. Teachers whose students perform poorly in academics are targets for dismissal. Teachers whose students raise their test scores are rewarded for the students' academic success. A concentrated focus on the teacher need not exceed the education budget. To make the plan work, valid teacher assessment is needed, as is a system of accountability. Much recent attention has focused on teacher evaluation and accountability, but controversy continues to surround the belief that the teacher is the primary causal agent of student improvement. Sociologists of education need to address the critical task of conceptualizing other determinants of learning, in addition to teacher performance, to identify the mechanisms that link these factors to student growth in achievement and attainment.

In Chap. 8, Schneider, Grogan, and Maier address several issues pertaining to teachers, including assessment and accountability. Researchers frequently estimate value-added models of student growth in achievement to estimate teacher effectiveness. The authors note the widespread use of value-added models in evaluating teacher effectiveness in large surveys of students and teachers. Urging researchers not to allow the accessibility of national and statewide data to dominate the study of teacher assessment, Schneider and colleagues encourage sociologists of education to conduct observational studies to complement survey analyses.

- *The transition from school to work*: Legislation mandates that all students in the USA obtain a first- through twelfth-grade education. While attendance at a public school is tuition free, higher education in its various forms is not. Consequently, continuing schooling beyond high school represents a considerable financial burden for many families. To make higher education possible and worthwhile, students, parents, and guidance counselors must work together to select a school and program with a high probability that the student will succeed. Information about prerequisites, required courses, credits, costs, graduation rates, and employment rates are essential to making wise decisions about higher education. Counselors and admissions officers can create obstacles for students by failing to provide information about the costs and benefits of continuing one's education after high school. Moreover, it is critical that counselors and parents help students choose an educational institution that matches the student's abilities and realistic expectations. While some comprehensive studies on the transition from high school to college are available, more are needed, given the obstacles that high school graduates confront as they face career choices in an economically stressed climate. Sociological research on college choices is particularly important for educators and counselors whose heavy workloads do not give them time to study these issues. The transition to college is an ideal area for sociologists of education to study and to demonstrate the important role that school counselors play in contributing to educational and occupational success.

In Chap. 9, Rosenbaum, Rosenbaum, and Stephan examine the process of student decision making in the transition to higher education. They show that some counselors discourage students from enrolling in a 4-year college, arguing that many students are academically ill prepared for college and by attending, would incur an unnecessary financial burden with little assurance of success. Other counselors may encourage students to pursue a 4-year college degree regardless of the student's ability, determination to succeed, or financial situation. Rosenbaum and colleagues examine these two situations, stressing the critical role that information plays in the process of preparing a student for a future career. They encourage sociologists of education to conduct studies to demonstrate the factors that influence career choice and college admissions and to illustrate how best to prepare students for future employment.

- *Institutional influences on education*: Structural and cultural change is endemic to all societal institutions. The growth and decline of these institutions can be seen in the attitudes, values, and behaviors of members. Societal change in demographics, economics, politics, religion, medicine, and other institutions has resulted in structural and cultural adaptations in all institutions at both national and local levels. Sociologists of education could contribute to this vital area of research by examining the social and institutional changes that pressure schools, the ways educators and students respond to them, and how their responses affect the structure and culture of a school community.

In Chap. 10, Hamilton, Werum, Steelman, and Powell examine how change in the structure and culture of a family influences student educational outcomes. They argue that recent dramatic changes in traditional family structure have altered the way families influenced learning in the past. Among these structural changes in contemporary families are single-parent families, stepfamilies, and same-sex families. Contextual and normative changes such as these have altered the importance of economic privilege and parental involvement in their child's formal schooling. These changes also modify the cultural image of what a normal family is and shape a student's participation in informal social networks of adults and students that may be beneficial to learning. Hamilton and colleagues urge sociologists of education to study how to utilize family structure and culture to promote students' educational achievement and attainment.

In conclusion, time gaps exist between educational research, practice, and policy. These gaps occur at the federal, state, and local levels. As a result, most decisions about education are made in the absence of input from the research community. For example, insufficient research was available when school administrators were charged with evaluating teacher quality, as mandated by No Child Left Behind. As a result, ill-informed, and ultimately unsuccessful policies were implemented, which did little to advance student learning.

Coordinating the time researchers need to complete a study and make findings available with the time policymakers take to decide on and implement a reform is necessary to make education decisions more efficient and effective. Sociologists of education can come close to making this goal a reality by anticipating factors that will shape the evolution of education in the USA and the global society and by beginning studies as soon as these factors can be identified. This would increase the likelihood that basic and applied research is available when educators and policymakers need it. By doing so, sociologists would make an important contribution to the quality of future education.

The *Frontiers in Sociology of Education* challenges researchers to reduce the time lag between research, practice and policy. The hope is that the chapters and essays in the volume will motivate sociologists of education to conduct future-oriented research to have theory and empirical findings available for educators and policymakers when they make decisions about practice and policy. By accepting this challenge, they will exert a more powerful influence on schooling in the future than they have in the past.

References

Bidwell, C.E. 1965. The school as a formal organization. In *The handbook of organizations*, ed. J.G. March, 922–1022. Chicago: Rand McNally.
Boudon, R. 1974. *Education, opportunity, and social inequality: Changing prospects in western society*. New York: Wiley.
Bryk, A.S., V.E. Lee, and P. Holland. 1993. *Catholic schools and the common good*. Cambridge: Harvard University Press.
Coleman, J.S. 1961. *The adolescent society*. Glencoe: The Free Press.
Coleman, J.S. 1988. Social capital in the creation of human capital. *American Journal of Sociology* 94: S95–S120.
Coleman, J.S. 1990. *Foundations of social theory*. Cambridge: The Belknap Press of Harvard University Press.
Dreeben, Robert. 1968. *On what is learned in school*. Reading: Addison-Wesley.
Durkheim, E. 1961. *Moral education: A study in the theory and application of the sociology of education*. Trans. E. K. Wilson and H. Schnurer. New York: The Free Press.

Entwisle, D.R., and K.L. Alexander. 1994. Winter setback – the racial composition of schools and learning to read. *American Sociological Review* 59: 446–460.

Granovetter, M. 1995. *Getting a job: A study of contacts and careers*, 2nd ed. Chicago: University of Chicago Press.

Jencks, C., and M. Phillips (eds.). 1998. *The black-white test score gap*. Washington, DC: The Brookings Institution Press.

Kerckhoff, A.C. 1976. The status attainment process: Socialization or allocation? *Social Forces* 55(2): 368–381..

Kerckhoff, A.C. 1993. *Diverging pathways: Social structure and career deflections*. Cambridge: Cambridge University Press.

Mare, R.D. 1981. Change and stability in educational stratification. *American Sociological Review* 46: 72–87.

Meyer, J.W. 1977. The effects of education as an institution. *American Journal of Sociology* 83: 55–77.

Weber, M. 1978. *Economy and society*. Trans. G. Roth and C. Wittich. Berkeley: University of California Press.

Part I
Research Articles: Theoretical and Empirical Analyses of Schooling

Chapter 2
The Future of the Schooled Society: The Transforming Culture of Education in Postindustrial Society

David P. Baker

The education revolution has transformed postindustrial society. Along with a few other major phenomena, such as global capitalism and democracy, schooling whole populations to complete a widening array of educational degrees changes both individuals and institutions that make up the core of society. The education revolution is a cultural phenomenon more than a material or political one, although it has major material and political consequences. Widespread education in a postindustrial society creates cultural ideas about new types of knowledge, new types of experts, new definitions of personal success and failure, a new workplace and conception of jobs, and new definitions of intelligence and human talent. At the same time, educational achievement and degree attainment have come to dominate social stratification and social mobility, superseding and delegitimizing forms of status attainment left over from the past. The global impact of formal education on postindustrial society has been so extensive that it can be argued that mass education is a founding social revolution of modernity (Parsons 1971).

Even though there is ample evidence of the broad impact of education as a social institution, it is by and large an underappreciated social revolution among intellectuals (Baker forthcoming; Baker et al. 2010c). When scholars think about dramatic social events during the nineteenth and twentieth centuries that are responsible for the way people live, they rarely include the remarkable activity of schooling all children for long periods of time. Other transforming forces receive credit for the modern world. Industrial production, technology, science and medicine, capitalism, the rise of the nation-state and democratic politics, large-scale warfare, decline of religion, and rise of rationalized bureaucracies are seen as shaping most of what humans have become in a relatively short time. Likewise in thinking about the creation of the modern individual, scholars rush to include the psychological impact of

D.P. Baker (✉)
Penn State University, University Park,
PA 16802-3203, USA
e-mail: dpb4@psu.edu

a culture of individualism on elaborated and complex personalities and changes in the family as the main transforming events of the last several centuries. Rarely is the impact of mass schooling considered among the list of major forces that have created modern society.

When mass education is mentioned in accounts of the most transforming events in modern society, it is presented as a collective mistake—too much unneeded education resulting in educational credential inflation. For example, in the late 1960s, the notion of runaway schooling as overeducation, that is, too many people receiving unnecessary education for the job that they will eventually obtain, became a topic of wide concern (Dore 1976). Economists, professional educators, sociologists, and other experts proclaimed that the education revolution was a growing and threatening social problem. Too many children would receive too much education, causing them to become frustrated and alienated when they could not find suitable jobs for the level of their educational credentials. Economists predicted an inefficient labor market where jobs requiring little skill would be given to those with more education than needed.

Yet these negative consequences never came to pass (Baker 2009; Burris 1983). There was no revolt against expanding education for large sections of the world's population. Indeed, people from various cultural heritages and nations have embraced the idea of education as both a personal and common good. Demand for education continues at such a pace that it often surprises social scientists. Western professionals, such as economists, assisting developing nations in expanding their economies are often amazed at the persistent demand for more education among populations (e.g., UNESCO 2002). In every corner of the world, even among the poorest of people, after basic nutrition and health needs are met, parents demand education for their children as the central way to help them achieve a better life. Since the overeducation debate 50 years ago, rather than a burst of an inflationary educational bubble, the rise of a robust culture of education has changed ideas about many major institutions in society. The core values and social meanings behind education have become remarkably similar worldwide; so much so that there is an increasing trend among nations to develop and employ a similar model of formal education from the earliest grades up through graduate study at the university (Baker and LeTendre 2005).

The demography of the education revolution is well known to sociologists of education. Gross enrollment rates have risen consistently over the past 150 years, justified as preparing all children for the adult world. Near full enrollments have been attained, first in wealthier nations, and since the middle of the twentieth century have spread globally (Benavot and Riddle 1988; Fuller and Rubinson 1992). Consequently, 80% of all persons aged 15 or older are able to read and write a short statement about their life. This phenomenon would have been hard to imagine 50 years ago and unthinkable 100 years ago (UNESCO 2002).[1] Along with the diffusion of mass education, the normative standard of educational attainment has risen with each new generation of schooled parents. For example, the USA has led the way in developing mass education. A hundred years ago about half of all US school-aged children were

---

[1] Most people who are still illiterate are living in very poor nations and seven out of ten are women (UNESCO 2002).

enrolled in school, whereas the proportion rose to 75% within the next 40 years and to almost 90% over the next 20 years. Today, more than 12 years of schooling is the median attainment (US Department of Education 1993). Over the past several decades, mass education has flowed into the higher education sector in many nations, and the beginnings of mass post- and undergraduate education are observable (Schofer and Meyer 2005). In the academic year 2006–2007, the entire American higher education system graduated approximately 1.5 million students with a B.A. and 755,000 students with graduate degrees, yielding a ratio of one graduate degree for every two B.A. degrees (US Department of Education 2008).

As the charge of this book is to project major education trends into the future and consider these as new frontiers for the sociological investigation of education and society, this chapter argues that the already robust global culture of education will likely intensify its transformation of postindustrial society into the foreseeable future. The argument stems from emerging conclusions based on over four decades of research on two central questions from the sociology of education. The first question, and the one that has commanded the most sustained research, is: What role does formal education play in the social stratification of postindustrial society, and what social mechanisms has it developed to play its role? The second question, attracting a significant but smaller volume of research, is: To what extent has the education revolution become institutionalized worldwide and what effect does this have on postmodern society beyond the stratification process?

Sociological research on these questions points to a future society where education performance will be the singular dominant factor in social status attainment, and education will be one of the most transforming of social institutions. In fact, to a large extent this has already happened and an advanced version of the schooled society is evident in a number of nations. The prediction offered here is that the stage now is set for an intensification of both phenomena into the future. Thus, a full understanding of the consequences of the education revolution for postindustrial society is a major frontier facing the sociological investigation of education.

This prediction is related to an older one advanced by some intellectuals as they observed the spread of mass higher education in developed nations in the mid-1960s, as well as the rise of big science and the knowledge conglomerate in the American research university (Bell 1973; Galbraith 1969; Parsons 1971). Even without the benefit of the last 50 years of research on education and its role in society, mass education was predicted to become a central institution in postindustrial society. And although some early speculations on the consequences of this change proved to be overblown (i.e., a fully rationalized, technological expert society), the overall idea was prophetic. Meyer, in his 1977 seminal article on the transforming power of the education revolution, hypothesized that education has two emerging societal functions that are mutually reinforcing and, hence, will generate significant institutional power. One is the growing allocative function of education and the other is its expanding cognitive function.[2]

---

[2] *Cognitive* will be used here instead of Meyer's original 1977 formulation of *socialization*, as the former more accurately represents what schooling does, plus the latter is an older term now rarely used and conveys other unneeded meanings.

Allocation is shorthand for the role formal education performs in the attainment of social status, which includes, but is not limited to, occupational attainment. Cognition stands for the change in thinking processes that occurs among schooled individuals. This process includes at least three main facets: (1) learning the manifest curriculum; (2) developing deeper reasoning, problem solving, and rational thought; and (3) expanding conceptual images of the self and the world.

Specifically, Meyer's (1977) hypothesis predicts that over time and across increasingly more individuals, allocative and cognitive functions of schooling will reinforce one another and form a significant ideology about the centrality of formal education, which in turn will intensify each function's legitimacy. Meyer's additional insight was that this symbiotic process lends to formal education the cultural capability to change not only individuals, but, and perhaps most relevant to sociology, other social institutions too.

The duality of the societal functions of formal education and its potential for symbiotic interaction is at the heart of the prediction here that the education culture of postindustrial society will intensify and continue its significant transformation of other social institutions. This underscores the regrettable fact that Meyer's sweeping hypothesis has gone untested. The primary impact of the 1977 article focused research on the demography and politics of the expansion of mass education as a prerequisite to assessing the original argument about the effects of education on society. Moreover, a test of the hypothesis would require complex data about educational development, social stratification, and cognitive effects of education across societies varying in the pace of institutionalization of education. As these data do not exist yet, a formal test is not attempted here. Instead, there is first a brief description of the broader theoretical argument behind the predicted future impact of the education revolution. Second, with the aid of findings from a range of related research, the extent to which allocative and cognitive functions of formal education have intensified for individuals over the development of the schooled society is illustrated. Third, to demonstrate the potential of a symbiotic process between these functions capable of transforming other social institutions, a sampling of research is reviewed indicating the consequences for occupational credentialing and the nature of work in postindustrial society. Lastly, related research agenda are suggested as topics from which to study the intensifying education culture in postindustrial society.

Institutional Impact: Education as a Primary Institution

Generally there has been one traditional model of education's institutional role in society. By educating students through teaching and curriculum, schooling plays a helping role in creating the overall social and economic complexity of society. Hence education is seen as a reproducer of society among each successive generation of children. This image depicts formal education as producing a replica of society in children's minds, as well as conveying the skills needed to participate in society. As such, on an institutional level, education is considered a secondary institution.[3]

This traditional model of education as a secondary institution is the most common image held both by social scientists and the public. It frequently is found in a range of social thought, from a Marxian perspective, which considers education as forming an exploited pool of labor (i.e., social class reproduction), to conservative notions of classical elite education (i.e., elites and elite cultural reproduction), and to the technological functionalism of human capital theory (i.e., skill reproduction) (Bowles and Gintis 1976; Schultz 1961). Although these theories predict radically different outcomes of schooling's reproductive nature, at the core of each is the traditional institutional model of education and society. This model is also popular among educational policymakers and is a central assumption in many public debates about education.

In part, the traditional model is so common because education's broader influence is often hard to observe in societies, such as the USA, where education and its effects are already ubiquitous. Although the expansion of schooling is readily obvious, and becoming more so around the world, it is a distinctly quiet change, even though it profoundly changes society in multiple ways. The traditional model assumes that the social and economic positions to which adults are allocated by educational credentials are fixed by the society at large, changing only as a function of noneducational phenomena. The traditional perspective of education and society tends to consider the education revolution as either relatively trivial, or even as a troubling educational inflation that wastes peoples' time and energies.

Neoinstitutional theory, as used by Meyer (1977) to develop his hypothesis, reverses the traditional view of the relationship between education and society, and instead considers that society follows education more than the other way around. Therefore, formal education is judged to be a massive constructivist force in society. A strong case can be made that schooling, as practiced over the past century and a half, is far more than a preparatory exercise for youth following only where the technological and social demands of society dictate. Rather, the education revolution has constructed, for better or worse, many of the basic ideas, beliefs, and human capabilities that underpin human society at the beginning of the twenty-first century. For example, ideas such as universalistic values and knowledge, human empowerment, social justice, citizenship, scientific truth claims, meritocracy, and rationality all have infused modern culture because of the success of formal education as a social institution from early childhood education to graduate study at universities. In the schooled society, not only is everyone considered to be a student capable of academic learning that will provide him or her with important competencies, in addition, society is transformed in the process of educating all (Meyer 1977).

---

[3]The distinction here between primary and secondary institutions applies to the difference in their role in creating society, not to the older sociological idea of face-to-face versus formally organized.

The schooled society has far reaching implications for human life, some of which are seen as positive and others as disconcerting. Beyond documenting the considerable impact of education on the individual, a substantial amount of research finds evidence of the institutional impact of the educational revolution on the ideas, values, and norms of other institutions, such as work and occupations (Baker 2009), parenting roles and normative behavior (Schaub 2010), structure and processes of polity and civic culture in democratic societies (Kamens 2009), definitions of knowledge and truth claims (Kamens et al. 1996; Young 2008), valuation of central human capabilities (Martinez 2000; Blair et al. 2005), organization of religious communities and theology (Schwadel 2003), definitions of personal success and failure (Smith 2003), spread and dominance of formal organizations (Stinchcombe and March 1965), rising belief in professionalism and scientization of society (Drori et al. 2006), and the foundational image of society itself (Frank and Gabler 2006).

While there is considerable evidence about the effects of schooling as a primary institution on a host of societal institutional processes, identifying such effects does not explain how education has come to have the significant transformative power it apparently does. Meyer's (1977) hypothesis suggests this. In addition, a growing amount of research supports the basic argument of the duality of the allocative and cognitive functions of formal education as a central transforming process.

The Narrowing Educational Road to Social Status: Allocation of Individuals

Since the main findings of the investigation of social mobility and the causal modeling of status attainment are well known, there is no need to recount these in general. It is essential, however, to consider the historical development of the role of formal education in the mobility and status attainment process of society because its rise and dominance has been sociologically swift and revolutionary. From historical accounts and the earliest systematic investigation of social mobility, it is clear that prior to a century and a half ago, formal education played almost no role in the process of intergenerational mobility over the entire history of human society (Collins 1979). For example, although in late European feudal society a small stratum of elite and semi-elite positions were allocated based on university training, the vast majority of all positions were not defined by educational attainment (Ackroyd 1998). Much later, just before the advent of the education revolution, a variety of decidedly noneducational allocation mechanisms and criteria dominated intergenerational mobility in preindustrial and early industrialization societies, such as family origin and position in a social stratum, status inheritance, sinecure, marriage, age, gender, religious charisma, guild training, patronage, caste, and land ownership.

But with the initiation of mass education circa the second half of the nineteenth century, this began to change radically. In his historical analysis of the economic development of American society for example, Hogan (1996) captures the essence of this sociological shift in the USA. He argues that

> Whereas the class position of most Americans in 1840 was almost entirely a function of their ownership of property, a century later educational credentials had become the primary and proximate determinant of class position for most people by virtue of the capacity of educational credentials to regulate access to the occupational structure. (p. 243).

By the 1960s, when modern statistical methods first were applied to analyze social mobility data from large samples of individuals, the education revolution was in full swing in the USA. Not surprisingly, the groundbreaking research of Blau and Duncan (1967) showed that educational attainment had become a causal factor to a degree never before seen in human society. And contrary to expectations held before the study, education played two roles once thought to be mutually exclusive—education had become central to intergenerational reproduction *and* the achievement of status (Hout and DiPrete 2006). In other words, while educational attainment had become the main route to an individual's adult status, educational attainment was influenced by both social origins (i.e., parents' socioeconomic status [SES]) and factors independent of social origins (i.e., success or failure at schooling due to effort, intelligence, and motivation). This shift was a substantial one, as the direct influence of social origin on the adult child's status was now remarkably weak, particularly compared to what it is presumed to have been prior to the education revolution. Further, parental SES was itself increasingly a function of educational allocation. Consequently, over just several American generations, education had thoroughly saturated intergenerational mobility. This conclusion has been widely replicated in the USA and other heavily schooled nations (Breen and Luijkx 2007; Hout 1988; Ishida 1993; Shavit and Blossfeld 1993; Treiman and Ganzeboom 1990).

The next historical shift in intergenerational mobility witnessed an even greater saturation of education. Hout's landmark 1988 (see also 1984) American study finds that in the late 1980s, parental social origin still influenced allocation processes through the child's education attainment, but the strength of this relationship had declined by a full third from what it had been in the 1960s. Furthermore, the relationship was disconnected completely among offspring completing a college degree. In other words, for the first time, evidence showed that allocation based on the educational achievement of the individual independent of social origin had become a dominating process.

In a comprehensive study of American social status attainment, Torche (2010) and Brand and Xie (2010) replicate Hout's findings and show that the trend has continued since the late 1980s. Using recent data, Torche reports that social origin is a causal factor in determining the adult child's occupational status, earnings, and total economic worth for those with a high school degree or less; while for those who attended college and earned a degree, adult status remains disconnected from social origin. Thus, once one is into the higher education arena, allocation becomes based solely on educational achievement, such as better academic performance in college, majors selected, and perhaps between-college effects of a variety of types.[4] While there is still an influence of social origin on postsecondary attendance, this influence is weakening with the worldwide growth in this sector. Given the increasing homogenization of schooling's influence, it is not surprising that this new trend in stratification has been replicated in Sweden, France, and Germany (Vallet 2004; Breen and Jonsson 2007; Breen and Luijkx 2007).

Often the shift toward educational allocation is attributed merely to greater economic and social complexity, particularly from both social class reproductive and human capital theories that employ the traditional model of education as a secondary institution. Certainly economies have changed, family-owned farms and small businesses declined, but what often is missed in this social change is that to replace age-old social mobility mechanisms in such a rapid and total fashion as the education revolution has done takes far more sociological change than general economic and social complexity. With the exception of the apprenticeship, the noneducational mechanisms of status attainment just listed are not well known to most in modern society. Yet before the education revolution, these were deeply embedded in societies and considered completely legitimate ways to sort individuals to adult status, including to occupations. But the rise of education as the sole arbitrator of allocation has been so complete that former allocative processes—sinecure, occupational inheritance, marriage, religious charisma, guild training, patronage, caste—appear now as exotic social relics. While formal education controlled access to a few elite positions in a number of premodern societies, the fact that it now singularly does so for nearly all status positions would have been an alien idea just 100 years ago. Although educational allocation seems to many contemporaries as a natural way to allocate, it is in fact a sweeping sociological construction at the very foundation of postindustrial society.

Now obvious in hindsight, the historical rise and intensification of the allocative function of formal education is precisely what Meyer's hypothesis predicted in 1977. And the shift from reproductive to achieved educational allocation is further an evidence of the continued intensification of the culture of education into the present. This evidence sets the stage for assessment of the second intensifying function of education—the rise of the widely assumed idea that cognition is the master human capacity.

Academic Intelligence as the Privileged Human Capability

Along with the fact that educational attainment is now the dominating legitimate allocative process, the education revolution also spreads the notion that academic achievement reigns supreme for the making of a productive and broadly capable

---

[4] Torche also found some evidence suggesting that among the Americans who are earning postgraduate degrees, social origin again explains some portion of adult status. While yet to be replicated, the finding does raise speculation about the interaction between allocation processes and expansion of new educational degrees (see the following third future research suggestion).

human. This cognitive function of schooling is accepted so widely that it often is overlooked when social and behavioral scientists examine the impact of education on society. Of course everyone with personal experience with schooling (which today is almost everyone in heavy-schooled nations) knows that academic achievement is important to an individual's school success and in turn to his or her future. What is missed is how the idea of academic achievement itself has a massive impact on society.

Institutionally, schooling has made academic achievement both an objective in and of itself and a publicly celebrated quality of the individual. Academic achievement is an accomplishment to celebrate not only because it leads elsewhere, but also because it has become defined as the central component of progress toward the general development of the individual. Also, academic subjects themselves increasingly have become more overtly cognitive in their approach, further linking cognition and the idea of the developed individual.

Literacy, numeracy, and mastery of other academic subjects still are seen as skills needed for adult life, but over the course of the education revolution their connection to the individual's future has broadened and been generalized to the point that academic performance becomes synonymous with the successfully developed person. An individual with considerable academic achievement who later fails in adult society is described by many as wasting talent, that is, wasting a record of academic achievement. Meanwhile, few commend the adult failure who was a low school achiever. In fact, the failure of this adult confirms for all the belief in the connection between success and academic performance. Students themselves learn to value academic intelligence as a generalized human potential, as demonstrated by Norwegian youth who think that undertaking upper-secondary schooling directed to particular types of occupations and not to more general academic training is a waste of good grades (Hegna and Smette 2010). American parents of college-bound high school seniors proudly and publicly celebrate the status of the admitting college as conformation of their child's academic prowess and by inference their parenting of such achievement.

Included in the impact of the cognitive function of education is that the underlying cognitive nature of academic achievement assumes greater importance than specific skill mastery. Also, schooling inculcates a sense of empowerment on the part of the schooled individual to use general cognitive abilities. This is witnessed in the tendency of the education establishment to use terms such as higher order thinking, critical thinking skills, and problem solving as reified objectives of schooling. Given this, the centrality of academic achievement makes cognitive skill the widely recognized central human capability in postindustrial society (Martinez 2000). Of course, intelligence has always been valued in human society, but the schooled society intensifies this to the point where intelligence, enhanced and validated through formal education, is assumed essential for the performance of social roles of all types, from the world of work to modern soldiering, to parenting.

In the schooled society, what can be called academic intelligence has become the foundational human capability, with education as the institution that develops, defines, and acknowledges this celebrated central quality in individuals (Baker forthcoming).

Over the historical course of the education revolution, schooling has produced an elaborate culture of academic intelligence, where a student's mastery over many years of mathematics, language skills, science, and other key subjects is considered a value in and of itself, as well as being accepted as a crucial gatekeeper to further education and an assumed happy future (Labaree 1986; Meyer 2000). Academic intelligence is rewarded by the growing social relevance of formal education. At the same time, this construction runs in the other direction too, so that academic intelligence shapes our ideas about intelligence in general. Academic achievement, as well as its everyday manifestations as grades, test scores, teacher recommendations, and educational promotions, is the central currency of formal schooling, so much so that a person's intelligence is largely judged in public through indicators of their schooling performance such as formal degrees attained (Baker 2011). All of the attributes that were once the valued goals of good parenting and early forms of education, such as moral character, ability to work hard, and even erudite knowledge, are surpassed by the value of the smart youth who does well in school, or more accurately phrased, the one celebrated as smart because she achieves in school (Schaub 2010).

The importance and celebration of academic intelligence is so ubiquitous in the schooled society that it is difficult to observe the historical intensification of this cognitive function of schooling over the course of the education revolution, but there are three lines of research that offer unique vantage points.

The Schooling Effect on Cognitive Development

Research shows that the learning process aimed at literacy, numeracy, and other subjects, even in rudimentary conditions for only a few years of schooling, leads to a number of metacognitive enhancements that cause schooled individuals to think and reason in a fashion significantly different from unschooled individuals. Metacognition, or what cognitive psychology refers to as *domain-general cognition* in terms of working memory, inhibitory control, and attention-shifting processes, as well as components of decision making and problem solving, have been shown to be enhanced by exposure to formal education (Nisbett 2009). Reading, writing, and understanding numbers and basic operations are themselves a transforming set of skills, but there is evidence that in the process of learning these skills, domain-general cognition is enhanced as well.

For example, in the 1930s, when large numbers of unschooled Russian peasants lived alongside those who had had access to some schooling as children, psychologists Vygotsky and Luria (1976) reported evidence of differences in thinking styles between unschooled and schooled adults. Adults with even small amounts of exposure to formal school showed greater propensity to use cognitive abstraction and reasoning to solve new problems, while unschooled adults tended to rely on their concrete experiences even at the risk of finding an incorrect solution (1976). Since this initial finding, the impact of schooling on the ability to reason more abstractly and solve problems in new and unique situations has been demonstrated in related research in other cultures (Cole 1996; Stevenson and Chuansheng 1989; Tulviste 1991).

In the USA, before the inception of widespread mass schooling, a host of studies comparing unschooled and schooled individuals with various methods showed schooling's influence on domain-general cognition beyond specific skills and factual knowledge. A detailed meta-analysis of over 50 of these studies using naturalistic observation, post hoc statistical comparisons, and cohort-sequential analysis concludes that there is a stable and robust association between schooling and the enhancement of cognitive skills (Ceci 1991). Estimating across the studies, schooling enhances IQ (measures of which can be heavily influenced by domain-general cognition) by .3 to .6 of a point for every year, and with the usual standard deviation set at 15 points over even a modestly long school career add up to significant enhancement. Importantly, the association between IQ and exposure to formal education is not due to high aptitude children staying in school longer. Instead, by comparing children similar on family social background and initial intelligence with different exposures to schooling, these studies support a nonspurious statistical association between schooling and domain-general cognition.

Recent advances in instrumentation for measuring domain-general cognition enable a detailed and exhaustive study of schooling effects on cognition. In a natural experiment among Ghanaian substance-level famers who as children experienced different levels of schooling, Peters et al. (in press) find robust schooling effects on measures of domain-general cognition, decision-making skills, and new problem-solving tasks. A related study on nationally representative samples from nine sub-Saharan African nations finds a similar schooling effect on reasoning ability (Baker et al. 2010b).

As mass schooling spread over the twentieth century and its cognitively intense environment reached greater portions of the world's population, more individuals were exposed not only to the specific skills of literacy and numeracy, but also to new ways of thinking and reasoning. It is not surprising then that evidence of domain-general cognition shows significant improvement across populations of adults over successive generations during the past 100 years. A wealth of data from developed nations, shows rising fluid IQ (essentially domain-general cognitive skills), which has been dubbed the "Flynn effect" (Nisbett 2009; Flynn 1998). Rising too fast to be attributed to genetic influence, a case can be made that the expansion of education, with its intensified focus on cognitive skills, is a major cause of the Flynn effect (Blair et al. 2005).

The Cognitive Curriculum

A second line of research demonstrates that over the course of the education revolution, traditional and narrow learning objectives of schooling give way to broader, universal, and ultimately cognitively more complex objectives. Over the second half of the twentieth century, vocational training as a goal of schooling has become obsolete and is replaced by the idea that schooling is about the cognitive and social development of the multifaceted individual. Not only has enrollment in vocational education dropped, but also the idea of vocationalism itself has been replaced. As increasingly more aspects of human life become incorporated within the domain of education, the schooled society constructs the image of the student as far more than just a future worker (Frank and Gabler 2006). While the notion of schooling as preparation for the future is still part of the educational mission, or package, it is less focused on particular kinds of jobs and skill acquisition, and based more on cognitive enhancement that is assumed effective for all kinds of activities after the educational experience.

As mass schooling began in North America and Western Europe at the beginning of the twentieth century, vocationalism was one of its core ideas. By 1950, a fourth of all students worldwide were enrolled in vocational education, as were a third of all secondary students in North America and Western Europe and 50% in Eastern Europe (Benavot 1983). But 1950 was the tipping point as these were the largest enrollment shares vocational education was to have for the rest of the century. By 1975, it had dropped to 16% worldwide and has kept declining. Today, vocational training comprises only about 10% of all secondary school programs. Further, this drop was uniform across most nations, and neither the level of industrial output nor size of the industrial labor force in nations slowed the decline. Therefore, the death of vocationalism is likely a result of a shift in the central values and ideas behind schooling and its curricula, rather than a reaction to the rhythms of industrial and postindustrial economies. The vocational programs that still exist are themselves less apt to be terminal degrees (i.e., for a specific job) and are more broadly academically cognitive with emphasis on gaining yet additional academic education in students' futures (Kamens and Benavot 2006).

Further, a study by the US Department of Education (2003) shows that in the USA, the downward trend in vocational education continues. The percentage of public secondary school students concentrating in occupationally oriented curricula declined from the early 1980s through the 1990s. With the exception of computer technology, all programs geared to occupations were declining within the overall secondary curricula. At the same time, student concentration in academic courses increased, and the content of the remaining vocational courses included more academic material. As this trend intensifies in formal education, on-the-job training is also shifting toward a distinctive academic goal. Several studies of such training find that while some narrow technical training remains, the major growth has been in the spread of more diffuse education from human relations skills to self-enhancement techniques including cognitive skills (Monhan et al. 1994).

At the other end of the spectrum of central educational goals existing before the education revolution is the classicism of elite education or the idea that the highest form of knowledge and knowing revolves around the appreciation and replication of classical Western art, language, and scholarship in the styles of Greek and Roman antiquity. Yet, like the ending of vocationalism, historical evidence shows a significant decline in classicism in the secondary school curricula. It dropped substantially worldwide from the 1930s when a third of all national secondary curricula were based on the classicism approach to knowledge, to only 9% by 1980 (Kamens et al. 1996).

In educational systems across the world, what has replaced both vocationalism and classicism is the idea that all students should have access to, and mastery of, core academic subjects such as mathematics, science, and language skills now taught in comprehensive systems of education. By 1980, these subjects taught in a comprehensive format made up 90% of all secondary schooling worldwide (Kamens et al. 1996). And increasingly the content of these subjects aims to develop one's domain-general cognition along with the learning of some specific knowledge.

As mental problem solving, effortful reasoning, abstraction and higher order thinking, and the active use of one's intelligence take center stage, they take the place of mental skills, such as recitation, disputation, memorization, formalistic debate, formulae application, rote accuracy, and authoritative text reading and exegesis taught in a traditional preschooled society. A recent content analysis of over 28,000 pages from 141 widely used American elementary school mathematics texts from first through sixth grade level published during the twentieth century shows that beginning in the mid-1960s there was a significant increase in textbook approaches including problems requiring domain-general cognition skills related to the mental retention of multiple pieces of information, understanding multiple strategies to solve problems, and shifting attention between salient pieces of information (Baker et al. 2010a). The change is evident across the range of grades and continued over the rest of the twentieth century. The goal of the content is clear, namely, to learn mathematics, the young learner must develop and apply domain-general cognitive skills to use and learn mathematics. Evidence also reveals that exposure to such a curriculum has cognitive effects (see also Downey et al. 2004).

Academically Intelligent Children and a Successful Nation

An emerging set of studies demonstrates how widely the idea of cognitive development has penetrated the culture as a result of the education revolution. In an historical analysis of American mothers' activities with preschool children, Schaub (2010) finds a significant increase in the teaching of basic academic skills in preparation for schooling. In the early 1950s one half of mothers report reading to their preschool-aged children, yet by 2001 nearly all mothers report reading to their child regularly. Statistical modeling of these trends finds a two-part historical process by which, first, more educated mothers led the way in activities related to the cognitive demands of schooling, and second, over the past 50 years, less educated mothers have closed the gap as they, too, now engage in a similar array of these activities. As each generation of mothers enters parenthood with more formal education, their parenting reflects the values and ideas embedded in this cognitive focus of schooling.

Lastly, over the past few decades, the reach of the schooled society and its culture of academic intelligence can be observed in how academic achievement has become defined as a collective good leading to an array of assumed societal benefits. Measures of the academic achievement of national student bodies are believed to indicate the economic and social health of nations. Widespread reactions to international academic achievement test results and comparing students from a host of nations mirror the deep reverence modern society holds toward school-created and certified cognitive abilities. Witness the national condemnation incurred by low national scores across many nations and the rhetoric of societal decline in media that accompanies this condemnation (Baker and LeTendre 2005). It is a noteworthy occurrence when large, robust nations with huge labor forces, complex economies, technological militaries, celebrated histories, and other indicators of national prowess condemn their own future on the basis of an 8th or 12th grade math test. However, it happens often, given the importance of academic achievement to the modern psyche as a result of the education revolution.

Symbiotic Consequences: The Educational Transformation of Occupational Credentials and Work

The intensifying functions of status allocation and cognitive development, along with the deeply held cultural values that they create, make formal education in all its forms a transforming institution. And, as listed above, symbiotic effects from the greater institutionalization of these two functions are evident for the postindustrial social institutions of the family, politics, public policy, production of knowledge, life course, military, religion, formal organization, science, and individuality. Among these, the related institutions of occupational credentials and work have witnessed some of the most dramatic changes as a function of the education revolution. Two recently published essays chronicle this empirical change (Baker 2011, 2009). One is on the dominance of the education institution on occupational credentialing, and the other on the educational transformation of occupations and the workplace. Brief highlights from these analyses illustrate the symbiotic effect between the allocative and cognitive functions of education.

The Dominance of Educational Credentialing

As education comes to solely define status allocation based solely on academic degree attainment won through mastery of an increasingly cognitive curriculum, a pervasive belief in the power of degrees to both allocate individuals in the labor market and to serve as job requirements in the occupational structure has taken root (Baker 2011). While often observed at the level of individual status attainment, less research on the penetration of the effect of the educational revolution into the structure of occupations in postmodern society is available, although this is changing.

Collins (1979) provided the founding analysis of the rise of educational credentials among American occupations. What he initially attributed to interoccupational competition has over time given way to a normative pattern of the use of educational credentials across many occupations. In the complex organized workplaces of the late twentieth century, educationally defined exclusive groups of professionals lay claim to privileged functions accompanied by competition for significant amounts of fluid resources (Baker 2011; Collins 1979; Shanahan and Khagram 2006). And, as educational credentialing gains wider use and credibility, noneducational credentials are increasingly delegitimized and made formally illegal.

Data from 2004 to 2006 compiled by the US Bureau of Labor Statistics (Hecker 2005) on change in occupations shows the trend toward greater educational credentialing. Among the 45 fastest growing occupations in the American economy, three fourths of them required an education credential and over half required a bachelor degree or higher. Twenty-five percent of these fastest growing occupations required a graduate or professional degree, including occupations such as medical scientists (Ph.D.), occupational therapists (M.S.), postsecondary teachers (Ph.D.), mental health counselors (M.S.), and veterinarians (Ph.D.). While absolute job growth was dominated by noneducation credentialed occupations, 30% of the largest job growth was in occupations requiring an educational credential, with most among these requiring a bachelor degree. Lastly, the 30 occupations experiencing the largest job decline were all noneducationally credentialed. This example is cross sectional and only of the occupations experiencing the greatest changes, but it is illustrative of the degree to which education credentialing penetrates the occupational structure.

In addition to education controlling the access to more occupations, educational credentialing has intensified across specific jobs in many different occupations. For example, occupational licensing and its related occupational certification are a transforming trend in the occupational structure in postindustrial society that rests on intensification of educational credentialing (Bills 2004; Kleiner 2006; Kleiner and Krueger 2008). Certainly financial, quality control, and competitive motivations are behind the organizing of occupations through a licensure process, but the trend signifies a deeper motivation. Sociologically, occupational licensing is a form of mass professionalization of jobs that has arisen with the education revolution, particularly with mass higher education (Parsons 1971; Baker 2009). Many occupations use a form of licensing that is heavily influenced and controlled by professional associations based on specific educational degrees, and the licensing process itself is dominated by educational requirements. Not only is access controlled educationally, but licensure maintenance and job tenure increasingly require additional education. As of 2005, 34% of working American adults reported that their occupation had legal or professional requirements for continuing education (US Department of Education 2005).

Of course, there is varying fidelity across occupations to the high form of the original professions (medicine, law, and theology). However, a major professionalizing component of the licensing process for most occupations is the establishment and maintenance of formal educational requirements, usually verified by academic degrees, for entry and renewal of a license to practice an occupation. At the same time many of these educationally intensifying occupations are discontinuing use of, or required to follow legal sanctions regarding, traditional noneducational qualities of credentials such as experience, age, and gender.

Finally, the centrality and value of educational credentials are such that when mass fraud is suspected, it is defined as a widespread social problem. Diploma mills that produce counterfeited degrees are a billion-dollar industry (Ezell and Bear 2005). Although reliable data on the extent of fraud are virtually nonexistent, and many estimates appear wildly exaggerated, the perception of credentialing fraud is salient enough that to date, major congressional investigations into fraudulent educational credentials have occurred in the USA. Relying mostly on anecdotal evidence, the tone of the investigations seems intended to create greater levels of concern over fraud. Moreover, the fear of credentialing fraud and the taboo itself has created a new line of business in the verification and investigation of educational credentials, along with translation of the foreign educational credentials into the American system of educational degrees. This is, without a doubt, an effect of the growing globalization of upper levels of the occupational structure along with a worldwide convergence on the meaning and centrality of educational credentials.

In the schooled society, social costs of committing educational credentialing taboos can be extreme. Mass media often report on the fall of successful persons for misrepresenting their educational credentials, adding a measure of public shame and reinforcing the value of educational credentials. CEOs and CEFs of well-known corporations such as RadioShack and Bausch and Lomb, a Head of the US Olympic Committee, a Dean of Admission at a prestigious university, various university athletic coaches, and others all have been the subject of recent widely publicized stories of education credentialing fraud.[5]

Educational credentialing is so widespread and publically accepted within the occupational structure of most advanced economies that it is now clear that the original perspective on the earliest observations of this process, akin to the idea of overeducation and known as educational credentialism, was never the best way to conceive of the trend sociologically (Collins 1979). The education revolution has transformed the entire institution of occupational credentialing, not in a false or inflationary way, but along its own institutional terms. A similar transformation has occurred for work.

The Educated Job and Workplace

The first piece of evidence of the educational transformation of the institution of jobs and work in postindustrial society is precisely how wrong the dire predictions were that the education revolution would produce extensive overeducation and thus

---

[5]Details about each of these examples can be found on the *Wall Street Journal*'s Web site under "Careers" November 13, 2008, with summaries and references from *Wall Street Journal* original articles.

social upheaval (Dore 1976; Bowles and Gintis 1976; Clogg 1979; Freeman 1975, 1976; Rumberger 1981; Smith 1986; Witmer 1980). When sociologists searched for social unrest due to the education revolution, they could not see even the remotest of traces. For example, in an analysis of a large, nationally representative example of working Americans, Burris (1983) finds no substantial differences between people who are overly educated for their jobs and those with an adequate education when compared across job satisfaction, political radicalism, political alienation, unionism, and allegiance to an achievement ideology (Spenner 1988; see also Vaisey 2006 for modest effect on job satisfaction).[6] The education revolution did not cause social unrest among less wealthy nations, nor did it create the predicted downgrading of its own effectiveness in curricular content, instruction, and student motivation (Baker 2009). If anything, evidence shows an upgrading of the influence of the education revolution on curriculum, instruction, and motivation across academic content (Baker et al. 2010a). Extrapolating from Meyer's (1977) hypothesis, educational expansion and deeper institutionalization of its functions likely led to a transformation of the world of work in terms of job context and working conditions. Three prime examples of this change can be noted.

First, as formal education becomes the dominating institution of social and occupational allocation based on greater generalization of academic intelligence, a new image of the worker emerges defined by his cognitive skills and related capabilities, increasingly credentialed by the attainment of academic degrees. Contrary to older visions of jobs and skills, new evidence suggests that as larger numbers of educated individuals enter the labor market, employed in large complex organizations, a sustained shift occurs toward the creation of jobs with more higher order cognitive activities, and managerial and communicative components, or in other words, the mass professionalization of work (Drori et al. 2006).

Research demonstrates this point. An analysis of changes in job content across a consistent set of 264 occupations and 64 industries from 1960 to 1985 found significant growth in the cognitive skills of analytical reasoning (i.e., use of mathematics, language, and reasoning) and synthetic reasoning (i.e., working with new ideas and concepts through effortful thinking and new problem solving) as job requirements (Howell and Wolff 1991). Similarly, the jobs with higher cognitive complexity attracted large gains among professionals and technical workers. They increased their share of the overall labor market from 4% in the early part of the twentieth century to 23% by the beginning of the twenty-first century, an absolute expansion from 1.7 million to over 30 million workers (Wyatt and Hecker 2006). Correspondingly, over the twentieth century there was massive growth in computer specialists, engineers, accountants, auditors, healthcare professionals, educators at the university level, and teachers. Certainly a proportion of this expansion is due to an increase in technical components of jobs but it is also due to the growth in jobs with professional qualities.

---

[6]The one small difference found was on job satisfaction for very highly educated people working in menial jobs.

Second, research on technology adoption and job content in private firms shows that the education level of employees causes substantial change in basic job activities related to use of technology. This change is the opposite of what usually is assumed in the traditional model of education and society. Recently, labor economists have been exploring complementary technology, or the process by which the educated worker transforms the workplace through the expectations of what s/he is capable of and hence what technologies will be most productive and profitable (Acemoglu 1998). The technology that is complimentary to more educated workers is what labor economists refer to as pervasive skill-biased technology and it is transforming the workplace (Berman et al. 1998; Levy and Murnane 1996; Autor et al. 1998). A rising supply of more educated people entering the labor market leads to greater use of pervasive skill-biased technology, resulting in jobs within production plants rapidly being upgraded through a complimentary relationship between education and technology. This transformation is happening across nations within both the same industries and the same plants within those industries, thus ruling out many exogenous factors that could influence the composition of the labor force. The trend is significant. In many developed nations from 1979 to 1987, a 71% shift to more educated workers within plants occurred. This increase in a production factor is more than eight times more influential than increased trade (Berman et al. 1998).

Lastly, evidence from econometric modeling of historical macroeconomic development of several nations over the twentieth century shows that a significant force in economic development is the upward spiraling interplay between rising human capital through educational expansion of the working population and technological change (Goldin and Katz 2008; Rubinson 1986). In other words, the educational transformation of jobs and the workplace has a causal role in economic development.

Into the Future

The educational transformations of access to jobs and work demonstrate how the combined functions of allocation and cognitive development connect the institution of education to other core institutions in postmodern society. Educational credentialing and rising cognitive content of jobs are two of the factors that influence the symbiotic intensifying functions of education. Meyer's (1977) hypothesis can be generalized beyond work and occupations to all types of institutions. A case can also be made that current educational transformations of other institutions adds future legitimation to the institution of education itself. An upward spiraling process of greater institutional influence followed by greater institutionalization into society has long been recognized as the hallmark of primary institutions at their most robust stage (Berger and Luckmann 1966). Therefore, it is relatively easy to predict that the transformative qualities of the education revolution will continue worldwide into the foreseeable future. This provides at least three frontiers for sociological investigation of education.

Functionalism Revisited

Since the late 1960s, the influence of social origin on adult status chiefly occurred through the influence of social origin on the child's educational attainment. This relationship has become a primary focus of the sociological investigation of schooling. Understanding schooling as a conduit for social reproduction through differentiation in educational access, quality, and opportunity remains at the heart of the field. Yet, as productive as this research effort has been, one can speculate on whether this success came at the expense of less sociological investigation into the rise of allocation based on education achievement. It can be argued that as a result, the sociology of education may be less prepared intellectually to integrate the evidence of a vanishing impact of family social origin and a rising influence of educational performance on adult status.

Rather than viewing social class reproduction and functional models of education and society in a zero-sum fashion, one could consider them as two ends of a continuum. Empirical evidence indicates that education can play both roles at once and the balance between them can shift over time. However, in the past four decades, theoretical models proposed by sociologists of education in the USA and Europe have tended to concentrate primarily on reproduction. Projecting the impact of the education revolution into the future suggests that sociological investigation attaching more importance to function and less to class reproduction could add greatly to our understanding of the impact of education on postmodern society. Because it avoids a number of the theoretical problems limiting older structural functionalism approaches, a neoinstitutional perspective may engender an effective functional analysis (Luhmann 1990). Beyond the research summarized here, perhaps most promising would be a research agenda that fully explores Meyer's (1977) hypothesis about the greater institutionalization of education and its transforming effects on other institutions.

Educational Stratification as Meritocracy

A meritocratic educational system is considered to be highly desirable in postindustrial society. Many sociologists of education view educationally determined status as a step toward basing social status on merit instead of privilege. Others criticize the equating of educationally determined status with merit, citing a host of studies showing that in practice, education rarely offers equal opportunity to succeed in school for everyone for various noneducational reasons (Baker and LeTendre 2005). Whether widespread education could be meritocratic if opportunity to succeed educationally were unencumbered by noneducational factors related to social privilege has not been determined even though some empirical analyses reviewed above show that the impact of noneducational factors on educational attainment has substantially declined with the expansion of education.

What is missing in the debate over an educational meritocracy is a discussion of the basic assumption underlying the arguments, namely, that if fairly achieved, educational attainment is, if not completely meritocratic, then at least the most legitimate accomplishment on which to base future opportunity. Considerable agreement may be found in postindustrial society that formal education is the proper context for merit. This belief could be education's central triumph as an institution over the course of the education revolution. In a sense, the world that Young envisioned in his 1958 dark satire on intelligence has come about, although it is likely less dark, less oppressive, and less hierarchical than he predicted. Whether educational achievement is true merit is not the correct sociological question to ask. In past societies, celebrated noneducational contexts of merit, such as military prowess, were viewed as meritorious. Today, academic intelligence is constructed as merit in the schooled society.[7] Over the past century and a half, education has been accepted worldwide as the one appropriate, legitimate basis on which to compete for merit. Sociological inquiry into how education shapes the terms of merit and accomplishment is a promising avenue for future research.

Educational Expansion and Research on Social Stratification

The educational transformation of occupational credentialing and work are two examples indicating the broader trend that, as the institution of education changes, so does the nature of social stratification. Neoinstitutional study of educational expansion has so far missed an important opportunity to examine the dynamics between expansion and stratification.[8] Once the overeducation argument is discarded, the relationship between the educational revolution and social stratification is problematized anew. A central research question along this line is how the creation of new educational degrees, which at first are rare and then over time become more widely attained, shape stratification processes at each stage of expansion.

Lastly along this line, it should be noted that the neoinstitutional perspective on education does not rule out all influence of other social institutions on education. Certainly other robust institutions in postindustrial society, such as capitalism and democratic politics, can influence education as an institution, just as they have been transformed by education (Baker 2009; Kamens 2009). This represents an interesting research question for the future: Even though education is a robust institution, under what conditions can it be transformed? For example, while there is no evidence that prior economic downturns changed the development of the fundamental role of education in allocation reviewed above, the unprecedented

---

[7] In fact, this is so much so that modern militaries themselves prefer educational credentials as prior training to be an effective solider (Boesel et al. 1998).

[8] See Dougherty 1988 for an account of similar shortcoming of functional and conflict perspectives.

current world recession might retard educational expansion, and this may have uncharted consequences for social mobility.

These frontiers are only three of several new topics for research that the schooled society presents to sociologists of education. The implications of the neoinstitutional model of education and society significantly broaden the future scope of theory and empirical research in this area. Investigating the full range of individual and institutional transformations caused by the worldwide expansion of the schooled society is a major intellectual challenge facing sociologists of education and will determine the continued success of this field of sociology.

References

Acemoglu, D. 1998. Why do new technologies complement skills? Directed technical change and wage inequality. *Quarterly Journal of Economics* 113: 1055–1089.

Ackroyd, P. 1998. *The life of Thomas More*. New York: Anchor Books.

Autor, D.H., L.F. Katz, and A.B. Krueger. 1998. Computing inequality: Have computers changed the labor market? *Quarterly Journal of Economics* 113: 1169–1213.

Baker, D. 2009. The educational transformation of work: Toward a new synthesis. *Journal of Education and Work* 22: 163–193.

Baker, D. Forthcoming. *The schooled society: How the quiet education revolution transforms society*.

Baker, D. 2011. Forward and backward, horizontal and vertical: Transformation of occupational credentialing in the schooled society. *Research in Social Stratification and Mobility: A Journal of the International Sociological Association* 29(1): 5–29.

Baker, D., and G.K. LeTendre. 2005. *National differences, global similarities: World culture and the future of schooling*. Stanford: Stanford University Press.

Baker, D., H. Knipe, E. Cummings, J. Collins, J. Leon, C. Blair, and D. Gamson. 2010a. One hundred years of American primary school mathematics: A content analysis and cognitive assessment of textbooks from 1900 to 2000. *Journal of Research on Mathematics Education* 41(4): 383–423.

Baker, D., J. Leon, and J. Collins. 2010b. Facts, attitudes, and health reasoning about HIV and AIDS: Explaining the education effect on condom use among adults in Sub-Saharan Africa. *AIDS and Behavior* 11. doi: 10.1007/s10461-010-9717-9.

Baker, D., J. Leon, E. G. Smith, J. Collins, and M. Movit. 2010c. *Education and population health: A reassessment*. Working Paper Series, #WP1003, Population Research Institute, Pennsylvania State University.

Bell, D. 1973. *The coming of post-industrial society*. New York: Basic Books.

Benavot, A. 1983. The rise and decline of vocational education. *Sociology of Education* 56: 63–76.

Benavot, A., and P. Riddle. 1988. The expansion of primary education, 1870–1940: Trends and issues. *Sociology of Education* 61: 191–210.

Berger, P., and T. Luckmann. 1966. *The social construction of reality: A treatise in the sociology of knowledge*. Garden City: Anchor Books.

Berman, E., J. Bound, and S. Machin. 1998. Implications of skill-biased technological change: International evidence. *Quarterly Journal of Economics* 113: 1245–1279.

Bills, D. 2004. *Sociology of education and work*. Malden: Blackwell Publishing.

Blair, C., D. Gamson, S. Thorne, and D. Baker. 2005. Rising mean IQ: Cognitive demand of mathematics education for young children, population exposure to formal schooling, and the neurobiology of the prefrontal cortex. *Intelligence* 33: 93–106.

Blau, P.M., and O.D. Duncan. 1967. *The American occupational structure*. New York: Wiley.

Bowles, S., and H. Gintis. 1976. *Schooling in capitalist America: Educational reform and the contradictions of economic life*. New York: Basic Books.

Brand, J., and Y. Xie. 2010. Who benefits most from college? Evidence for negative selection in heterogeneous economic returns to higher education. *American Sociological Review* 75: 273–302.

Breen, R., and J. Jonsson. 2007. Explaining change in social fluidity: Educational equalization and educational expansion in twentieth-century Sweden. *The American Journal of Sociology* 112: 1775–1810.

Breen, R., and R. Luijkx. 2007. Social mobility and education: A comparative analysis of period and cohort trends in Britain and Germany. In *From origin to destination: Trends and mechanisms in social stratification research*, eds. S. Scherer, R. Pollak, G. Otte, and M. Gangl, 102–124. New York: Campus.

Burris, V. 1983. The social and political consequences of overeducation. *American Sociological Review* 48: 454–67.

Ceci, S.J. 1991. How much does schooling influence general intelligence and its cognitive components? A reassessment of the evidence. *Developmental Psychology* 27: 703–722.

Clogg, C. 1979. *Measuring underemployment: Demographic indicators for the United States*. New York: Academic.

Cole, M. 1996. *Cultural psychology: A once and future discipline*. Cambridge: The Belknap Press of Harvard University Press.

Collins, R. 1979. *The credential society*. New York: Academic.

Dore, R. 1976. *The diploma disease: Education, qualification and development*. Berkeley: University of California Press.

Dougherty, K.J. 1988. The politics of community college expansion: Beyond the functionalist and class-reproduction explanations. *American Journal of Education* 96: 351–293.

Downey, D.B., P. von Hippel, and B. Broh. 2004. Are schools the great equalizer? Cognitive inequality during the summer months and the school year. *American Sociological Review* 69: 613–635.

Drori, G., J. Meyer, and H. Hwang. 2006. *Globalization and organization: World society and organizational change*. Oxford: Oxford University Press.

Ezell, E., and J. Bear. 2005. *Degree mills: The billion-dollar industry that has sold over a million fake diplomas*. Amherst: Prometheus Books.

Flynn, J.R. 1998. IQ gains over time: Toward finding the causes. In *The rising curve: Long term gains in IQ and related measures*, ed. U. Neisser, 25–66. Washington, DC: American Psychological Association.

Frank, D., and J. Gabler. 2006. *Reconstructing the university: Worldwide shifts in Academia in the 20th century*. Stanford: Stanford University Press.

Freeman, R. 1975. Overinvestment in college training. *The Journal of Human Resources* 10: 287–311.

Freeman, R. 1976. *The overeducated American*. New York: Academic.

Fuller, B., and R. Rubinson (eds.). 1992. *The political construction of education: The state, school expansion, and economic change*. New York: Praeger Publishers.

Galbraith, J. 1969. *The affluent society*. New York: Houghton Mifflin.

Goldin, C., and L. Katz. 2008. *The race between education and technology*. Cambridge: Harvard University Press.

Hecker, D. 2005. Occupational employment projections to 2014. *Monthly Labor Review*, November 2005, 86–125.

Hegna, K. and I. Smette. 2010. *Educational horizons: The role of agency, class and gender in the choice of upper secondary education*. Working Paper, Norwegian Research Council.

Hogan, D. 1996. 'To better our condition': Educational credentialing and 'the silent compulsion of economic relations' in the United States, 1830 to the present. *History of Education Quarterly* 36: 243–270.

Hout, M. 1984. Status, autonomy, and training in occupational mobility. *The American Journal of Sociology* 89: 1397–1409.

Hout, M. 1988. More universalism, less structural mobility: The American occupational structure in the 1980s. *The American Journal of Sociology* 93: 1358–1400.

Hout, M., and T.A. DiPrete. 2006. What have we learned? RC28's contributions to knowledge about social stratification? *Research in Social Stratification and Mobility* 24: 1–20.

Howell, D., and E. Wolff. 1991. Trends in the growth and distribution of skills in the U.S. workplace, 1960–1985. *Industrial & Labor Relations Review* 44: 486–502.

Ishida, H. 1993. *Social mobility in contemporary Japan educational credentials class and the labor market in cross-national perspective*. Stanford: Stanford University Press.

Kamens, D. 2009. The expanding polity: Theorizing the links between expanded higher education and the new politics of the post-1970s. *American Journal of Education* 116(1): 99–124.

Kamens, D., and A. Benavot. 2006. Worldwide models of secondary education, 1960–2000. In *School knowledge in comparative and historical perspective: Changing curricula in primary and secondary education*, eds. A. Benavot and C. Braslavsky, 135–54. Amsterdam: Springer.

Kamens, D.H., J.W. Meyer, and A. Benavot. 1996. Worldwide patterns in academic secondary education curricula. *Comparative Education Review* 40: 116–138.

Kleiner, M.M. 2006. *Licensing occupations: Ensuring quality or restricting competition?* Kalamazoo: W. E. Upjohn Institute.

Kleiner, M.M. and A.B. Krueger. 2008. *The prevalence and effects of occupational licensing*, Working Paper 14308. Cambridge, MA: National Bureau of Economic Research.

Labaree, D. 1986. Curriculum, credentials, and the middle class. *Sociology of Education* 59(1): 42–57.

Levy, F., and R. Murnane. 1996. With what skills are computers a complement? *The American Economic Review* 86: 258–262.

Luhmann, M. 1990. The paradox of system differentiation and the evolution of society. In *Differentiation theory and social change*, eds. J. Alexander and P. Colomy, 409–440. New York: Columbia University Press.

Luria, A.R. 1976. *Cognitive development: Its cultural and social foundations*. Cambridge: Harvard University Press.

Martinez, M. 2000. *Education as the cultivation of intelligence*. New Jersey: Erlbaum Associates.

Meyer, J.W. 1977. The effects of education as an institution. *The American Journal of Sociology* 83: 55–77.

Meyer, J. 2000. Reflections on education as transcendence. In *Reconstructing the common good in education*, eds. L. Cuban and D. Shipps, 206–222. Stanford: Stanford University Press.

Monhan, S.C., J.W. Meyer, and W.R. Scott. 1994. Employee training: The expansion of organizational citizenship. In *Institutional environments and organizations*, eds. W.R. Scott and J.W. Meyer, 255–269. Thousand Oaks: Sage.

Nisbett, R.E. 2009. *Intelligence and how to get it: Why schools and cultures count*. New York: W. W. Norton and Company, Inc.

Parsons, T. 1971. Higher education as a theoretical focus. In *The sociologies of Talcott Parsons and George C. Homans*, eds. H. Turk and R.L. Simpson, 233–252. Indianapolis: Bobbs-Merill.

Peters, E., D. Baker, N. Deickmann, J. Leon, and J. Collins. 2010. Explaining the education effect on health: A field-study from Ghana. *Psychological Science* 21(10):1369–1376

Rubinson, R. 1986. Class formation, politics, and institutions: Schooling in the United States. *The American Journal of Sociology* 92: 519–548.

Rumberger, R. 1981. The rising incidence of overeducation in the U.S. labor market. *Economics of Education Review* 20: 199–220.

Schaub, M. 2010. Parenting of cognitive development: Mass education and the social construction of parenting 1950–2000. *Sociology of Education* 83: 46–66.

Schofer, E., and J. Meyer. 2005. The worldwide expansion of higher education in the twentieth century. *American Sociological Review* 70: 898–920.

Schultz, T.W. 1961. Investment in human capital. *The American Economic Review* 51: 1–17.

Schwadel, P. 2003. The Persistence of religion: The effects of education on American Christianity. Ph.D. Dissertation, Pennsylvania State University.

Shanahan, S., and S. Khagram. 2006. Dynamics of corporate responsibility. In *Globalization and organization: World society and organizational change*, eds. G.S. Drori, J.W. Meyer, and H. Hwang, 196–224. Oxford: Oxford University Press.

Shavit, Y., and H.P. Blossfeld. 1993. *Persistent inequality: Changing educational achievement in thirteen countries.* Boulder: Westview Press.

Smith, H. 1986. Overeducation and underemployment: An agnostic review. *American Sociological Association* 59: 85–99.

Smith, T. 2003. Who values the GED? An examination of the paradox underlying the demand for the general educational development credential. *Teachers College Record* 105(3): 375–415.

Spenner, K.I. 1988. Social stratification, work and personality. *Annual Review of Sociology* 14: 69–97.

Stevenson, H., and C. Chuansheng. 1989. Schooling and achievement: A study of Peruvian children. *International Journal of Educational Research* 13(8): 883–894.

Stinchcombe, A., and J. March. 1965. *Handbook of organizations.* Chicago: Rand McNally.

Torche, F. 2010. *Is a college degree still the great equalizer?* Intergenerational mobility across levels of schooling in the U.S. Working Paper, New York University Center for Advanced Social Science Research

Treiman, D.J., and H.B.G. Ganzeboom. 1990. Comparative status attainment research. *Research in Social Stratification and Mobility* 9: 105–127.

Tulviste, P. 1991. *The cultural-historical development of verbal thinking.* Commack: Nova Science.

U.S. Department of Education. 1993. *120 years of American education: A statistical portrait.* Washington, DC: U.S. Government Printing Office.

U.S. Department of Education. 2003. *Trends in high school vocational/technical coursetaking: 1982–1998.* NCES 2003–025, by Karen Levesque. Washington, DC.

U.S. Department of Education. 2005. *The Institute of Education Sciences, National Center for Education Statistics, Adult Education Survey of the 2005 National Household Education Surveys Program* [Public-use data file].

U.S. Department of Education. 2008. *National Center for Education Statistics Digest of Educational Statistics.* Washington, DC: U.S. Government Printing. Retrieved October 13, 2010 (http://nces.ed.gov/Programs/digest).

UNESCO. 2002. *Education for all: Is the world on track?* EFA Monitoring Report. Paris: UNESCO.

Vaisey, S. 2006. Education and its discontents: Overqualification in America, 1972–2002. *Social Forces* 85: 835–864.

Vallet, L. 2004. Change in intergenerational class mobility in France from the 1970s to the 1990s and its explanation: An analysis following the CASMIN approach. In *Social mobility in Europe*, ed. R. Breen, 115–145. Oxford: Oxford University Press.

Witmer, D.R. 1980. Has the golden age of American higher education come to an abrupt end? *The Journal of Human Resources* 15: 113–120.

Wyatt, I. and D. Hecker. 2006. Occupational Changes during the 20th Century. *Monthly Labor Review*, March 2006, 35–57.

Young, M. 1958. *The Rise of the meritocracy, 1870–2033: The new elite of our social revolution.* New York: Random House.

Young, M. 2008. *Bringing knowledge back in: From social constructivism to social realism in the sociology of education.* New York: Routledge.

Chapter 3
Frontiers in Comparative and International Sociology of Education: American Distinctiveness and Global Diversity

Claudia Buchmann

Many of the questions examined in US sociology of education today are quite grounded, practical, or policy oriented. Sociologists of education ask questions about the specifics of the US educational system, about the details of how students move through the system, and about the implications of these features for inequalities in achievement, attainment, and other outcomes. Much research in the field seeks to describe empirical relationships regarding social problems related to schooling, most often in the USA. This focus contributes detailed knowledge of the society in which many researchers and their audiences are based. It is rooted in the goal of understanding real issues and problems in education and speaking to the formation of national and state level policies pertaining to education.

But in its quest for understanding US-specific schooling, the American sociology of education has lost sight of another primary goal of social research: improving and expanding theories of education to refine their explanatory power. Critics of this current state of affairs have bemoaned the narrowness of the field (Meyer quoted in Bromley 2010) and its apparent lack of "concern for theory testing or the accumulation of propositional knowledge about schooling and society" (Brint 2009:13). Because many recent analyses in the sociology of education have been "conceptually shallow and empirically incremental…few have made a major contribution to our understanding of the role of today's schools in a rapidly changing global society" (Hallinan 2011:1).

One reason for the theoretical shallowness of the field is its disproportionate focus on education in the USA. Overt concern with a single nation limits progress in advancing general theories of education, because "important elements of the societal context are held constant and therefore may not be subject to even implicit consideration"

C. Buchmann (✉)
Department of Sociology, The Ohio State University, Columbus, OH 43210, USA
e-mail: buchmann.4@sociology.osu.edu

(Broaded 1997:36; see also Meyer 1987). In fact, extensive detailed knowledge of a single case may be counterproductive to the goal of advancing general theory, if scholars erroneously generalize knowledge from an atypical case (Ragin 1994).

In the quest to advance general knowledge and theories about education and educational processes in a global society, comparative and international approaches offer leverage over US-centric approaches on two fronts. First, comparative and international research can provide fresh insights to longstanding questions in the sociology of education, which serve to refine and expand existing theories. When comparative research addresses similar questions but reveals different answers from those provided by US-based research, the theoretical leverage gained is most readily apparent. Second, comparative and international research can pose new questions rarely considered in US-focused research that are crucial to developing a general sociology of education and new theoretical perspectives. In these ways, comparative research holds the promise to lead the American sociology of education in bold new directions to make contributions to the study of schooling and educational systems in the global era.

This chapter assesses the degree to which the American sociology of education is comparative and international in scope and briefly considers why the attention devoted to comparative and international research has remained relatively stable over time. It then explains the distinctive role of comparative and international research for advancing new insights on longstanding substantive questions and provides examples of prior studies that have done so. Beyond calling for more international and comparative research, it advocates for greater dialogue and integration between the US-focused and comparative and international streams of research in sociology of education. The chapter then discusses some pressing questions rarely considered by US-based research that constitute frontiers for a more globally oriented and theoretically expansive sociology of education.

How Comparative?

There is no doubt that the American sociology of education has been largely a US-centric enterprise. But in light of globalization of the past 20 years or so, to what degree has the field become more internationally comparative? One way to capture the extent to which the American sociology of education is comparative in scope is to examine the proportion of all articles in the discipline's leading journal, *Sociology of Education,* that are internationally or comparatively oriented.[1] Between 1990 and

---

[1] *Sociology of Education* is one of the highest ranking education journals in the USA and nearly exclusively publishes research by sociologists of education. Thus, it can be said to reflect the "forefront of current sociological thinking about education in the USA" (Brint 2009:8). Articles (excluding special features, comments, and replies) were coded as international and comparative if they focused on one or more societies other than the USA. Case studies of a single society other than the USA, research comparing at least two societies (one of which could be the USA), and cross-national research comparing many nations were all coded as international and comparative.

1999, 35 of the 169 research articles (20.7%) published in the journal were comparative or internationally oriented. In the next decade, 2000–2009, 27 of the 159 research articles published (16.9%) were comparative or international in their orientation. Thus, on average, since 1990 roughly 19% of the research articles published in the leading journal in the American sociology of education were comparative and international in scope.

When these results are compared with those from an analysis for an earlier period (Ramirez and Meyer 1981), it is clear that the quantity of content devoted to international research in the *Sociology of Education* has increased, albeit slightly. Ramirez and Meyer (1981) found that between 1964 and 1981, 15% of the articles published in the journal were comparative or international in their scope.

From this evaluation we can conclude that the quantity of comparative and international content has remained relatively stable over the past four decades and that it has never comprised more than 20% of the content in the *Sociology of Education*. A content analysis of a single journal offers only one lens on the field's degree of internationality, but other approaches, such as examining books or papers presented at the annual meetings of the American Sociological Association, likely would reveal a similar picture of a field that focuses about one fifth of its efforts on comparative and international research.

Perhaps it is not surprising that the majority of pages of the leading American journal devoted to the sociology of education should be focused on the education in the USA (Baker 1994). On the other hand, in this era of globalization and the rapid expansion of international data sources in recent decades, a parallel expansion in international and comparative research might have been expected. This is true especially in light of the "ritual deference" to the need for more comparative international research in the field (Ramirez and Meyer 1981). Editors of *Sociology of Education* often explicitly appeal for more international research in the pages of the journal when they begin their editorship (see e.g., Alexander 2003; Schneider 2006; Bills 2009). Schneider stated it this way: "One area that the sociology of education has devoted limited attention to is globalization, both as it relates to mass education and with respect to how education is serving minority groups within the USA and other countries. We encourage submissions from scholars in the USA and abroad on these issues" (2006:1).

Why have such appeals for more globally focused education research gone largely unheeded? Perhaps it is because calls for more comparative and international research in the field have seldom explained why such research is needed or described the broad intellectual returns it could bring to the field generally. Comparative and international research and the theoretical leverage it offers are seldom emphasized in graduate training in sociology of education. Instead, in this era of ever-increasing expectations for publications, many graduate programs "encourage students to make their careers by exploring under-investigated empirical relationships rather than working on testing or developing theory" (Brint 2009:14). Moreover, comparative and international research is difficult and time consuming. Scholars interested in comparative research have to work harder to find and compile data,[2] to gain the substantial knowledge necessary to conduct research on societies about which they initially may know little, and to convince a disproportionately US-centric audience of the broad relevance of their research. These challenges of comparative and international research clearly will not appeal to all scholars, but those scholars who rise to these challenges also have great opportunities to reap the rewards.

The Value of a Comparative Lens for Extending Theory

Across a significant number of characteristics, the American educational system is distinctive from most other educational systems in the world today. The American educational system is marked by decentralized, local control of the main components of schooling and the propensity for multiple grassroots reforms. In contrast to highly standardized educational systems found in much of the world, the US educational system is marked by a lack of standardization. Teacher training, school budgets, examinations, and a host of other factors are determined at the local and state levels, not at the national level (Kerckhoff 2001). This low level of standardization in the American educational system has implications for a wide array of educational processes and outcomes. For example, Park (2008) finds that in less standardized educational systems, like that of the USA, parents of low socioeconomic status face more barriers to necessary knowledge about schooling, due to the lack of accountability and transparency in such educational systems. In contrast, the greater accountability and transparency of standardized education systems enables parents from all socioeconomic backgrounds to assess and monitor the child's performance in comparison to established standards.

American secondary education also is distinctive in that virtually all high schools award the same credential, the high school diploma (Müller and Shavit 1998; Kerckhoff 2001). In many other countries, different types of secondary schools provide different credentials to their students. As a result, American schooling tends to be less vocationally oriented relative to schooling in other industrialized countries and has a weaker capacity to structure the flow of students out of educational institutions and into the labor market (Kerckhoff 1996, 2000; see also Mortimer and Krueger 2000). The American system is rife with second chances for students who do not complete a particular level of schooling by a certain age (Turner 1960; Clark 1985; Brint and Karabel 1989; Levin and Levin 1991), such as the possibility of graduating from high school by means of a GED for students who drop out of high school (Milesi 2010). For all these reasons, "it is best to think of the American institutional structure as an outlier in comparison to other systems" (Baker 1994:59).

---

[2] Fortunately, data constraints have eased in the past decade with the development of several high quality, comparative international data sets related to education. These include the Trends in International Math and Science Study (TIMSS), Progress in International Reading Literacy Study (PIRLS), the International Adult Literacy Study (IALS) and, perhaps most notably, the Program for Student Assessment (PISA) of the Organization for Economic Cooperation and Development (OECD).

Precisely because the US system of education is distinctive in many ways, comparative and international research has an especially important role to play in the sociology of education. It can determine the degree to which propositions formulated in the USA can apply to other contexts. Comparative and international research on education also can generate important questions for further research that would not be considered if only a US-centric lens were used. Finally, a comparative lens can serve to caution scholars to resist the tendency to generalize knowledge from the often atypical case of the American educational system.

Nearly half a century ago, Marsh noted the centrality of comparative analysis to the goal of generating universal propositions in the social sciences:

> A science strives to formulate universal propositions. Once a proposition has been tentatively formulated, the task of research is to replicate it, attempt to state limiting conditions and intervening variables, and analyze exceptional cases. In this process, inter-societal comparative analysis is but a necessary extension of intra-societal comparative analysis. It is a necessary step, but one that many sociologists fail to take (Marsh 1967:11).

Marsh astutely critiqued the tendency of sociologists to formulate universal propositions prematurely from a single case. He also noted the crucial role of inter-societal analysis to refine and extend general theories.

Other scholars have described the process of theory building as the search for mechanisms behind any observed or predicted systematic relationship between two events or variables. A mechanism is simply "an account of how change in some variable is brought about" (Sorensen 1998:240). When scholars search for generative mechanisms, they are able to distinguish between "genuine causality and coincidental association" and thus come closer to "understanding why we observe what we observe" (Hedstrom and Swedberg 1998:9).

Comparative research is one particularly promising strategy in the search for mechanism-based explanations of social processes because comparative, intersocietal research lays bare the effects of context and structure. "Although structural and contextual effects are not themselves mechanisms (Sorensen 1998:253), they are proxies for mechanisms that vary across settings" (Reskin 2003:14). By examining relationships between events or variables in diverse societies, scholars get closer to understanding the mechanisms behind those relationships. In some cases, research will demonstrate that a relationship appears to be consistent in a wide variety of settings. But in other instances, where the relationship found in some contexts does not hold in others and the outcomes are quite different, the theoretical leverage to be gained from comparative and international research is most readily apparent.

Consider three examples that demonstrate the power of comparative and international research to advance theory. In each case, the research explores a relationship that has been of longstanding concern in the American sociology of education. In each case, the research yields findings quite different from those well established in the USA and as a result, refines thinking about the mechanisms underlying the relationships of interest.

The first example is drawn from the study of family structure and children's educational outcomes. Much US-based research found that having many siblings is detrimental to an individual's educational performance and attainment (Steelman et al. 2002). The inverse relationship between the number of siblings and educational outcomes came to be viewed as "one of the most consistent findings in the status attainment literature" (Downey 1995:746). A prominent explanatory mechanism for this relationship is resource dilution, that is, with each additional child in the household, there are fewer material resources and less parental attention available to each individual child. Finite resources must be distributed across more children. Fewer resources per child, in turn, lead to lower academic performance and attainment.

More recently, comparative research has examined this longstanding relationship to find that the negative relationship between sibship size and educational outcomes tends not to hold in some societies. Instead, in many developing countries, the number of siblings a child has is either neutral or beneficial for his or her educational performance and attainment. In Vietnam, the negative relationship between sibship size and enrollment disappeared when controls for socioeconomic status were added (Anh et al. 1998). In Kenya, Buchmann (2000) found no effect of sibship size on children's probability of enrollment. In Botswana, the number of 7- to 14-year-old children in the household was positively related to educational enrollment and attainment (Chernichovsky 1985). In China, Lu and Treiman (2008) found that effects of sibship size on educational attainment varied over time in response to changing state educational policies. When schooling opportunities were limited and expensive, children in large families obtained less schooling. When schooling expanded and became less expensive, the negative relationship between many siblings and educational attainment disappeared.

The extended family systems common in developing countries can provide resources, economic or otherwise, that facilitate children's schooling. In some societies, older children also are expected to contribute their earnings and other resources to finance the education of younger children. Thus, the relationship consistently found in the USA is not generalizable to all countries. Taken together, evidence from developing and developed nations suggests that there is no axiomatic relationship between family size and schooling (Buchmann and Hannum 2001). Rather, the relationship varies according to a society's level of development; the USA represents only one context in a continuum of societies. Moreover, the diversity of patterns in the relationship between family size and school outcomes across different societies improves our understanding of the mechanisms underlying the family size–educational attainment relationship. Family resources do indeed play a key role in individual children's educational success, but societal variations in the structure of families (e.g., nuclear or extended) can give rise to different family strategies to procure those resources.

Another example of the value of international research for refining general theory comes from research on how interpersonal influences shape students' educational expectations. After more than 30 years of US-based research on this relationship, the consensus became that peers and parents "shape ambitions more directly and with greater impact than any other source" (Spenner and Featherman 1978:392). When highly comparable international survey data became available in the mid-1990s, Buchmann and Dalton (2002) examined the reach of this well-known relationship and found that in some countries, peers and parents had little or no impact on students' educational expectations. They reasoned that whether or not these significant others are influential for students' educational expectations depends, in large part, on the structural features of the educational systems in which they operate. In the US system of relatively open, undifferentiated secondary schooling, peer and parental attitudes about academic performance significantly influence adolescents' own attitudes and aspirations, net of other factors. The diffuse charter of US secondary schools (Meyer 1977) means that schools have little influence on the expectations and self-conceptions of their students. But in educational systems where students are sorted into different educational pathways at an early age, their expectations are determined in large part by the type of secondary school they attend; there is far less room for significant others' attitudes to influence students' educational expectations (2002).

Like the example of the relationship between sibship size and children's educational outcomes, this second example demonstrates how a social process of central interest, the role of significant others in this case, is not fixed or finite; rather, its effects depend on the context in which it operates. Awareness of such variations in the relationship between significant others and adolescent educational expectations can give rise to a more nuanced understanding of the process of attitude formation among adolescents which, in turn, can lead to more elaborate theories.

A final example comes from the study of curricular differentiation within academic subjects (tracking) and its relationship to inequality of opportunity and achievement. Much US-based research has shown that tracking tends to magnify inequality of achievement because minority and low-income students often are assigned disproportionately to lower tracks (Gamoran and Mare 1989; Hallinan 1991, 1992; Lucas 1999) and students enrolled in lower tracks have lower achievement than students enrolled in higher tracks (Oakes et al. 1992; Gamoran 1987). These results have led many scholars to be critical of tracking, viewing the practice as "a segregative mechanism that…builds inequalities into schools that both devalue and materially disadvantage those groups who are least able to defend themselves" (Oakes 1994).

Comparative and international research on curricular differentiation demonstrates that tracking does not lead necessarily to inequalities in learning or achievement outcomes; rather, the effect of tracking depends on other features of the educational system in which tracking is implemented. In a comparative study of Israel and the USA, Ayalon and Gamoran (2000) found that in Israel tracking is associated with higher average achievement and lower achievement inequality, while in the USA, in line with prior research, they found that differentiation in academic programs reinforces inequalities. They attribute these differences to structures of the secondary education systems in the two countries. Israel's standardized curriculum and national examination system offer clear incentives for achievement among teachers and students in all levels of academic courses, whereas the absence of a standardized curriculum and national examination system in the USA leads tracking to reinforce inequality without raising average scores.

Research on Taiwan provides further evidence that the effects of tracking depend on features of the educational system in which it is implemented. Like Israel, Taiwan's educational system includes a highly standardized curriculum and national examinations (Broaded 1997). These features create high incentives for teachers and students to work hard and perform to the best of their ability, regardless of their track placement (1997:39). They also ensure that schools place students with the greatest aptitude for taking standardized tests into high ability tracks, with little or no regard to their social class backgrounds.

Knowledge of cases where tracking appears to have achieved the desired effects of both low inequality and high overall achievement is relevant for theory as well as US educational policy. It underscores how the effects of tracking can be better understood when aspects of both the school environment and the societal context are considered. These findings are also provocative for policymakers. In debates about how to achieve the desired goals of tracking without its detrimental effects in the USA, evidence about the effects of tracking from Israel and Taiwan could give rise to deeper reflection about other distinctive features of the US educational system that might be manipulated toward this goal. This is just one example of the benefits of greater integration between the US-focused and comparative and international streams of research in sociology of education.

These examples all demonstrate the power of comparative and international research to extend the theoretical and empirical scope of the questions sociologists of education ask and examine. In each case, new evidence from non-US contexts generates new ideas about a longstanding relationship of interest and extends and refines prior theories of these relationships.

The Value of a Comparative Lens for Developing New Global Theories of Education

> In the USA, ours has been a nationalist sociology of schooling, not a sociology of all forms of education in global society (Brint 2009:15).

Beyond extending the reach of general theories and highlighting the distinctive nature of the US educational system, comparative and international research is uniquely suited to pose new questions about education on a global scale that will be of great consequence in the next decade. With globalization, as economic, social, and cultural linkages and exchanges throughout the world have intensified they have stimulated powerful socioeconomic and demographic changes. These changes are challenging educational systems and schools everywhere in the world (Suarez-Orozco and Sattin 2007). As globalization promotes greater universalism and homogenization across national boundaries and regions, there are clear trends toward convergence in educational institutions and processes on a global level. The increasing standardization of curricula and core teaching practices (Baker and LeTendre 2005; Ramirez 2006; Meyer et al. 2010), the global spread of school choice principles (Forsey et al. 2008), and the rapid rise of shadow education throughout the world are just three examples of educational phenomena becoming more common in the course of globalization.

Within these and other trends of global convergence, there remain important differences across societies and their educational systems that significantly impact educational inequalities and outcomes for individuals and groups within those societies (Kerckhoff 2001). Institutional variations in educational systems lead to different processes whereby youth are sorted into educational trajectories and subsequent occupational destinations (Kerckhoff 1995, 2000, 2001; Shavit and Blossfeld 1993; Müller and Karle 1993; Shavit and Müller 1998). These institutional variations also impact various educational outcomes such as academic achievement (see Van de Werfhorst and Mijs 2010, for a review) and students' educational and occupational expectations (Buchmann and Park 2009). Two trends constitute particularly promising frontiers for future research: the global spread of shadow education and stability and change in educational stratification.

The Global Spread of Shadow Education

Shadow education, or out-of-school educational activities that supplement formal schooling, has grown rapidly throughout the world. These activities include tutoring and extra classes, offered either online or in learning centers, that are intended to increase students' chances of navigating the allocation process (Stevenson and Baker 1992:1640). A recent study of more than 40 nations found that more than a third of all seventh and eighth graders participate in tutoring, cram schools or other forms of shadow education in these nations (Baker et al. 2001; see also Bray 1999).

The prevalence of shadow education and its goals vary across nations. Shadow education can be remedial, when it is used to help struggling students improve their performance in school, or enriching, when it provides supplementary learning and skills beyond what is taught in school (Baker and LeTendre 2005). Shadow education of the enrichment variety often flourishes in educational systems where high-stakes testing serves as a gatekeeper to future educational opportunities (Stevenson and Baker 1992; Buchmann 2002; Yamamoto and Brinton 2010; Buchmann et al. 2010; Park et al. 2011). One form of shadow education in need of further research is the rapid growth of private learning center franchises. Private learning centers provide a host of remedial and enrichment supplemental educational services. The Sylvan Learning Company, with more than 2,000 franchises in North America and Europe, is the largest private learning company in the world (Sylvan Learning 2007). Aurini and Davies (2004) predict that this form of market-based shadow education is the wave of the future (see also Davies 2004; Aurini 2006).

The rapid growth of shadow education across the globe raises several important questions for further research. First, what factors have given rise to this global trend? Mori and Baker (2010) argue that the growth of shadow education is one consequence of the global spread of the schooled society (Baker 2011:11) and that "the use of shadow education is motivated by the dominant logic of educational expansion in all its forms" (2010:40). Scholars from human capital or conflict orientations may well have other interpretations about the mechanisms underlying the spread of shadow education throughout the world. A second set of questions involves the consequences of shadow education for educational inequalities and national educational systems. Does the emergence and expansion of shadow education magnify inequalities? Does it confound a nation's ability to provide equitable and high-quality education to the general population? The United Nations Educational, Scientific and Cultural Organization (UNESCO) has expressed concern that the rapid expansion of privatized shadow education could influence formal educational systems negatively in terms of both equity and quality (Bray 2009). It also is possible that national governments will seek to incorporate shadow education into formal schooling, such that "in the near future in most places mass shadow education will be a legitimate part of education itself" (Mori and Baker 2010:46). Whether and how these process occur and their consequences for educational systems, stratification and student performance remain to be seen.

Stability and Change in Educational Inequalities on a Global Scale

The dramatic expansion of education that has occurred since the mid-twentieth century generates new questions about educational inequalities within societies, across societies, and on a global scale. A core concern for the American sociology of education has been to understand how individuals come to be stratified in educational experiences and outcomes on the basis of class, gender, race, and immigrant status. A comparative lens illuminates how over the course of educational expansion, some stratification trends have been marked by substantial change and fluidity, while others have remained remarkably constant. An ongoing challenge for sociologists of education and stratification is to make sense of these patterns and trends and explain why some forms of educational inequality are resistant to change while others are changing rapidly.

Socioeconomic Status

The effect of social background on educational attainment has remained stable in almost all industrialized countries over the course of the past 20 years, despite educational expansion and various national policy interventions to reduce inequality (Mare 1981; Shavit and Blossfeld 1993; Torche 2005; Pfeffer 2008). This finding of persistent inequality underscores that educational expansion alone does not change the relative position of social groups in the education queue; already privileged groups manage to maintain their status by getting more education than the masses (Walters 2000). The persistent inequality phenomenon further highlights the need to consider separately the effects on educational inequality of an overall increase in the size of the educational system (school expansion) and changes in the rules by which educational opportunities are allocated (school reform) (Walters 2000:254). An enduring puzzle, then, is to explain why socioeconomic inequalities often prove resistant to educational expansion and policy change.

Gender

In contrast to the stability found in socioeconomic inequalities in education, trends in gender inequalities in education have seen remarkable fluidity in recent decades. A particularly dramatic shift has been the rapid rise of women in higher education throughout much of the world. Prior to the 1980s, women lagged behind men in the number of tertiary degrees completed in most nations. In the 1980s, women began to reach parity with men and in many cases surpassed men in the amount of education they received (Bradley and Ramirez 1996; Buchmann and DiPrete 2006). By 2000, more college-age women than men were enrolled in higher education in both the USA and the European Union (Eurostat 2002). Moreover, in most industrialized societies, females have made substantial gains in all realms of education and now generally outperform males on several educational benchmarks (for a review, see Buchmann et al. 2008). Even in developing countries, gender gaps in education increasingly favor, rather than discriminate against, females. Boys are still slightly more likely than girls to enroll in school, but girls now progress through school on pace with or at faster rates than boys and have equal or greater educational attainment than boys in most developing regions (Grant and Behrman 2010).

Projections suggest that the trend of growing female educational advantages throughout the world will continue well into the future. Old paradigms of comprehending gender differences in education as solely due to widespread obstacles to girls and women no longer help guide research. Sociologists of education are beginning to examine the forces that have led women to surpass men in educational attainment in many industrialized countries including the USA and similar trends in many developing countries, but much work remains. Fruitful explanations include different trends in the returns to education for men and women (DiPrete and Buchmann 2006), changes in the educational aspirations of postfeminist women (McDaniel 2010), and changes in the way parents invest resources in their sons and daughters (Buchmann and DiPrete 2006). Understanding why the educational attainment and performance of males has stagnated in some realms relative to females also is crucial. Clearly, the nature, causes, and consequences of the changing gender gaps in education throughout the world constitutes an important research frontier for sociologists of education.

Ethnic and Immigrant Status

Globalization, coupled with changes in immigration policies, has spurred a recent wave of immigration to industrialized world regions. The magnitude of this wave of immigration is unprecedented and it raises important questions about the impact on receiving nations and on the lives of both immigrants and nonimmigrants within these nations. For the large portion of the immigrant population that is young, prospects for social mobility largely stem from their experiences in the educational system.

While much research examines the determinants of academic achievement for children of immigrants in the USA (Kao and Tienda 1995; Zhou and Bankston 1998; Portes and Rumbaut 2001; Suarez-Orozco and Todorova 2007), very few studies have examined educational attainment and achievement gaps between immigrant and native-born students in a comparative and international context. Research that illuminates how and why immigrants differ from nonimmigrants in terms of their educational performance and attainment across societies constitutes an important frontier for sociologists of education. Prior predominantly US-based research focuses on individual-level explanations, such as differences in family background, sociocultural adaptation, and language ability, to explain the educationally disadvantaged position of immigrant students. But at the contextual level, features of the country of destination as well as features of the country of origin may impact immigrants' adaptation processes and subsequent educational achievements, over and above variations in individual and family level characteristics.

Nations differ in their historical experiences with immigration, the degree to which they promote immigration, and public acceptance of immigrants within the host society (Portes 1997). By attending to national-level variations in the receptivity toward immigrants, scholars can determine the degree to which national policies are exclusionary toward immigrants and then predict how these institutional variations relate to aspects of immigrants' experiences, including their educational achievement and attainment. Using this strategy, Buchmann and Parrado (2006:347) find that immigrant–native student achievement gaps are largest in nations with exclusionary immigration regimes and smallest in nations with inclusionary immigration regimes. Levels et al. (2008) improve on this approach and use an innovative double comparative research design to examine the extent to which macrolevel characteristics of immigrants' destination countries as well as their origin countries explain differences in immigrant children's educational achievement. They find that attributes of both host countries and origin countries explain achievement differences among immigrant children. For example, selective immigration laws in the host country explain immigrant children's better educational performance in traditional immigrant-receiving countries, while political instability in the country of origin is related to the weaker educational performance of immigrant children.

Countries differ not only in their immigration polices but also in the structural features of their educational systems, including level of differentiation across schools and their retention policies. Park and Sandefur (2010) demonstrate the importance of national educational systems for determining cross-national variations in the degree of educational integration of immigrant students. Like other studies mentioned, such research illuminates how the institutional arrangements of educational systems impact educational outcomes of different groups, in this case for immigrants. More research should examine how other institutional arrangements or features of educational systems shape how immigrant students fare relative to nonimmigrant groups. Both of these studies (Levels et al. 2008; Park and Sandefur 2010) serve as valuable models for future research on immigrant education and demonstrate how intersocietal analysis can generate new theories of immigrant educational adaptation. Through a comparative lens that considers a range of diverse contexts beyond the USA, such scholarship places the social and educational processes in the USA into a much larger spectrum.

Conclusion

In its goal to understand US-specific schooling, the American sociology of education increasingly has lost sight of the goal of improving and expanding general theories of education. More comparative and international research on education can remedy the current narrowness of the field by providing fresh insights to longstanding questions in the sociology of education. Because comparative, intersocietal research lays bare the effects of context and structure, it is one particularly promising strategy in the search for mechanism-based explanations of social and educational processes. By examining relationships between events or variables in diverse societies, scholars get closer to understanding the mechanisms behind those relationships. In some cases, research will demonstrate that a relationship appears to be consistent in a wide variety of settings. But in other instances, where the relationship found in some contexts does not hold in others and the outcomes are quite different, the theoretical leverage to be gained from comparative and international research is greatest.

The field's overt concern with a single nation also has limited progress in advancing general theories of education. Comparative and international research can pose new questions rarely considered in US-focused research that are crucial to developing a general sociology of education and new theoretical perspectives. For these reasons comparative research holds the promise to lead the American sociology of education in bold new directions to make contributions to the study of schooling and educational systems in the global era. To realize these goals, more American sociologists of education must rise to the challenge of conducting comparative and international research. US-focused scholars of education must read and reflect upon the findings of research conducted in diverse contexts and integrate these findings into their work. Only through greater dialogue and integration between the US-focused and comparative and international streams of research in sociology of education can the great value of a comparative lens be realized.

Acknowledgments This chapter is dedicated to Alan Kerckhoff, John Meyer, and David Baker—three scholars whose provocative research and writings have deeply influenced my thinking about comparative and international sociology of education. I also thank Maureen Hallinan and a reviewer for thoughtful comments and suggestions that have refined and improved this chapter.

References

Alexander, Karl L. 2003. Editorial notice. *Sociology of Education* 76: 1.
Anh, T.S., John Knodel, David Lam, and Jed Friedman. 1998. Family size and children's education in Vietnam. *Demography* 35: 578–70.
Aurini, Janice. 2006. Crafting legitimation projects: An institutional analysis of private education businesses. *Sociological Forum* 21: 83–111.
Aurini, Janice, and Scott Davies. 2004. The transformation of private tutoring: Education in a franchise form. *Canadian Journal of Sociology* 29: 419–438.
Ayalon, Hanna, and Adam Gamoran. 2000. Stratification in academic secondary programs and educational inequality in Israel and the United States. *Comparative Education Review* 44: 54–80.

Baker, David P. 1994. In comparative isolation: Why comparative research has so little influence on American Sociology of Education? *Research in Sociology of Education and Socialization* 10: 53–70.

Baker, David P. 2011. The future of the schooled society: The transforming culture of education in postindustrial society. In *Frontiers in sociology of education*, ed. Maureen T. Hallinan, 1–8. Dordrecht: Springer.

Baker, David P., and Gerald K. LeTendre. 2005. *National differences, global similarities: World culture and the future of schooling*. Stanford: Stanford University Press.

Baker, David P., Motoko Akiba, Gerald K. LeTendre, and Alexander W. Wiseman. 2001. Worldwide shadow education: Outside-school learning, institutional quality of schooling, and cross-national mathematics achievement. *Educational Evaluation and Policy Analysis* 23: 1–17.

Bills, David. 2009. From the incoming editor of the sociology of education. *Sociology of Education Section Newsletter* 12(2): 3–7.

Bradley, Karen, and Francisco O. Ramirez. 1996. World polity and gender parity: Women's share of higher education, 1965–1985. *Research in Sociology of Education and Socialization* 11: 63–91.

Bray, Mark. 1999. *The shadow education system: Private tutoring and its implications for planners*. Paris: International Institute for Educational Planning, United Nations Educational, Cultural and Scientific Organization.

Bray, Mark. 2009. *Confronting the shadow education system: What government policies for what private tutoring?* Paris: International Institute for Educational Planning, United Nations Educational, Cultural and Scientific Organization.

Brint, Steven. 2009. The 'collective mind' at work: A decade in the life of U.S. Sociology of Education. *Sociology of Education Section Newsletter* 12(1): 7–15.

Brint, Steven, and Jerome Karabel. 1989. American Education, Meritocratic Ideology and the legitimation of inequality: The Community College and the problem of American Exceptionalism. *Higher Education* 18: 725–735.

Broaded, C. Montgomery. 1997. The limits and possibilities of tracking: Some evidence from Taiwan. *Sociology of Education* 70: 36–53.

Bromley, Patricia. 2010. Five questions to John Meyer. *Sociology of Education Section Newsletter* 13(1): 7–8.

Buchmann, Claudia. 2000. Family structure, parental perceptions and child labor in Kenya: What factors determine who is enrolled in school? *Social Forces* 78: 1349–1378.

Buchmann, Claudia. 2002. Getting ahead in Kenya: Social capital, shadow education, and achievement. *Research in the Sociology of Education* 13: 133–159.

Buchmann, Claudia, and Ben Dalton. 2002. Interpersonal influences and educational aspirations in twelve countries: The importance of institutional context. *Sociology of Education* 75: 99–122.

Buchmann, Claudia, and Thomas A. DiPrete. 2006. The growing female advantage in college completion: The role of parental resources and academic achievement. *American Sociological Review* 71: 515–541.

Buchmann, Claudia, and Emily Hannum. 2001. Education and stratification in developing countries: A review of theories and research. *Annual Review of Sociology* 27: 77–102.

Buchmann, Claudia, and Hyunjoon Park. 2009. Stratification and the formation of expectations in highly differentiated educational systems. *Research in Social Stratification and Mobility* 27: 245–267.

Buchmann, Claudia, and Emilio Parrado. 2006. Educational achievement of immigrant-origin and native students: A comparative analysis informed by institutional theory. In *The impact of comparative education research on institutional theory*, eds. David P. Baker and Alexander W. Wiseman, 345–377. Oxford: Elsevier Science.

Buchmann, Claudia, Thomas A. DiPrete, and Anne McDaniel. 2008. Gender inequalities in education. *Annual Review of Sociology* 34: 319–337.

Buchmann, Claudia, Dennis Condron, and Vincent Roscigno. 2010. Shadow education, American style: Test preparation, the SAT and college enrollment. *Social Forces* 89: 435–462.

Chernichovsky, Dov. 1985. Socioeconomic and demographic aspects of school enrollment and attendance in rural Botswana. *Economic Development and Cultural Change* 33: 319–332.

Clark, Burton. 1985. *The higher education system*. Berkeley: University of California Press.

Davies, Scott. 2004. School choice by default? Understanding the demand for private tutoring in Canada. *American Journal of Education* 110: 233–255.

DiPrete, Thomas, and Claudia Buchmann. 2006. Gender-specific trends in the value of education and the emerging gender gap in college completion. *Demography* 43: 1–24.

Downey, Douglas B. 1995. When bigger is not better: Family size, parental resources, and children's educational performance. *American Sociological Review* 60: 746–761.

Eurostat. 2002. *The life of women and men in Europe: A statistical portrait*. Luxembourg: Eurostat.

Forsey, Martin, Scott Davies, and Geoffrey Walford. 2008. *The globalisation of school choice?* Oxford: Symposium Books.

Gamoran, Adam. 1987. The stratification of high school learning opportunities. *Sociology of Education* 60: 135–155.

Gamoran, Adam, and Robert D. Mare. 1989. Secondary school tracking and educational inequality: Reinforcement, compensation, or neutrality? *The American Journal of Sociology* 94: 1146–1183.

Grant, Monica J., and Jere R. Behrman. 2010. Gender gaps in educational attainment in less developed countries. *Population and Development Review* 36: 71–89.

Hallinan, Maureen T. 1991. School differences in tracking structures and track assignments. *Journal of Research on Adolescence* 1: 251–275.

Hallinan, Maureen T. 1992. The organization of students for instruction in middle school. *Sociology of Education* 65: 114–127.

Hallinan, Maureen T. 2011. Improving the interaction between sociological research and educational policy. In *Frontiers in sociology of education*, ed. Maureen T. Hallinan, 1. Dordrecht: Springer.

Hedstrom, Peter, and Richard Swedberg. 1998. Social mechanisms: An introductory essay. In *Social mechanisms: An analytical approach to social theory*, eds. Peter Hedstrom and Richard Swedberg, 1–31. Cambridge: Cambridge University Press.

Kao, Grace, and Marta Tienda. 1995. Optimism and achievement: The educational performance of immigrant youth. *Social Science Quarterly* 76: 1–19.

Kerckhoff, Alan. 1995. Institutional arrangements and stratification processes in industrial societies. *Annual Review of Sociology* 21: 323–347.

Kerckhoff, Alan. 1996. *Generating social stratification: Toward a new research agenda*. Boulder: Westview Press.

Kerckhoff, Alan. 2000. The transition from school to work in comparative Perspective. In *Handbook of the sociology of education*, ed. Maureen T. Hallinan, 453–474. New York: Kluwer Publishers.

Kerckhoff, Alan. 2001. Education and social stratification processes in comparative perspective. *Sociology of Education* Extra Issue: 3–18.

Levels, Mark, Jaap Dronkers, and Gerbert Kraaykamp. 2008. Immigrant children's educational achievement in western countries: Origin, destination, and community effects on mathematical performance. *American Sociological Review* 73: 835–853.

Levin, J., and W.C. Levin. 1991. Sociology of educational late blooming. *Sociological Forum* 6: 661–679.

Lu, Yao, and Donald Treiman. 2008. The effect of sibship size on educational attainment in China: Period variations. *American Sociological Review* 73: 813–834.

Lucas, Samuel Roundfield. 1999. *Tracking inequality: Stratification and mobility in American High Schools*. New York: Teachers College Press.

Mare, Robert. 1981. Change and stability in educational stratification. *American Sociological Review* 46: 72–87.

Marsh, Robert M. 1967. *Comparative sociology: A codification of cross-societal analysis*. New York: Harcourt, Brace and World.

McDaniel, Anne. 2010. Cross-national gender gaps in educational expectations: The influence of national-level gender ideology and educational systems. *Comparative Education Review* 54: 27–50.

Meyer, John W. 1977. The effects of education as an institution. *The American Journal of Sociology* 83: 55–77.

Meyer, John W. 1987. Implications of an institutional view of education for the study of educational effects. In *The social organization of schools: New conceptualizations of the learning process*, ed. Maureen T. Hallinan, 157–176. New York: Plenum Press.

Meyer, John W., Patricia Bromley, and Francisco Ramirez. 2010. Human rights in social science textbooks: Cross-national analyses, 1970–2008. *Sociology of Education* 83: 111–134.

Milesi, Carolina. 2010. Do all roads lead to Rome? Effect of educational trajectories in educational transitions. *Research in Social Stratification and Mobility* 28: 23–44.

Mori, Izumi, and David P. Baker. 2010. The origin of universal shadow education: What the supplemental education phenomenon tells us about the postmodern institution of education. *Asian Pacific Education Review* 11: 36–48.

Mortimer, Jeylan T., and Helga Krueger. 2000. Pathways from school to work in Germany and the United States. In *Handbook of the sociology of education*, ed. Maureen T. Hallinan, 475–497. New York: Kluwer Publishers.

Müller, Walter, and Wolfgang Karle. 1993. Social selection in educational systems in Europe. *European Sociological Review* 9: 1–23.

Müller, Walter, and Yossi Shavit. 1998. The institutional embeddedness of the stratification process: A comparative study of qualifications and occupations in thirteen countries. In *From school to work: A comparative study of educational qualifications and occupational destinations*, eds. Yossi Shavit and Walter Müller, 1–48. Oxford: Oxford University Press.

Oakes, Jeannie. 1994. One more thought. *Sociology of Education* 67: 91.

Oakes, Jeannie, Adam Gamoran, and Reba N. Page. 1992. Curriculum differentiation: Opportunities, outcomes and meanings. In *Handbook of research on curriculum*, ed. Philip W. Jackson, 570–608. New York: Macmillan.

Park, Hyunjoon. 2008. The varied educational effects of parent-child communication: A comparative study of fourteen countries. *Comparative Education Review* 52: 219–243.

Park, Hyunjoon, and Gary Sandefur. 2010. Educational gaps between immigrant and native students in Europe: The role of grade retention. In *Quality and inequality of education: Cross-national perspectives*, ed. Jaap Dronkers, 113–136. Dordrecht: Springer.

Park, Hyunjoon, Soo-yong Byun, and Kyung-keun Kim. 2011. Parental involvement and students' cognitive outcomes in Korea: Focusing on private tutoring. *Sociology of Education* 84: 3–22.

Pfeffer, Fabian. 2008. Persistent inequality in educational attainment and its institutional context. *European Sociological Review* 24: 543–565.

Portes, Alejandro. 1997. Immigration theory for a new century: Some problems and opportunities. *International Migration Review* 31: 799–825.

Portes, Alejandro, and Ruben G. Rumbaut. 2001. *Legacies: The story of the immigrant second generation*. Berkeley: University of California Press.

Ragin, Charles. 1994. *Constructing social research: The unity and diversity of method*. Thousand Oaks: Pine Forge Press.

Ramirez, Francisco O. 2006. Beyond achievement and attainment studies: Revitalizing a comparative sociology of education. *Comparative Education* 42(3): 431–449.

Ramirez, Francisco O., and John W. Meyer. 1981. Comparative education. In *The state of sociology: Problems and prospects*, ed. James F. Short, 215–238. Beverly Hills: Sage Press.

Reskin, Barbara. 2003. Including mechanisms in our models of ascriptive inequality. *American Sociological Review* 68: 1–21.

Schneider, Barbara. 2006. Editorial statement. *Sociology of Education* 79: 1.

Shavit, Yossi, and Hans-Peter Blossfeld. 1993. *Persistent inequality: Changing educational attainment in thirteen countries*. Boulder: Westview Press.

Shavit, Yossi, and Walter Müller. 1998. *From school to work: A comparative study of educational qualifications and occupational destinations*. Oxford: Oxford University Press.

Sorensen, Aage B. 1998. Theoretical mechanisms and the empirical study of social processes. In *Social mechanisms: An analytical approach to social theory*, eds. Peter Hedstrom and Richard Swedberg, 238–266. Cambridge: Cambridge University Press.

Spenner, Kenneth I., and David L. Featherman. 1978. Achievement ambitions. *Annual Review of Sociology* 4: 373–420.

Steelman, Lala Carr, Brian Powell, Regina Werum, and Scott Carter. 2002. Reconsidering the effects of sibling configuration: Recent advances and challenges. *Annual Review of Sociology* 28: 243–269.

Stevenson, David, and David P. Baker. 1992. Shadow education and allocation in formal schooling: Transition to university in Japan. *The American Journal of Sociology* 97: 1639–1657.

Suarez-Orozco, Marcelo M., and Carolyn Sattin. 2007. Introduction: Learning in the global era. In *Learning in the global era: International perspectives on globalization and education*, ed. Marcelo M. Suarez-Orozco, 1–43. Berkeley: University of California Press.

Suarez-Orozco, Marcelo M., and I. Todorova. 2007. *Learning in a new land: The children of immigrants in American Schools*. Cambridge: Harvard University Press.

Sylvan Learning. 2007. Retrieved May 23, 2007 (http://tutoring.sylvanlearning.com).

Torche, Florencia. 2005. Privatization reform and inequality of educational opportunity: The case of Chile. *Sociology of Education* 78: 316–343.

Turner, Ralph. 1960. Sponsored and contest mobility and the school system. *American Sociological Review* 25: 855–867.

Van de Werfhorst, Herman G., and Jonathan J.B. Mijs. 2010. Achievement inequality and the institutional structure of educational systems: A comparative perspective. *Annual Review of Sociology* 36: 1–22.

Walters, Pamela Barnhouse. 2000. The limits of growth: School expansion and school reform in historical perspective. In *Handbook of the sociology of education*, ed. Maureen T. Hallinan, 163–187. New York: Kluwer Academic.

Yamamoto, Yoko, and Mary C. Brinton. 2010. Cultural capital in East Asian Educational Systems: The case of Japan. *Sociology of Education* 83: 67–83.

Zhou, Min, and C. Bankston. 1998. *Growing up American: How Vietnamese children adapt to life in the United States*. New York: Russell Sage.

Chapter 4
Toward a Theory of the Political Construction of Empty Spaces in Public Education

Pamela Barnhouse Walters

For some time, the intellectual center of gravity in sociology of education has been the study of determinants of students' academic achievement and attainment.[1] In their rush to study these important consequences of schooling, however, sociologists have paid insufficient attention to a prior and equally important issue, namely, why we have the kinds of schools we have, teaching what they do, providing the kinds of educational opportunities they do. Every parent in the USA understands that there are vast differences in educational opportunities and resources between good schools and bad schools, and a vast body of scholarship documents that the divides in the quality of public schooling available to privileged versus disadvantaged children have been remarkably impervious to various reform movements intended to make schooling more equal (see Brint 2006). Given these understandings, it is surprising that scholars have paid so little attention to questions about what factors shape the educational opportunity structure itself and why efforts to reform it have made so little headway.

In this chapter, I argue that we need to develop a good understanding of the policy processes that create the empty spaces into which students are sorted and allocated (the outcome that has been studied in depth by status attainment and mobility scholars). We need to reconceptualize education policy development as a process that is deeply embedded within American politics, and to that end, I propose what might constitute the essential elements of a political theory of the structure of empty spaces in American K–12 public education. I then illustrate the usefulness of this approach to understanding how and why the structure of empty spaces in

---

[1] For a careful analysis of all articles published over a 10-year period in the subfield's leading journal, *Sociology of Education*, that corroborates this point, see Brint (2009).

P.B. Walters (✉)
Department of Sociology, Indiana University, Bloomington, IN 47405, USA
e-mail: walters@indiana.edu

American education is constructed politically through a brief analysis of an interrelated set of national policy development episodes that, taken as a whole, helps explain why we have such a durable racial divide in public educational opportunities in the USA, albeit one that appears in new forms and was achieved through new political means in the period following the landmark 1954 US Supreme Court decision in *Brown v. Board of Education* than before. I show that the persistence of a sharp racial divide in students' access to good schools is the result of a series of *interrelated* policy processes, the politics of which can only be understood by examining the combination of institutional and noninstitutional means and contexts in which political battles occurred. As I explain in greater detail later, the set of policies whose development we need to consider include not only the race-conscious policies of desegregation and busing (and their eventual defeat), but also the peculiar twists and turns of school finance reform and the movement for school vouchers, policies that are formally race neutral.

The foundational piece of any theory that attempts to explain the construction of the K–12 public educational opportunity structure, I argue, is the simple observation that education is a *political* institution, as deeply imbedded in American politics as any other institution that provides state social goods or services. It is political officials and agencies that fund and control public education. Sociologists have, however, paid little attention to the politics through which a vast range of political and policy decisions about American public schools are made. Examples include rules about access, resource allocation, curriculum, staffing, the basis of school finance and governance, and how political boundaries are drawn around schools and school districts. Yet it is precisely these sorts of decisions that, taken together, give us the opportunity structure of American education at any given point in time.[2] Our ability to understand why we have the existing opportunity structure in education is hampered severely by a lack of research examining the political, social, and cultural factors that shape the policy development process in education and that consider the interrelated histories of seemingly disparate educational policies.

To be sure, there is a substantial existing body of research on educational policy development, much of it undertaken by education scholars and published in education

---

[2] I focus on public K–12 education rather than private because the vast majority of American elementary and secondary students are enrolled in public rather than private schools, because the factors that determine the opportunity structure in K–12 private schooling are less political, and because family affluence is a more important factor governing access to private schooling than access to public schooling. (I note, however, that the state shapes private K–12 education in important if generally unacknowledged ways: State policies influence the availability of private schooling and determine the terms under which it can be offered.) I focus on K–12 education rather than higher education, even though I grant that for purposes of understanding student achievement and attainment, the organization and opportunity structure of American higher education is as, if not more, important at present than the organization and opportunity structure of K–12 education. Nonetheless, the processes that account for the former are quite different from the processes that account for the latter. The higher education opportunity structure is influenced by market processes to a far greater degree than is the case for K–12 education, and political authority over higher education is far more fragmented than is the case in K–12 education.

rather than social science journals. While that research is informative in many respects, it has serious limitations for understanding why we have the extant system of empty spaces in public education. The first limitation is that the research generally pays attention to politics and the political process only among a narrow set of actors and institutional settings, confined mostly within the institution of public education itself. Education is not viewed as embedded within the larger system of politics that governs and produces policy outcomes in other important policy arenas, such as welfare or health care policy (for similar points, see McDonnell 2007).[3] A partial exception to this pattern is the literature on urban school reform, which does situate the politics of urban schooling within the larger politics of cities. That is, it pays attention to mayors, political parties, unions, the business community, organized social groups, perhaps the courts, and the like (Anyon 1997; Henig et al. 1999; Hess 1999; Payne 2008; Rich 1996). But, its understandable focus on urban areas—after all, urban schools are generally the most distressed in the country—leaves it silent on the political and policy reasons why we have the larger system of education within which urban schools are embedded and which, arguably, is responsible for the dire challenges faced by urban schools and by educators and students in urban areas.

A second important limitation of the extant education policy research with respect to understanding why we have the system of empty spaces we do is that much of it focuses not on the development of the policies themselves but on their consequences. Such studies have addressed, for example, questions about whether voucher students perform better than similar students who remain in the public schools (Howell and Peterson 2006; for a heated debate over these findings, see Krueger and Zhu 2004; Peterson and Howell 2004) and whether students in better-funded schools have higher academic achievement than students in poorly funded schools (Hanushek 1989; for a heated debate over these findings, see Hedges et al. 1994a, b; Hanushek 1994). Many sociological and historical studies that address long-term processes of school reform similarly focus on questions of whether the reforms had the intended effects; for example, whether Irish school reforms intended to reduce class inequality in access to schooling have done so (Raftery and Hout 1993) and whether Head Start really helped close the achievement gap between poor and affluent children (Hasci 2002). Such studies treat the reform itself (its adoption and implementation) as an exogenous factor. To understand why we have the system of empty spaces we do, the reform process needs to be the outcome studied. And the outcome of interest must include policy implementation as well as adoption.

The closest we come to analyses that situate education reform or policy development within a broader political context is a literature that focuses on class conflict over education or on the efforts of disadvantaged groups to press their own interests with respect to public schooling, despite the fact that they stand largely outside of

---

[3] That is, the attention is to the politics within the educational system and bureaucracy; other political institutions and actors are relevant primarily to the degree in which they interact with political actors within education. The point holds even for those excellent historical treatments of school reform that do deal well with the messy (within-education) politics of reform, such as Tyack and Cuban (1995) and Ravitch (2000).

the power structure of formal politics. Even groups with no formal political voice at all, such as blacks after disfranchisement and prior to the Civil Rights era (Strong et al. 2000) and women before they had the vote (Reese 1986), have under some conditions worked outside of the formal political structure to at least partially realize their educational interests. While this focus on noninstitutional politics is useful, these studies do not place alongside that analysis a comparison of the politics within formal political institutions. (Examples of studies of more recent events include Binder 2002; Davies 1999; Dougherty and Sostre 1992; Stevens 2001.) In their emphasis on noninstitutional politics, this body of research has a great deal in common with scholarship on social movements in sociology and political science which focuses on outsiders to formal politics and political institutions. This is a form of politics that we ignore at our peril but it does not constitute the complete picture. Nonetheless, this literature reminds us that understanding the interests of competing groups is not sufficient; we also must examine the political means through which they act on their interests.[4] Further, our analyses need to interweave an analysis of the formal, institutional political process with the noninstitutional means through which various groups work to realize their interests.

A Theory of the Political Construction of Empty Spaces

For good theoretical models of the ways in which larger political factors shape policy development, we have to look outside of the literature on educational reform or education policy development. Sociologists and political scientists have conducted a body of research on the development of American redistributive policies and key forms of state social provision, examining such important outcomes as the development of the American welfare state and health care policies. This research weaves together an emphasis on the political and policy interests of competing social groups and an analysis of the political processes through which they attempt to realize their interests—both within formal political institutions and through noninstitutional means. The highly influential field of American political development, for example, emphasizes policy development constraints posed by existing state institutional structure and rules of governance. New institutional forms are seen as most likely to emerge during periods when the institutional landscape is marked by contradiction or fragmentation (Orren and Skowronek 2004). Similarly, scholars studying American policy development within the historical institutionalist tradition in political science give analytical priority to two main explanatory factors: the way that political institutions constrain and enable policy development and the way in which previously enacted policies create legacies that make some policy options

---

[4] Failure to identify the means by which elites were able to realize their interests with respect to schooling is perhaps the single most important limitation of class-domination theories of education reform (Bowles and Gintis 1976; Katz 1968; Spring 1972).

more likely to be adopted than others, over and above their perceived merit or level of political support (Pierson 1994; Skocpol 1992; Mahoney 2000).[5] Social science research on the development of the American welfare state also has highlighted structural factors and conditions such as the configuration of political parties (Amenta 1998; Manza 2000; Hicks and Swank 1992), the fragmented nature of American government (Amenta 1998; Orloff 1993; Quadagno 2005), the weakness of American labor unions (Korpi 1983; Stephens 1979),[6] and the strength of the business community (Berkowitz and McQuaid 1988; Manza 2000; Orloff 1993).[7] Much of this literature identifies a more important causal role of noninstitutional politics, including but not limited to social movements, than does the literature on American political development or historical institutionalism.

Work in all of these traditions stands apart from extant research on education policy development in that it pays careful attention to elected and appointed state officials outside the educational sector (both their interests and their institutional capacity to act on them) and the institutional rules and procedures for making and implementing state policies (Domhoff 1990; Skocpol 1995). This body of work further shows that what happens inside state bureaucracies may be as important as debates and actions within legislatures, state and federal executive branches, or the judiciary (Pedriana and Stryker 1997; Stryker 2001).

Attention to policy legacies has been particularly important in the literature that seeks to address the question of why we have the set of institutional arrangements for the delivery of state-provided social goods (e.g., in the welfare system or the health insurance system) that we do at present. Studies have shown that policies and arrangements put in place early in the policy development process wield a disproportionate influence on later policy development possibilities through the administrative procedures and organizational arrangements they lock in place. Those procedures and arrangements, in turn, generate constituencies and clients that defend them against later policy development changes (Pierson 1994, 2000, 2004; Skocpol 1992; Quadagno 2005; Mahoney 2000; Hacker 2002). This path dependency or analysis of policy legacies not only suggests that we must look at the policy development process over a long period of time; it also suggests that we need to look at how the development over time of seemingly different policies may be interrelated, especially in the ways in which the politics surrounding one particular policy create powerful constituencies whose interests and influence may shape the development of other policies (Skocpol and Amenta 1986). To illustrate, the politics of black disfranchisement and the creation of a one-party system in the South at the turn of the twentieth century left southern senators and congressmen with enormous national political power until the 1960s (particularly through the disproportionate

---

[5] This latter factor often is referred to as path dependence or policy feedback.

[6] Historical work on class conflict in American education has similarly pointed to the importance of teachers' unions for school reform (see Wrigley 1982; Hogan 1982; McDonnell and Pascal 1988).

[7] Work on class domination in the revisionist history tradition similarly suggests that the business community wields enormous influence over the course of school reform and educational policy development (Bowles and Gintis 1976; Katz 1968; for more recent work, see Sloan 2008; Saltman 2007).

control of committee leadership that came from their seniority). This allowed them to shape decades of welfare-state policy development in ways that excluded or disadvantaged blacks (Quadagno 2005). Many otherwise excellent studies of school reform tend to treat the reforms one at a time rather than recognizing the ways in which their policy histories are interwoven and interdependent (e.g., Hochschild and Scovronick 2003).

Thus far, I have highlighted research on policy development that focuses on the causal influence of institutional and noninstitutional political processes; that identifies a range of relevant actors, both within and outside the formal policy, that have particular interests in policy development; and that emphasizes ways in which legacies of previously enacted policies constrain and enable policymaking. A recent body of work points us in an additional explanatory direction, by showing that ideas, political claims and debates, and the language in which political discourse unfolds are also causally important in policy development (for reviews, see Beland 2005; Campbell 2002; Lieberman 2002). The key point is that political ideas and cultural traditions constrain policymaking by limiting the range of policies considered reasonable or rational and enable policymaking by giving actors a repertoire of ideas with which to legitimate the policies they favor (see Campbell 1998; Dobbin 1994). More specifically, the terms groups use to articulate grievances and make claims for state redress for grievances shape the public's and policymakers' willingness to acknowledge the legitimacy of expressed grievances and adopt new social policies to grant those claims (Polletta 2000). Grievances are more likely to be seen as legitimate and claims are more likely to be viewed as realistic policy options when they are expressed in language that conforms to taken-for-granted norms and political ideologies that lurk in the background of American political culture (Benford and Snow 2000; Ferree 2003; Oliver and Johnston 2000). For example, core American political values shape the definition of public problems that warrant policy intervention (Burstein and Bricher 1997) and are invoked by those seeking policy redress to put issues on the policy agenda, enact policy, or interpret and enforce court decisions (Burstein and Linton 2002; Pedriana and Stryker 1997; Stryker 2001). There is also a path-dependent process that applies to the development of persuasive frames. New policy proposals that are consistent with familiar cultural ways of talking about public problems and their solutions are more likely to garner political support (Levitsky 2008; McCann 1994; Polletta 2000).

Finally, research on the development of American redistributive policies reminds us that we cannot forget the important role of race in American policy development. Welfare-state scholars, for example, have emphasized that race is always a factor in welfare policymaking (even with respect to policies that are not explicitly remedies for racial inequality and do not use race as a criterion for eligibility—see Quadagno 1988, 1994; Gilens 1999; Omi and Winant 1994; Lieberman 1998). The explanations of the ways in which race shapes the development of nominally color-blind welfare policies do not stop by showing that policymakers, policy influentials, or the American public have an interest in maintaining racial inequality. It also examines the political institutional means through which they manage to realize their interests (as in the previous example of the disproportionate influence of southern congressmen and senators in national policy development prior to the Civil Rights Movement).

An analysis of policy development in education is more complicated than are analyses of the social insurance and social assistance policies (e.g., Social Security and Aid to Families with Dependent Children [welfare], respectively) on which most analyses of American redistributive policymaking focus. Most importantly, in the USA, political responsibility for K–12 public schooling falls primarily to local and state officials and agencies rather than to federal ones.[8] Nonetheless, educational policy development within states is nestled within a national policy development environment. That is, there is a national educational policy development narrative as well as different state narratives. The national narrative—especially the one focused on desegregation—is commonly viewed through the lens of US Supreme Court decisions. And indeed, those decisions often initiate a trajectory of policy development, in desegregation as well as with respect to other educational policies. Other federal factors, however, often are consequential for launching a new educational policy initiative. Consider, for example, the Education for All Handicapped Children Act, passed in 1975, which occasioned radical change in classrooms throughout the country in arrangements for education for special needs children. No Child Left Behind is an important recent example. Failed attempts at federal legislation also matter: They constitute opportunities that, by virtue of having failed once, possibly never appear again. We also need to determine whether political factors that shape policy development differ systematically from policies that originate through different political means, for example, ones initiated through a court decision versus legislation versus (as is possible in some states) a referendum.

There is a national political culture and climate that shape not only federal policymaking but also state-level policy developments. Some of this is represented by shifts in policy regimes. The national conversation about the most pressing problems concerning public education, for example, changed radically with the publication of *A Nation at Risk* in 1983 (National Commission on Excellence in Education 1983): It marked a turn to an era of accountability and standards and away from concerns about equality and access. Some of it is represented by common, often tacit, understandings of what counts as good, reasonable, and responsible ways for government to solve educational problems. National political debates and changes in broad public support for particular educational policies also shape developments within states. Further, a policy decision within an individual state can reverberate throughout the national political culture, granting greater legitimacy to some policy options and discrediting others. The first school finance decisions, in Texas and California in the early 1970s, for example, put school finance reform on the national policy agenda and helped frame it as a legitimate federal effort (Walters et al. 2009a). Years later, the Kentucky Supreme Court's 1989 school finance decision in *Rose* signaled a shift in standards for redress from equality to adequacy—a shift that influenced all

---

[8] The situation changed somewhat in 1965 with the passage of the Elementary and Secondary Education Act (ESEA), which provided for the first time substantial federal funding to state and local school districts. ESEA is an antipoverty measure; funds are provided to school districts based on the proportion of children from low-income families they enroll (see Cross 2004; Urban and Wagoner 2000). However, when averaged across school districts, this federal funding has accounted for only about 10 percent of total spending on K–12 public education in the USA.

subsequent state supreme court decisions concerning school finance (Ladd et al. 1999). The establishment of the first voucher program in Milwaukee in 1990 helped to establish the political legitimacy of such programs and eased their adoption in other places, partly because the new inclusion of blacks in the political coalition that supported vouchers in Milwaukee made possible a new language of equality with which advocates could make the case for vouchers (Dougherty and Sostre 1992).

To make manageable the outline I present here of an analysis of the politics of policy development that has left us with a sharp racial divide in American education, I focus on the national policy development narrative and briefly hint at ways in which this was shaped by developments within individual states. This national narrative illustrates the range of influences that must be taken into account in any analysis of the politics of policy development, and it is consequential in its own right. It opens some doors to state-level developments and closes others. It is not the whole story, however. Particularly for questions about why educational policy development differed across states, attention would have to be focused on variation in the ways that states responded politically to those limits and possibilities established through the national policy development process as well as to policy developments and political factors unique to a particular state. Nonetheless, I expect that the state-level counterparts of the same class of factors that shape national educational policymaking shape state-level educational policy development as well.

Analyzing Racial Inequality in the Structure of Empty Spaces in American Public Schools

To illustrate the ways in which a more fully developed political theory can help us understand why we have the system of empty spaces in education that we do, I now turn to a brief outline of an analysis of the policy development process that explains the persistence of racially segregated and unequal schools in the half century since the US Supreme Court, in *Brown v. Board of Education*, attempted to dismantle separate and unequal schooling. Race is the most enduring social divide in American education (Brint 2006), and it is a divide that is important to understand in its own right as well as a useful case for understanding the phenomenon of persisting inequality in access to education more generally.[9] American public schools today are almost as racially segregated as they were in the late 1960s, which is when the federal government made its first systematic efforts to enforce *Brown* (Orfield and Lee 2004). Further, in ways that are not captured by simple data on between-district differences in per-pupil expenditures, districts that enroll a disproportionate number of minority students continue to enjoy fewer of the educational resources that most

---

[9] The narrowing since the 1960s of the gap between blacks and whites in scores on achievement tests (see Jencks and Phillips 1998; Hedges and Nowell 1998) shows that modest progress has been made in some aspects of the racial divide. Nonetheless, the racial divide in access to what are considered to be good schools remains substantial.

scholars consider necessary for student learning and achievement, such as adequate buildings, sufficient instructional materials, and well-trained teachers.[10]

It is one matter to establish that a stark racial divide in educational opportunities persists in the USA. It is quite another to understand how and why that is the case. A theory of the politics of educational policy development should be able to answer the how and why questions and reveal the processes and mechanisms through which outcomes are produced. The answer typically provided to the how and why questions about the durable racial divide remains limited to the singular policy history of *Brown*. A vast literature maintains that the reasons American schools remain highly racially segregated and racially unequal is that desegregation and busing were derailed by white parents' unwillingness to send their children to racially mixed schools (Anderson et al. 2004; Clotfelter 2006; Irons 2002; Ogletree 2004b). I grant that desegregation and busing were largely derailed by white opposition (albeit in a wide range of forms), but I take issue with the sole focus on desegregation and busing as the policies that contributed to the longevity of the racial divide in American education. In contrast, my analysis of how and why the racial divide persists puts alongside desegregation and busing two major colorblind reforms[11] of the past half century, namely, school funding equalization and school vouchers. Neither of these policies uses race as a criterion for eligibility. Yet, both were proposed as ways to help close the racial gap in educational opportunities. Equally importantly, the development of each policy was shaped in significant ways by the racial politics of school desegregation and busing. Simply put, I demonstrate that the politics of these three reforms constitutes a single path-dependent process[12] and that a full

---

[10] For compelling descriptions, see Kozol (1992, 2005); for comprehensive data on the degree to which schools in California that disproportionately enroll poor and minority students suffer such resource inadequacies, see Oakes (n.d.) and California Postsecondary Education Commission (1998). These kinds of data on instructional resources are not routinely collected by federal agencies. Also see Walters (2007).

[11] By color blind, I mean that race is not an explicit criterion for eligibility for benefit or assignment. School desegregation and busing are, in contrast, color-conscious policies in that race was used as a basis for school assignment.

[12] Little existing scholarship recognizes this path dependency. There are four exceptions, to the best of my knowledge. The first is Dougherty's (2004) historical analysis of Milwaukee, which presents school desegregation, school finance reform, and vouchers in a sequential, path-dependent process but is limited by its primary focus on within-city politics. That focus causes him to miss the concurrently intertwined paths of the three reforms, because those connections are more apparent at the federal level. The second is Ryan's (1999a) analysis of the complicated legal connections between desegregation and school finance reform, which shows clearly how race influenced both, but misses the ways in which both shaped and were shaped by the voucher movement. The third is Minow's (2010) legal analysis of the legacies of *Brown* for a variety of subsequent equality-in-education movements undertaken by or on behalf of other social groups. While her analysis establishes a legal policy legacy from *Brown* to school vouchers, it misses the intertwined histories of school finance reform and *Brown*. The fourth is Ryan's (2010) study of racial inequalities in educational opportunities a half-century after *Brown*, which beautifully shows that the histories of school desegregation, school finance reform, and vouchers are connected via a politics of race. Like his prior work and Minow's, however, Ryan's 2010 study is limited by a disproportionate attention to court decisions as the primary engine of the policy development process. That said, these four analyses are rich and insightful, and none of them are intended to address the question I pose about the broad political determinants of the durable racial divide. Further, although some of the literature on school finance reform and vouchers shows that racial politics shape support for these reforms (see Ryan 1999b; Reed 2001a), little attention has been paid to similarities and differences in the ways these policies are racialized.

understanding of the persistence of the current racial divide requires attention to the politics of policy adoption, policy implementation, and resistance to both in all three reform efforts.

As described in more detail later, school funding equalization policies follow from decisions in individual states' supreme courts and are implemented (or not) by governors, state legislatures, and state school boards. The intent of such decisions is to reduce the disparities in resources between high- and low-resource school districts within a state, the latter of which disproportionately educates poor and minority students. School voucher programs, in contrast, have been put in place by state legislation (referenda are another pathway in some states, but all such efforts to date have failed). The current programs generally target students in failing school districts and provide publicly funded scholarships for the poor, disproportionately minority children enrolled therein to attend nearby private schools or public schools in neighboring districts. The intent is to give poor students, especially minorities, access to schools of higher quality that also might be less racially isolating than those available in the urban public school districts in which they live.

Just as the history of school desegregation often is told through the lens of *Brown* and subsequent court decisions, the following discussion will make clear that court decisions are pivotal in school finance reform and play a role in the voucher movement as well. Nonetheless, court decisions should not be considered the exclusive or primary explanatory factor. A legal history alone is inadequate for capturing the full range of political and social influences on the singular, intertwined policy development process under consideration.

First, the analysis reported here shows that legislation and executive decisions are consequential as well, and sometimes in ways that are independent of court decisions. For example, court decisions are not the only way to initiate school finance reform. There was a national episode in the early 1970s when federal legislation to equalize school resources was proposed, strongly supported, and might have been successful. Second, court decisions do not translate directly into change in educational policy or practice. Instead, they close some policy development options and open others. It is important to keep in mind that the courts do not implement their own decisions. Implementation falls to federal and state executive and legislative bodies and to government bureaucracies, and the possibilities for resistance to or reshaping of the court's intent must be considered carefully. The process of implementing court decisions is heavily influenced at times by popular, contentious politics that may include mobilized social groups acting outside of the boundaries of the formal political process. For example, protests, riots, and strategic use of violence were used by opponents of desegregation and busing to stall both. In sum, institutional and noninstitutional politics can influence the degree to which court decisions are translated into changes in educational policy and practice. The same is true for passed legislation; it also must be implemented.

In some cases, organized resistance to court decisions by policymakers and/or vocal social groups has been sufficient to forestall implementation for long periods of time, as was the case with the resistance in the South to *Brown*, which staved off systematic enforcement for almost 15 years. In other cases, political opposition and stonewalling have, in practice, reversed a court's decision. The fate of the Ohio Supreme Court's 1997 school finance decision in *DeRolph v. State* provides such an example. In the aftermath of the original decision, the governor, the legislature, and an alliance of property-rich school districts engaged in bitter political battle with the court over its implementation. The court rejected as inadequate four different education reform measures passed by the legislature, and eventually, apparently tiring of the legislature's pattern of ignoring its mandates, it vacated its original decision in *DeRolph* in 2003 (Walters et al. 2009a, b). That is, the court was "effectively waving the white flag and washing its hands of the dispute" (Koski 2004:1170), an act that released the state from its court-ordered obligation to overhaul its school finance system even as it recognized the continued need for overhaul.

Finally, in those cases when court decisions open possibilities for policy development (as opposed to mandating them), whether those possibilities are pursued is a political rather than a legal matter. For example, the 2002 US Supreme Court decision in *Zelman v. Simmons-Harris*, a case that upheld the Cleveland school voucher program allowing participants to use their vouchers in private, religious schools, opened the door to more widespread adoption of voucher programs. But it did not compel political authorities elsewhere to establish voucher programs. Those that were adopted elsewhere in the aftermath of *Zelman* originated through local and state political processes.

Policy Origins: **Brown** *and Beyond*

We can start the story of this intertwined policy history of desegregation and busing, school finance reform, and vouchers with the 1954 US Supreme Court decision in *Brown v. Board of Education*. Before *Brown*, most whites and blacks attended white-only or black-only schools as a matter of state policy and by policy black schools received fewer resources than white schools. In the form in which it existed prior to *Brown*, separate and unequal education functioned as a racial set-aside system that reserved the best educational opportunities for white students.[13] In its declaration that separate and unequal schooling for whites and blacks would no longer be accepted, *Brown* and the busing measures adopted later as part of the efforts to implement *Brown* were the centerpieces of efforts to provide greater educational opportunity for black Americans in the second half of the twentieth century (Kluger 1977). Even though *Brown* challenged separate, and not unequal, the assumption behind *Brown* was that racial equality in educational resources would be accomplished through integration.[14]

---

[13] Explicitly and directly so in those states that practiced *de jure* segregation; indirectly so in those states that practiced *de facto* segregation.

[14] *Brown* and busing were not expected to do it all alone, however. The federal government mounted other efforts in education that disproportionately benefited blacks without using race as a criterion for receiving social benefits (that is, they were color blind), among which were the antipoverty educational programs of the 1960s, such as Head Start and federal funding for school districts that educate disproportionate numbers of poor and at-risk students. None of these programs, however, directly attacked separate (that is, segregation). Nor was equality the goal; rather, the emphasis was on reducing hardship among the disadvantaged.

The *Brown* decision established the principle that separate could not be equal, a principle that has held an iconic status in American political culture since the 1950s. The importance of dismantling segregation was consistent with the position adopted by the National Association for the Advancement of Colored People (NAACP) and other national black Civil Rights organizations in the years immediately preceding *Brown*,[15] and it provided moral force to Civil Rights organizations' efforts to have *Brown* enforced in the 1950s and 1960s. As I describe next, however, the unwillingness of the Civil Rights leadership to accept segregated schools, even as part of a package that might increase the resources in those schools, was highly consequential for the policy history of school finance reform. In this case, it was an *idea* embraced by political leaders with great moral authority that created an important policy legacy. The *Brown* decision itself did not establish a legal legacy that limited the possibilities for a national policy of school finance reform.

In practice, racial equality in school resources did not follow from *Brown* and busing because desegregation efforts were stymied. From 1954 to the late 1960s, southern white segregationists used a range of noninstitutional means to launch a massive resistance campaign to federal attempts to enforce desegregation[16] that largely succeeded in keeping southern schools segregated. It was through this campaign that the policy history of vouchers became intertwined with the policy history of school desegregation, and in the process, the policy history of the former was transformed.

Vouchers had their debut as a policy proposal when neoconservative Milton Friedman (1955) recommended them in an attempt to introduce market competition into public schools. At the time, vouchers were unrelated to race or school desegregation. However, the political history of vouchers and desegregation became closely intertwined shortly thereafter. Throughout the 1950s and 1960s, southern segregationists used vouchers and voucher-like plans, such as voluntary pupil assignment plans, freedom of choice plans, and tuition tax credits for private schools, to undermine and thwart the intent of *Brown* (O'Brien 1997; Patterson 2001; Futrell 2004). Resistance to *Brown* in the South and the unwillingness or inability of federal authorities to enforce it prior to the late 1960s put the black Civil Rights leadership into the position of constantly working for enforcement of *Brown* for the first 15 or so years after the ruling. During that period, the Civil Rights leadership, including the NAACP and the National Urban League, opposed vouchers and all voucher-like plans

---

[15] Note, however, that the NAACP did not always hold that separate could not be equal. In fact, its early litigation campaigns to improve educational opportunities for blacks represented an attack on unequal: Throughout the 1930s and 1940s, the NAACP pressed the courts to enforce equality of state-funded educational facilities available to whites and blacks by bringing equalization suits against one school district and state after another throughout the South (Williams 2004; Anderson et al. 2004; Ogletree 2004a, b; Patterson 2001). Their many successful challenges improved black teachers' salaries and the quality of black schools and opened up new opportunities for graduate and professional study for African Americans. By the 1950s, however, the NAACP considered the pursuit of equal while letting segregation stand to be a violation of its core principles.

[16] Until the 1973 US Supreme Court decision in *Keyes v. Denver School District*, which extended the protections of *Brown* to students in districts that had practiced de facto segregation prior to *Brown*, most of the conflict over school desegregation was confined to the South.

because of their close association with efforts to circumvent school desegregation. As a national policy effort, vouchers were tainted by their association with die-hard segregationists and thus obtained little political traction until much later.

The black Civil Rights leadership also was opposed to efforts to equalize resources between minority and white schools throughout the 1950s and 1960s, albeit for different reasons than the ones for opposing vouchers. In their eyes, such efforts would constitute a retreat from the overarching goal of school integration. The *Brown* decision, of course, gave the NAACP and other black Civil Rights organizations legal ammunition and rhetorical legitimacy to fight segregated schooling. To the NAACP leadership, foregrounding integration did not mean they were abandoning the goal of achieving equality; integration was, rather, the ticket to equality. As the NAACP put it in a 1969 report: "There is such an enormous difference [in resources between black and white schools] that it is impossible to compensate in any other way but by integration, by the end of segregation. Jim Crow can't teach."[17]

Although working for integration was not at odds with the goal of equality, the reverse did not hold for black Civil Rights leaders following their embrace of the principle that separate could not be equal. Even in the face of slow progress on school desegregation in the 1960s and early 1970s, accepting greater equality without pushing for integration was understood as an abandonment of core Civil Rights principles rather than a means of achieving them. That is, integration would lead to equality, but equality could not and would not lead to integration. Hence, when the first school finance reform suits were filed in 1968, in Texas and California, black plaintiffs and black Civil Rights organizations were not party to them. This is a clear example of path dependency between seemingly unrelated policy domains.

There is another way in which the history of school finance reform is intertwined with the history of political struggles over racial inequality in American schools, albeit with Hispanics rather than blacks in the forefront. Prior to and for almost 20 years following *Brown*, Hispanics also were largely segregated into inferior schools, but the divide between Hispanics and others was maintained largely through *de facto* rather than *de jure* means. Because the *Brown* decision originally applied only to school districts that practiced *de jure* segregation, as was the case in most of the South and in a few districts in the North, it was not until 1973, in the US Supreme Court decision in *Keyes v. Denver School District*, that Hispanics and other nonblack minorities were afforded constitutional protection against segregated schooling.[18] In other words, between 1954 and 1973, Hispanics did not have the same constitutional basis as blacks for fighting the form of school segregation they experienced. Thus

---

[17] Library of Congress, Manuscript Division, Records of the National Association for the Advancement of Colored People, Group IV. Box A69, folder titled "Schools California 1966–69," mimeo titled "Education Committee Report on Compensatory Education," dated 2/11/1966.

[18] In its 1973 decision in *Keyes v. Denver School District No. 1*, the US Supreme Court extended the right to desegregated schooling to Latinos, as well as African Americans who lived outside southern states that had practiced *de jure* segregation. Prior to *Brown*, the segregation of Latinos from white children had been accomplished by *de facto* means, as had the segregation of blacks from whites outside the South.

prior to the 1970s, Hispanics were not participants in the struggles to desegregate schools, nor were they engaged in busing battles (San Miguel 1982, 1983; Ferg-Cadima 2004; Wilson 2003).[19] In the absence of strong legal and political means to fight segregation, they became involved in attacks on inequalities in resources among schools and school districts by becoming party to the two early school finance suits.

Thus, while African Americans were engaged in fighting the white counterassault on efforts to dismantle separate, the Mexican American community mounted a direct assault on unequal. In 1968, Mexican American families in poor school districts in Texas and then California filed court suits charging that the discrepancies in per-pupil funding among school districts in their states violated their constitutional rights (*San Antonio Independent School District v. Rodriguez* and *Serrano v. Priest*, respectively). These suits were understood by the plaintiffs to be remedies for racial inequality, despite the fact that the common understanding of school finance reform today is that it is a race-neutral practice. The court decisions in force at the time precluded them from engaging in the same kinds of battles against segregated schools in which black Civil Rights leaders were involved, but their decision to fight the inequality in resources between predominantly minority and predominantly white schools and to frame school finance reform as a redress for racial inequality was a political choice.

Consider the first of these two school finance cases, *Rodriguez*, which was filed by Mexican American parents in Texas and supported by a number of Mexican American grassroots political organizations (Schragger 2007). The original complaint in *Rodriguez* alleged that the Texas school finance system was unconstitutional because it discriminated against racial minorities, specifically Mexican Americans. The racial inequality at issue in San Antonio was illustrated and represented in a contrast between the Edgewood Independent School District, poorly funded and populated primarily by poor Mexican Americans, and the Alamo Heights Independent School District, well funded and with an almost exclusively white and wealthy student population.

Similarly, in its original formulation, the arguments in support of *Serrano* made explicit that it was intended to be a redress for racial inequality, particularly segregation and inequality of educational opportunity between Mexican Americans and Anglos. For example, in an amicus brief filed in support of the plaintiffs in *Serrano*, the Mexican American Legal Defense and Education Fund (MALDEF) and the Congress of Mexican American Unity asserted

> that the distribution of state educational resources is directly related to the wealth of the school district and that the quality of education a child receives is, in large part, determined by the position of the child's school district on the wealth spectrum.... Mexican Americans in particular are severely damaged educationally by the state school financing scheme in that they generally live within the poorer school districts.[20]

---

[19] In fact, many Hispanic parents opposed desegregation, in part because they worried that desegregated schools would not offer bilingual education. See Peter Roos to Ben Williams, Jan. 9, 1978, Stanford University Libraries, Department of Special Collections, Mexican American Legal Defense and Education Fund Records, 1968–1984, RG5, Box 107, Folder 5.

[20] Stanford University Library, Department of Special Collections, Mexican American Legal Defense and Education Fund Collection. Series Legal Programs/Litigation files, 1968–1982/ LA alphabetical files. MO 673, RG#5, Box 1127, file 1: *Serrano v. Priest*. Amicus brief, filed 12/31/1970, p. 3.

Further, MALDEF provided statistical data that poorer school districts in California had greater concentrations of Mexican Americans than wealthier districts, leading to the conclusion "that Mexican Americans are suffering and will continue to suffer discrimination in educational opportunity simply because they remain in the economically deprived core of the central cities."[21]

The Texas case, *San Antonio Independent School District v. Rodriguez*, was initially decided in favor of the plaintiffs (the Mexican American families), but upon appeal the US Supreme Court ruled in 1973 that education was not a fundamental right in the US Constitution. Thus after 1973, redress for funding inequality could be found only by appeal to state constitutional guarantees. In 1976, in *Serrano v. Priest*,[22] the California Supreme Court made the first of what would be a series of post-*Rodriguez* state Supreme Court decisions that ordered states to redress the district-to-district inequalities in school spending that resulted from heavy reliance on local property taxes to fund public schools (Ryan 1999a; Wong 1999; Reed 2001a; Corcoran et al. 2003). The policy legacy of *Rodriguez* was substantial: Not only did it make school finance reform a matter of state rather than federal policymaking, but as the following section shows, it also closed down a national political discussion that had by 1973 framed school finance reform as desirable and appropriate and made federal legislation to accomplish it appear to be inevitable.

Desegregation and Federal Policy Debates About School Finance Reform and Vouchers

Between the initial Texas ruling and the 1973 US Supreme Court decision in *Rodriguez*, school finance reform came to be regarded in highly positive terms within federal policy circles.[23] Further, the national policy discussion about school finance reform linked it with the problems of racial discrimination and inequality

---

[21] Schragger (2007):5–6. For more details on the politics of Mexican Americans' battles over segregation and school finance reform, see Walters et al. 2008:14–21.

[22] The 1976 California case is known as *Serrano II*. The first *Serrano* case, decided in 1971, was based on US constitutional guarantees and was thus rendered invalid by the US Supreme Court's decision in *Rodriguez*.

[23] To cite one example, in 1972 testimony before the House Education and Labor Committee concerning proposed federal legislation to require states to reduce school funding disparities, Terry J. Hatter Jr. of the Western Center on Law and Poverty declared that after the state court's decision in 1971 in *Serrano*, which was followed closely by similar rulings in Texas, Minnesota, and New Jersey, "Almost overnight the matter of school financing has become one of the major domestic issues of the decade." The directive of the court, he continued, is: "There is to be equalization of basic education for all; there is to be the opportunity for education for all; and everybody is to pay his fair share!" See "Public Education Finance." CQ Electronic Library, CQ Almanac Online Edition, cqal72–1249347. Originally published in *CQ Almanac 1972* (Washington: Congressional Quarterly, 1973). http://library.cqpress.com/cqalmanac/cqal72–1249347 (accessed February 21, 2008).

that school desegregation efforts were intended to address. According to the *Washington Post*, for example, "…the legal attacks on racial discrimination and on financial discrimination are converging. Eventually, in most cities as in Detroit, they are going to overlap" (1972:A18). Writing in the *New York Times*, Rosenthal (1972:1) makes the connections even more explicit, noting that funding equalization cases "are not literally desegregation cases. But rich districts are often composed of whites and poor districts are often composed of blacks or minority groups"; thus "mixing poorer children with more affluent children…is often tantamount to saying 'desegregation.'" The *Los Angeles Times* saw equalization of school quality (the issue at the center of funding equalization debates) as crucial for the pursuit of racial equality: "When quality and security are equalized among the schools, the greatest barriers to integration will have been eliminated" (1972b:B2).

Building on the prevailing cultural understanding in the early 1970s that school desegregation and school finance reform were closely linked and were both about race, in 1971 and 1972, new federal policymaking brought the histories of school desegregation and busing, school finance reform, and school vouchers together in new ways. The triggering event was widespread opposition to school busing, which had become a new policy tool for enforcing *Brown* in 1971 with the US Supreme Court decision in *Swann v. Charlotte-Mecklenburg Board of Education*. After *Swann* brought busing to school districts throughout the country, the Nixon administration attempted to render void the Court's decision by proposing federal anti-busing legislation. Busing of public elementary and secondary students to achieve racial balance in the nation's public schools was the most heated political issue about American education in the early 1970s. The debate over school busing, and school desegregation efforts more generally, provided the institutional opportunity for both school finance reform and vouchers to garner support, albeit through different institutional mechanisms. To briefly preview the important parts of this policy episode upon which the following sections expand, the policy history of school finance reform was shaped significantly by a national legislative proposal backed by President Nixon that coupled an initiative to increase federal funding for poor school districts with an initiative to dismantle busing. The other important and interrelated part of the national policy episode was a voucher-like plan offered by President Nixon as part of his 1972 reelection campaign and strategy for courting the vote of whites in the South. Nixon's proposal breathed new political life into the voucher movement. His plan was nonetheless all-too-similar to strategies used by southern segregationists to evade the intent of *Brown v. Board of Education* throughout the 1950s and 1960s, and supporters were not able to overcome the taint of that association.

School finance equalization. In light of the fact that the first state-level attempts to reduce inequalities in school funding had been cast as desegregation efforts, it is ironic that the earliest sustained federal policy proposals to reduce between-district funding disparities were part of efforts to oppose school desegregation and busing. In 1972, President Nixon proposed a measure called the Equal Educational Opportunities Act. In a televised address to the nation on March 16, the President outlined his proposal to "improve the education of minority children in the central cities without busing them to the suburbs" by providing "compensatory" relief to minority schools (Semple 1972:1). He proposed to channel $2.5 billion in federal funds into schools in poor neighborhoods to guarantee "equal educational opportunity to every person regardless of race, color or national origin." His proposal to increase funding to poor school districts was a complement to his anti-busing proposals: "What I am proposing is that at the same time we stop more busing we move forward to guarantee that the children currently attending the poorest schools in our cities and in rural districts be provided with education equal to that of the good schools or their communities" (Toth 1972:A1). In addition to federal funds, the proposed Equal Educational Opportunities Act contained provisions requiring "each school district" to spend as much on schools in poor areas as it did on schools in wealthy areas, or "it would not be eligible for federal funds" (Beckman 1972:S1).

The mainstream black Civil Rights leadership vociferously opposed the Equal Educational Opportunities Act because its price was to back off of a commitment to desegregation and busing.[24] A spokesperson for the Leadership Conference in Civil Rights, declared that "…for those who have dedicated their lives to an integrated America, [the Equal Educational Opportunities Act] is indeed D-day for civil rights."[25] Similarly, the NAACP opposed efforts to improve ghetto schools as an

---

[24] Not all black activists or black activist organizations embraced the separate-cannot-be-equal tenet. Extending back into the nineteenth century, one strand of black political culture – black nationalism – embraced autonomy, self-determination, and various degrees of segregation from white America alongside the quest for equality (Dawson 2001). Although most of the established Civil Rights organizations were united in their calls for enforcement of *Brown* and in support of school desegregation efforts through the 1960s, in September 1970, the Congress of Racial Equality (CORE) broke with the mainstream Civil Rights leadership over school desegregation and busing as a means to obtain equal educational opportunity for blacks. In a demonstration of the flexibility of core ideological concepts, CORE called for "desegregation without integration" (Wooten 1970:1). CORE and other voices for black nationalism continued to espouse equality in the context of segregated schooling throughout the early 1970s. Nonetheless, none of these voices for segregation carried much weight in the policy debates. For example, in February 1972, CORE denounced the Congressional Black Caucus (the 13 black members of the House) for its failure to include the organization in a national meeting about educational goals for black children, an exclusion it attributed to its support for "separate but really equal schools" (Lardner 1972:A3). In March 1972, participants in the first National Black Political Convention, a meeting dominated by separatists, passed a resolution condemning racial integration of schools, despite opposition by the NAACP (Johnson 1972:1). This position did not sway elected black policymakers: Within a few days of the passage of this resolution, the Black Political Caucus again reaffirmed its commitment to integration (Wentworth 1972:A1). The NAACP continued to represent its position as the true sentiment of the black community, arguing that polls consistently showed that the majority of African Americans supported school integration (Wilkins 1972). In sum, it was the integrationist arguments of the mainstream black Civil Rights organizations such as the NAACP and the National Urban League that held most sway in the national policy debates about educational equality for blacks in the early 1970s.

[25] Library of Congress, Manuscript Division, Records of Leadership Conference in Civil Rights. Box I:114, "A Breakthrough for Higher Education." Letter to the editor of *Washington Post*, May 31, 1972, by Joseph Rauh (lawyer for LCCR).

alternative to busing,[26] and the National Urban League stated its opposition to Nixon administration proposals to increase funding for ghetto schools. "Though not stated by its proponents, the proposal seems to offer a bribe to accept resegregation."[27] In a separate statement, the National Urban League argued that:

> [Rather than bus, President Nixon] proposes instead that the ghetto be guilded [sic], money poured into black schools that will remain all-black, thus insuring the continued division of this nation into two societies, one white the other black.[28]

Simply put, acceptance of racially segregated schools was an unacceptably high price for the Civil Rights leadership to pay for equality in resources and opportunities between black and white schools. Ironically, the major political actors in favor of a substantial increase in funding for black schools were white elected officials opposed to busing[29]—a position that also has to be understood as a clear policy legacy of the desegregation fights.

There also was opposition to any federal attempt to intervene in state and local school finance matters from some political conservatives that was expressed as a defense of the local control of schooling. For example, the greatest worry of many officials and taxpayers opposed to school finance was "the possible loss of local control, the fear that once money is no longer raised locally, decisions will no longer be made locally either" (Greenhouse 1972:1). Another news article represented the worry as follows: "Often left unmentioned by advocates of the Federal-support proposal is what its effect would be on local control of schools. It is difficult to conceive of Congress picking up one-third of the school costs without building in a system of controls and accountability over the way the money is used" (Maeroff 1972:E7).

The strong objections of the established Civil Rights leadership and some political conservatives notwithstanding, anti-busing sentiment came close to carrying the day: In August of 1972, the Equal Educational Opportunities Act was passed by the House. The federal policy debate on school finance reform came to a conclusion in October, however, when the Senate took up the bill and "moved to stop debate before a word was spoken" (*Chicago Tribune* 1972:3). By the following year, the

---

[26] Library of Congress, Manuscript Division, Records of the National Association for the Advancement of Colored People, Group VIII. Box 146, folder 1: Busing 1975–1979. Nathaniel R. Jones (General Counsel) to The Editor, *Long Island Newsday*, August 5, 1975.

[27] Library of Congress, Manuscript Division, Records of the National Urban League, Part III. Box 17, folder 7: Communication Department, busing Mar–Sept 1972, n.d. Draft position paper, "The Facts about Busing," March 29, 1972.

[28] Library of Congress, Manuscript Division, Records of the National Urban League, Part III. Box 17, folder 7: Communication Department, busing Mar–Sept 1972, n.d. Strategy paper titled "The Anti-Busing Crisis," 3 pages, n.d.

[29] While, as previously described, the Congress for Racial Equality and other black separatist organizations and individuals were on the same side of this policy debate as whites opposed to busing, these groups lacked the political legitimacy of the more mainstream Civil Rights organizations and thus their policy preferences received little attention in the general debate.

US Supreme Court decision in *Rodriguez* [30] took school finance reform off the national policy agenda and returned it to individual states, making it more difficult to mount political claims based on the rights of children in poor districts to equality of educational opportunity.

One may speculate about what might have happened if federal legislation that increased funding for schools in resource-poor districts had been passed in the early 1970s, before *Rodriguez*. Not only might the stark inequality of resources among school districts that are apparent today not exist, but there is reason to believe that minorities might not be as isolated in predominantly minority schools as is the case today. If schools with significant proportions of minorities enjoyed the same resources and provided the same educational opportunities as predominantly white schools, white parents would have one less reason to avoid the former.

School choice and tuition tax credits. In March 1972, the President's Commission on School Finance recommended that, alongside efforts to promote greater within-state, between-district equality in school funding, the federal government adopt proposals to allow parents tax credits for tuition paid at private K–12 schools (Herbers 1972a:1). This policy had a long association with efforts to circumvent the intent of desegregation orders by easing white southern parents' withdrawal of their children from public schools in favor of enrollment in private white flight academies. Tuition tax credits were also in direct opposition to a series of court decisions disallowing the use of public funds for private schools (Herbers 1972b:E3). In August 1972, tuition tax credits took their place on the national policy agenda when the Nixon administration backed a plan to provide tax credits for tuition at private schools, a proposal that the media acknowledged as an effort to attract southern segregationist votes because it would provide financial assistance to "those who send their children to segregated private academies in the South" (Shanahan 1972:19).

Civil rights organizations opposed tax credits, vouchers, and choice plans because those policies represented long-standing efforts to circumvent federal desegregation orders.[31] They were joined by many long-time friends of public education, central among which were teachers unions. The California Teachers Association, for example, argued in 1972 that "vouchers would cripple or destroy the public schools" (Fairbanks 1972a:D2; Fairbanks 1972b:A3); the editors of the *Los Angeles Times*

---

[30] *San Antonio Independent School District v. Rodriguez*, 411 US 1 (1973). The lower federal court had held that the traditional financing method using property taxes imposed by local school districts was unconstitutional in violation of the equal protection clause of the US Constitution. The Supreme Court reversed, holding that wealth was not a "suspect classification" and that education was not a fundamental right. Consequently, the state's decision to use traditional school finance schemes was not subject to heightened judicial scrutiny but rather subject to the deferential rational basis test. The Court concluded that the state's purpose of providing local control over education met that test. In contrast, the decision in *Serrano*, 487 P.2d 1241 (Cal. 1971), was based on a finding that unequal funding violated the state constitution. The *Serrano* decision initiated a wave of similar school finance lawsuits in other states.

[31] The US Supreme Court struck down freedom of choice plans in 1971 in *Swann v. Charlotte-Mecklenburg Board of Education*.

wondered how Americans could "countenance the siphoning off of general funds [from public schools] for private schools or for parents who prefer to send their children to them"? (1972a:D6). Voucher supporters, in contrast, did not directly counter the charges that vouchers and/or tuition tax credits would harm blacks or public schools. Rather, they relied on a language of political conservatism used to support vouchers since Milton Friedman first introduced the idea, arguing that "vouchers would improve education by stimulating competition among schools" (Fairbanks 1972a:D2) and would "free schools from bureaucratic resistance to innovation" (Rosenthal 1972:46).

By late 1972, bills to provide tax credits for private-school tuition costs remained in committee in both the House and the Senate, from which they did not emerge (*New York Times* 1972:24). In the early 1970s, therefore, the taint of school choice measures due to their close association with efforts to fight desegregation proved fatal. It took an entirely different set of political conditions in the late 1980s to revitalize school choice—in the form of school vouchers—as a reform that would promote racial equality in public schooling by allowing poor, predominantly minority parents the same right to choose their children's schooling that white middle-class parents had long enjoyed.

Beyond the 1970s

Shortly after the Nixon administration's failure to pass anti-busing legislation, progress on desegregation and busing was sharply curtailed by the 1974 US Supreme Court decision in *Milliken v. Bradley*, which with few exceptions made it unconstitutional to bus students across school-district boundaries. This ruling limited the degree to which busing could be used to meet desegregation goals since many urban public school systems enrolled small proportions of white students by that time. Ultimately, busing and desegregation efforts were further undermined by a series of US Supreme Court decisions in the 1980s and 1990s that dismantled both policies (Orfield et al. 1996). Nonetheless, the histories of both school finance reform and vouchers continued to be shaped by the legacies of busing and desegregation long after the early 1970s.

In the aftermath of the 1973 US Supreme Court decision in *Rodriguez*, state supreme courts in almost 20 states ordered overhauls of their states' school finance systems. In no state, however, have the courts' decisions been implemented as intended, and resource inequality between affluent and poor districts remains high (Corcoran et al. 2003). Funding equalization decisions were contested in most states in which they were adopted. In an attempt to maintain their communities' competitive edge in school quality, white and affluent communities have mobilized to delay, dilute, or discontinue attempts to implement the court decisions (Carr and Fuhrman 1999; Ladd et al. 1999; Paris 2001; Reed 2001b; Wong 1999). In states where funding disparities among districts have been partly eliminated, parents in affluent districts have responded in some cases with private resources to bolster the facilities or programs at their children's schools (Ryan and Heise 2002). Opposition to school finance reform, then, has taken both institutional and noninstitutional forms. However, public opinion polls have shown consistently high levels of support for the equal funding of schools (Carr and Fuhrman 1999; Rose and Gallup 2002).

Consistent with the terms used to argue the original school finance cases in Texas and California, proponents of school finance reform generally use a language of equality and rights to state their claims and legitimize their proposals. Students in resource-poor districts have a right to good schools or, more recently, adequate ones—a right that allegedly is denied by long-standing reliance on local property taxes as the main source of school funding. A redistribution of school funding is an appropriate and necessary way to end between-district inequality in educational resources (see Walters et al. 2009a; Lamber et al. 2009). Opponents, on the other hand, do not attempt to undermine equality explicitly. Instead, they depict attempts to take money from rich districts to give to poor districts as unfair, in some cases labeling them a Robin Hood plan. Such language was used to great effect in political battles over court-ordered school finance reform in Texas, Vermont, and Ohio (Folbre 1992; Goodman 1999; Walters et al. 2009a; Lamber et al. 2009). Other common counterarguments are expressed more clearly in a language of political conservatism. The decisions would require an irresponsible increase in taxes, would undermine local control of schools, or would constitute judicial activism (Walters et al. 2009a, b, c). Returning to the case of Ohio, for example, the state budget director argued that *DeRolph* would "likely result in a significant state tax increase and an erosion of local control of schools" (Leonard 1997:1A). A state senator declared "We will not be bullied or browbeaten into… bayoneting the people of Ohio with a massive—and unnecessary—tax increase" (Candisky 1999:1A). The Republican legislative leadership "insisted that school finance was a matter for the legislative institution" (Koski 2004:1149).

While there is a voluminous state-by-state literature on the history of school finance reform, there has been insufficient attention to the racialized basis of opposition to it. Some survey research, however, finds that whites make an association between funding equalization and urban blacks, one that undermines their support for it (Ryan 1999b; Reed 2001a). Further, in poll after poll, minorities express considerably more support for funding equalization than whites (Moe 2001; Hochschild and Scovronick 2003; Tedin 1994). This level of support extends even to minorities who reside in the suburbs (Walters et al. 2003), a group that would have to share their schools' resources with less affluent districts if reforms were implemented.

By the late 1980s, many minorities were weary of waiting for the promise of *Brown* to be fulfilled. The attempt to attack separate had not produced either integrated or equal education, nor had the attack on unequal resources produced much change (Dougherty 2004).[32] First in Milwaukee, and then elsewhere, groups of

---

[32] Part of the reason for the elimination of progress on school desegregation is a series of US Supreme Court decisions in the 1980s and 1990s that curtailed busing and put such severe restrictions on desegregation plans that it was effectively dismantled (Orfield et al. 1996).

influential minority activists joined with social and religious conservatives to support school vouchers as a means to help poor urban parents secure a better education for their children. This new social movement succeeded in giving vouchers a political legitimacy they had lacked in the 1960s and 1970s (Chubb and Moe 1990; Carl 1996; Mintrom 2000; Moe 2001; Wolfe 2003; Kahlenberg 2003). Recall that the original arguments for vouchers were not cast in a language of equality. Rather, political conservatives who were early voucher proponents argued that vouchers would introduce market competition into the public education sector and thereby reform inefficient bureaucracies (Chubb and Moe 1990; Friedman 1962). Voucher proposals framed in these conservative terms were easily defeated by charges of inegalitarianism (Dougherty and Sostre 1992). The inclusion of poor urban minorities into the new voucher coalition in the late 1980s, however, made possible a substantial shift in the language in which the voucher case could be made. With poor urban students in general, and poor black students in particular, as the new public face of would-be voucher recipients, a new equality argument was able to displace the original anti-big-government argument: Vouchers give poor parents the same right to choose their children's schools as rich parents always have enjoyed (Hochschild and Scovronick 2003; Moe 2001).[33] The now-conspicuous presence of black activists and parents in the voucher coalition made it possible to present vouchers indirectly as a form of racial justice as well. The new coalition and language it adopted allowed the nation's first voucher program to be established in Milwaukee in 1990 (Moe 2001). More generally, a body of scholarship corroborates that the public face of vouchers at present is minorities, especially urban blacks, and further shows that, in contrast to the racial politics of welfare, the association in the public mind of vouchers with minority recipients increases public support (Dougherty and Sostre 1992; Shokraii 1996; Wolfe 2003).

Opponents of vouchers generally depicted them as an abandonment rather than reform of public schools and as a policy that would further disadvantage students who already suffered disproportionately in bad schools. For example, opponents of Cleveland's voucher program argued that it "will drain badly needed money and the best students from the Cleveland schools without doing anything to improve the system" (McLarin 1996:B9). The *Los Angeles Times* wrote that critics of vouchers "contend such plans would drain scarce public funds from public school systems" (Chen 1996:A10). Sounding a similar note, the president of the Connecticut Education Association argued that "The minute you take tax dollars from local school budgets, you're seriously affecting the programs of the children left behind" (Miller 1996:1). People for the American Way (PFAW), an advocacy organization

---

[33] A new pro-voucher advocacy organization, the Black Alliance for Educational Options (BAEO), was established in the late 1990s by African Americans who broke from the NAACP over their opposition to vouchers. The BAEO supports vouchers as a way to "empower low-income and working-class Black families." See www.baeo.org. They ran a series of print pro-voucher ads shortly after their founding that featured photos of young black children with the tag line that "parental school choice is widespread – unless you're poor." See Kane (2001).

devoted to the cause of equality and a diverse democratic society, depicts vouchers as an assault on public schools, an institution central to the proper functioning of a democratic society.[34] With the NAACP and the Ad Council, in 1997, PFAW set up a separate advocacy organization devoted to championing public education, Partners for Public Education, that—although currently defunct—ran a $100 million advertising campaign between 2000 and 2003 urging African American and Latino parents to become more involved in their public schools rather than accepting a voucher and thus turning their back on public education (*The Crisis* 2001:73). The NAACP, the National Urban League, and other mainstream Civil Rights organizations "oppose vouchers because of the threat they believe the system presents to public education" (Kane 2001:42). Teachers' unions and professional education associations also have argued that support for vouchers amounts to an abandonment of public education.[35]

The fact that vouchers, like funding equalization, are formally color blind[36] did not prevent it from being cast as a policy that will disproportionately help urban minorities secure an education for their children that is more equal to the education received by affluent white children. The rhetoric and coalition proved powerful beyond their origin in Milwaukee. Voucher programs were established in Cleveland in 1995, Florida in 1999, the District of Columbia in 2004, and Utah in 2005. Vouchers, then, let separate stand unchallenged and do not attempt to redistribute resources among schools or school districts. Instead, they promise to improve the educational experiences of some poor children by redistributing the children themselves to better schools, although the schools available to voucher students do not necessarily offer better material resources than the failing schools they are fleeing. In effect, voucher proponents promise equality (in the form of an equal right to choose) while letting stand racially segregated schooling and resource differences between predominantly white and predominantly minority school districts.

The politics of vouchers have been racialized in ways that go beyond the inclusion of blacks in the pro-voucher coalition and the showcasing of black children as primary recipients. In recent years, voucher supporters have increasingly drawn on a language of racial equality in their rhetoric, for example, referring to vouchers as the Civil Rights struggle of our era. Clint Bolick, a prominent pro-voucher activist, described the litigation over the constitutionality of the Cleveland voucher program "the most important education case since *Brown*" (Bumiller 2002:1). President Bush reiterated many of the racial equality rhetorical points in a speech he gave after the US Supreme Court upheld the constitutionality of Cleveland's program in *Zelman v. Simmons-Harris* 2002. In this speech, he declared the ruling "just as historic" as *Brown* in that "our nation cannot have two separate educational systems…, one for African Americans and one for whites" (Bumiller 2002:1).

---

[34] See http://www.pfaw.org/, accessed March 10, 2010.

[35] See, for example, the websites of the National Education Association and the American Federation of Teachers (www.nea.org and www.aft.org).

[36] That is, eligibility is based on family income, not on students' race.

The political boost the voucher movement obtained from its association with black beneficiaries and from its advocates' adoption of a rhetoric of racial equality is at odds with a body of research on the racial politics of redistributive policy showing that the policies believed to disproportionately benefit minorities are stigmatized. There are two reasons, I argue, for the apparent anomaly. First, the public face of vouchers is not just blacks—it is young black children. And children, especially those depicted in pro-voucher materials, are generally seen as innocent and hence deserving of public benefits (Walters et al. 2009b). Second, the association of vouchers with deserving, innocent black children as beneficiaries has its limits. It only rallies the support of affluent whites when the voucher program is limited to schools inside the city and when it constitutes no threat to their children's schools. Suburban residents have consistently opposed voucher proposals that would have included the suburbs (Broder 2002; Ryan and Heise 2002). Further, every statewide voucher referendum that included affluent, predominantly white suburban districts has been defeated. Although the Cleveland and Milwaukee voucher plans give the option of participating to school districts that are contiguous to the central city, not one of those districts has participated. Affluent suburban parents who work to keep voucher programs limited to private schools in the city do so for the same reason they historically have opposed busing: They are unwilling to share the superior educational opportunities in their schools with poor urban children (Ryan and Heise 2002). "Suburban parents oppose vouchers, as they did busing, in part because they do not want to open up their schools to students from the cities" (Zernike 2002:3). Thus, in practice, voucher recipients in Cleveland and Milwaukee are restricted to private schools within the district boundaries. Even though vouchers' proponents have prevailed in many places, the plans that exist were adopted presumably because they do not hold much promise for reducing racial isolation in our schools.

Conclusions

In this essay, I trace a path-dependent political process that links desegregation and busing to school funding equalization, and both in turn to school vouchers. I show that we cannot understand the reasons why and how we continue to observe sharp racial divides in American K–12 public educational opportunities without considering the policy histories of a series of policies that, taken together and if adopted as intended, might have produced less racial segregation and more racial equality in public educational opportunities. The racial divide is a product of color-blind as well as color-conscious policies whose histories are linked through a politics of race. The political process involved both noninstitutional means of opposition to and demand for state policies as well as politics that worked through formal political channels. The policy progression from *Brown* and busing to funding equalization and vouchers has narrowed the scope of the attack on racial inequality. What began as a color-conscious attack on separate that also carried the promise of equal evolved into a color-blind attack on unequal that would have reduced racial inequalities in educational opportunities. Still later, it became a strategy promoted as a form of racial justice that attempts to put in place a new form of equality—a parent's equal right to choose—but lets stand the forms of both separate and unequal that *Brown* was intended to dismantle. More specifically, I show that desegregation and busing created enduring policy legacies that led to both school funding equalization and school vouchers, and that in turn the policy history of desegregation was shaped by the politics of school finance reform and vouchers.

Contrary to much of the extant work on racial inequality in American education that views court decisions as the most pivotal events, this analysis shows that it is not just the courts. There are other institutional arenas of formal politics in which policies may originate and through which implementation proceeds. But, even adding legislatures and the White House or governors' offices does not provide the whole picture. Other important individuals and groups who stand outside of formal political institutions matter greatly: advocacy groups, other mobilized social groups, and even the unorganized acts of individual parents who choose some schools for their children and avoid others.[37]

This analysis also shows that the institutional arena in which a policy originates (for the ones considered here, the contrast is mostly between courts and legislatures) is consequential for the degree to which powerful and challenger groups can have their interests realized and the means available to them to do so. When a policy originates because of a court decision, more opportunities appear to exist for the claims presented by challenger groups to be realized. An important constraint on the courts as instigators of school reform, however, is that those claims have to be expressed in a language the courts will recognize and must be presented by a group or groups the courts view as entitled to make such a rights claim. The inability of Mexican Americans to seek legal redress for school segregation prior to 1973 is a case in point. Nonetheless, there is considerable room for creativity even within what often appears to be the tight constraints of the legal system. For example, *Rodriguez* and *Serrano* were filed in part as remedies for racial discrimination in education.

An adopted policy has little chance of changing educational practices, however, unless it is implemented. That phase of policy development appears to favor the powerful, because they have greater access to institutional and noninstitutional means of political influence. Desegregation, school finance reform, and school vouchers were all stymied, circumvented, or greatly limited by powerful opponents who resisted the most redistributive ways in which each could have been implemented.

I have shown that policy legacies work through ideas as well as institutional arrangements. For example, the ways in which school finance reform and vouchers became tainted through their association with segregationists during the anti-busing wars of the early 1970s turned the black Civil Rights leadership against them at

---

[37] To be clear, however, these parental choices are enabled and constrained by decisions made by policymakers, including decisions about how to draw school district boundaries and how sacrosanct those boundaries are (Walters 2001).

important historical junctures and shaped the policy processes of school finance reform and vouchers. The policy legacies of important and powerful ideas are significant in ways that sometimes are surprising. For example, the principle that separate cannot be equal proved a great advantage to the Civil Rights movement as it worked to desegregate schools, but it ironically limited the degree to which they could or would work for school finance reform at a critical moment of opportunity in the early 1970s. If the Civil Rights leadership had thrown its moral capital and political weight behind the proposed federal legislation to increase funding for urban schools, American public schools might not be as racially segregated as they are today. Recall the sentiment of the editors of the *Los Angeles Times* when the federal debate was underway: "When quality and security are equalized among the schools, the greatest barriers to integration will have been eliminated" (1972b:B2). Another example of the power of ideas is the new political life that was breathed into the voucher movement when its leaders introduced a new set of equality arguments to make the case for vouchers—a change that was made possible in part by bringing into the coalition a group of blacks who had broken from the anti-voucher position of black Civil Rights organizations and who were able to make a credible equality argument in ways that white conservatives could not.

The illustrations provided in this chapter have focused on the interrelated policy development processes that have left us with the biggest social divide in American education, namely, the gap in educational opportunities between whites and minorities. A similar approach would be useful in understanding other major social inequalities in educational opportunities, such as gender and class divides. Another topic for scholarly inquiry is the question of why American policymakers and the public have tolerated the geographic divides in access to what are understood to be good schools. Attempts to close the divides between suburban, urban, and rural schools are addressed to some degree in the literature on school finance reform, but that literature has not explored adequately the reasons why school district boundaries are a more consequential determinant of access to good schools in some states than others. And, the policy question of unequal access to good schooling that exists among states has received scant attention, despite the well-known fact that between-state variation in school resources is higher than within-state variation. A similar analysis of the reasons why geography acts as a major divide in school resources and opportunities would need to address questions about why certain conceivable policy developments did not occur. For example, why, with the exception of Hawaii, we do not have statewide school districts and why is there so little national funding over and control of public education in the USA? It is as important to explore the policy roads not taken as it is to explore the reasons why the policy development process took the turns that it did.

Finally, the present analysis illustrates the importance of studying the politics of school reform and educational policy development as processes that are part of the larger politics of social provision in the USA. Such an analysis needs to identify the educational interests of a broad group of actors and organizations both within and outside of formal politics and the terms in which those interests are expressed. It needs to pay close attention to their capacities to act on their interests. Such capacities may derive from formal political institutions or be realized through noninstitutional means. Perhaps most importantly, questions about the structure of empty spaces in American education—questions that are logically prior to questions about how some students get sorted into good spaces and others get consigned to bad ones—cannot be addressed adequately by studying school reform or policy development in a singular fashion. The opportunity structure results from the cumulative effects of related series of policies whose histories are tightly interwoven.

References

Amenta, Edwin. 1998. *Bold relief: Institutional politics and the origins of modern American social policy*. Princeton: Princeton University Press.

Anderson, James, Dara N. Byrne, and Tavis Smiley (eds.). 2004. *The unfinished agenda of Brown v. Board of Education*. New York: Wiley.

Anyon, Jean. 1997. *Ghetto schooling: A political economy of urban educational reform*. New York: Teachers College Press.

Beckman, Aldo. 1972. U.S. maps antibusing plan. *Chicago Tribune*, Mar. 18, p. S1.

Beland, Daniel. 2005. Ideas and social policy: An institutional perspective. *Social Policy and Administration* 39: 1–18.

Benford, Robert D., and David A. Snow. 2000. Framing processes and social movements: An overview and assessment. *Annual Review of Sociology* 26: 611–639.

Berkowitz, Edward, and Kim McQuaid. 1988. *Creating the welfare state: The political economy of twentieth-century reform*. New York: Praeger.

Binder, Amy. 2002. *Contentious curricula: Afrocentrism and creationism in American public schools*. Princeton: Princeton University Press.

Bowles, Samuel, and Herbert Gintis. 1976. *Schooling in capitalist America: Educational reform and the contradictions of economic life*. New York: Routledge.

Brint, Steven. 2006. *Schools and societies*, 2nd ed. Stanford: Stanford University Press.

Brint, Steven. 2009. The 'Collective Mind' at work: A decade in the life of U.S. sociology of education. *Sociology of Education Section Newsletter*, Spring, pp. 7–15. Retrieved August 2, 2010 (http://www2.asanet.org/soe/misc/Newsletter_spring09.pdf).

Broder, David. 2002. Lines dividing vouchers. *Washington Post*, July 7, p. B07.

Bumiller, Elisabeth. 2002. Bush calls ruling about vouchers a 'historic' move. *New York Times*, July 2, p. A1.

Burstein, Paul, and Marie Bricher. 1997. Problem definition public policy: Congressional committees confront work, family, and gender, 1945–1990. *Social Forces* 76: 135–168.

Burstein, Paul, and April Linton. 2002. The impact of political parties, interest groups, and social movement organizations on public policy: Some recent evidence and theoretical concerns. *Social Forces* 81: 381–408.

California Postsecondary Education Commission. 1998. *Toward a greater understanding of the state's educational equity policies, programs, and practices*. Sacramento: California Postsecondary Education Commission.

Campbell, John L. 1998. Institutional analysis and the role of ideas in political economy. *Theory and Society* 27: 377–409.

Campbell, John L. 2002. Ideas, politics, and public policy. *Annual Review of Sociology* 28: 21–38.

Candisky, Catherine. 1999. Two senators propose to amend state constitution. *Columbus Dispatch* March 4: 1A.

Carl, Jim. 1996. Unusual allies: Elite and grass-roots origins of parental choice in Milwaukee. *Teachers College Record* 98: 266–285.

Carr, Melissa C., and Susan H. Fuhrman. 1999. The politics of school finance in the 1990s. In *Equity and adequacy in education finance: Issues and perspectives*, eds. H.F. Ladd, R. Chalk, and J.S. Hansen, 136–174. Washington, DC: National Academy Press.

Chen, Edwin. 1996. Dole pushes plan for low-income students to select school of choice. *Los Angeles Times*, July 19, p. A10.

Chicago Tribune. 1972. Cloture motion made on busing bill in Senate. *Chicago Tribune* Oct. 7: 3.

Chubb, John E., and Terry M. Moe. 1990. *Politics, markets, and America's schools*. Washington, DC: Brookings Institutions Press.

Clotfelter, Charles T. 2006. *After "Brown": The rise and retreat of school segregation*. Princeton: Princeton University Press.

Corcoran, Sean, William N. Evans, Jennifer Godwin, Sheila E. Murray, and Robert M. Schwab. 2003. The changing distribution of education finance: 1972–1997. Working Paper, Russell Sage Foundation.

Cross, Christopher T. 2004. *Political education: National policy comes of age*. New York: Teachers College.

Davies, Scott. 1999. From moral duty to cultural rights: A case study of political framing in education. *Sociology of Education* 72: 1–21.

Dawson, Michael C. 2001. *Black visions: The roots of contemporary African-American political ideologies*. Chicago: University of Chicago Press.

DeRolph v. State, 78 Ohio St. 3d 193, 197 (1997), (*DeRolph I*).

Dobbin, Frank. 1994. *Forging industrial policy: The United States, Britain, and France in the railway age*. Cambridge: Cambridge University Press.

Domhoff, G.William. 1990. *The power elite and the state: How policy is made in America*. New York: Aldine de Gruyter.

Dougherty, Kevin J., and Lizabeth Sostre. 1992. Minerva and the market: The sources of the movement for school choice. *Educational Policy* 6(June): 160–179.

Dougherty, Jack. 2004. *More than one struggle: The evolution of black school reform in Milwaukee*. Chapel Hill: University of North Carolina Press.

Fairbanks, Robert. 1972a. Education voucher bill passes test in senate. *Los Angeles Times*, March 23, p. D2.

Fairbanks, Robert. 1972b. Senate group rejects voucher education plan. *Los Angeles Times*, July 11, p. A3.

Ferg-Cadima, James A. 2004. Black, white and brown: Latino school desegregation efforts in the pre- and post-*Brown v. Board of Education* era. Mexican American Legal Defense and Educational Fund. Retrieved Mar 10, 2006 (http://www.maldef.org/pdf/LatinoDesegregation.pdf).

Ferree, Myra Marx. 2003. Resonance and radicalism: Feminist framing in the abortion debates of the United States and Germany. *American Journal of Sociology* 109: 304–344.

Folbre, Nancy. 1992. Remembering Alamo Heights. *Texas Observer*, Nov 13, pp. 6–9.

Friedman, Milton. 1955. The role of government in education. In *Economics and the public interest*, ed. Robert A. Solo. New Brunswick: Rutgers University Press.

Friedman, Milton. 1962. *Capitalism and freedom*. Chicago: University of Chicago Press.

Futrell, Mary Hatwood. 2004. The impact of the *Brown* decision on African American educators. In *The unfinished agenda of* Brown v. Board of Education, eds. James Anderson, Dara N. Byrne, and Tavis Smiley, 79–98. New York: Wiley.

Gilens, Martin. 1999. *Why Americans hate welfare: Race, media, and the politics of antipoverty policy*. Chicago: University of Chicago Press.

Goodman, David 1999. America's newest class war. *Mother Jones*, pp. 68–75.

Greenhouse, Linda. 1972. Property tax reform enthusiasm lags. *New York Times*, December 19, pp. 1, 36.

Hacker, Jacob S. 2002. *The divided welfare state: The battle over private and private social benefits in the United States*. Cambridge: Cambridge University Press.

Hanushek, Eric A. 1989. The impact of differential expenditures on school performance. *Educational Researcher* 18: 45–65.

Hanushek, Eric A. 1994. Money might matter somewhere: A response to Hedges, Laine, and Greenwald. *Educational Researcher* 23(4): 5–8.

Hasci, Timothy A. 2002. *Children as pawns: The politics of educational reform*. Cambridge: Harvard University Press.
Hedges, Larry V., Richard D. Laine, and Rob Greenwald. 1994a. Does money matter? A meta-analysis of studies of the effects of differential school inputs on student outcomes. *Educational Researcher* 23(3): 5–14.
Hedges, Larry V., Richard D. Laine, and Rob Greenwald. 1994b. Money does matter somewhere: A response to Hanushek. *Educational Researcher* 23(4): 9–10.
Hedges, Larry V., and Amy Nowell. 1998. Black-white test score convergence since 1965. In *The black-white test score gap*, eds. Christopher Jencks and Meredith Phillips, 149–181. Washington, DC: Brookings Institution Press.
Henig, Jeffrey R., Richard C. Hula, Marion Orr, and Desiree S. Pedescleaux. 1999. *The color of school reform: Race, politics and the challenge of urban education*. Princeton: Princeton University Press.
Herbers, John. 1972a. School financing by states urged in federal study. *New York Times*, March 7, p. 1.
Herbers, John. 1972b. A new way to foot the bill. *New York Times*, March 12, p. E3.
Hess, Frederick M. 1999. *Spinning wheels: The politics of urban school reform*. Washington, DC: Brookings Institution Press.
Hicks, Alexander M., and Duane H. Swank. 1992. Politics, institutions, and welfare spending in industrialized democracies, 1960–82. *American Political Science Review* 86: 658–674.
Hochschild, Jennifer, and Nathan Scovronick. 2003. *The American dream and the public schools*. New York: Oxford University Press.
Hogan, David. 1982. Making it in America: Work, education, and social structure. In *Work, youth, and schooling*, eds. Harvey Kantor and David Tyack, 142–179. Stanford: Stanford University Press.
Howell, William G., and Paul E. Peterson. 2006. *The education gap: Vouchers and urban schools*, Revised ed. Washington, DC: The Brookings Institution.
Irons, Peter. 2002. *Jim crow's children: The broken promise of the* Brown *decision*. New York: Viking.
Jencks, Christopher, and Meredith Phillips. 1998. The black-white test score gap: An introduction. In *The black-white test score gap*, eds. Christopher Jencks and Meredith Phillips, 1–54. Washington, DC: Brookings Institution Press.
Johnson, Thomas A. 1972. Black assembly voted at Parley. *New York Times*, March 13, p. 1.
Kahlenberg, Richard (ed.). 2003. *Public school choice vs. private school vouchers*. New York: Century Foundation Press.
Kane, Eugene. 2001. Voice for school choice. *The Crisis*, September/October, pp. 42–45.
Katz, Michael. 1968. *The irony of early school reform*. Cambridge: Harvard University Press.
Keyes v. School District No. 1 413 U.S. 189 (1973).
Kluger, Richard. 1977. *Simple justice*. New York: Vintage.
Korpi, Walter. 1983. *The democratic class struggle*. London: Routledge.
Koski, William S. 2004. The politics of judicial decision-making in educational policy reform litigation. *Hastings Law Journal* 55: 1077–1133.
Kozol, Jonathan. 1992. *Savage inequalities: Children in America's schools*. New York: Harper Perennial.
Kozol, Jonatham. 2005. *The shame of the nation: The restoration of apartheid schooling in America*. New York: Crown.
Krueger, Alan B., and Pei Zhu. 2004. Another look at the New York City school voucher experiment. *American Behavioral Scientist* 47: 658–698.
Ladd, Helen F., Rosemary Chalk, and Janet S. Hansen. 1999. *Equity and adequacy in education finance: Issues and perspectives*. Washington, DC: National Academy Press.
Lamber, Julia C., Pamela Barnhouse Walters, Jean C. Robinson, and Emily Meanwell. 2009. Equality talk, claims making, and educational reform: Reconsidering 1996. Paper presented at the annual meeting of the Law & Society Association, Denver.
Lardner, George, Jr. 1972. CORE leaders assail black caucus. *Washington Post*, February 11, p. A3.
Leonard, Lee. 1997. Budget process to go on. *Columbus Dispatch* Mar 26: 1A.

Levitsky, Sandra R. 2008. 'What rights?' The construction of political claims to American health care entitlements. *Law and Society Review* 42: 551–590.
Lieberman, Robert C. 1998. *Shifting the color line: Race and the American welfare state.* Cambridge: Harvard University Press.
Lieberman, Robert C. 2002. Ideas, institutions, and political order: Explaining political change. *American Political Science Review* 96: 697–712.
Los Angeles Times. 1972a. Public education comes first. *Los Angeles Times*, July 12, p. D6.
Los Angeles Times. 1972b. Education and unity. *Los Angeles Times*, December 31, p. B2.
Maeroff, Gene I. 1972. A call for federal funds; public schools. *New York Times*, July 9, p. E7.
Mahoney, James. 2000. Path dependence in historical sociology. *Theory and Society* 29: 507–548.
Manza, Jeff. 2000. Political sociological models of the U.S. New Deal. *Annual Review of Sociology* 26: 297–322.
McCann, Michael W. 1994. *Rights at work.* Chicago: University of Chicago Press.
McDonnell, Lorraine M. 2007. The politics of education: Influencing policy and beyond. In *The state of education policy research*, eds. Susan H. Fuhrman, David K. Cohen, and Fritz Mosher, 19–39. Mahway: Lawrence Erlbaum Associates.
McLarin, Kimberly. 1996. Ohio paying some tuition for religious school students. *New York Times*, August 28, p. B9.
Miller, Julie. 1996. Schools, choices and tax dollars. *New York Times*, January 21, Section 13CN, p. 1.
Milliken v. Bradley 418 U.S. 717 (1974).
Minow, Martha. 2010. *In Brown's wake: Legacies of America's landmark legislation.* New York: Oxford University Press.
Mintrom, Michael. 2000. *Policy entrepreneurs and school choice.* Washington, DC: Georgetown University Press.
Moe, Terry M. 2001. *Schools, vouchers, and the American public.* Washington, DC: Brookings Institution Press.
National Commission on Excellence in Education. 1983. *A nation at risk: The imperative for education reform.* Washington, DC: U.S. Department of Education.
New York Times. 1972. Record of major Nixon legislative proposals and of action taken in the second session of 92d congress. *New York Times*, October 20, p. 24.
Oakes, Jeannie. N.d. Educational inadequacy, inequality, and failed social policy: A synthesis of expert reports prepared for *Williams v. State of California*. An expert report submitted on behalf of the plaintiffs. Retrieved May 24, 2006 (http://www.decentschools.org/expert_reports/oakes_report.pdf).
O'Brien, Molly Townes. 1997. Private school vouchers and the realities of racial politics. *Temple Law Review* 359: 372–394.
Ogletree, Charles. 2004a. All too deliberate. In *The unfinished agenda of* Brown v. Board of education, ed. James Anderson et al., 45–60. Hoboken: Wiley.
Ogletree, Charles. 2004b. *All deliberate speed: Reflections on the first half-century of* Brown v. Board of Education. New York: W. W. Norton.
Oliver, Pamela E., and Hank Johnston. 2000. What a good idea! Frames and ideologies in social movement research. *Mobilization* 4: 37–54.
Omi, Michael, and Howard Winant. 1994. *Racial formation in the United States.* Boston: Routledge.
Orfield, Gary, Susan Eaton, and the Harvard Project on School Desegregation. 1996. Dismantling desegregation: The quiet reversal of *Brown v. Board of Education*. New York: The New Press.
Orfield, Gary and Chungmei Lee. 2004. *Brown* at 50: King's dream or *Plessy's* nightmare? Harvard University: The Civil Rights Project (http://www.civilrightsproject.harvard.edu/research/reseg04/brown50.pdf).
Orloff, Ann Shola. 1993. *The politics of pensions: A comparative analysis of Britain, Canada, and the United States, 1880–1940.* Madison: University of Wisconsin Press.
Orren, Karen, and Stephen Skowronek. 2004. *The search for American Political Development.* New York: Cambridge University Press.

Paris, Michael. 2001. Legal mobilization and the politics of reform: Lessons from school finance litigation in Kentucky, 1984–1995. *Law and Social Inquiry* 26: 631–684.

Patterson, James T. 2001. Brown v. Board of Education: *A civil rights milestone and its troubled legacy*. New York: Oxford University Press.

Payne, Charles M. 2008. *So much reform, so little change: The persistence of failure in urban schools*. Cambridge: Harvard University Press.

Pedriana, Nicholas, and Robin Stryker. 1997. Political culture wars 1960s style: Equal employment opportunity-affirmative action law and the Philadelphia plan. *American Journal of Sociology* 103: 633–691.

Peterson, Paul E., and William G. Howell. 2004. Efficiency, bias, and classification schemes: A response to Alan B. Kreuger and Pei Zhu. *American Behavioral Scientist* 47: 699–717.

Pierson, Paul. 1994. *Dismantling the welfare state? Reagan, Thatcher, and the politics of retrenchment*. New York: Cambridge University Press.

Pierson, Paul. 2000. Increasing returns: Path dependence and the study of politics. *American Political Science Review* 94: 251–267.

Pierson, Paul. 2004. *Politics in time: History, institutions, and social analysis*. Princeton: Princeton University Press.

Polletta, Francesca. 2000. The structural context of novel rights claims: Southern civil rights organizing, 1961–1966. *Law and Society Review* 34: 367–406.

Quadagno, Jill. 1988. *The transformation of old age security*. Chicago: University of Chicago Press.

Quadagno, Jill. 1994. *The color of welfare: How racism undermined the war on poverty*. New York: Oxford University Press.

Quadagno, Jill. 2005. *One nation, uninsured: Why the U.S. has no national health insurance*. New York: Oxford University Press.

Raftery, Adrian E., and Michael Hout. 1993. Maximally maintained inequality: Educational stratification in Ireland. *Sociology of Education* 65(January): 41–62.

Ravitch, Diane. 2000. *Left back: A century of failed school reforms*. New York: Simon & Schuster.

Reed, Douglas S. 2001a. *On equal terms: The constitutional politics of educational opportunity*. Princeton: Princeton University Press.

Reed, Douglas S. 2001b. Not in my schoolyard: Localism and public opposition to funding schools equally. *Social Science Quarterly* 82: 34–50.

Reese, William J. 1986. *Power and the promise of school reform*. Boston: Routledge.

Rich, Wilbur C. 1996. *Black mayors and school politics: The failure of reform in Detroit, Gary, and Newark*. New York: Garland Publishing, Inc.

Rose v. Council for Better Educ. Inc., 790 S.W.2d 186, 194 (Ky. 1989).

Rose, Lowell C. and Alec M. Gallup. 2002. The 34th annual Phi Delta Kappa/Gallup Poll of the public's attitudes toward the public schools. *Phi Delta Kappan*, pp. 41–57.

Rosenthal, Jack. 1972. Major integration test confronts U.S. in 1972. *New York Times*, January 20, p. 1.

Ryan, James E. 1999a. Schools, race, and money. *Yale Law Journal* 109: 249.

Ryan, James E. 1999b. The influence of race in school finance reform. *Michigan Law Review* 98: 432–481.

Ryan, James E., and Michael Heise. 2002. Taking school choice to the suburbs. *Pittsburgh Post-Gazette*, July 7, p. B1.

Ryan, James E. 2010. *Five miles away a world apart: One city, two schools, and the story of educational opportunity in modern America*. New York: Oxford University Press.

Saltman, Kenneth J. 2007. *Capitalizing on disaster: Taking and breaking public schools*. Herndon: Paradigm Publishers.

San Antonio Independent School District v. Rodriguez, 411 U.S. 1 (1973).

San Miguel, Guadalupe. 1982. Mexican American organizations and the changing politics of school desegregation in Texas, 1945 to 1980. *Social Science Quarterly* 63: 701–715.

San Miguel, Guadalupe. 1983. The struggle against separate and unequal schools: Middle class Mexican Americans and the desegregation campaign in Texas, 1929–1957. *History of Education Quarterly* 23: 343–359.

Schragger, Richard. 2007. *San Antonio v. Rodriguez* and the Legal Geography of School Finance Reform. University of Virginia Law School, Public Law and Legal Theory Working Paper Series, Paper # 64. Retrieved July 23, 2007 (http://law.bepress.com/cgi/viewcontent.cgi?article=1104&context=uvalwps).

Semple, Robert B., Jr. 1972. Nixon asks bill imposing halt in new busing orders; seeks education equality. *New York Times*, March 17, p. 1.

Serrano v. Priest, 487 P.2d 1241, 1246 (Cal. 1971), (*Serrano I*).

Serrano v. Priest, 557 P.2d 929, 931 (Cal. 1976), (*Serrano II*).

Shanahan, Eileen. 1972. 2 Parties push nonpublic school aid with bill for tax credits to parents. *New York Times*, August 7, p. 19.

Shokraii, Nina. 1996. Free at last: Black America signs up for school choice. *Policy Review* 80: 20–26.

Skocpol, Theda. 1992. *Protecting soldiers and mothers: The political origins of social policy in the United States*. Cambridge: Belknap Press.

Skocpol, Theda. 1995. *Social policy in the United States*. Princeton: Princeton University Press.

Skocpol, Theda, and Edwin Amenta. 1986. States and social policies. *Annual Review of Sociology* 12: 131–157.

Sloan, Kris. 2008. The expanding educational services sector: Neoliberalism and the corporatization of curriculum at the local level in the U.S. *Journal of Curriculum Studies* 40: 555–578.

Spring, Joel. 1972. *Education and the rise of the corporate state*. Boston: Beacon.

Stephens, John D. 1979. *The transition from capitalism to socialism*. New York: MacMillan.

Stevens, Mitchell. 2001. *Kingdom of children: Culture and controversy in the homeschooling movement*. Princeton: Princeton University Press.

Strong, David, Pamela Barnhouse Walters, Brian Driscoll, and Scott Rosenberg. 2000. Leveraging the state: Private money and the development of public education for blacks. *American Sociological Review* 65: 658–681.

Stryker, R. 2001. Disparate impact and the quota debates: Law, labor market sociology, and equal employment policies. *Sociological Quarterly* 42: 13–46.

Tedin, Kent. 1994. Self-interest, symbolic values, and the financial equalization of the public schools. *Journal of Politics* 56: 628–649.

Tyack, David, and Lary Cuban. 1995. *Tinkering toward utopia: A century of public school reform*. Cambridge: Harvard University Press.

The Crisis. 2001. The NAACP Today. *The Crisis*. Sept/Oct, p. 73.

Toth, Robert C. 1972. Nixon asks congress to bar new racial busing orders. *Los Angeles Times*, March 17, p. A1.

Urban, Wayne, and Jennings Wagoner. 2000. *American education: A history*, 2nd ed. Boston: McGraw Hill.

Walters, Pamela Barnhouse. 2001. Educational access and the state: Historical continuities and discontinuities in racial inequality in American education. *Sociology of Education*, Special Issue: 35–49.

Walters, Pamela Barnhouse. 2007. Explaining the durable racial divide in American Education: Policy development and opportunity hoarding from *Brown* to vouchers. Presented at The Conference on the Social Dimensions of Inequality Sponsored by the Russell Sage Foundation and Carnegie Corporation, UCLA, January.

Walters, Pamela Barnhouse, Josh Klugman, Jenny Stuber, and Michael Rosenbaum. 2003. Race, redistribution, and Americans' educational policy preferences. Presented at The Annual Meeting of the American Sociological Association, August, Atlanta.

Walters, Pamela Barnhouse, Julia C. Lamber, and Jean C. Robinson. 2008. American political culture and discourses of equality: How can separate be equal? Presented at The Annual Meeting of the Law & Society Association, June, Montreal.

Walters, Pamela Barnhouse, Julia C. Lamber, Jean C. Robinson, and Emily Meanwell. 2009a. Equality talk, claims making, and educational reform: Reconsidering 1972. Presented at The Annual Meeting of the Western Political Science Association, Vancouver.

Walters, Pamela Barnhouse, Julia C. Lamber, Jean C. Robinson, and Emily Meanwell. 2009b. Political discourse and policy regime change: Constructions of deservedness in education reforms, 1972 to 1996. Presented at The Annual Meeting of the Law & Society Association, Chicago.

Walters, Pamela Barnhouse, Julia C. Lamber, Jean C. Robinson, and Julie Swando. 2009c. Policy development, political culture, and the courts: The cases of school finance reform in Kentucky and Ohio. Presented at The Annual Meeting of the American Sociological Association, San Francisco.

Washington Post. 1972. On court orders and school budgets. *Washington Post*, August 17, p. A18.

Wentworth, Eric. 1972. Black caucus affirms its support for busing. *Washington Post*, March 16, p. A1.

Wilkins, Roy. 1972. Nixon: Principal polarizer of the races. *Los Angeles Times*, June 6, p. D7.

Wilson, Steven H. 2003. Brown over 'other white': Mexican Americans' legal arguments and litigation strategy in school desegregation lawsuits. *Law and History Review*, 21(1).

Wolfe, Alan. 2003. The irony of school choice: Liberals, conservatives, and the new politics of race. In *School choice: The moral debate*, ed. Alan Wolfe, 31–50. Princeton: Princeton University Press.

Wong, Kenneth S. 1999. *Funding public schools: Politics and policies*. Lawrence: University Press of Kansas.

Wooten, James T. 1970. CORE gives up integration to back separatism. *New York Times*, September 7, p. 1.

Wrigley, Julia. 1982. *Class politics and public schools: Chicago, 1900–1950*. New Brunswick: Rutgers University Press.

Zelman v. Simmons-Harris, 536 U.S. 639 (2002).

Zernike, Kate. 2002. Vouchers: A shift, but just how big? *New York Times*, June 30, section 4, p. 3.

Chapter 5
Methodological Transactionalism and the Sociology of Education

Daniel A. McFarland, David Diehl, and Craig Rawlings

In recent years, Social Network Analysis (SNA) has become increasingly common in numerous sociological subdisciplines, the result being a host of innovative research that tackles old and new problems alike. Students of the sociology of knowledge, for example, use networks of journal co-citations as a novel method for tracking the diffusion of new ideas through the academy (e.g., Hargens 2000; Moody 2004). Political sociologists are drawing on SNA to understand the dynamics of collective action (Diani 1995; Tarrow 1994). Organizational sociologists use formal and informal work networks to study organizational learning (Hansen 1999; Rawlings et al. 2010; Reagans et al. 2004; Singh 2005). And educational sociologists apply social network methodologies in their study of teacher communities, classroom conduct and learning (Bidwell and Yasumoto 1999; Frank et al. 2008; McFarland 2001; Pittinsky and Carolan 2008). In this chapter, we focus our attention on educational sociology and relate how SNA has the potential to substantially reshape the future of this subfield.

Generally defined, SNA is the statistical study of the structure of interaction as it occurs between persons and/or other social units. The goal of most SNA is to understand how these configurations of relationships relate to some phenomenon of interest, such as actor behaviors or attitudes. The last several decades have witnessed an explosion of awareness about networks, not only within various parts of the academy as discussed above, but within the larger cultural consciousness as well. It is now common to colloquially speak of one's social network because of the ubiquitous use of networking platforms like Linked-In or Facebook as well as the new array of social media affixed to cell phones. This consciousness about networks has spread to educational phenomena as well, such that it is now common for educational practitioners and stakeholders to discuss networks when managing teacher professional

---

D.A. McFarland (✉) • D. Diehl • C. Rawlings
School of Education, Stanford University, Stanford, CA 94305-3084, USA
e-mail: dmcfarla@stanford.edu; diehld@stanford.edu; craigr@stanford.edu

communities (Penuel et al. 2009; Wiley 2001), school redesign networks (Daly and Finnigan 2010), cyber bullying (Kowalski and Limber 2007), and the integration of technology into schools (Frank et al. 2004). We believe that the growth of network thinking in educational research will only continue, but before elaborating on how we imagine this will look, it is worth beginning with a brief discussion of *why* it is that networks have become so popular in recent years in order to help clarify exactly what the potential research value is.

There are several reasons new inferential methods are advanced and adopted, each of which is evident in the particular case of SNA. The first reason is that new methods are developed to help answer what would otherwise be intractable problems related to foundational disciplinary theory. While SNA is becoming an increasingly interdisciplinary endeavor, it was largely developed within sociology and anthropology (Wasserman and Faust 1994:10–16). This is not a coincidence as SNA and sociology share the goal of explaining important social phenomena in terms of how particular units (such as people) are embedded in interconnected systems. This view extended to education early on as well, and one can find many early empirical works in SNA that studied relationships in classrooms (Almack 1922; Wellman 1926).

Within both SNA and sociology, however, there has always existed a gap between their theoretically informed vision about the nature of social process and the ability to capture them empirically. While some have argued that paradigmatic statistical methods, especially general linear modeling, distort sociologists' view of the world (Abbott 1988), there is a long history of scholars cautioning that many of the basic assumptions of common methods, such as independence and normality, are at odds with classical theory's description of social reality (Emirbayer 1997; Martin 2003). Many methods common today were originally advanced precisely to help close this gap between theory and empirical reality. The development of hierarchical linear modeling offers a good example of this (Bryk and Raudenbush 1992). Standard linear models assume independence among actors, but this clearly is not the case when studying students who are nested in classrooms, which in turn are nested in schools. By allowing variance to be measured at multiple levels, hierarchical linear modeling presents a method more in line with our understanding of how schools are actually structured.

Similarly, SNA was also developed as an alternative methodology for studying social phenomenon, but until recently its ability to fulfill this goal has been severely hindered by limitations of computational power and statistical methodology. Work in SNA has most commonly concentrated on small groups and static networks because network data are difficult to gather and smaller datasets have been all that could be computationally managed. Over the past few decades, however, statistical breakthroughs and substantial increases in computing power have allowed for the development of progressively more sophisticated techniques. SNA models can now handle millions of nodes and new methods for dynamic and temporal features of networks continue to be at the forefront of the field (Boyack et al. 2009). Much of what SNA potentially offers sociology and the study of education, then, is a means for better capturing complex interdependencies and fluid dynamics than many current and more popular methods are able to do.

It is worth asking, then, why did general linear modeling itself become so popular? Part of the answer is certainly that it proved itself capable of helping sociologists tackle many long-standing problems as discussed above. There is another reason as well, however, one having to do with the second motivation for creating new methods, namely the availability of new types of information. After World War II, the social survey became the main source of data in sociology and the development and adoption of linear multivariate analysis was the result of the need to find more sophisticated ways to analyze them (Clogg 1992; Converse 1987). We can see a strong parallel here with the current state of SNA. Numerous changes in the contemporary world, perhaps again most importantly the growth of the Internet, have provided abundant new sources of rich data. Most of these data are relational in nature and new statistical tools are required for their analysis. In much the same way that survey research created the necessity for more complicated multivariate models, so too does our burgeoning ability to collect massive interdependent data sets increase the need for more sophisticated network techniques.

These two rationales for the development of new methods are interrelated. As statistical tools become more advanced and their explanatory power more evident, they come to be applied to a growing number of areas and problems. This in turn raises new questions, again often requiring the development of even more sophisticated tools in order to find answers. Through this iterative process, SNA helps us refine and reconceptualize our very understanding of the social phenomenon in which we are interested. We can see this happening within education as many emerging streams of research focus on network aspects of schooling processes. For example, network and relational thinking is helping reframe teaching and learning by focusing our attention on the role of trust (Bryk and Schneider 2002), relations among teachers (Coburn and Russell 2008), and the effect of social capital on student outcomes (Morgan and Sørensen 1999).

For each of these three reasons – the ability to close the gap between theory and empirical reality, the capacity to deal with complex new forms and amounts of data, and the capability to help refine our theoretical lenses and questions in light of social change – we expect SNA to become an increasingly central part of the sociology of education and bring about a paradigm shift from methodological individualism to methodological transactionalism. Throughout the rest of this chapter, we make this argument using research on classroom processes and status attainment as substantive examples.

More specifically, we argue that sociologists of education can adopt SNA and the network perspective in increasingly comprehensive ways. First, SNA can be used to augment topics by applying network variables and constructs in current statistical models. Here, we add relational variables to standard models to better account for interdependencies. Next, SNA can help us reconceptualize research topics reframing the phenomenon of interest in network terms. Generally, this means seeing complex social interdependencies not only as part of the explanation for some individual level outcome, but also as part of the phenomenon to be explained. That is, we come to reconceptualize educational processes as being understood in terms of the fluid and changing relationship between actors and the networks in which they are embedded.

Finally, we conclude the chapter with a brief and speculative discussion about how cutting-edge technological breakthroughs in methods for both collecting and analyzing network data hold the possibility for revolutionizing the field. Here, we describe the potential impact of new methods like reality mining (Eagle and Pentland 2006) where technological tools are used to automatically collect features of human behavior. The results are massive data sets of actual instances of interaction that can be used to directly model patterns of transaction.

We begin with a discussion of how current data and methods in SNA can be deployed to augment and reconceptualize our approach to classroom processes – an important but somewhat understudied area in the sociology of education. We then move on to examine how the network perspective can inform our understanding of status attainment processes – an area at the core of the sociology of education, and one which can clearly be augmented with SNA, but where a network reconceptualization may only become fully possible through future advances in data mining and computation.

Network Perspectives on Classroom Processes

Methodologically, the most common approaches to the quantitative study of classrooms have treated them as groups of isolated individuals whose behavior and attitudes are influenced by personal and family attributes on one hand, and the characteristics of instruction, teachers, and school organization on the other (Lubbers 2003:309). Yet the underlying statistical assumptions of independence are at odds with the implications of both sociological theory and diverse qualitative ethnographic work, each of which presents classrooms as complex interdependent social environments. Teachers and students simultaneously construct and are molded by the social context they jointly enact through moment-by-moment social transactions (Wells 1993). This view is rarely captured, however, in the statistical methods typically used to study classroom processes.

By more thoroughly incorporating network perspectives and tools into the sociology of education, especially cutting-edge work on network dynamics, we argue that we will be able to better understand and study the interdependent relational processes that are the hallmark of classrooms. One of the central contributions of SNA has been the conceptualization of the individual's attitudes and behaviors as significantly related to the pattern of his or her relationships. Within SNA, these patterns have generally been taken to be a social structure itself (Freeman and Romney 1987:310). Over the past 15 years, however, there has been a shift both theoretically and methodologically in the network research community toward a more dynamic and processual view of relational structures. This has entailed a growing interest in network change as well as in identifying the ongoing interactional micromechanisms that give rise to the formal properties of global level networks (e.g., Robins et al. 2005). We think what is especially exciting about these developments is that as SNA becomes more sophisticated it allows us to quantitatively study the classroom in ways that match our current qualitative and theoretical view of them as interdependent and processual social contexts.

And so here we articulate two broad categories for how network analysis might be incorporated into our current study of classroom processes. These approaches differ in the degree that they integrate assumptions of interdependence as well as the level of methodological sophistication they entail. In this way we can think of them as constituting a continuum that, as we travel across it, moves us progressively further away from our current variable-centric methods and toward more transactional models. On one end, network measures are used to study the distribution of some dependent variable on individual actors; on the other end, network ties and individual attributes are modeled as changing in relation to each other through time.

Augmentation: Improving Individual-Level Explanations

We first look at the approach we refer to as *augmentation*. While not directly addressing issues of causation (which we will discuss in more detail in the next section), network data in an augmenting approach are used to create explanatory variables for use in standard regression models. The goal here is to use network measures to help explain variation in the distribution of some outcome measured at the individual level. This is probably the most common means of utilizing SNA in educational research because it can be done within standard models, thereby allowing the researcher to incorporate networks measures within a familiar and recognizable framework.

These individual-level explanatory variables can be constructed in one of two ways. The first corresponds to what is referred to in SNA as the *relational* perspective (Burt 1980). Here the focus is on how individuals are affected by the behaviors and attitudes of the people to whom they are connected. Common to this approach are social influence and peer effects models that attempt to find the amount of influence that friends have on individual attitudes or behaviors. This work has shown, for example that an adolescent's level of delinquency is influenced by the delinquency of his or her friends (Haynie 2002) and that peers help shape stability and change in individual identity (McFarland and Pals 2005). Research in this area also looks at the effect of membership in subgroups or cliques. Bidwell and Yasumoto, for example, found that shared norms in teacher collegial groups are associated with higher student achievement (1999). In each of these examples, we find that the nature of relationships helps explain variation in what most studies treat as individuals' level attributes or behaviors.

The second general approach to constructing individual-level variables is based on measures of an actor's position in a network (Burt 1980). Here the importance of networks is seen not in terms of the characteristics of the people to whom the individual is tied, but rather in the location of the individual within the overall pattern of relationships (e.g., as bridge, as peripheral, etc.). This is, perhaps, a less intuitive account of the importance of networks than the relational perspective. There are two reasons position in a network can be important. First, those in similar positions within or across networks may have similar attitudes or behaviors. Van Rossem and Vermande, for example, find that preschoolers in equivalent locations in classroom friendship networks have similar levels of school adjustment (2004). Second, there are advantages to being centrally located in a network, or in controlling positions through which important resources flow. In one well-known study, for example, Friedkin and Slater (1994) find that school-level standardized test scores were positively correlated with the centrality of the principal in the relational network of the school.

Reconceptualization: Explaining Relational Structures

While the augmentation approach helps us better understand the impact of networks on individual behavior and attitudes, we ultimately want to know how the connection runs in the other direction as well. That is, we want to understand not only how actors are influenced by the pattern of their embeddings in their networks, but also how the individuals who compose it shape the structure of the network. One of the important emerging areas in SNA is methods for modeling global features of a network in terms of the probabilistic nature of underlying social and behavioral processes that give rise to it (Morris 2003). The methods for analyzing complete networks are less than a few decades old, most of them extensions of the p* family of models (Frank and Strauss 1986; Wasserman and Pattison 1996), more commonly known now as the exponential family of random graph models, or ERGMs (see Hunter et al. 2008 for a detailed explanation).

The relative newness of ERGMs and related methods means that there is a scarcity of empirical studies utilizing them, but educational studies are quite well represented among the work that has been done. Research on both classrooms (Lubbers 2003) and schools (Goodreau et al. 2009) has found that patterns of friendship are the result of individual preferences, group composition, and endogenous network processes like reciprocity and transitivity. The importance of such findings is that it shows that networks emerge out of complex and interdependent social processes, not just independent individual choices about ties. Most of our standard statistical tools cannot directly model this kind of interdependence.

Dropping independence assumptions and modeling tie formation directly helps us better capture interdependencies in classroom processes, but it does not deliver the fully dynamic view we are after. Such models cannot, for example, help us tease apart selection versus influence processes in tie formation, one of the stickiest issues in the study of behavioral dynamics (Baerveldt and Van Rossem 2008). An assumption with ERGMs is that the network under study is at equilibrium but in reality most social networks are inherently dynamic, with ties constantly being created, maintained, and dissolved (Snijders et al. 2010). To capture this empirically, we need to be able to simultaneously treat the network as both explanatory and dependent variable. This requires longitudinal modeling that captures how individual traits and interdependent relationships mutually influence and construct each other over time.

The longitudinal analysis of social networks has long been the "Holy Grail" for network researchers (Wasserman et al. 2005:6). It is only within the past few years that accessible methods for longitudinal network analysis have been developed. The most well known of these methods are the stochastic-based models developed by Tom Snijders and his colleagues, available in the statistical package SIENA (Steglich et al. 2006). These models are essentially longitudinal ERGMs that combine regular panel data (e.g., individual attitudes) with network panel data (i.e., relational measures collected at separate time points). Importantly, even though network data in this work is generally measured at discrete intervals, the methodological assumption is that relationships are (potentially) evolving states that may change between observations.

This empirical work utilizing longitudinal network methods is just in its earliest stages, but early work on adolescent friendship networks is already beginning to tease apart selection and influence processes related to issues such as drug use (Pearson et al. 2006) and smoking (Mercken et al. 2009). In both cases the authors find that over time there is a process of both selection and influence as peers both seek out other "deviants" as well as influence each others' behavior. Existing work outside of the network tradition has already argued for this reciprocal relationship between selection and influence, but utilizing dynamic network analysis allows researchers to better specify the mechanisms at work and understand how they shape each other through time.

We end this section with a brief discussion about how dynamic SNA might help us reconceptualize the study of trust in schools. Recent research has linked trust to numerous important classroom and school outcomes, including the success of school-wide improvement efforts (Spillane and Thompson 1997), the fostering of a sense of community (Louis 2007), and student academic achievement (Hoy et al. 2006). This is a case, however, where there is a mismatch between our theories about trust and the tools we use to study it. Conceptually, we do not think that trust directly affects the outcomes listed above, but rather that its presence shapes the nature of various types of interactions and behaviors. And so while relational trust is commonly defined as something that is "forged in daily social exchanges" (Bryk and Schneider 2002:136), we have tended not to study it in terms of patterns of interactions but rather as an individual level variable collected through self-reports. These self-reports are often then aggregated to create a school-level measure of trust.

The result is a black box where we know that trust shapes the nature of relationships in schools, but cannot say how trusting relationships emerge or identify the mechanisms through which trust fosters desired outcomes. Dynamic network analysis that models the coevolution of individuals and networks offers the potential for opening up this particular aspect of classroom life. The key is in bringing together work on the characteristics of individuals and schools related to the presence of trust with research on the network evolution of social structure (Van de Bunt et al. 2005). By collecting data about both actor and institutional attributes as well as longitudinal network data, we start to understand just how it is that trust matters and can begin to test hypotheses about possible causal mechanisms. Doing so is key if we hope to better understand how to foster conditions in classrooms and schools that not only engender trust among teachers and students, but also maximize the link between trust and the outcomes we care about.

Network Perspectives and Status Attainment

We now move on to discuss how SNA can better inform an area at the core of the sociology of education (see Brint 2009). While there are fairly straightforward ways SNA has been incorporated into status attainment research to augment existing models, there are many frontiers within this new terrain that remain underexplored. Fairly straightforward opportunities to augment attainment processes abound, while more conceptual ways to think about attainment as broader "structuration" processes (Giddens 1984) in which individuals are both enabled and constrained by a complex network of institutional arrangements (Kerckhoff 1995) require reconceptualizing how attainment research might be conducted. We are confident that because status attainment researchers have long been at the methodological frontier of the sociology of education, SNA will become increasingly important within the core, although the more radical reconceptualizations may not take hold as quickly as in microlevel areas such as classroom dynamics with more clear affinities with existing network tools.

As a brief illustration of how we see new data and SNA tools poised to change attainment research, consider the early sociograms of adolescent social structure by Coleman (1961). They were painstaking to create because they relied on survey data and manual visualization. Compared with the relative ease of collecting rich network data from various online sources and the various data reduction and visualization techniques now available, these early attempts appear heroic. Of course, the researcher cannot simply rely on more advanced tools to provide an in-depth analysis; these changes are not simply methodological in nature and have opened up whole new vistas on adolescent society that are substantively important. If Coleman's main point was that adolescents are living in greater isolation from adult society, this is probably nowhere more evident today than in various online social arenas. Clearly, many of the *relational* issues of peer influence are taking place through digital media, and SNA is poised to extract and analyze the traces of such relationships. New data sources and methods afford new opportunities to think about enduring questions of peer influences on students' beliefs and behaviors that are central for achievement. While opportunities for augmenting existing models abound, getting at the broader structural conditions that create and recreate the fragmented institutions and alienation of adolescent society as a largely autonomous social world will require more creative use of broader network mapping techniques. In short, we are poised to elaborate and extend Coleman's approach by collecting and comparing data on samples of adolescent societies' social structures.

In what follows, we discuss these various issues in greater depth. We begin with a discussion of various attempts to augment attainment research using SNA. We then discuss how SNA affords a broader set of opportunities to reconceptualize this core of the sociology of education.

Augmentation: Networks and Individual Resources

Status attainment research has long epitomized the strengths of sociological approaches to agent-centered models – that is, models that incorporate social variables into explanations of an individual's behaviors and beliefs. Since nearly its inception, this area of research has also incorporated inherently relational social factors into explanations of achievement, although a shortage of network data and techniques for modeling such data for many years prevented a more nuanced way of getting at many of these processes. Researchers have necessarily approximated many relational effects using individual-level characteristics and standard regression frameworks.

The original status attainment model argues that an individual's family background characteristics tend to reproduce intergenerational mobility, but that years of schooling moderate the tendency toward social reproduction (Blau and Duncan 1967). The reproduction process – or rather, correspondence process – is even mapped out as a set of probabilities (Fig. 5.1a). This was elaborated as the Wisconsin Model (e.g., Blau and Duncan 1994:321 [1967]) by augmenting it with relational influences (e.g. peer, parental, and neighborhood effects) to improve the overall fit of the predominant view of attainment.

At the same time that status attainment researchers were advancing these models, social network scholars were developing ways to more properly parameterize the formal properties of social structures. These scholars created sophisticated ways to model peer influence and reduce complex sociometric data into graph-level indicators (e.g. network density, clustering, etc.). Through the structural features of such concepts as social capital – that is, parental social network closure – some of these concepts have been incorporated into models of individual student achievement (Carbonaro 1998; Morgan and Sørensen 1999). Yet the main strategy in this work is still that of incorporating network properties as individual-level characteristics. Only a few studies have approached education from a structural network perspective,

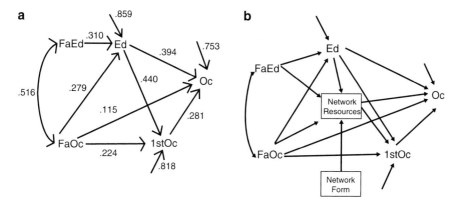

Fig. 5.1 (**a** and **b**) Blau and Duncan model and its network augmentation

as organized opportunities to establish long-term connections with implications for attainment (Bergesen 2007; Stuber 2006).

Introducing measures of social capital or variables reflective of some structural location interjects a relational set of factors within the flow of attainment paths. Here, one can introduce a variety of individual-based structural measures as independent and moderating variables to the standard OLS representation as an individual trait (as in many ego-centric network analyses) as opposed to a situational condition or conditional resource that depends on which third party is present (as in the formal study of roles and positions). In the social capital augmented version of attainment, the factor salient to an outcome is the resource a network affords (Lin 2001; Sandefur and Laumann 1998). Hence, a student may have a dense group of friends, but if these friends expose the student to antisocial behaviors, the resources in that network will be of a different type than if they were high-achieving students. In many peer-influence models, the effects of such processes are modeled as "linear-in-means" – that is, influences from one's associates are typically portrayed as a "mean on variable X" and used as an additional predictor of a given attainment outcome (i.e., attending college). This is often a first approximation of a more correctly weighted peer influence process (Friedkin and Marsden 1994).

Introducing the structure of one's networks as a moderator allows the attainment model to become even more sociological and interesting, because it shows that attainment may not only rely on the content of network resources but also the form of network structures. The characteristics of individuals in networks are important in accessing important material and symbolic resources; however, the ways that these individuals come together to form a relational structure of ties is also central to various processes. In most models, the structural moderator of choice is most likely the cohesiveness of the friendship group (closure, closeness, cliquing, etc.) (see Fig. 5.1b; see Friedkin 1998 for review). The point here is that being situated within a dense group of friends or a popular group of friends may (1) intensify access to the resources and behaviors of those actors and (2) serve as more enduring resources in the future because of the strength of such ties. There may be trade-offs in such moderator effects. For example, belonging to a cohesive group may be particularly advantageous in higher status settings, but particularly disadvantageous in lower status settings; while forming many weaker ties may be helpful to the extent that it leads to connecting with individuals who differ in their broader connections (Granovetter 1973; Horvat et al. 2003).

While such augmentations are proving informative, we are presented with a number of unmet opportunities to unpack questions derived from this literature: Are the forms and contents of social networks more important than an individual's grades or other achievements in structuring status attainment? Does schooling organize opportunities for network formation and thus naturalize social closure? Do women and minorities have different network-formation strategies that may be implicated in subsequent differences in attainment?

Of course, in answering these questions we confront issues of causation so salient today in econometrics and currently being imported into sociology. For many classes of causal models, the interunit dependencies and spillovers in social networks are violations of regression models' nonindependence assumptions, while for a few scholars, network effects are substantively important but difficult to estimate (Manski 1995; Jackson 2008). In peer-influence models, one wonders if students behave as they do because of their peers, or from factors that led them to associate with their peers in the first place. Ideally, we would have attitudinal measures preceding these networks that capture an individual's propensity for a certain belief or behavior, and then compare this to some change associated with exposure to a specific peer-influence process. Of course, beliefs and behaviors are likely confounded with prior experiences with the peers of one's peers, so we may constantly have an infinite regress of reflected and reciprocal influence rather than a story of ultimate causal origins. And yet, longitudinal network models will allow for greater causal analysis along these various reciprocal chains and therefore represent exciting opportunities to disentangle various interdependencies and spillovers.

Estimating such models has become more sophisticated and capable of handling various aspects of social embeddedness. As Frank (1998) was early to notice, the advent of multilevel models is particularly promising for allowing network properties to be incorporated within existing cross-sectional and longitudinal designs. Today, these advances have opened up a new frontier for better capturing a number of processes that are important for attainment research in education. Another approach often discussed is agent-based simulation (McFarland and Rodan 2009). What is nice about these characterizations of social phenomena like attainment is that they can relate a system of factors in explicit form (e.g., decision processes with their feedback loops, accruals, interdependencies). However, many of these applications lack empirical grounding and merely reveal the limits of theories. Even when grounded in real data, we have more of a correspondence model of verification, much like a computer program can mirror the mind's output and appear like a person (e.g., chess computers, avatars, etc.), but it is still not clear that it actually represents the way the mind works.

Ultimately, social network approaches may also afford a shift away from the strategy of incorporating relational characteristics into linear models of attainment processes toward a broader approach to the various social landscapes upon which individual attainment processes are carried out. Rather than focusing on augmenting an individual-centered model, network approaches afford a reconceptualization of attainment as an ecology of linked institutions. We discuss the potential for such a future shift in attainment research next.

Reconceptualization: Macrolevel Opportunity Structures as Networks

Social network approaches tend to move beyond focusing on individual characteristics – even relational ones – to take into account the consequences of *positions* within a larger network *structure* for various processes, especially those concerning the flow of various beliefs or behaviors (White et al. 1976). Positions can often be equated with "statuses" that imbue individuals with certain properties – both good and bad – that often have the property of being acts of "social magic" (Bourdieu 1984) or self-fulfilling prophecies (Meyer 1977). If we consider attainment processes as occurring within various opportunity structures that are properties of no single individual (Blau 1994), but of social contexts, then there is a natural affinity between network approaches and broader explanations of attainment (Small 2009). Stevens et al. (2008) have recently called for this broader vision in studies of higher education by approaching colleges and universities as "hubs" through which "the economy, the family and the state intersect and are connected to other domains." In this imagery, it is individuals who are "flowing" through a larger set of linked organizational and institutional structures – and in so doing, recreating these larger pathways.

This broader vision harkens back to the institutional roots of educational inquiry by showing attainment *as* patterned and networked. Early social theorists saw schooling as the predominant mechanism through which individuals are socialized and sorted into status positions. For Durkheim, the content of the schooling process was the central concern because it socialized individuals into functionally differentiated roles but also inculcated a broader sense of the moral underpinnings to the division of labor (Durkheim 1973). For Weber and Sorokin, the content of schooling was important, but was approached within a broader ecology of institutions (families, professions, states) that intersected in ways that legitimate various status groups (Weber 1968:249; Sorokin 1959). These fundamental processes have been elaborated over generations of sociological research. Theories of attainment contend that a variety of socialization experiences, institutions, and organizations tend to recreate status inequalities; however, the structures upon which attainment is carried out are rarely studied. The social network perspective is poised to reconceptualize status attainment approaches at both the intra-schooling and broader institutional levels in a manner that is more consistent with these earlier conceptualizations but also informed by later institutional and structural theories of attainment.

We propose that the metaphor of a cityscape – with a system of roads, origins, destinations, maps (knowledge), and types of cars (resources) – can be anchored in network concepts and analytical tools to better show how attainment unfolds through a set of individual decisions and happenstance that are situated within a fundamentally differentiated and linked institutional environment. Educational organizations are indeed hubs in a differentiated space, linking origins and destinations as well as numerous constituencies. Just as mobility can be situated within urban environments, which are structured so that opportunities are unequally distributed (Massy and Denton 1993; Small 2009), we can think of networks between organizations and institutions in formal terms. The network approach allows us to consider the formal properties of the ways that organizations and institutions are linked, how these enable and constrain individual mobility, and how in the course of moving through these structures that individuals either forge new paths or further pave existing ones. While augmenting existing individual-centered attainment models can provide a first approximation of many of these processes, especially in how they structure various life-course transitions (Fernandez and Weinberg 1997; Granovetter 1995), the broader cityscape metaphor is in many ways more intellectually satisfying because it is inherently relational and deals directly with structuration processes – how individuals navigate through social structures and in the process tend to recreate these structures (Giddens 1984). Mapping this broader cityscape is becoming increasingly plausible.

This also draws our attention to the consequences of organizational and institutional differentiation for attainment. If social networks are structured in part by contexts of opportunity, then clearly the number of years of education are not as important as *where* one goes to school, what one studies as one's educational path – and how these opportunities are internally organized as well as externally linked to other institutional contexts. For example, the vast literature on tracking could benefit from this expanded metaphor and network approach. Students are indeed tracked, but we seldom *see* these tracks – how they are linked in intersecting trajectories with turning points, or how some are wider and are fast tracks to certain levels of attainments. Friedkin and Thomas (1997) and McFarland (2006) used network conceptualizations of course-taking to uncover such internal schooling pathways (see Fig. 5.2). McFarland's work reveals common pathways or highly traveled routes in different parts of the curriculum that have different speeds, volumes, and points of confluence. Analyses of pathway mobility reveal that "traffic" matters and opportunities for movement are limited in certain positions, and that the "driver's" resources in terms of experience and capacity for coursework also affect which pathway they can enter and remain within (McFarland 2006; McFarland and Rodan 2009). Advances in network approaches are making it easier to collect data and summarize the formal properties of such tracks. In addition to creating a richer *image* of the tracking process, we may be able to take a more variable-centered approach to various tracks themselves and how these properties help channel students in certain directions.

Mapping internal and external pathways and connections offers opportunities for understanding the broader landscape upon which attainment takes place – at the interorganizational level we can ask which organizations are more central hubs and which are typical linkages in terms of important life transitions? There is a growing sense that various higher educational specializations have become increasingly linked to different occupational pathways (see Gerber and Cheung 2008 for review). As the *level* of educational attainment has increased, the number of qualitatively different routes to attainment have proliferated (Davies and Guppy 1997; Lucas 2001; see also Ayalon and Yogev 2005). Differential access to specific college majors and unpaid internships may become more important as the roads to higher levels of education have widened for all. Mapping these networks of major highways and emerging back-road shortcuts to attainment stands to reveal more than correlations between origins and destinations, or studies of how networks structure a single life-course transition. Studies of road networks could offer greater insight into the complex institutional environments wherein individuals struggle for various forms of capital and exchange them for status rewards (Bourdieu and Passeron 1977).

Finally, rather than looking at such networks as static, we may examine macrolevel linkages as dynamic structures. Institutional change sometimes affords

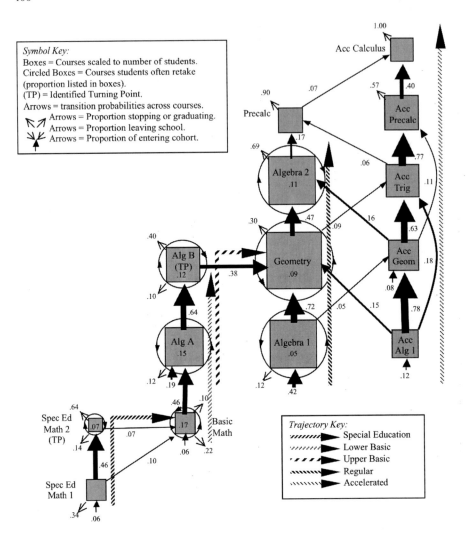

Fig. 5.2 Example of "Cityscapes" and "Traffic Patterns" in attainment: Rural High from McFarland 2006

the creation of new roads and destinations. For example, the creation of the land-grant system of colleges and universities provided a new set of academic roads (especially agriculture credentials) that helped create a number of professional destinations (Rawlings and Bourgeois 2004). Some of these new status destinations, including the occupation of professor in a land-grant institution, were of a level that was absent from rural American life until the creation of the institution. The son of a sharecropper could well become a professor in a neighboring town. This suggests that the macro-institutional environment in which attainment takes place is constantly under construction, and information on new occupational destinations may be one particularly important source for first-mover advantages in attainment. That such information is contained within social networks that are themselves organized by schools is an understudied and potentially vital source of social reproduction.

Of course, many of the techniques for reducing complex images into sets of formal properties are still in their infancy. However, we believe an important frontier for future research will be to extend these more case-based approaches to more representative samples of different linkages in order to better understand the attainment implications for various hidden meso- and macrolevel social structures.

A New Empirical Watershed: Methodological Transactionalism

To this point in the chapter, we have laid out not only an argument for the importance of social network analysis in the sociology of education, but also presented a continuum on which it can be used to both augment and reconceptualize existing research traditions. We applied this to both the microlevel processes of classroom interaction and instruction and the macrolevel issue of status attainment. In this last section, we will talk about the final point on our continuum, the point where network theory facilitates a revolutionary rethinking about fundamental understandings in the sociology of education. More specifically, we argue, the frontier of network methods offers the possibility of empirically capturing the commonplace but interactionally complex social phenomenon in the inherently relational undertaking of education on both the proximal and distal levels.

There is a long history in the social sciences of seeing through network analysis, both theoretically and methodologically, a more processual and transactional view of the social world that could serve as an alternative to the variable-centered methodological individualism that now dominates (White et al. 1976; Emirbayer and Goodwin 1994; Emirbayer 1997). When thinking about the future of social network analysis, it is worth reflecting briefly on how methodological individualism came to hold the dominant position it now does. In the early years of sociology's disciplinary development, there was a shared recognition that important social phenomenon was cultural, situated, and interdependent. This was (and still is) difficult to capture, and early sociologists relied on formalisms like historical narratives and ethnographic accounts and typically performed case studies of small groups, communities, or firms. The difficulty of collecting rich qualitative data and the lack of statistical sophistication helped shape the kinds of questions these early sociologists asked as well as the ontological assumptions that undergirded them.

When the survey watershed took hold in the 1940s, it dramatically altered the study of old sociological questions (Converse 1987; Platt 1996). By methodologically rendering individuals into atomic vessels of categorical attributes and social phenomenon as particular combinations of these atoms, some social scientists came to actually view the world in these terms (Abbott 1988). The approach was so widely performed that some even argued that the public began to view social reality in these individualized terms (Igo 2006). And yet, toward the end of this century, some of the leading proponents of methodological individualism openly wondered if the approach should be adapted so as to recapture the social and communal aspects of educational life that had been so important prior to the survey watershed (Coleman 1994). We have a story, then, of early sociology having limited means of data collection and a great reliance on narrative accounts that resulted in portrayals of social phenomena as situated communities composed of interdependent, culturally informed actors, and then we have a survey watershed which entailed the massive collection of individualized responses and reliance on statistical modeling that resulted in portrayals of social phenomena as aggregates of individuals and their central tendencies.

Now in 2011, we stand at the edge of another empirical watershed. With the advent of computing and the Internet, we have witnessed data collection and storage techniques growing exponentially more sophisticated. Today, we are able to collect enormous bodies of rich information on the form and content of communicative transactions. The result of this new watershed, we posit, will be a diminishment of the primacy of methodological individualism and methodological transactionalism being placed on equal footing (Lazer et al. 2009). In methodological transactionalism, dynamic networks and communication processes are the primary focus of data collection. Because transactions entail changing networks of communication, they can represent the duality of persons and groups (Breiger 1974). In effect, persons are intersections of transactions, and communities or groups are temporary equilibriums of aggregates. Hence, transactional data likely affords the means of bringing back early studies of groups and sustaining accounts of individuals while making room for changing situations and the communicative acts that form all of them.

But a reader might stop at this point and correctly remark that network analysis has long been touted as the new revolution that has never happened, so why is now any different? The most important development in recent years is simply that there is more and significantly richer communication data with which researchers can work. Most obviously, this refers to the familiar assortment of streaming and interconnected information that is readily available on the Internet in the form of information ranging from text, images, videos, communication, and organizational records that can be rendered into network relations. Even beyond this already available data are the technological advancements that are making the collection of streaming behavior more feasible. One well-known example of this kind of work comes from the Reality Mining project at MIT (Eagle and Pentland 2006). As part of this project, research participants were given cell phones that continuously recorded their location, the presence of other participants, and all phone calls and text messages. Using these data, researchers could directly model the network of interaction between participants and study its contents in terms of communicative features such as expressions of sentiment in text usage, and voicing qualities. One could easily imagine extensions that would also allow collecting biophysical data like physiological change and shifts in body position during interactions.

One potential challenge brought by the availability of such rich data is that of overload. We still must answer the question of how we derive useful findings from the glut of data available to us now. The two primary challenges here have to do with, first, rendering digital materials into usable information, and next, the creation of complex data structures that will allow us to analyze this data in a variety of possible ways. With computer science, for example, there are already methods for parsing records and texts into spreadsheets of information; Natural Language Processing (NLP) is already quite advanced and capable of rendering texts and voices into an assortment of streaming features tested for meaningful information in other scholarly domains; and data management techniques in computer science (and corporations) have far outpaced the usual simple structures social scientists use to compile their information on individuals.

And alongside these developments in rendering digitized material into usable information have been advances in sheer computing power and novel statistical techniques. In prior decades, dyadic or network modeling was often performed separately from individual models and therefore did not alter or challenge the primacy of the OLS paradigm. Today, the statistical tools and computational power of computers make it feasible to study detailed longitudinal information on the coevolution of network structures, individual attributes, and interactional processes. From the perspective of network analysis and the sociology of education, these data and concomitant methodological watershed offer the same promise. In both areas we hold a view of important social phenomenon as relational and dynamic, but for practical reasons have been long forced to reify social processes into cold and static variables in order to statistically study them. Increasingly, however, we can perform computational ethnography and directly capture the more vibrant, active and "warm" view seen in qualitative research.

Revolutionizing the Study of Trust in Schools

We end with a brief thought experiment about what a shift toward methodological transactionalism might mean for the sociology of education by looking at a more concrete issue, namely trust in schools. First, we would need to collect appropriate data. At the classroom level, we might install panoramic video cameras placed in ceilings and small voice recorders on individuals, and then couple this with digitized textual information on student work. Outside of the classroom, we could use cell phone readings to trace the daily movements of students and teachers across various social settings, their voicing, and the patterns of their communication with others (e.g., colleagues, peers, principals and parents). At the district and school level, we could data mine for various types of transactions, like student course assignments, test scores, grades and extracurricular activities and teacher administrative teams, professional development and parent contacts. We could even acquire digital copies of all policies and curricula and render them into analyzable texts to see how they correspond with voiced texts.

And so imagine now that we had managed to collect the kind of rich digital data described above. What this presents us with is not simply more information about classroom processes (though this is of course part of it), but even more importantly, an opportunity to fundamentally revolutionize our perception of what constitutes interaction and the role that trust plays in it. If we begin to see the classroom not, as we often do now, as a collection of semiautonomous individuals and their attributes, but instead in terms of an ongoing stream of multilayered, communicative interactions, we can start to see the phenomenon of teaching and learning anew. We can begin to conceptualize the classroom now as an intricate dance in which teachers and students must coordinate their behavioral moves in constant relation to each other, where the pace, rhythm, and temporality of exchanges influence their success and the affective experience of their participants, and knowledge is an emergent feature of shared communication.

Envisioning the classroom as a dance permits a shift away from seeing trust as a mental structure and toward a feature of interactions between people. We can start to study trust, in other words, not only in terms of how it facilitates the choice of exchange partners, but also the quality and nature of the transactions themselves. And what is exciting here is that just as dancing involves a complex combination of body control, cognitive scripts, affective feeling and social and partner awareness, so too can we potentially study the trustfulness of classroom transactions on numerous levels. Audio of classroom talk, for example, could be assessed for intensity and pitch features emblematic of emotions associated with the presence or lack of trusting, such as calmness or anger (Jurafsky et al. 2009). Pulse and facial temperature readings can be used to gauge excitement and embarrassment, which can in turn be linked to subjective feelings of trust. Eye movement can be used to gauge focus of attention and physical gestures can be recorded to measure levels of gestural synchronicity, each of which could be connected to feelings of trusting. These findings could then be connected to other attitudes or behaviors, to student academic outcomes, and records.

The point is that we can imagine numerous ways of directly measuring differences and variances in classroom transactions and the way that they are mediated by trust. Moreover, our current methods for studying trust in schools is a methodological compromise in which, for reasons of practicality, we render our theoretically microdynamical construct into something abstract and largely static. It is as if we were studying real dances by asking people if their feelings of trust toward their partners influenced their performances. Such an approach certainly might yield useful post hoc information, but it would likely tell us little about actual variance in the nature of the dance itself – for example, do differences in levels of engrossment exist, or are bodies positioned differently depending on their levels of trust? And just as importantly, what precisely does a person do while dancing to make their partner trust them more? The point here is that, just as with classrooms, our real concern is with the activity that people are collectively engaged in, and trust only in so far as it helps us understand the nature of experience in that activity. The incredible new vistas opening up to us through new ways of collecting and analyzing streaming behavioral data suggest that methodological transactionalism affords a revolutionizing means to capture the dance of social life more faithfully than our standard models.

References

Abbott, Andrew. 1988. Transcending general linear reality. *Sociological Theory* 6(2): 169–186.
Almack, John C. 1922. The influence of intelligence on the selection of associates. *School and Society* 16: 529–530.
Ayalon, Hanna, and Abraham Yogev. 2005. Field of study and students' stratification in an expanded system of higher education: The case of Israel. *European Sociological Review* 21: 227–241.
Baerveldt, Chris, Beate Völker, and Ronan Van Rossem. 2008. Revisiting selection and influence: An inquiry into the friendship networks of high school students and their association with delinquency 1. *Canadian Journal of Criminology and Criminal Justice* 50(5): 559–587.
Bergesen, A. 2007. Exploring the impact of social class on adjustment to college: Anna's story. *International Journal of Qualitative Studies in Education* 20: 99–119.
Bidwell, Charles E., and Jeffrey Y. Yasumoto. 1999. The collegial focus: Teaching fields, collegial relationships, and instructional practice in American high schools. *Sociology of Education* 72(4): 234–256.
Blau, Peter. 1994. *Structural contexts of opportunities*. Chicago: University of Chicago Press.
Blau, Peter M., and Otis D. Duncan, with the collaboration of Andrea Tyree. 1994[1967]. The process of stratification. In *Social stratification: Class, race, and gender in sociological perspective*, ed. David Grusky, 317–329. Boulder: Westview Press.
Bourdieu, Pierre. 1984. *Distinction: A social critique of the judgement of taste*. Trans. R. Nice. Cambridge: Harvard University Press.
Bourdieu, Pierre, and Jean-Claude Passeron. 1977. *Reproduction in education, society and culture*. Trans. R. Nice. London: Sage Publications.
Boyack, Kevin W., Katy Börner, and Richard Klavans. 2009. Mapping the structure and evolution of chemistry research. *Scientometrics* 79(1): 45–60.
Breiger, Ronald L. 1974. The duality of persons and groups. *Social Forces* 53: 181–190.
Brint, Steven. 2009. The 'Collective Mind' at work: A decade in the life of U.S. sociology of education. *Sociology of Education Newsletter* 12: 7–15.
Bryk, Anthony, and Stephen Raudenbush. 1992. *Hierarchical linear models: Applications and data analysis methods*, 2nd ed. Thousand Oaks: Sage Publications.
Bryk, Anthony S., and Barbara L. Schneider. 2002. *Trust in schools: A core resource for improvement*. New York: Russell Sage Foundation.
Burt, Ronald S. 1980. Models of network structure. *Annual Review of Sociology* 6: 79–141.
Carbonaro, William. 1998. A little help from my parent's friends: Intergenerational closure and effects on educational outcomes. *Sociology of Education* 71: 295–313.
Clogg, Clifford C. 1992. The impact of sociological methodology on statistical methodology. *Statistical Science* 7(2): 183–196.
Coburn, Cynthia E., and Jennifer L. Russell. 2008. District policy and teachers' social networks. *Educational Evaluation and Policy Analysis* 30(3): 203.
Coleman, James S. 1961. *Adolescent society: The social life of the teenager and its impact on education*. New York: Greenwood Press.
Coleman, James S. 1994. A vision for sociology. *Society* 32(1): 29–34.
Converse, Jean M. 1987. *Survey research in the United States: Roots and emergence 1890–1960*. Berkeley: University of California Press.
Daly, Alan J., and Kara S. Finnigan. 2010. A bridge between worlds: Understanding network structure to understand change strategy. *Journal of Educational Change* 11: 111–138.
Davies, Scott, and Neil Guppy. 1997. Fields of study, college selectivity, and student inequalities in higher education. *Social Forces* 75: 1417–1438.
Diani, Mario. 1995. *Green networks: A structural analysis of the Italian environmental movement*. Edinburgh: Edinburgh University Press.
Durkheim, Emile. 1973. *Moral education*. New York: Free Press.

Eagle, Nathan, and Alex Pentland. 2006. Reality mining: Sensing complex social systems. *Personal and Ubiquitous Computing* 10(4): 255–268.

Emirbayer, Mustafa. 1997. Manifesto for a relational sociology. *American Journal of Sociology* 103(2): 281–317.

Emirbayer, Mustafa, and Jeff Goodwin. 1994. Network analysis, culture, and the problem of agency. *American Journal of Sociology* 99: 1411–1154.

Fernandez, Roberto, and Nancy Weinberg. 1997. Sifting and sorting: Personal contacts and hiring in a retail bank. *American Sociological Review* 62: 883–902.

Frank, Kenneth A. 1998. Quantitative methods for studying social context in multilevels and through interpersonal relations. *Review of Research in Education* 23: 171–216.

Frank, Ove, and David Strauss. 1986. Markov graphs. *Journal of the American Statistical Association* 81(395): 832–842.

Frank, Kenneth A., Yong Zhao, and Kathryn Borman. 2004. Social capital and the diffusion of innovations within organizations: The case of computer technology in schools. *Sociology of Education* 77(2): 148.

Frank, Kenneth A., Chandra Muller, Kathryn S. Schiller, Catherine Riegle-Crumb, Anna S. Mueller, Robert Crosnoe, and Jennifer Pearson. 2008. The social dynamics of mathematics coursetaking in high school. *American Journal of Sociology* 113(6): 1645–1696.

Freeman, Linton C., and A. Kimball Romney. 1987. Words, deeds and social structure: A preliminary study of the reliability of informants. *Human Organization* 46(4): 330–334.

Friedkin, Noah. 1998. *A structural theory of social influence*. New York: Cambridge University Press.

Friedkin, Noah, and Peter Marsden. 1994. Network studies of social influence. In *Advances in social network analysis: Research in the social and behavioral sciences*, eds. Stanley Wasserman and Joseph Galaskiewicz, 3–25. Thousand Oaks: Sage Publications.

Friedkin, Noah E., and Michael R. Slater. 1994. School leadership and performance: A social network approach. *Sociology of Education* 67(2): 139–157.

Friedkin, Noah, and Scott L. Thomas. 1997. Social positions in schooling. *Sociology of Education* 70: 239–255.

Gerber, Theodore, and Sin Yi Cheung. 2008. Horizontal stratification in postsecondary education: Forms, explanations, and implications. *Annual Review of Sociology* 34: 299–318.

Giddens, Anthony. 1984. *The constitution of society: Outline of the theory of structuration*. Cambridge: Polity Press.

Goodreau, S.M., J.M. Kitts, and M. Morris. 2009. Birds of a feather, or friend of a friend? Using exponential random graph models to investigate adolescent social networks. *Demography* 46(1): 103–125.

Granovetter, Mark. 1973. The strength of weak ties. *The American Journal of Sociology* 78: 1360–1380.

Granovetter, Mark. 1995. *Getting a job: A study in contacts and careers*. Chicago: University of Chicago Press.

Hansen, Morten T. 1999. The search-transfer problem: The role of weak ties in sharing knowledge across organization subunits. *Administrative Science Quarterly* 44: 82–111.

Hargens, Lowell L. 2000. Using the literature: Reference networks, reference contexts, and the social structure of scholarship. *American Sociological Review* 65: 846–865.

Haynie, Dana L. 2002. Friendship networks and delinquency: The relative nature of peer delinquency. *Journal of Quantitative Criminology* 18(2): 99–134.

Horvat, Erin McNamara, Elliot B. Weininger, and Annette Lareau. 2003. From social ties to social capital: Class differences in the relations between schools and parent networks. *American Educational Research Journal* 40: 319–351.

Hoy, Wayne K., C. John Tarter, and Anita W. Hoy. 2006. Academic optimism of schools: A force for student achievement. *American Educational Research Journal* 43(3): 425.

Hunter, David R., Mark S. Handcock, Carter T. Butts, Steven M. Goodreau, and Martina Morris. 2008. Ergm: A package to fit, simulate and diagnose exponential-family models for networks. *Journal of Statistical Software* 24(3).

Igo, Sarah. 2006. *The averaged American: Surveys, citizens, and the making of a mass public*. Cambridge: Harvard University Press.
Jackson, Mathew. 2008. *Social and economic networks*. Princeton: Princeton University Press.
Jurafsky, Dan, Rajesh Ranganath, and Daniel McFarland. 2009. Extracting social meaning: Identifying interactional style in spoken conversation. In *Proceedings of NAACL HLT 2009*, Boulder.
Kerckhoff, Alan C. 1995. Institutional arrangements and stratification processes in industrial societies. *Annual Review of Sociology* 15: 323–347.
Kowalski, Robin M., and Susan P. Limber. 2007. Electronic bullying among middle school students. *Journal of Adolescent Health* 41(6): 22.
Lazer, David, A. Sandy Pentland, Lada Adamic, Sinan Aral, Albert L. Barabasi, Devan Brewer, Nicholas Christakis, et al. 2009. Life in the network: The coming age of computational social science. *Science* 323(5915): 721–2323.
Lin, N. 2001. *Social capital: A theory of social structure and action*. Cambridge: Cambridge University Press.
Louis, Karen S. 2007. Trust and improvement in schools. *Journal of Educational Change* 8(1): 1–24.
Lubbers, Miranda J. 2003. Group composition and network structure in school classes: A multilevel application of the p* model. *Social Networks* 25(4): 309–332.
Lucas, Samuel R. 2001. Effectively maintained inequality: Education transitions, track mobility, and social background effects. *American Journal of Sociology* 106: 1642–1690.
Manski, Charles. 1995. *Identification problems in the social sciences*. Cambridge: Harvard University Press.
Martin, John Levi. 2003. What is field theory? *American Journal of Sociology* 109: 1–49.
Massy, Douglas, and Nancy A. Denton. 1993. *American apartheid: Segregation and the making of the underclass*. Cambridge: Harvard University Press.
McFarland, Daniel A. 2001. Student resistance: How the formal and informal organization of classrooms facilitate everyday forms of student defiance. *American Journal of Sociology* 107(3): 612–678.
McFarland, Daniel A. 2006. Curricular flows: Trajectories, turning points, and assignment criteria in high school math careers. *Sociology of Education* 79(3): 177–205.
McFarland, Daniel, and Heili Pals. 2005. Motives and contexts of identity change: A case for network effects. *Social Psychology Quarterly* 68(4): 289.
McFarland, Daniel A., and Simon Rodan. 2009. Organization by design: Supply- and demand-side models of math careers. *Sociology of Education* 82(4): 315–343.
Mercken, Liesbeth, Math Candel, Paul Willems, and Hein de Vries. 2009. Social influence and selection effects in the context of smoking behavior: Changes during early and mid adolescence. *Health Psychology* 28: 73–82.
Meyer, John. 1977. The effects of education as an institution. *American Journal of Sociology* 83: 55–77.
Moody, James. 2004. The structure of a social science collaboration network: Disciplinary cohesion from 1963 to 1999. *American Sociological Review* 69: 213–238.
Morgan, Stephen L., and Aage B. Sørensen. 1999. Parental networks, social closure, and mathematics learning: A test of Coleman's social capital explanation of school effects. *American Sociological Review* 64(5): 661–681.
Morris, Martina. 2003. Local rules and global properties: Modeling the emergence of network structure. In *Dynamic social network modeling and analysis: Workshop summary and papers*, eds. Ron L. Brieger, Kathleen M. Carley, and Philippa Pattison. National Research Council. National Academic Press. Washington DC.
Pearson, Michael, Christian Steglich, and Tom Snijders. 2006. Homophily and assimilation among sport-active adolescent substance users. *Connections* 27(1): 51–67.
Penuel, William, Margaret Riel, Ann Krause, and Kenneth Frank. 2009. Analyzing teachers' professional interactions in a school as social capital: A social network approach. *The Teachers College Record* 111(1): 124–163.

Pittinsky, Matthew, and Brian V. Carolan. 2008. Behavioral versus cognitive classroom friendship networks. *Social Psychology of Education* 11(2): 133–147.

Platt, Jennifer. 1996. *A history of sociological research methods in America, 1920–1960.* Cambridge: Cambridge University Press.

Rawlings, Craig M., and Michael D. Bourgeois. 2004. The complexity of institutional niches: Credentials and organizational differentiation in a field of American higher education. *Poetics* 32: 411–437.

Rawlings, Craig M., Daniel McFarland, Linus Dahlander, and Dan Wang. 2010. *Funnels and filters: When networks channel intra-organizational knowledge flows.* Working Paper, Stanford University, Stanford.

Reagans, Ray E., Ezra W. Zuckerman, and Bill McEvily. 2004. How to make the team: Social networks vs. demography as criteria for designing effective projects in a contract R&D firm. *Administrative Science Quarterly* 49: 101–133.

Robins, Gary, Philippa Pattison, and Josie Woolcock. 2005. Small and other worlds: Global network structures from local processes. *American Journal of Sociology* 110(4): 894–936.

Sandefur, Rebecca, and Edward Laumann. 1998. A paradigm for social capital. *Rationality and Society* 10(4): 481–501.

Singh, Jasjit. 2005. Collaborative networks as determinants of knowledge diffusion patterns. *Management Science* 51: 756–770.

Small, Mario L. 2009. *Unanticipated gains: Origins of network inequality in daily life.* New York: Oxford University Press.

Snijders, Tom A.B., Gerhard G. Van de Bunt, and Christian E.G. Steglich. 2010. Introduction to stochastic actor-based models for network dynamics. *Social Networks* 32(1): 44–60.

Sorokin, Pitirim. 1959[1927]. *Social and cultural mobility.* New York: Free Press.

Spillane, James P., and Charles L. Thompson. 1997. Reconstructing conceptions of local capacity: The local education agency's capacity for ambitious instructional reform. *Educational Evaluation and Policy Analysis* 19(2): 185–203.

Steglich, Christian, Tom A.B. Snijders, and Patrick West. 2006. Applying SIENA. *Methodology: European Journal of Research Methods for the Behavioral and Social Sciences* 2(1): 48–56.

Stevens, Mitchell, Elizabeth Armstrong, and Richard Arum. 2008. Sieve, incubator, temple, hub: Empirical and theoretical advances in the sociology of higher education. *Annual Review of Sociology* 34: 127–151.

Stuber, Jenny. 2006. Talk of class and discursive repertoires of white working and upper-middle class college students. *Journal of Contemporary Ethnography* 35: 285–318.

Tarrow, Sidney. 1994. *Power in movement: Social movements, collective action and politics*, 2nd ed. New York/Cambridge: Cambridge University Press.

Van de Bunt, Gerhard G., Rafael P.M. Wittek, and Maurits C. de Klepper. 2005. The evolution of intra-organizational trust networks: The case of a German paper factory: An empirical test of six trust mechanisms. *International Sociology* 20(3): 339–369.

Van Rossem, Ronan, and Marjolijn M. Vermande. 2004. Classroom roles and school adjustment. *Social Psychology Quarterly* 67(4): 396.

Wasserman, Stanley, and Katherine Faust. 1994. *Social network analysis: Methods and applications.* New York: Cambridge University Press.

Wasserman, Stanley, and Philippa Pattison. 1996. Logit models and logistic regressions for social networks: I. An introduction to Markov graphs and p. *Psychometrika* 61(3): 401–425.

Wasserman, Stanley, John Scott, and Peter J. Carrington. 2005. Introduction. In *Models and methods in social network analysis*, eds. Peter J. Carrington, John Scott, and Stanley Wasserman. Cambridge: Cambridge University Press.

Weber, Max. 1968. *Economy and society.* Berkeley: University of California Press.

Wellman, Beth. 1926. The school child's choice of companions. *The Journal of Educational Research* 14(2): 126–132.

Wells, Gordon. 1993. Reevaluating the IRF sequence: A proposal for the articulation of theories of activity and discourse for the analysis of teaching and learning in the classroom. *Linguistics and Education* 5(1): 1–37.

White, Harrison C., Scott A. Boorman, and Ronald L. Breiger. 1976. Social structure from multiple networks. I. Blockmodels of roles and positions. *American Journal of Sociology* 81(4): 730–780.

Wiley, Susan D. 2001. Contextual effects on student achievement: School leadership and professional community. *Journal of Educational Change* 2: 1–33.

Chapter 6
Designing Instruction and Grouping Students to Enhance the Learning of All: New Hope or False Promise?

Adam Gamoran

For more than a century, educators have struggled to find the right balance between providing common instruction to all students and targeting instruction to meet students' specific needs. Whereas targeted instruction seems like an appropriate response to differences among students, all too often it has resulted in unequal learning opportunities, to the particular detriment of students from disadvantaged backgrounds (Gamoran 2010).

Despite the challenges, educators and researchers have continued to seek successful approaches to grouping students and targeting instruction because high-achieving students have fared well under such approaches (unlike their low-achieving counterparts), and because common instruction for academically diverse students has not been very successful. A new scientific, data-rich wave of research offers great promise for innovative approaches to grouping students and designing instruction in response to student differences. The new research takes advantage of advances in assessment, technology, and research design to develop and test new approaches for matching students to instruction. Yet despite the advances, the scope of the challenge is so great that the question of how best to organize students for instruction has not yet been resolved. Moreover, the findings have implications for sociological concerns about school organization and inequality, and attention from sociologists could enhance the value of the new findings. This chapter reviews the new research, assesses its prospects for resolving the age-old dilemma, and considers the consequences for the sociology of education and for social inequality more broadly.

A. Gamoran (✉)
Department of Sociology, University of Wisconsin, Madison, WI 53706, USA
e-mail: gamoran@ssc.wisc.edu

The Debate over Differentiation

The fact that students in the same grade cohort exhibit different levels of academic performance is well established (e.g., Bloom 1964), but the optimal response to these differences is a matter of intense debate. Grouping students into relatively homogeneous subsets, either within or between classes, for one subject at a time (ability grouping) or for the whole day (tracking) is a common response because it allows teachers to tailor instruction to the relatively restricted range of performance levels within a group. While this practice seems to benefit students assigned to classes with other high-performing students, it is detrimental to the achievement of students assigned to classes with low-achieving peers. As a result, tracking tends to have no effect on overall academic performance, or productivity, but it tends to widen the dispersion of achievement, that is, it increases inequality, because high-track students gain while low-track students fall further behind (Gamoran 2010).[1]

These findings have been reviewed extensively by past writers (e.g., Kulik and Kulik 1982; Slavin 1987, 1990; Gamoran and Berends 1987; Oakes et al. 1992; Harlen and Malcolm 1997; Hallam 2002; Gamoran 2004, 2010). A key mechanism that links tracking to achievement inequality is the unequal distribution of instruction across classes at different track levels. Whereas high-track students tend to progress rapidly through more complex material, low-track students tend to encounter more fragmented information at a slower pace. Even taking account of low-track students' less-advanced starting points, teachers tend to underestimate their capabilities and fail to provide challenging instruction. As one writer put it, low-track students encounter a vicious cycle of low expectations, in which teachers expect little of them, so they exert little effort, reinforcing teachers' expectations, and so on (Page 1991; see Gamoran 1993, for an exception that proves the rule). Because students from economically disadvantaged and minority ethnic backgrounds are assigned disproportionately to low tracks and underrepresented in high tracks, tracking tends to reinforce social inequalities that are present in the wider society.

Writers who differ in their views of tracking and ability grouping tend to talk past one another instead of engaging one another's arguments. Whereas supporters focus on the benefits for high-achieving students, critics focus on the losses incurred by low-achieving students. Yet both processes tend to occur. The debate remains unsettled because supporters view tracking students for instruction as a neutral organizational device intended to optimize the matching of instruction to student needs, while critics claim that such efficiency is impossible to attain. According to the critics, biases embedded in the wider society prevent teachers of low tracks from

---

[1] The terms tracking and ability grouping are often used interchangeably. For brevity, I use tracking as a generic term for the differentiation of students for instruction on the basis of prior academic performance. However, when I distinguish among the different forms of instructional differentiation, I use tracking to refer to systems that divide students into classes or bands of classes for all subjects, and ability grouping to divisions of students on a subject-by-subject basis. Ability grouping can occur within or between classes.

providing challenging instruction targeted to the needs of such students and, even if appropriate instruction could be identified, it could not be delivered effectively nor could students engage successfully because of the stigma of assignment to a low track. Because each approach to arranging students for instruction has both strengths and limitations, education systems tend to swing back and forth from one approach to the other (Gamoran 2002).

The argument over efficiency versus inherent inequality reached its height in a 1994 debate between Maureen Hallinan and Jeannie Oakes that appeared in the esteemed academic journal, *Sociology of Education*. In Hallinan's words:

> Tracking is an organizational practice whose aim is to facilitate instruction and to increase learning. The theory of tracking argues that tracking permits teachers to tailor instruction to the ability level of their students. A good fit between a student's ability and the level of instruction is believed to maximize the effectiveness and efficiency of the instructional process (1994, p. 79).

Most of the negative consequences, Hallinan argued, derived from the way tracking typically is implemented. Pervasive segregation, low social status, failure to form classes in which the variance of student ability actually is reduced, poor instruction in low tracks, and perceptions of stigma among low-track students are implementation problems that can be eliminated or at least mitigated by educators who arrange students and organize instruction in systematic and thoughtful ways.

Oakes (1994, p. 85), by contrast, argued that tracking reflects social norms that link class and group assignments to assumptions about students' future directions. Strategies to mitigate the harmful effects of tracking are unworkable because "few students miss the clear status message carried by racially identifiable tracking in high-status academic classes" (p. 86). Track assignments are discriminatory and in the end, Oakes argued, "the inequalities of tracking are nothing other than the normative and political guises of tracking itself" (pp. 88–89).

The empirical literature has done little to adjudicate between these competing positions. Indeed, Hallinan and Oakes were speaking from the same set of facts, and subsequent studies have done little to bridge the gap (Oakes 2005). Decades of research suggest that implementing tracking without increasing inequality is rare and difficult to accomplish (Gamoran 2010). At the same time, detracking also is hard to enact with success (2010). Existence proofs of successful detracking tend to reflect special conditions such as extra resources that permit additional instructional time for low-achieving students—another form of instructional differentiation (Gamoran and Weinstein 1998; Burris et al. 2006, 2008). Oakes (1992) has insightfully identified three barriers to detracking: normative (people believe that young persons differ, so it seems sensible to group them according to differences), political (some persons have vested interests in maintaining tracking), and technical (teachers lack preparation to instruct groups of students with widely varying performance levels). In her view, overcoming normative and political barriers would provide a context in which the technical problems can be solved (1992). An alternative view is that surpassing the technical challenges would provide the evidence needed to leap over the normative and political obstacles.

Recent international research on grouping and tracking lend credence to both sides of the argument (see Gamoran 2010 for a review). On the one hand, the general pattern from studies of tracking across the globe is similar to that found in the USA: The use of tracking is associated with a greater dispersion of achievement across schools or classrooms (depending on where the sorting of students occurs), that is, tracking tends to magnify inequality (e.g., Ono 2001; Park 2009; Hoadley 2008; Ayalon 2006; Cheng et al. 2007; Van Houtte 2004; Van de gaer et al. 2006; Ireson et al. 2002; Ivinson and Duveen 2005). On the other hand, international studies also provide evidence of cases in which the impact of tracking on inequality is mitigated or eliminated. Research from Taiwan (Broaded 1997), Israel (Ayalon and Gamoran 2000), and Australia (Stanley and MacCann 2005) suggests that outside the USA, programs that promote challenging standards for low-achieving students tend to be associated with lower levels of inequality. Within the USA, standards-raising efforts have not yet resulted in less damaging uses of tracking (Sandholtz et al. 2004; Lewis and Cheng 2006; Mickelson and Everett 2008). However, a familiar finding is that Catholic schools in the USA, which make greater academic demands on low-track students than public schools, also yield less achievement inequality between tracks than public schools (Gamoran 1992). These findings suggest that the effects of tracking are context dependent (Gamoran 2010). They are consistent with Oakes' (2005) position in that track effects on inequality reflect political and normative conditions in which students in low tracks are systematically denied high-quality opportunities for learning. Yet they also are consistent with Hallinan's (1994) view that if tracking is implemented in a way that brings challenging academic demands to low achievers, skill-based grouping does not result necessarily in greater inequality. Whereas rigid forms of tracking that stratify students for the entire school day largely have been discredited (Lucas 1999; Gamoran 2010), the use of more flexible ability grouping is as hotly contested as ever.

Where does this debate stand today? Is there any evidence that a systematic and thoughtful use of ability groups to differentiate instruction—within or between classes—can boost overall productivity without exacerbating inequality? Or does the assignment of students to groups or classes based on prior performance unavoidably result in slower growth for students who start out behind, as compared to an approach in which students are assigned to mixed-ability classes? Recent literature offers hints that yield promising answers to these questions and points toward a need for well-designed research to provide more secure answers in the future.

New Evidence on Matching Students to Learning Opportunities

Two distinct bodies of work begin to answer the question of whether there are conditions under which assigning students to groups or classes based on their prior academic performance may result in both greater learning and more equal distributions of learning. One set of writing focuses on diagnosing students' needs, arranging students in groups according to their documented needs, and responding to needs with well-targeted instruction. This approach may be termed, diagnosis and instructional response. The second body of work focuses more on teachers than on students. It relies on an analysis of which teachers tend to be successful with which students and suggests that achievement may be maximized by placing students with the teachers who are most adept at working with students who exhibit their particular academic profiles. This approach may be termed, optimal matching of teachers and students. The approaches share the notion that ability grouping may be a useful device for improving learning of all students if it is implemented carefully to match teaching with students' learning needs. In the sections that follow, I will present each approach, highlight a specific line of work at the leading edge of the approach, explore evidence of the approach's viability, and consider its implications for sociological research on education.

Diagnosis and Instructional Response

Education researchers and designers of instruction have long recognized that students who vary in their prior skills respond differently to the same instruction. Researchers termed this phenomenon the aptitude–treatment interaction (Cronbach and Snow 1977; Snow 1989). This notion is reflected in a number of learning theories, including Vygotsky's (1978) zone of proximal development, which maintains that students are best equipped to learn from instruction that builds on a foundation of their existing knowledge and encourages them to move beyond their starting points. Instructional designers responded with the notion of scaffolding, the idea that teachers can foster learning by erecting supports for students that meet them at their skill-based starting points and elevate them to further heights of learning (Palincsar and Brown 1985). In principle, findings about the aptitude–treatment interaction and related work imply that students' instructional needs can best be met by dividing students into groups based on prior skills and differentiating instruction to meet their skill-specific needs—exactly as intended by those who view ability grouping as an organizational device to promote learning.

A major limitation to translating theory into practice has been a lack of well-specified theory and corresponding evidence on how instruction can be differentiated optimally in response to students' varied starting points. As a result, even the most well-intentioned uses of ability grouping are vulnerable to a failure to target instruction appropriately and, especially, to a tendency to provide low-quality instruction in low-ability groups. In the absence of clear knowledge about what instruction is not responsive to particular learning needs, teachers may underestimate the ability of low-achieving students to meet instructional challenges (Gamoran 1986; Page 1991). Moreover, ambiguity about instructional design coupled with an ideology of teacher autonomy (Jackson 1968; Lortie 1975) tends to obscure the fact that low performance in low-ability groups reflects not only differences among students, but differences in students' experiences of instruction. These challenges lie at the heart of the difficulty of implementing ability grouping in a way that does not widen the achievement gap between high- and low-performing students.

Recent work by Connor and colleagues (e.g., Connor et al. 2004a, b, 2007, 2009) suggests that it may be possible to overcome this limitation and consequently to use grouping as an effective tool for matching instruction to students' needs. Working within the area of early reading instruction—the instructional area for which perhaps the greatest volume of research has been undertaken and the highest degree of consensus exists—Connor's research began within the aptitude–treatment-interaction framework. Prior research laid the foundation for this work by providing detailed knowledge about the nature of early reading instruction, and well-specified assessment instruments that permitted the researchers to test hypotheses about the relation between instruction and learning. With these two key resources, the researchers carefully modeled the relation between instruction and student achievement growth. They demonstrated that different aspects of instruction were effective differentially for students, depending on their measured starting points (Connor et al. 2004a, b). For example, teacher-managed comprehension activities promoted higher achievement for initially low-performing students, whereas child-managed instructional activities contributed more to achievement of students who began with higher achievement scores (Connor et al. 2004a). A second complex analysis mapped the specific associations between more fine-grained instructional activities and multiple measures of student performance (Connor et al. 2004b).

Armed with these findings, the researchers developed an instructional intervention that matched initial assessment results with specific instructional prescriptions that, theoretically, would maximize achievement gains. They further developed a computer algorithm that accomplishes the matching process in three steps: first, the researcher inputs student initial assessment results; second, the algorithm identifies small groups of students with similar needs; and third, it recommends specific instructional allocations for each group. Outputs from the "Assessment to Instruction" (A2i) software consists of recommendations for both how to group students and what specific instructional activities to allocate to each group. For students who are behind their peers in reading, the prescriptions set an advanced target so that low-performing students would narrow the gap over the course of the school year (Connor, 2010).

In a series of field experiments, the investigators have tested the impact of the A2i intervention on student achievement. They found that first-grade students in classes whose teachers were assigned randomly to use the A2i software exhibited more achievement growth than students in control classrooms (Connor et al. 2007, 2009). Moreover, the research team demonstrated that in experimental classrooms in which teachers used the A2i software extensively, students with low vocabulary scores in the fall closed the gap with higher scoring students on the spring assessment of reading comprehension, while students whose teachers made little use of the A2i software did not close the gap (Connor et al. 2007). A detailed analysis of instructional differences between experimental and control classes suggested that the mechanism through which the experimental effects occurred consisted of teachers following the A2i instructional recommendations. Among the recommended activities was the use of small, skill-based groups, and teachers in the experimental group were more likely to use small groups than teachers in the control condition (Connor et al. 2009).

Additional Work Needed

The series of studies by Connor and her colleagues provides clear evidence of how skill-based grouping can be used to promote achievement among students whose achievement is low initially as well as among their higher achieving peers. Indeed, there is some evidence that this approach can have a compensatory effect, in that the use of the A2i diagnostic and prescriptive software led to smaller gaps in spring reading comprehension among students with varied fall vocabulary scores. Yet despite the promise of these findings, substantial additional work is necessary before we can settle the debate over the use of ability grouping. First, Connor's work takes place in an arena for which there is relatively strong evidence about effective instruction for low performers. Other content domains and grade levels lack such established wisdom. Indeed, there are many areas in which we have good evidence about what does not work—for example, providing general math courses in high school for students with poor arithmetic scores (Gamoran and Hannigan 2000), but much less knowledge about what does work. Hence the prescriptions of the National Mathematics Advisory Panel (2008) are much less precise than those of the National Reading Panel (2000). For this work to result in a more general approach to grouping students and allocating instruction, therefore, we need much more research on what instruction works best for students with particular prior skills. In the absence of such knowledge, teachers exercise their professional judgments about matching instruction to students' needs, but as is revealed in the research literature on tracking, this commonly results in widening rather than narrowing gaps.

A second requirement for expanding the use of this approach to arranging students is high-quality assessments to which instructional strategies can be linked. Work in this area falls under the heading of formative assessment (Black and Wiliam 1998), the practice of gauging students' progress frequently and modifying instruction in response to student performance. Commonly, formative assessment is used in combination with "flexible skill grouping" so that teachers can respond to students in small groups rather than one-on-one.[2] The bank of assessment items for such approaches constitutes an essential resource for precise diagnosis of student needs.

The use of student assessment data to guide instruction also may be viewed as part of a broader movement toward the use of data-based decision making in classrooms. The first recommendation of the US Department of Education's recent "practice guide" on *Using Student Achievement Data to Support Instructional Decision-Making* (Hamilton et al. 2009) is to "make data part of an ongoing cycle of instructional improvement" (p. 9). However, the authors acknowledged that evidence supporting this practice is limited. Moreover, the practice guide does not address questions about how best to arrange students for instructional delivery. Thus, substantial work remains to link data on student performance to instructional strategies, to consider grouping arrangements in light of strategies, and to test the productivity of these arrangements.

---

[2] See, for example, the Northwest Education Association's Measures of Academic Progress: http://www.nwea.org/products-services/computer-based-adaptive-assessments/map.

Nearly 25 years ago, Slavin (1987) reached conclusions on the basis of a research synthesis that resonate with the latest findings: ability grouping could be an effective approach to organizing students for instruction if enabling conditions were met: if students were assigned to groups on the basis of the specific skill to be taught; if instruction was targeted carefully to address the specific skill; and if grouping was flexible so that assignments could change as the focus of instruction shifted. The work of Connor et al. (2007) both demonstrates the validity of this conclusion and shows that we have far to go before such an approach can be broadly implemented.

Potential Contributions from Sociologists

The implementation of instructional diagnosis would benefit from sociological research that considers the social context of instructional differentiation. Connor and colleagues' (2009) experimental study took place in an ethnically and economically diverse Florida school district. However, the results reported to date do not examine whether the intervention resulted in smaller achievement gaps between students of different ethnic, linguistic, or economic backgrounds. Yet this issue is paramount when it comes to considering the merits of assigning students to groups or classes on the basis of academic performance because of the historic links between academic performance and social background.

Not only can sociologists contribute to the effectiveness of instructional diagnosis and prescription, they also have much to learn from this line of research. The work of Connor and her colleagues, and the broader field of scientific studies of reading (e.g., National Reading Panel 2000), demonstrate that to identify the mechanisms through which achievement inequality is created, one must examine student experiences of instruction inside classrooms. Despite a recognition that unequal learning opportunities play a key role in within-school variation in achievement, research on the relation between teaching and learning, particularly research that yields data from observations, remains relatively sparse among sociologists, with only a few studies in this vein (e.g., Barr and Dreeben 1983; Gamoran et al. 1995; Gamoran and Kelly 2003; Rowan and Correnti 2009). Sociologists could advance this agenda by collaborating with learning theorists and content area specialists to derive new insights about the relation between learning opportunities and achievement inequality. Attention to students' experiences of instruction also is important sociologically to understand the core technology of schooling, that is, teaching and learning in classrooms. The sociologist's depictions of how schools work (Barr and Dreeben 1983) remain incomplete without greater attention to what occurs inside classrooms.

Optimal Matching of Teachers and Students

A second approach to organizing students for instruction in a way that may boost achievement growth of low as well as high achievers takes off from the widespread current interest in distinguishing between effective and ineffective teachers by monitoring the achievement growth of each teacher's students. Researchers, politicians, educators, and the public are engaged in vigorous debates about whether student achievement growth linked to teachers provides information that bears sufficient reliability and validity so as to support high-stakes decisions about teachers, including employment and salary decisions. As a result of federal law, students in all states are tested annually in reading and mathematics in grades 3–8. This practice yields achievement trajectories of up to 6 years for each student and permits researchers to calculate value-added scores for teachers: a measure of how much a given teacher contributes to a student's achievement trajectory, over and above the trajectory the student was already on as he or she entered the teacher's classroom.

A side point in the value-added debate—but a central concern for this chapter— is whether teachers differ in their effectiveness for different students. Are some teachers more effective with low achievers and others with high achievers? Or is an effective teacher effective regardless of the skill level of his or her students, and likewise are ineffective teachers ineffective with students across the achievement spectrum? Educational statisticians and policymakers concerned with teacher effects care about this issue because it affects how value-added scores are calculated. For example, a teacher might appear ineffective (i.e., exhibit a low value-added score), but if teacher effects vary by student performance levels, then the same teacher might be more effective if he or she had a different class of students. Consequently, the value-added score could be misleading and result in an improper or unfair decision about the teacher's employment prospects or salary. In addition, policymakers hope to use value-added scores to identify effective teachers who can then be incentivized to work with the lowest achieving students. However, if measures of effectiveness are sensitive to the achievement levels of students being taught, then the strategy of luring high-performing teachers to work with low-performing students may be futile if teachers who are effective with high-achieving students cannot bring the same value added to initially low-achieving students. Hence, the calculation of differential teacher effects as reflected in differential value-added scores is a high priority for researchers and school districts (Meyer and Dokumaci 2010).

While differential teacher effects matter for value-added analyses in general, they are important especially for addressing the question of optimally assigning students to classrooms. In principle, differential value-added scores would allow educators to match teachers and students in a way that optimized achievement growth. Low-achieving students could be assigned to teachers who tend to be most successful for such students, and similarly for high-achieving students. If differential teacher effects exist, schools could resolve the debate over grouping by matching low-achieving students with teachers who are most likely to elevate their learning, while at the same time linking high-achieving students to teachers who will be most effective in their classes.

Although the idea seems straightforward, the calculation of differential teacher effects is difficult to carry out in practice. Value-added models of teacher effects require, at a minimum, 2 years of achievement data on each student, before and after a student's experience with the student's teacher. Moreover, even though such models take account of prior performance in estimating teacher effects on subsequent achievement, they are subject to selection bias because some teachers may have the opportunity to instruct students who are already on steeper achievement trajectories than others, even if their test scores are the same at a given point in time. Adjusting for this sort of selectivity requires at least three test scores on each student. Estimating stable teacher effects also requires a large number of students per teacher; the usual twenty students per teacher often found in elementary classrooms may be insufficient for reliable estimation of teacher value-added scores, and for estimating differential effects the elementary context may fall short of the data requirement. As a result, estimation of differential teacher effects requires multiple years of data on teachers as well as on students, and may be suited best for middle schools where a mathematics or reading teacher may instruct as many as five classes of 25 students each (i.e., 125 students per year), in contrast to perhaps 20 students per teacher per year at the elementary level. Finally, to separate teacher effects from peer effects—which is important in the estimation of differential teacher effects so as not to confuse possible effectiveness of a teacher with the benefits of having a class full of high-achieving students—it is necessary to have data on several different classes for each teacher, again pointing to middle schools as a likely source of useful data. In short, estimation of differential teacher effects is possible theoretically, but carries extensive data demands.

The rigorous data demands have, until very recently, forestalled sophisticated efforts to estimate differential teacher effects. Sanders and Rivers (1996), early pioneers in value-added methodology, examined the issue in a rudimentary way by comparing effects of teachers sorted into quintiles of effectiveness with achievement growth of students categorized according to the average of prior and current test scores. They reported that teacher effects varied to some degree across categories of students' prior achievement. By contrast, case studies by Wharton-McDonald et al. (1998) suggested that teachers who were effective with high achievers also succeeded with low achievers.

A breakthrough in the analysis of differential teacher effects was accomplished by Lockwood and McCaffrey (2007) in their analysis of longitudinal achievement data from three urban districts. While the authors' main purpose was to assess the generalizability of teacher value-added scores, they recognized that "such information [on differential teacher effects] could also lead to more efficient assignment of student-teacher pairings that leveraged each teacher's relative strengths" (p. 442). The approach they took was to estimate value-added models in which teacher effects varied across students according to each student's predicted achievement in the current year, where predicted achievement was identified on the basis of a vector of past achievement scores. The authors reported strong evidence of differential teacher effects, in the sense that value-added models that included interactions of teacher effects by prior student achievement provided a significantly better fit for the observed data than did models without the interactions. The magnitude of the interactions was not large, with about 10% of the variance of teacher effects across students attributable to teachers' differential effectiveness with students who differ in their prior achievement trajectories. The authors also examined the distribution of differential teacher effects, and found that the pattern varied across districts. In two of the districts, teachers who were effective overall tended to be effective particularly with students who were already embarked on a high-achieving trajectory. In the third, teachers who tended to have larger teacher effects overall tended to have particularly high value-added scores with low-performing students. The latter case is of particular interest in the present discussion because it suggests the possibility of using class assignment in a compensatory manner to reduce inequality.

Additional Work Needed

In the context of accountability for student test performance as well as increasing use of value-added models, school districts are keenly interested in the possibility of using value-added achievement data to equalize achievement growth among students at different starting points. Meyer and Dokumaci (2010) reported estimating differential teacher effects in three major cities: New York, Chicago, and Milwaukee. Thus far, however, no one has compared a system in which differential teacher effectiveness is used as the basis for assigning students to classes to a system in which that is not the case. Yet that is a logical next step for researchers and local decision makers if teachers really do have differential effects, as suggested by Lockwood and McCaffrey.

Once differential teacher effects can be consistently and reliably measured, substantial implementation challenges will remain before they can be employed in a practical solution to the problem of arranging students for instruction. Two challenges seem paramount. First, it is not clear that there will be enough teachers who excel with low-achieving students to make this approach viable. What if there are many teachers who are more productive with high than with low achievers, but the opposite is rare? That would undermine the usefulness of calculating differential value added for matching teachers and students. Even so, such data would make it possible to ensure that low-achieving students are not assigned repeatedly to ineffective teachers—which is probably the case under current tracking regimes. So, it might be possible to curtail some of the worst consequences of tracking, but whether students can be optimally assigned remains to be seen. Second, even if there is a wide range of teacher effects, implementation will require careful experimentation. For example, discovering a teacher who is unusually effective with low-achieving students does not mean that teacher will be effective with an entire class of low-achieving students. These issues can be addressed, but it should be clear that we are a long way from optimal student assignment.

Potential Contributions from Sociologists

The use of value-added models to test for possible differential teacher effects has the potential to open up a new agenda for sociologists. The value-added approach is essentially a production function, which examines inputs (prior achievement) and outputs (subsequent achievement) and links them by noting who gets taught by whom at what points in time. Yet Barr and Dreeben (1983) argued long ago that the production function is too limiting an approach for sociologists. As Lauen and Tyson (2009) recently explained, sociologists are uniquely positioned to examine not only the effects of educational practices, but the mechanisms through which effects occur, that is, what constitutes the practices and how they come about. Sociological understanding of schools as organizations requires researchers to develop concepts and evidence about what instruction teachers provide and how students experience instruction. Research on teacher decision making in light of accountability pressures moves in this direction (e.g., Anagnostopoulos 2003; Booher-Jennings 2005), but does not illuminate the outcomes of teachers' instructional decisions. Are some teachers more effective with low achievers because they adapt instruction to the needs of such students? Or do such teachers always instruct in the same manner, and their approach happens to work better with low-achieving students? In light of the connection between prior achievement levels and long-standing bases of inequality such as race/ethnicity and social class, sociologists also may be driven to ask whether differential effects that seem to correspond to prior achievement actually reflect differences by social background. Sociologists can open the "black box" of differential effects by increasing their attention to interaction between teachers and students in the social and organizational contexts of the classroom.

Conclusions: Implications for Inequality

Inequality in schooling outcomes is central to the agenda of sociologists of education, and approaches that seem to mitigate inequality must draw our attention. Two promising streams of research suggest that it may be possible to differentiate instruction within and between classes in a way that maximizes the learning trajectories of students irrespective of their starting points. Both approaches are at very early stages, having established proofs of concept but demanding more extensive research to assess their applicability to a broad range of subject areas and grade levels and the feasibility of widespread implementation.

Of the two approaches, the system of diagnosis and instructional response exemplified by the work of Connor and her colleagues is farther along in many ways. First, it provides a model of translation from theory to practical application, although within a single content domain and limited age range. Second, it offers evidence of closing gaps between high and low achievers over the course of a school year. Third, it provides a product in the form of an assessment system and diagnostic software that, in principle, can be transferred to other locations. It also demonstrates how other researchers may go about developing similar systems of assessment, diagnosis, and instructional prescriptions in other subjects and grade levels.

Nonetheless, the implications of this approach for inequality have yet to be fully explored. If the system helps low achievers to catch up to their higher achieving peers, then even if disadvantaged students are overrepresented in low groups, inequality will not be magnified as usually occurs when students are grouped by ability because students in low groups will be helped rather than held back. Questions remain, however, as to whether the system is powerful enough to overcome the stigma of low-group assignment. The flexible rather than permanent use of groups that is advocated in this system may help prevent perceptions of low status from arising. As teachers follow the instructional prescriptions and see their students making rapid progress, the vicious cycle of low expectations may be avoided. More explicit attention to the context of implementation and the backgrounds of participants would help assess these possibilities.

The implications of the second approach for inequality are less clear. To the extent that measures of differential teacher effects permit optimal matching of teachers and students, inequality may be mitigated as low-achieving students benefit from teachers who are adept especially at responding to their needs. Yet this possibility has not yet been tested. Moreover, it is not clear that teacher effects revealed with one group of students would carry over if class compositions were manipulated deliberately to match teachers with students whose profiles correspond to those whom teachers have helped in the past. Problems of social stigma and racially identifiable classrooms may be compounded if large numbers of low achievers are assigned to teachers who have exhibited success previously with such students, especially if the prior success occurred with smaller concentrations of disadvantaged students. Still, the notion is promising enough to warrant further investigation.

The effects of grouping and tracking are not merely about perceptions of low status, they also reflect actual differences in resources that are commonly brought to bear on the teaching of advantaged and disadvantaged students. In this area, the new approaches exhibit substantial promise. Both may help ensure that low expectations for low achievers do not result in slow-paced, fragmented, dead-end instruction. On the contrary, both offer mechanisms for bringing high-quality instruction to low-achieving students: one by prescribing specific instruction that responds to students' skills, and the other by matching low-achieving students with teachers who have shown success with such students in the past. To the extent that differences in the manner and content of instruction are responsible for the increasing inequality commonly associated with tracking, the approaches examined here are likely to result in less inequality than typically occurs. For this reason, continued research and development are warranted.

Acknowledgments The author is grateful for helpful comments from Carol Connor, Maureen Hallinan, and an anonymous reviewer.

References

Anagnostopoulos, Dorothea. 2003. The new accountability, student failure, and teachers' work in urban high schools. *Educational Policy* 17: 291–316.
Ayalon, Hanna. 2006. Nonhierarchical curriculum differentiation and inequality in achievement: A different story or more of the same? *Teachers College Record* 108: 1186–1213.

Ayalon, Hanna, and Adam Gamoran. 2000. Stratification in academic secondary programs and educational inequality: Comparison of Israel and the United States. *Comparative Education Review* 44: 54–80.

Barr, R., and Robert Dreeben. 1983. *How schools work*. Chicago: University of Chicago Press.

Black, Paul, and Dylan Wiliam. 1998. Inside the black box: Raising standards through classroom assessment. *Phi Delta Kappan* 80(2): 139–149.

Bloom, Benjamin S. 1964. *Stability and change in human characteristics*. New York: Wiley.

Booher-Jennings, Jennifer. 2005. Below the bubble: 'Educational Triage' and the Texas Accountability System. *American Educational Research Journal* 42: 231–268.

Broaded, C. Montgomery. 1997. The limits and possibilities of tracking: Some evidence from Taiwan. *Sociology of Education* 70: 36–53.

Burris, Carol C., Jay P. Heubert, and Henry M. Levin. 2006. Accelerating mathematics achievement using heterogeneous grouping. *American Educational Research Journal* 43: 105–136.

Burris, Carol C., Ed Wiley, Kevin Welner, and John Murphy. 2008. Accountability, rigor, and detracking: Achievement effects of embracing a challenging curriculum as a universal good for all students. *Teachers College Record* 110: 571–607.

Cheng, Simon, Leslie Martin, and Regina E. Werum. 2007. Adult social capital and track placement of ethnic groups in Germany. *American Journal of Education* 114: 41–74.

Connor, Carol M. 2010. Child characteristics X instruction interactions: Implications for students' literacy skill development in the early grades. In *Handbook on early literacy*. 3rd ed. eds. S. B. Neuman and D. K. Dickinson. New York: Guilford Press.

Connor, Carol M., Frederick J. Morrison, and Leslie E. Katch. 2004a. Beyond the reading wars: Exploring the effect of child-instruction interactions on growth in early reading. *Scientific Studies of Reading* 8: 305–336.

Connor, Carol M., Frederick J. Morrison, and Jocelyn Petrella. 2004b. Effective reading comprehension instruction: Examining child X instruction interactions. *Journal of Educational Psychology* 96: 682–698.

Connor, Carol M., Frederick J. Morrison, Barry J. Fishman, Christopher Schatschneider, and Phyllis Underwood. 2007. The early years: Algorithm-guided individualized reading instruction. *Science* 315: 464–465.

Connor, Carol M., Shayne B. Piasta, Barry Fishman, Stephanie Glasney, Christopher Schatschneider, Elizabeth Crowe, Phyllis Underwood, and F.J. Morrison. 2009. Individualizing student instruction precisely: Effects of child by instruction interactions on first graders' literacy development. *Child Development* 80: 77–100.

Cronbach, Lee, and Richard Snow. 1977. *Aptitudes and instructional methods: A handbook for research on interactions*. New York: Irvington.

Gamoran, Adam. 1986. Instructional and institutional effects of ability grouping. *Sociology of Education* 59: 185–198.

Gamoran, Adam. 1992. The variable effects of high school tracking. *American Sociological Review* 57: 812–828.

Gamoran, Adam. 1993. Alternative uses of ability grouping in secondary schools: Can we bring high-quality instruction to low-ability classes? *American Journal of Education* 101: 1–22.

Gamoran, Adam. 2002. *CES briefing: Standards, inequality, and ability grouping*. Edinburgh: Centre for Educational Sociology.

Gamoran, Adam. 2004. Classroom organization and instructional quality. In *Can unlike students learn together? Grade retention, tracking, and grouping*, 141–155. Greenwich: Information Age Publishing.

Gamoran, Adam. 2010. Tracking and inequality: New directions for research and practice. In *The Routledge international handbook of the sociology of education*, eds. M. Apple, S.J. Ball, and L.A. Gandin, 213–228. London: Routledge.

Gamoran, Adam, and Mark Berends. 1987. The effects of stratification in secondary schools: Synthesis of survey and ethnographic research. *Review of Educational Research* 57: 415–435.

Gamoran, Adam, and Eileen C. Hannigan. 2000. Algebra for everyone? Benefits of college preparatory mathematics for students with diverse abilities in early secondary school. *Educational Evaluation and Policy Analysis* 22: 241–254.

Gamoran, Adam, and Sean Kelly. 2003. Tracking, instruction, and unequal literacy in secondary school English. In *Stability and change in American education: Structure, process, and outcomes*, eds. M.T. Hallinan, A. Gamoran, W. Kubitschek, and T. Loveless, 109–126. Clinton Corners: Eliot Werner Publications.

Gamoran, Adam, and Matthew Weinstein. 1998. Differentiation and opportunity in restructured schools. *American Journal of Education* 106: 385–415.

Gamoran, Adam, Martin Nystrand, Mark Berends, and Paul C. LePore. 1995. An organizational analysis of the effects of ability grouping. *American Educational Research Journal* 32: 687–715.

Hallam, Susan. 2002. *Ability grouping in schools*. London: University of London Institute of Education.

Hallinan, Maureen T. 1994. Tracking: From theory to practice. *Sociology of Education* 67: 79–84.

Hamilton, Laura, Richard Halverson, Sharnell S. Jackson, Ellen Mandinach, Jon A. Supovitz, and Jeffrey C. Wayman. 2009. *Using Student Achievement Data to Support Instructional Decision Making* (NCEE 2009–4067). Washington, DC: National Center for Educational Evaluation and Regional Assistance, Institute of Education Science, U.S. Department of Education. Retrieved November 12, 2010 (http://ies.ed.gov/ncee/wwc/publications/practiceguides/).

Harlen, Wynne, and Heather Malcolm. 1997. *Setting and streaming: A research review*. Edinburgh: Scottish Council for Research in Education.

Hoadley, U. 2008. Social class and pedagogy: A model for the investigation of pedagogic variation. *British Journal of Sociology of Education* 29: 63–78.

Ireson, Judith, Susan Hallam, Sarah Hack, Helen Clark, and Ian Plewis. 2002. Ability grouping in English secondary schools: Effects on attainment in English, mathematics, and science. *Educational Research and Evaluation* 8: 299–318.

Ivinson, Gabreille, and Gerard Duveen. 2005. Classroom structuration and the development of social representations of the curriculum. *British Journal of Sociology of Education* 26: 627–642.

Jackson, Philip W. 1968. *Life in classrooms*. New York: Holt, Rinehart, and Winston.

Kulik, Chen-Lin, and James A. Kulik. 1982. Effects of ability grouping on secondary school students: A meta-analysis of evaluation findings. *American Educational Research Journal* 19: 415–428.

Lauen, Douglas Lee, and Karolyn Tyson. 2009. Perspectives from the disciplines sociological contributions to education policy research and debates. In *The handbook of education policy research*, eds. Gary Sykes, Barbara Schneider, and David N. Plank, 71–82. Washington, DC: American Educational Research Association.

Lewis, T., and S.-Y. Cheng. 2006. Tracking, expectations, and the transformation of vocational education. *American Journal of Education* 113: 67–99.

Lockwood, J.R., and Daniel F. McCaffrey. 2007. Exploring student-teacher interactions in longitudinal achievement data. *Education Finance and Policy* 2: 439–467.

Lortie, Dan C. 1975. *Schoolteacher: A sociological study*. Chicago: University of Chicago Press.

Lucas, Samuel R. 1999. *Tracking inequality: Stratification and mobility in American high schools*. New York: Teachers College Press.

Meyer, Robert H., and Emin Dokumaci. 2010. *Value-added models and the next generation of assessments*. Princeton: Educational Testing Service.

Mickelson, Roslyn A., and Bobbie J. Everett. 2008. Neotracking in North Carolina: How high school courses of study reproduce race and class-based stratification. *Teachers College Record* 110: 535–570.

National Mathematics Advisory Panel. 2008. *Foundations for success: Final report of the National Mathematics Advisory Panel*. Washington, DC: U.S. Department of Education.

National Reading Panel. 2000. *Teaching children to read: An evidence-based assessment of the scientific research literature on reading and its implications for reading instruction*. Washington, DC: National Reading Panel.

Oakes, Jeannie. 1992. Can tracking research inform practice? Technical, normative, and political considerations. *Educational Researcher* 21(4): 12–22.

Oakes, Jeannie. 1994. More than misapplied technology: A normative and political response to Hallinan on tracking. *Sociology of Education* 67: 84–91.

Oakes, Jeannie. 2005. *Keeping track: How schools structure inequality*, 2nd ed. New Haven: Yale University Press.

Oakes, Jeannie, Adam Gamoran, and Reba N. Page. 1992. Curriculum differentiation: Opportunities, outcomes, and meanings. In *The handbook of research on curriculum*, ed. P.W. Jackson, 570–608. New York: Macmillan.

Ono, Hiroshi. 2001. Who goes to college? Features of institutional tracking in Japanese higher education. *American Journal of Education* 109: 161–195.

Page, Reba N. 1991. *Lower-track classrooms: A curricular and cultural perspective*. New York: Teachers College Press.

Palincsar, Annemarie S. and Ann L. Brown. 1985. Reciprocal teaching: Activities to promote 'Reading with Your Mind.' In *Reading, thinking and concept development: Strategies for the classroom*, eds. T. L. Harris and E. J. Cooper, 147–158. New York: The College Board.

Park, Hyunjoon. 2009. Growing curricular differentiation and its implications for inequality in Korea. Presented at *the Annual Meeting of the Association of Asian Studies*, March 2009, Chicago.

Rowan, Brian, and Richard Correnti. 2009. Studying reading instruction with teacher logs: Lessons from the study of instructional improvement. *Educational Researcher* 38(2): 120–131.

Sanders, William L., and June C. Rivers. 1996. *Cumulative and residual effects of teachers on future student academic achievement*. Knoxville, TN: University of Tennessee Value-Added Research and Assessment Center.

Sandholtz, Judith H., Rodney T. Ogawa, and Samantha P. Scribner. 2004. Standards gap: Unintended consequences of local standards-based reform. *Teachers College Record* 106: 1177–1202.

Slavin, Robert E. 1987. Ability grouping and achievement in elementary schools: A best-evidence synthesis. *Review of Educational Research* 57: 293–336.

Slavin, Robert E. 1990. Achievement effects of ability grouping in secondary schools: A best-evidence synthesis. *Review of Educational Research* 60: 471–499.

Snow, Richard. 1989. Aptitude-treatment interaction as a framework for research on individual differences in learning. In *Learning and individual differences*, eds. P. Ackerman, R.J. Sternberg, and R. Glaser, 13–59. New York: W.H. Freeman.

Stanley, Gordon, and Robert G. MacCann. 2005. Removing incentives for 'Dumbing Down' through curriculum re-structure and additional study time. *Educational Policy Analysis Archives* 13: 1–10.

Van de gaer, E., H. Pustjens, J. Van Damme, and A. De Munter. 2006. Tracking and the effects of school-related attitudes on the language achievement of boys and girls. *British Journal of Sociology of Education* 27: 293–309.

Van Houtte, M. 2004. Tracking effects on school achievement: A quantitative explanation in terms of the academic culture of school staff. *American Journal of Education* 110: 354–388.

Vygotsky, Lev. 1978. *Mind in society*. Cambridge: Harvard University Press.

Wharton-McDonald, Ruth, Michael Pressley, and Jennifer M. Hampston. 1998. Literacy instruction in nine first-grade classrooms: Teacher characteristics and student achievement. *Elementary School Journal* 99: 101–128.

Chapter 7
Getting Ideas into Action: Building Networked Improvement Communities in Education

Anthony S. Bryk, Louis M. Gomez, and Alicia Grunow

Reorganizing Educational Research and Development[1]

Background

In a recent essay, we argued that our current educational research and development (R&D) infrastructure fails to connect to enduring problems of improvement in our nation's schools and colleges (Bryk and Gomez 2008). An all too well-known sample of these problems includes: ethnically based gaps in academic achievement, too many adolescents dropping out of high school, too few children learning to read

---

[1] We would like to acknowledge the contributions of our senior partners in the Carnegie Community College Initiative: Catherine Casserly, Bernadine Chuck Fong, James Stigler, Uri Treisman, and Guadalupe Valdes. This essay has benefited from numerous conversations with them about the general work of improving applied R&D in education and the specific case of developmental mathematics education used throughout this essay. We also wish to thank participants in our seminar on Networked Improvement Communities held jointly this past winter (January through April 2010) at the University of Pittsburgh and the Carnegie Foundation for the Advancement of Teaching. The give and take around problems and ideas stimulated much of what follows. This work has been undertaken through a joint funding initiative of the Carnegie Corporation of New York, the William and Flora Hewlett Foundation, Bill and Melinda Gates Foundation, Lumina Foundation, Kresge Foundation, and the Carnegie Foundation for the Advancement of Teaching. We wish to acknowledge their collective support, noting that the authors alone are responsible for the arguments offered here.

A.S. Bryk (✉) • A. Grunow
Carnegie Foundation for the Advancement of Teaching, Stanford, CA 94305, USA
e-mail: bryk@carnegiefoundation.org; grunow@carnegiefoundation.org

L.M. Gomez
School of Education, University of Pittsburgh, Pittsburgh, PA 15260, USA
e-mail: lgomez@pitt.edu

proficiently, and very low student success rates in our community colleges. We noted that educational problems like these continue to be vexing even though they have gained public policy attention and stimulated an extraordinary array of activity within the research and development community. Despite this activity, most assessments conclude that the R&D enterprise has not helped as much to date as one might hope and expect. A small but growing cadre of scholars and policy organizations have coalesced around an argument that the social organization of the research infrastructure is badly broken and a very different alternative is needed (e.g., Burkhardt and Schoenfeld 2003; Coburn and Stein 2010; Committee on a Strategic Education Research Partnership 2003; Hiebert et al. 2002; Kelly 2006; National Academy of Education Report 1999).

In response, we argued for a more problem-centered approach that joins academic research, clinical practice, and commercial expertise in sustained programs of Design, Educational Engineering and Development (DEED). We sketched out three overlapping phases of effective DEED, beginning with a set of alpha trials where a promising idea is attempted in a small number of places (Bryk and Gomez 2008; Bryk 2009). Extending this activity are beta investigations where DEED efforts deliberately focus on adapting the innovation so that it might be implemented with efficacy in more diverse settings. This, in turn, would lead to gamma-level activity that exploits evidence from large-scale use to continue to improve the innovation.

To engage such inquiries would require a profound shift in the social arrangements of R&D. Heretofore, nominal roles of researcher and practitioner have differentiated the arrangements of inquiry. Researchers, primarily those with PhDs in a cognate or applied discipline, did the intellectual heavy lifting at the front end of the idea pipeline, while practitioners, those with on-the-ground experience, were expected to implement and adapt idealized innovations. Practitioners simultaneously engaged in local problem solving; however their efforts were rarely seen as significant in the infrastructure of educational R&D. The ideas seeded in our earlier essay and further developed here take a different perspective. We argue that the complex problems of practice improvement demand that a diverse mix of skills be brought to bear and require reconsideration of when and how in the arc of problem solving this diversity of expertise is best exploited. It demands new arrangements for disciplined inquiry where the work of research and practice join in a more dynamic and interactive fashion. It invites strong scholars to engage in applied R&D, but now in quite different ways in the pursuit of a science of improvement.

We detail in this essay how the social organization for such work might actually be carried out. Toward this end, we introduce the idea of a networked improvement community. We focus primarily on how research and practice communities might join in initiating such an enterprise. Our inspiration for the discussion below draws on insights from successful R&D activities occurring in diverse fields outside of education, including the semiconductor industry, the Linux development community, and efforts at broad-scale quality improvements in health services. In each of these examples, large networks have been organized around complex problems and have brought about remarkable change. Understanding these developments better, extracting core ideas, and translating them into more productive institutional arrangements for educational R&D pose important questions for learning scientists, organizational sociologists, and political scientists interested in how expertise networks advance social improvement.

Orienting Ideas

Improving the organization of educational R&D requires answers to three seemingly straightforward questions: First, what problem(s) are we trying to solve? Second, whose expertise is needed to solve these problems? And third, what are the social arrangements that will enable this work? While these questions appear to be simple, in the last decades our field's responses to them have been confused. When the answers to these questions are disorganized, the natural result is a cacophony of questions and innovations that fail to accumulate into real progress on core concerns.

Consider community college graduation rates, which is now a major concern for public policy. There is a broad public consensus that community colleges are an important opportunity resource for a large segment of America. In the research and development community, we recognize that improving community college graduation rates is an important priority. Is this level of agreement enough for sustained progress so that more students will successfully graduate? We argue no. Once problems like this cross some public policy threshold, a spate of uncoordinated research and development activity ensues. Some scholars might say community college failure rates are high because "it is the textbooks"—we need to develop better and open source materials. Others might say "it is a student motivation problem"—let us organize learning communities to improve students' social connection to study groups across the college. Still others say "what we're teaching doesn't make sense when we look at students' educational and career goals"—so let us design/create more meaningful math courses. Still others say "it is an institutional leadership failure"—let us get serious about leadership development initiatives. In short, for this and most other significant problems in education, there are many voices that attempt to characterize the problem.

We argue that large societal concerns such as improving community college success are complex problems composed of multiple strands (with numerous embedded microlevel problems) that play out over time and often interact with one another. More specifically, graduation rates in community colleges are an aggregate consequence of numerous processes such as courses taken, advising systems, course scheduling, etc. One does not improve graduation rates directly except by decomposing this big presenting problem into its constituent component processes, then analyzing the interconnections among them. It is within the problem system where students actually progress or fail.

Another question is "Who should be doing the work?" If the listing of problem parts above captured even a small part of the problem ecology, then a very diverse colleagueship of expertise will be necessary to make progress (Bryk and Gomez 2008). Furthermore, these actors must be organized in ways that enhance the efficacy of individual efforts, align those efforts, and increase the likelihood that a collection of such actions might accumulate toward efficacious solutions. While innovations abound in education, we argue that the field suffers from a lack of purposeful collective action. Instead, actors work with different theories of the same problem, activities are siloed, and local solutions remain local.

In this essay, we focus on an alternative social organization for this activity network: How might one structure and guide the varied and multiple associated efforts necessary to sustained collective action toward solving complex improvement problems? Drawing on Englebart (1992), we call this kind of organization a networked improvement community. We detail a set of structuring agents necessary for productive R&D to occur across such a community. We attend to how this form of social organization might come into existence and sustain participation over time in order to advance real improvements for significant numbers of students.

Networked Improvement Communities

In an arena such as education, where market mechanisms are weak and where hierarchical command and control are not possible, networks provide a plausible alternative for productively organizing the diverse expertise needed to solve complex educational problems. Below we describe the organizing role that Networked Improvement Communities (NIC) might play here.

Networks as Design Communities

Networks enable individuals from many different contexts to participate according to their interests and expertise while sustaining collective attention on progress toward common goals. Organizational scholars have suggested that the novel interactions and information exchanges occurring within such networks make them particularly suitable for innovation and knowledge-intensive product design (Goldsmith and Eggers 2004; Podolny and Page 1998; Powell 1990). These more decentralized and horizontal work arrangements appear especially advantageous when, as von Hippel (2005) argues, "the problem-solving work of innovation requires access to 'sticky' information regarding user needs and the context of use." This knowledge is highly localized and thus costly to transfer. This latter consideration is especially significant in educational R&D where improving at scale requires coping productively with local diversity. The history of educational innovation is replete with stories that show how innovations work in the hands of a few, but lose effectiveness in the hands of the many (Gomez et al. 2010). At base here is a need for much better access to sticky knowledge. That is, we need designs and implementations which explicitly aim to function in the hands of diverse individuals working in highly varied circumstances. We know all too well from past experiences that such contextual knowledge is not transferred easily across institutional lines to the academic labs or publishing companies where many educational tools and products currently are designed. In contrast, a network organizational approach can surface and test new insights and enable more fluid exchanges across contexts and traditional institutional boundaries—thus holding potential to enhance designing for scale.

Networks as Learning Communities

The term network is used to describe a wide array of collectives. A networked improvement community is a distinct network form that arranges human and technical resources so that the community is capable of getting better at getting better (Englebart 2003). Englebart characterizes the work of organizations and organizational fields in terms of three broad domains of activity. In Englebart's terminology, A-level activity is the on-the-ground work of carrying out the organization's primary business. In the case of community colleges, A-level work is the frontline teaching and learning work of classrooms and includes units such as student support centers that offer tutoring services. Secondary or B-level activity describes within-organization efforts that are designed to improve the on-the-ground work. In the community college realm, the work of institutional research units offers one example. These shops collect data about student success rates and share that information with faculty and staff with the expectation that the data will inform subsequent improvements. C-level activity is interinstitutional, representing the capacity for learning to occur across organizations. Here, institutions engage in concurrent development, working on problems and proposed solutions that have a strong family resemblance. Concurrent activity across contexts puts relevant aspects of the context in sharp relief and can help each local setting see its efforts from new vantage points. This is a boon to problem solving. Englebart (2003) observes that C-level activity affords mechanisms for testing the validity of local knowledge, adjusting local understanding of the true nature of a problem, and advancing local support structures for improvement.

Applied inquiry in education has largely been about describing A-level activity, and on some occasions, evaluating it. Recently, we have seen a spate of interest in B-level activity, for example, in efforts to introduce evidence-based decision making as a guide to K–12 school reform. (See for example, Boudett et al. 2005). Likewise in community colleges, the Achieving the Dream initiative aims to develop local capacities to use data to inform improvement (see www.achievingthedream.org). This growing B-level activity is exciting because it lays the groundwork for the emergence of C-level inquiries and attendant possibilities for broad, interinstitutional social learning. Consequently, a more detailed account of how such networked improvement communities are initiated, organized, and governed could be useful in efforts to enhance the overall productivity of educational R&D. Beginning work toward such an account is the aim of this paper.

Exemplary Networked Improvement Communities (NICs)

To help ground our conversation about how networked organizations can arrange themselves to accomplish improvement at scale in educational research and development, we have identified three, extant organizational cases that share a significant number of the features detailed in Englebart's analysis. We use insights from the International Technology Roadmap for Semiconductors (ITRS) in which (sometimes competing) organizations from across the semiconductor industry coordinated their innovation efforts. The shared road map was instrumental in catalyzing unparalleled R&D-based improvements in microelectronics. We also look at Linux as a case of a loosely coupled collection of software professionals who volunteered their time to work cooperatively in an innovation network. Collectively, they produced a complex and highly sophisticated modern multipurpose operating system. And finally, we turn to the Institute for Healthcare Improvement (IHI) that is creating a new ethos for how healthcare organizations work at global scale to continuously advance better healthcare outcomes. Each of these cases offers insights as to how a more effective educational R&D might be institutionally arranged. We have drawn eclectically on these experiences, and related theoretical accounts, to detail framing elements of organizational structure, core work processes, and operating norms for an educational networked improvement community.

A Case of Learning Through Doing

As noted, reshaping educational R&D is a growing part of the contemporary scholarly and policy zeitgeist. This chapter contributes to this scholarship, and it has been informed by others. Only so much, however, can be learned through reflection; its natural complement is action to spur learning. That is, a concrete way to learn how a NIC might organize and carry out a better program of educational R&D is to build one. In this spirit, the Carnegie Foundation for the Advancement of Teaching has adopted a learning through doing orientation. Under the Foundation's umbrella, and in partnership with several other colleagues and institutions,[2] we are now initiating

---

[2] Of special note in this regard is the Foundation's partnership with the Dana Center at the University of Texas. Dana has lead design responsibility for developing the initial instructional kernel for Statway™. This includes pathway outcomes, a modular structure for the curriculum, classroom lessons, and assessments. In addition, the executive director of the Dana Center, Uri Treisman, also serves as a Carnegie senior partner. In this latter role, Treisman coleads the policy outreach and planning for scale team in the network.

a prototype NIC aimed at addressing the extraordinary failure rates in developmental mathematics in community colleges. As noted earlier, multiple processes combine to create observed community college outcomes. We sought to initiate a NIC around a high leverage wedge into this organizational system. Practitioners and researchers now agree that a key contributor, arguably the most important contributor, to low graduation rates in community colleges is the high failure rates of students in developmental mathematics courses (see for example, Cullinane and Treisman 2010). Redressing this is a well-specified problem around which a NIC can organize. In the pages that follow, we describe the rationale and design for this NIC and draw on emerging practices within it to illustrate how our framing ideas about NICs are becoming manifest in action.

The nation's 1,000 community colleges enroll more than 6 million students or upward of 40 percent of all postsecondary students in the USA.[3] These institutions are the front line in our nation's efforts to advance social equity and supply labor needs for a twenty-first century economy.[4] At present, however, many students enter community colleges with high aims and ambition, only to languish, sometimes for years, in developmental courses that are noncredit bearing and do not move them toward a degree, certificate, or transfer. This is true especially in mathematics. Recent studies report that between 60 and 70 percent of students who are referred to developmental mathematics do not successfully complete the sequence of required courses.[5] Many spend long periods of time repeating courses or simply leave college. Either way, they do not reach their career goals.

A careful analysis of this larger problem reveals a complex of subproblems operating within community colleges that contribute to the high failure rates. Instructional systems do not engage student interest in learning, student support systems inconsistently meet students' needs, human resource practices and governance structures create barriers for change, and there is insufficient access to data and insufficient use of data to inform improvements. Small gains may be possible by focusing on single elements, but dramatic change ultimately requires a systems view of how these elements (and others) interlock to create the overall outcomes currently observed.

---

[3] American Association of Community Colleges; Retrieved from http://www2.aacc.nche.edu/research/index.htm on September 11, 2009.

[4] The magnitude of community colleges' collective responsibility nearly doubled in July 2009 when President Obama called for an additional 5 million community college degrees and certificates by 2020. To achieve this scale under a constrained timeframe requires bold innovation. Entitled the American Graduation Initiative, the plan as proposed will invest 12 billion dollars to invigorate community colleges across the USA by funding improvements in physical infrastructure, developing challenge grant mechanisms, and creating a virtual course clearinghouse. Specifically the President highlights open, online education as a strategy for reaching more nontraditional students, accelerating students' progress, helping students persist, and improving instructional quality.

[5] Bailey et al. (2008) (revised April 2009). These data were obtained from Achieving the Dream campuses and compared to NELS 88 data.

The Carnegie Foundation has set out to catalyze and support the growth of a networked improvement community aimed at doubling the proportion of community college students who, within one year of community college enrollment, are prepared mathematically to succeed in further academic or occupational pursuits. Carnegie's first effort in this regard is to launch a Carnegie Statway™ Network.[6] This network seeks to redesign traditional developmental mathematics by creating a one-year pathway to and through statistics that integrates necessary mathematics learning along the way.

The first participants in the Statway network are 19 community college teams, each comprised of three faculty members, an institutional researcher, and an academic dean or vice president. These teams are now working together with Carnegie to codevelop a set of base resources for the network. Faculty members will develop, test, and refine an initial set of instructional resources. Common assessments and a lesson study methodology anchor their activity and set the stage for the continuous improvement of the instructional materials over time. The institutional researchers are working together to build common evidence systems to enable the network to measure, compare, and improve the performance of Statway students both within and across institutions. The deans and administrators from each college are addressing the multitude of logistical issues that arise in embedding an innovative design within their institutional contexts.

The work of these teams is supported, in turn, by expert others. As these pilot efforts proceed, the network will address concerns around faculty development, and where and how technology can add value. The network will form a robust information infrastructure to inform continuous improvement. It must consider how issues of literacy and language mediate mathematics learning and scrutinize how the vast array of extant academic, social, psychological/counseling services can be better integrated to advance student success. These are all key to advancing efficacious outcomes reliably at scale. Taken together, this assembled expertise provides the initiating social form for our NIC, which we call a Collaboratory. As the network evolves, Collaboratory membership will expand to other specialized practitioners, design-developers, and researchers as new needs and priorities come into focus.

The Statway design products codeveloped within the Collaboratory will belong to a growing networked improvement community and serve as base resources for the network to further improve over time. Involvement in the network also will advance participants' instructional and institutional expertise, thereby creating a cadre of leaders and champions for subsequent expansion of the network. Any intervention that is human and social resource intensive, as is the case for most educational improvement efforts, requires organizational and

---

[6] It is argued more generally that we need a small number of more structured pathways to success. Statway is Carnegie's first effort in this regard. The Foundation also will support efforts on a second pathway, called Quantway™, seeking to achieve similar goals for students with somewhat different career aspirations.

institutional structuring to build capacity. As such, attending to how to engender a proper organizing structure for problem solving in the alpha stage is a key issue for activity expansion into the beta phase (Bryk and Gomez 2008). We now turn to the issue of network structuring.

Structuring Agents

All networks have rules and norms for membership. They maintain narratives that detail what they are about and why it is important to affiliate. In one way or another, networked communities make clear who is allowed to join, how to join, and how to participate. Membership criteria may be very loose and broad. In a community like Facebook, for example, literally everyone can join. (There are, of course, within Facebook, many subcommunities with restrictions.) Facebook is essentially an open community.

Open networks abound in education. In the main, they function as free-floating idea bazaars, contexts for self-expression, and places to share information. In fact, the current social organization of educational R&D functions much like an open network. It is characterized by a multitude of voices lobbying for preferred approaches, but with weak mechanisms for directing intentional action that cumulates in coherent solutions to complex problems. In this regard, educational R&D's inability to orchestrate such improvement is akin to a market failure.

In contrast, a networked improvement community is an intentionally formed social organization. Its improvement goals impose specific demands on the rules and norms of participation. We detail here a set of structuring agents necessary to form participation in such an intentionally designed network so that coordinated R&D can occur on a focal problem. "Getting these agents right" is key to unleashing individual creativity, while also advancing joint accountability toward collective problem solving.

Common Targets and Measureable Ambitious Goals

The community of practice has become a prevalent organizational arrangement in education to support collaboration.[7] Communities of practice require that members have interests in common. For example, a community of practice devoted to teaching high school biology through open-ended and long-term project investigation centers its activities on sharing ideas about ways to accomplish projects more effectively in classrooms.[8] While communities of practice may form around a common concern,

---

[7] For a seminal text on this topic, see Wenger (1999).
[8] See for example Ruopp et al. (1992) and Schlager et al. (2002).

such as improving the execution of science projects in biology classes, their goal is to support individual action. In the best of cases, communities of practice may share some common artifacts, such as a rubric that specifies elements of science projects (e.g., developing a driving question). Rarely do these specifications, however, lead to the execution of common work, to shared outcome measures and to mechanisms for comparing results by which progress toward specified goals can be judged. Coordination in a community of practice is limited to maintaining a social focus on a common problem, akin to keeping members in the same idea ballpark.

In contrast, we posit that a networked improvement community requires more structured social arrangements. Participants in a NIC endorse shared, precise, measureable targets. Participants agree to use what is learned, from working toward meeting the targets, to setting new targets aimed at ever more ambitious goals. In this regard, shared measureable targets help a community stay focused on what matters, from the community's perspective. They catalyze discussions among participants as to why we should attend to this rather than that. They demand argument about what is likely to afford more immediate progress. They introduce some discipline in priority setting as it interacts with an individualistic rhetoric of "I am interested in…" NICs rebalance arguments from personal interests to targets. They also shift the location of goals from the personal "I" to the collective "we."

The semiconductor industry provides an illustrative example. Gordon Moore, cofounder of Intel, noted in 1965 that the number of transistors that could be placed cost effectively on an integrated circuit had doubled every year since the invention of the transistor. Moore saw no technical reason why this trend would not continue for at least the next 20 years. Moore's prediction turned out to be correct, and his observation was later named Moore's Law.

In the semiconductor industry, Moore's Law is a beacon. It guides work for a diverse collection of colleagues within and across firms in that industry. It shapes the activities of engineers who design and construct devices and it shapes how corporate leaders invest capital. Further, since Moore's Law is anchored in evidence about past performance and a perspective of feasible developments, it offers reason to believe that stretch targets are actually attainable. The combination of feasibility, and the knowledge that everyone is working in a common direction, can have significant disciplining power in a community. In essence the targets help create virtuous cycles of joint accountability.

This feature of targets also is visible in organizing the efforts of the Institute for Healthcare Improvement (IHI). In each IHI initiative, explicit attention focuses on specifying precise, measureable goals for each improvement. Participants work under a shared understanding that "some is not a number and soon is not a time."[9] Defining measureable outcomes and timelines to achieve those outcomes guides efforts in IHI's improvement communities.

---

[9] See for example the overview of IHI's 5 Million Lives campaign: http://www.ihi.org/IHI/Programs/Campaign/Campaign.htm?TabId=1.

Targets have at least one additional important benefit. They engender ongoing vetting processes. Targets are under constant negotiation in networked improvement communities. Take the case of Wikipedia. Most Wikipedia users think of it as a reference product. For its members, however, it functions as an argument platform. The peer-to-peer platform is a vehicle that structures and propels their conversation. The online encyclopedia is the very useful by-product of all that argument (Shirky 2008). In a similar way, the act of setting common targets in networked improvement communities is a way for community members to vet goals and sharpen shared understandings. The process draws people into regular conversations that develop into distinct communication forms that then structure behavior. Consequently, evolving targets are more than just a way to get to a product. The evolution is a process that, in and of itself, shapes and strengthens activity in a community.

The importance of targets has not been lost on educators. For example, it is a core element in the No Child Left Behind Act (NCLB). NCLB established a measureable goal of 100 percent proficiency on state tests in math and reading by 2014. This explicit target has, in many ways, encouraged the sort of behavior we might expect, given our previous discussion. In light of NCLB's target, learning standards were revised by professional societies, states, and cities across the country to align with the target. The assessment industry went into high gear to build tests to help states judge whether schools and students were meeting, or on track to meet, the standards. At the same time, researchers and designers pondered and piloted new assessments that might be better at judging progress. States and districts invested in data warehouses to report performance data that highlights, in granular detail, who is and who is not making average yearly progress (AYP) toward targets. School leaders focused attention and resources on disadvantaged children, especially those just below proficiency levels, as their progress was key to achieving AYP benchmarks. An industry of supplementary support services, especially individual student tutoring, grew rapidly as well. In short, a flurry of activity accrued in the wake of NCLB targets.

What did not cohere around NCLB was a full-fledged, networked improvement community. In comparison, the semiconductor industry took great care in creating targets that were viewed as attainable, whereas NCLB 2014 reading and math targets generated great skepticism.[10] For NCLB, there was no disciplining equivalent to Moore's Law. That law was anchored in empirical evidence about what had been achieved previously, combined with a shared field perspective that further improvements along these lines actually might be attainable. In contrast, NCLB goals represented an expression of valued social aims imposed by legislative action. No empirical evidence existed from past practice that the goals could be achieved and no community formed around their continued elaboration and refinement. To be sure, NCLB motivated individual actions, and many goods and services were purchased in an effort to reach the targets, but accumulating R&D for improvement was never vitalized.

---

[10] For example, Robert L. Linn of the National Center for Research on Evaluation is widely quoted as saying of NCLB: "There is a zero percent chance that we will ever reach a 100% target." (Paley 2007. http://www.washingtonpost.com/wp-dyn/content/article/2007/03/13/AR2007031301781.html). Also see Bryant et al. 2008.

These experiences have important implications as we think about targets in the context of Statway. We too lack the luxury of a disciplining framework like Moore's Law and worry that imposing socially valued outcomes by fiat lacks the organizing power needed. While we recognize the power of targets, we also understand that they must be valued and considered attainable by a community.

To begin a redress to this concern, each Collaboratory college will establish a performance baseline for students eligible to be served by Statway. This baseline will include common measures of student learning and program progress. In addition, we will collect data that refine our understandings about the student population being served, for example, their math course-taking history and proficiency, their language and literacy background and proficiencies, their motivation and determination to succeed in community college, etc.[11] Performance college-by-college in subsequent years will be judged against their local baselines. A distribution of effects will naturally emerge as the network accrues results from multiple sites implementing and refining Statway over several years. These results likely will vary from null findings in some situations to quite substantial improvements in others. We anticipate that somewhere along this distribution, say for example at the 75th percentile, a sense of feasible stretch goals should come into view.[12]

At base, two elements are key to establishing feasible targets that are generative toward improvement at scale. First, the variability in results achieved in the Statway network will be public to the Statway participants. And second, there will be a collective agreement to use results to continually refine targets in order to insure community ownership. As occurred in the semiconductor industry, we posit that a joint accountability dynamic will emerge through this process of reviewing network-wide results. Knowing that others engaged in the same endeavor may be achieving at higher rates creates incentives for learning how these successes are occurring. That is, as the network focuses on a comparative analysis of results for its ongoing target setting, the same processes also function to incent individual learning and improvements network wide.[13]

---

[11] This population definition process is now underway. It includes measures from student math and reading placement tests, and English language capabilities.

[12] Ideally, the Collaboratory would be able to draw results from previous institutional improvement efforts in the general domain of developmental mathematics education to set a network-wide goal. Absent the shared empirical discipline, such common data structures do not currently exist in the field. In contrast, were a community to embrace PDSA cycles as a common inquiry (see following section), such data might exist in the future. For an example of such a database in K–12, see research by the Consortium on Chicago School Research. Bryk et al. (2010), document rates of learning improvement across more than 400 elementary schools during a six-year period. These results provide an empirical basis setting improvement standards. Specifically, we know that improvements in annual learning gains of 10 percent or more in reading and 20 percent or more in mathematics are attainable.

[13] For an example in healthcare improvement, see Gawande's (2007) account of improvements in the treatment of cystic fibrosis across a health center network.

Mapping a Complex Problem–Solution Space: Forming a Shared Language Community

In addition to shared targets, mechanisms also are needed for coordinating efforts across diverse individuals and organizations engaged in a marketplace of parallel activity. The semiconductor industry uses an artifact called a roadmap to specify how targets become realized in the work of design, development, and engineering in different contexts. The terrain for possible innovation is vast and complex. The roadmap organizes the challenges to be confronted in this space in agreed upon ways. It establishes standards for how developments in different domains must fit together, and then sets microtargets, domain by domain. In these ways, the roadmap helps to coordinate the activity so that different innovations in hardware and software can be expected to interoperate at designated times in the future. In the industry's view, road mapping is a "practical approach to deal with the complex process of technological innovation" (Schaller 2004:13).

In essence, the roadmap reshapes accountability relationships that go beyond the confines of an individual firm or laboratory (Schaller 2004). Participants, both individuals and firms, are not autonomous actors operating within a disconnected marketplace. Rather, they form a densely connected network of peers who share a focused interest in common regions of the roadmap. Of note, today's technological climate includes the pervasive use of peer-to-peer collaboration tools, where individual activity is rapidly shared and transparent. For example, if network members working on common problems hear that others in the community have reached specified performance targets, it may spur the community to speed up work on competing products or push forward more rapidly on new products, given these reports.

For these reasons, the process of mapping the space for innovation development strikes us as another critical structuring agent for an educational improvement network. Problems such as dramatically improving student success in developmental math are not simple. Multiple processes happen simultaneously, and multiple subsystems within a community college are engaged around them. Each process has its own cause and effect logic, and these processes interact with one another over time to produce the overall outcomes we observe. Put simply, the extraordinary high failure rates in developmental mathematics in community colleges are a complex problem system.

The intrinsic complexity of such problem systems means that most participants appreciate only the parts of the system that seem particularly relevant to their role. Absent a working theory of the whole, interventions fail because of externalities not considered (also known as implementation failures), even though these are often predictable. For example, curriculum interventions often fail because of inadequate professional development. At base here is a natural human tendency to grasp for promising solutions or best practices without fully understanding how such solutions must be integrated with other solutions and preexisting organizational conditions.

In short, for a NIC to make headway toward constructive improvements on a complex problem, the community needs to detail the contours of its problem–solution space. Similar to the semiconductor industry, this includes elaborating various elements or subsystems that form it and the interrelations among them. Key here is to "carve the system at the joints" so that independent work can occur on pieces of the system and so that these components can be aggregated into more systemic solutions.

An important aspect of tools like the roadmap is that they help people see the challenges of innovation jointly and from multiple perspectives. For example, the semiconductor roadmap carved the problem at the level of individual devices while at the same time specifying the interoperability of the parts. This problem decomposition was then coupled with a temporal dynamic. That is, the roadmap also showed targets for technical performance, as they should unfold over time. The end product of such road mapping is a common language for organizing the diverse efforts occurring within a design and development community. Highly independent activities may occur across time and space, but the overall endeavor now coheres. Of note, the roadmap also provides the natural framework for accumulating field knowledge as it is developing. Over time, the roadmap is a persistent indicator that these joint efforts amount to tangible and important progress. In short, mapping the problem–solution space is key for coordinated work to occur and for improvement knowledge to accumulate.

Program Improvement Maps

We have developed two tools to assist efforts to decompose the problem–solution space confronted by the Statway Collaboratory. The first we call a program improvement map. The map seeks to align a network around a common understanding of the problem at hand. While decomposing a complex improvement problem into component parts, it also highlights the character of the system that embeds it. The anatomy of a problem is further detailed in terms of interacting subsystems, specified targets by domain, and the particular audiences for whom these outcomes are especially relevant. The map specifies the elements in how people currently work together to produce observed outcomes, and in so doing, organizes the challenges that must be confronted if substantial improvement is to occur.

The challenges faced by community colleges in seeking to use statistics as the curricular vehicle for revamping developmental math is by no means just an instructional system problem. While knotty curricular and pedagogical problems must be unraveled, to be successful Statway also must reach deeply into other institutional aspects of the community college and the policy infrastructure that surrounds it. The program improvement map encourages us to think through a detailed characterization of how these system elements operate in tandem with one another to produce the overall outcomes currently observed. The map also puts into relief how the efforts of other organizations beyond the colleges themselves, like curriculum providers and assessment developers, contribute to these outcomes. In so doing, it brings into focus how their efforts join the challenge space for innovation. In short, the program improvement map, like the roadmap, is a coordination device for diverse actors. It seeks to keep the improvement priorities of a network and their interconnections in explicit view as participants work on different parts of the problem.

7 Getting Ideas into Action: Building Networked Improvement Communities...

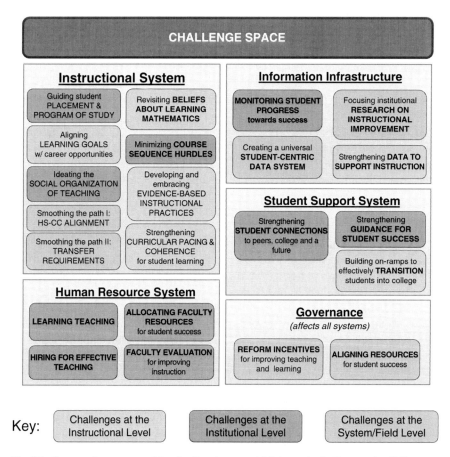

Fig. 7.1 Program Improvement Map for Developmental Mathematics in Community Colleges

Figure 7.1 offers a prototype program improvement map for guiding network activities in the Statway Collaboratory.[14] At first glance, it is apparent that this map aims to convey a systems perspective. The "challenge space" seeks to identify the organizational elements that need to be addressed in striving toward the targeted outcomes for students. For example, the map recognizes that improvement poses challenges for both the instructional and the human resource systems. This recognition is meant to stem the competing interventions problem that often results when policymakers, researchers, and practitioners gravitate toward one or another reform idea, believing that this is the silver-bullet solution. The program improvement map

---

[14] Our intent here is not to argue for the adequacy of the specific details offered, but simply to illustrate the system character of a problem and how it might be "carved at the joints" to guide subsequent efforts.

highlights the fact that there are no simple solutions. It documents how any specific solution likely will touch many other aspects of the problem space well beyond the confines of its own box. Consequently, the adaptive integration of a component solution within its larger organizational context is now placed firmly on the design table.

In short, the purpose of a tool like a program improvement map is to provide an end-to-end description of the challenge space. It encourages members of a networked improvement community to locate specific interventions in the larger problem space and begin to anticipate and problem solve around the systemic interconnections of any intervention. In this light, an intervention is, in essence, a hypothesized solution path through the program improvement map's space.

Driver Diagrams

Complementing the program improvement map is a second tool—the driver diagram. Drawing on a practice from improvement science (Langley et al. 1996), a driver diagram encourages network actors to explicate causal thinking; that is, how a proposed solution path responds to current understandings of the problem. The driver diagram requires attention to the specific hypotheses undergirding improvement solutions. These hypotheses are open to explicit study with common modes of inquiry. We now consider methods of inquiry.

In general, a driver diagram has three key elements: targets, primary drivers, and secondary drivers. The target is one of the community's agreed upon outcomes from the program improvement map. The primary drivers are the major causal explanations hypothesized to produce currently observed results. Secondary drivers, in contrast, are interventions in the system aimed at advancing improvement toward targets. Any argument for a specific secondary driver must explicate thinking about how a proposed intervention interconnects with understandings about primary causes or primary drivers for the outcomes currently observed. In so doing, an explicit causal explanation of problem–solution is developed. This can then be tested and refined against evidence.

Figure 7.2 illustrates a simple driver diagram. We begin with a specific target: Doubling the number of students that sustain effort to complete developmental mathematics in one year.[15] In this illustration, four primary drivers are hypothesized. The first focuses on problems associated with student course transitions. We know that we lose large numbers of students at transition points, for instance, when they complete one developmental course but may not enroll in the next. (Indeed, for many students, three to four developmental math courses may be required before reaching a credit-bearing class, and this may take two or more years to complete.)

---

[15]Given the space limits of the paper, we have constrained the example to a very rudimentary exposition. Our intent is simply to illustrate the tool rather than argue the merits of this particular instantiation.

7 Getting Ideas into Action: Building Networked Improvement Communities...

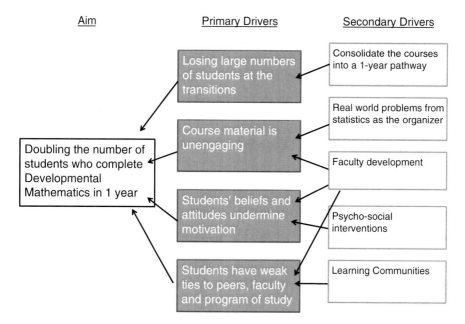

Fig. 7.2 Driver Diagram

Seeing the problem in this way led us to a specific change proposal: consolidate the pathway to one year of intensive instruction and have students enroll in a single pathway rather than separate courses where they have multiple opportunities to fall off the tracks. The latter is called a secondary driver.

Typically, a driver diagram includes multiple interrelated hypotheses about the presenting problem and plausible solutions.[16] Figure 7.2 offers three additional examples of primary drivers: the problem of unengaging course materials; students' beliefs that they are not good at math; and weak social ties that do not strongly connect students to peers, to faculty, and to a specific program of study. In turn, each of these primary drivers links to a specific secondary driver or hypothesized improvement intervention. To solve the problem of unengaging course materials, for example, we might use real-world concerns and analysis of relevant data as the backbone of instruction. To help students develop a stronger self-concept, we might introduce short-term psychosocial interventions that have proven to change student beliefs about efficacy of personal effort. And finally to develop more robust social ties, we might consider

---

[16] We note that in use the adequacy of a driver diagram is subject to empirical test. If all of the primary drivers have been identified, and an organization demonstrates change on each, then measureable improvements on the specified targets should occur. If the latter fails to materialize, some aspect of the driver diagram is underspecified. At base here is an organizing idea in science. Measurement and theory development move hand-in-hand. Theory sets out what we should measure; measurement in turn forces clarification on theory.

whether interventions such as learning communities might provide a vehicle for creating social capital for success. More generally, primary drivers may link to multiple interventions or secondary drivers. Likewise, a secondary driver also may respond to multiple primary drivers. For example, explicit attention may focus a faculty development initiative, a secondary driver, on both the importance of relational practices that sustain student engagement in instruction and the limited expectations that faculty may convey inadvertently about students' possibilities for success.

In sum, explicit problem decomposition coupled to explicit causal logic in intervention design is a critical agent guiding activity across a networked improvement community. Program improvement maps and driver diagrams are two promising, analytic tools that could be used to support coordinated work. Intellectually powerful forces anchored in personal belief and role-specific experiences tend to direct interveners away from systems thinking and toward silver-bullet solutions. A tool kit that includes program improvement maps and driver diagrams can discipline a community of interveners to see problems with larger, common eyes even as they may intervene in very specific ways. Regardless of whether the particular tools introduced here are actually used, we posit that the basic functions served by them must be addressed in some fashion for an improvement network to learn.

Common Protocols for Inquiry

Effective network action also requires common protocols that allow participants to share, test, and generalize local learning across a professional community of practice. As Hiebert et al. (2002) have noted, such common inquiry protocols distinguish activity aimed at building professional knowledge from individual clinical decision making.

We posit that a networked improvement community must engage in a disciplined approach to inquiry. For this purpose, we draw from core principles in continuous improvement pioneered by Deming, Juran, and others (e.g., Deming 2000; Juran 1962). We especially are indebted to insights gleaned from extensive use of these principles in advancing healthcare services improvement. Like education, health services are carried out through complex organizations. (Think of a hospital or a network of hospitals being comparable in complexity to a community college system that spans multiple campuses or a school district.) Like physicians, school and college faculty expect to have discretion to determine how best to respond to a particular set of presenting circumstances. Both enterprises are human and social resource intensive, and both operate under largely decentralized governance arrangements while also being subjected to increasing external regulation.[17]

---

[17] Of note, the primary mode of inquiry in this applied domain does not typically follow the clinical trials methodology that characterizes the development and marketing of new drug treatments. The more common protocol involves establishing a baseline of results and comparing subsequent performance against this baseline. See for example, Gawande (2007, 2009).

Research on health services improvement has surfaced recently in popular accounts such as Gawande's *Better* (2007) and more recently the *Checklist Manifesto* (2009). A dynamic group of leaders has been building this field for over two decades.[18] Particularly noteworthy are the efforts of Berwick and colleagues (2008) at the Institute for Healthcare Improvement (IHI) who pioneered a set of inquiry practices and conceptual frameworks that are now broadly applied to improving health services worldwide.

A core set of principles undergirds this work and forms a science of improvement (Berwick 2008).[19] As is customary in scientific inquiry, common protocols discipline the work carried out by individual participants. These protocols guide local efforts to introduce changes and examine whether these changes actually are improvements. This is akin to Englebart's "B-level learning activity" mentioned earlier. Simultaneously, these protocols also structure possibilities for accumulating evidence from diverse inquiries occurring across varied contexts and time. They afford data for examining the replicability of results, as is the focus of a meta-analysis. Even more important, the breadth of evidence generated, coupled with diversity among network contexts and participants, creates opportunities for new synthetic insights to arise that are unlikely to occur within any one study. In short, these common protocols operate as structuring agents for the systematic interorganizational learning that characterizes the C-level activity detailed by Englebart. Such learnings are largely missing in educational R&D at present. Instead, we live stuck between two polar views. On the one hand, a robust infrastructure has emerged for examining narrow, focused propositions through large, randomized field trials. On the other hand, there is a long tradition in education of local learning from the actions of individual practitioners. In the following, we discuss these two traditions of translational and action research and argue for a third way.

In its idealized form, translational research envisions a university-based actor drawing on some set of disciplinary theory, such as learning theory, to design an intervention. This activity is sometimes described as pushing research into practice (see, for example, Coburn and Stein 2010:10). After an initial pilot, the intervention is then typically field tested in a small number of sites in an efficacy trial. If this proves promising, the intervention is then subject to a rigorous randomized control trial to estimate an overall effect size. Along the way, the intervention becomes more specified and detailed. Practitioner advice may be sought during this process, but the ultimate goal is a standard product to be implemented by practitioners as designed. It is assumed that positive effects will accrue generally, regardless of local context, provided the intervention is implemented with fidelity.

In contrast, action research places the individual practitioner, or some small group of practitioners, at the center. The specification of the research problem is highly contextualized and the aim is localized learning for improvement. While both theory and evidence play a role, the structures guiding inquiry are less formalized.

---

[18] For a very readable historical narrative on this account, see Kenney (2008).

[19] Throughout this essay we use interchangeably the terms science of improvement and improvement research. One or the other may be more connotative depending upon context and audience.

Common constructs, measures, inquiry protocols, and methods for accumulating evidence typically receive even less emphasis. The strength of such inquiry is the salience of its results to those directly engaged. How this practitioner knowledge might be further tested, refined, and generalized into a professional knowledge, however, remains largely unaddressed (Hiebert et al. 2002).

A science of improvement offers a productive synthesis across this research–practice divide. It aims to meld the conceptual strength and methodological norms associated with translational research to the contextual specificity, deep clinical insight, and practical orientation characteristic of action research. To the point, the ideas sketched below are consistent with the basic principles of scientific inquiry as set out by the National Research Council (Shavelson and Towne 2002).[20]

A Continuous Improvement Ethic Engaged Across a Network

Shared narratives integrate collective experience. The main theme in the narrative for an improvement network is *learning through doing*.[21] Multiple cycles of design, engineering development characterize the improvement efforts occurring within a participating classroom, college, or individual commercial firm.[22] In principle, each cycle propels some bit of local learning. When parallel development activities occur in different sites at the same time, a network can learn from the ensemble of these experiences. This increases the overall odds of efficacious outcomes emerging more reliably at scale. This practice of learning through doing enlivens the mantra of continuous improvement that "deficits are a treasure."[23] Each process failure provides an opportunity to learn and to improve both locally and networkwide.

Cronbach sketched out this approach to the social organization of applied research over 30 years ago. Cronbach (1980) argued that sturdy evidence to inform improvement at scale is more likely to arise out of a fleet of studies rather than one big field trial. Although the causal warrant for results in any one small study may

---

[20] Shavelson and Towne (2002) identify six core principles. These include: specific questions to be investigated empirically, theory guides the investigation and generating cumulative knowledge is a goal, use of methods that permit a direct investigation of the question, a coherent and explicit chain of reasoning, efforts to replicate findings across a range of time and places and synthesize and integrate results, and open research to scrutiny and critique where objectivity derives from the enforced norms of a professional community. All of these are operationalized across an improvement research network.

[21] For a classic exposition of these ideas, see Lewin (1942).

[22] The ideas developed in this section apply equally to all participants in a networked improvement community. Depending upon the particular improvement objective, the units of interest might be individual classrooms, study centers within community colleges, departments, or entire colleges. They also apply to commercial firms developing new tools, goods, and services for this marketplace. In the interest of simplicity, we use the term colleges as a placeholder for this larger and more varied domain of participants.

[23] http://www.ihi.org/IHI/Topics/Improvement/ImprovementMethods/ImprovementStories/TreatEveryDefectasaTreasure.htm

well be weaker than the standards espoused for a rigorous clinical trial, a fleet of coordinated inquiries can generate much richer information about how an innovation actually functions when diverse participants are working in varied organizational contexts and time periods. The latter is essential knowledge for achieving efficacious outcomes more reliably at scale.[24]

This idea reminds us of the two spans of the inference problem identified by Cornfield and Tukey (1956). Getting a precise estimate about a treatment effect in a fixed setting, as for example in some nonrandomly selected set of sites studied in an educational randomized control trial, takes us only part way from data to practical inference. One must still negotiate a second span, which is the capacity of such data to actually guide improvement.[25] As Cornfield and Tukey point out, the two spans sit in some tension with one another and useable research entails effective compromise.[26] Applied research in education today has become hyper-concerned with the internal validity of the individual field trial. Treatises on modern causal inference place primacy on the word "cause" while largely ignoring concerns about the applicability of findings to varied people, places, and circumstances.[27] In contrast, improvement research must take this on as a central concern if its goal is useable knowledge to inform broad scale change. This consideration has important implications, as we will elaborate further.

The Central Role of Practical Measurement

While individual practitioners may rely on personal observations for their learning, improvement at scale entails common measurement.[28] The latter is key to learning across a network from the natural variation arising within it. Such measurement

---

[24] A close parallel to this in healthcare is the idea of complex treatment regimes. For a good example, see the *Patients Like Me* web site (http://www.patientslikeme.com/) as a knowledge base for chronic care. Patients have individual treatment histories and may be involved in multiple therapies simultaneously. Data to inform "what is right for me" involves more complex information structures than the on-average results derived from randomized control trials of individual therapies.

[25] Formally, Cornfield and Tukey (1956) used the term inference, meaning how one might apply the results of an experiment to a larger and different set of cases. Modern causal inference places primacy on the word "cause" and not the idea of "generalization." The latter in contrast is key to Cornfield and Tukey's argument.

[26] See also the classic distinction between internal and external validity introduced in Campbell and Stanley (1963) and further elaborated in Cook and Campbell (1979).

[27] See Weisberg (2010) for an explication of this argument.

[28] Note, we focus here on the common core of data that regularly informs the work of NIC participants and provides one basis for cross-network learning. A subnetwork within a NIC can, of course, also engage in specialized individual studies and one-time field trials. In fact, we are organizing as part of Statway an "alpha lab" that would bring an expanding array of applied researchers into this problem-solving research. The initial agenda for the alpha lab will focus on opportunities to deepen students' mathematics understandings, strengthen motivation for sustained work in the Pathway, and address literacy and language demands in statistics instruction.

includes longer term outcomes, both intended and unintended. It also requires attention to process measures and shorter term effects on students. For example, in our developmental mathematics education network, we will track long-term outcomes such as the percentage of students who successfully complete a college-level math course, or eventually earn an AA degree or transfer to a four-year institution. These are key summative measures, but they also tend to operate as lagging indicators. If some important process changes are affected, a jump in these aggregate indicators may accrue a year or two later. In general, real process improvements manifest in lagging indicators sometimes well after the actual improvements have occurred.

While summative lagging indicators are important, improvement research also needs data about specific program processes and student experiences as these occur in real time.[29] This evidence is key for informing more microlevel activities linked to longer term student success. For example, extant research suggests that the nature of students' initial engagement with their community college during the first two or three weeks of enrollment is critical.[30] Data about students' academic behaviors and experiences during these critical weeks are key to understanding whether a pathway design is reducing early disengagement. Such data also may be used formatively to improve quick outreach efforts to students before they actually disengage.

In short, the learning through doing orientation of a NIC requires data systems capable of informing ongoing activity. Data collection must be embedded into, rather than added on top of, the day-to-day work of program participants.[31] Inquiry now functions as a regular organizational activity rather than being thought of as a separate one-time enterprise. Consequently, improvement research requires the negotiation of an exchange relation between the time required for data collection and the utility of the information generated. To be sure, traditional psychometric concerns found in academic research still matter; but measurement in a continuous improvement context also places primacy on its informative quality for use in practice.[32] Such data must have prescriptive value, that is, provide evidence that might help clinicians think and act better given some specific problem at hand, and be accessible in a timely fashion

---

[29] We note that these also create a basis for more microlevel process targets. In doing so, a network may catalyze the formation of subnetworks working on improving the same microprocesses and aspiring to the same common microtargets. The overall logic of the NIC still applies but now at a more microlevel.

[30] See the extensive work on this topic using the Survey of Entering Student Engagement (http://www.ccsse.org/sense/).

[31] This idea has been developed in some detail at IHI. See: http://www.ihi.org/IHI/Topics/Improvement/ImprovementMethods/Measures/

[32] By way of example, there is great interest today in teacher assessments. Considerable attention now is directed toward developing protocols for rating classroom instruction and judging the quality of these protocols to the extent that they correlate with classroom level value-added measures of student learning. Predictive validity is viewed as the main criterion for judging instrument quality. One can envision instruments that rate relatively high by this standard, but afford little guidance as to what teachers need to learn or do differently to actually affect improvements in student learning. The latter is the informative quality of the assessment—does it signal what we value/want others to actually attend to?

to inform such decision making. We call this *practical measurement* and view it as a core agent structuring inquiry in a networked improvement community.[33]

Understanding Variability in Performance

Closely related to the emphasis on practical measurement is a second key feature structuring empirical activity in a NIC: attention to variability in performance and the multiple factors that may contribute to it. Most field trials formally assume that there is some fixed treatment effect (also known as a standardized effect size) to be estimated. If pressed, investigators acknowledge that the estimate is actually an average effect over some typically nonrandomly selected sample of participants and contexts. Given the well-documented experiences that most educational interventions can be shown to work in some places and not others, we would argue that a more realistic starting assumption is that interventions will have variable effects and these variable effects may have predictable causes. We expect, for example, that Statway effects will vary depending on specific characteristics of students, faculty, and the contexts in which they both work. This perspective leads to a very different organizing question for study. Rather than asking whether an "intervention works," a networked improvement community asks, "what works, when, for whom, and under what sets of circumstances?"

Put somewhat differently, improvement research focuses our attention on the information necessary to make interventions work reliably at scale. Rather than thinking about a tool, routine, or some other instructional resource as having proven effectiveness, improvement research directs efforts toward understanding how such artifacts can be adaptively integrated with efficacy into varied contexts, for different kinds of students, and for use by diverse faculty.

A Commitment to Contrasts and Comparisons

Understanding what works when, for whom and in which contexts, also places demands on how network participants design their individual inquiries so that practical inferences can be drawn about outcome variability. In principle, we need information from each improvement cycle on the outcomes that occurred, and how these link to specific characteristics of participants, contexts, and possibly time. Accumulating this evidence, and making comparisons and contrasts across it, provides the basis for examining variability both locally and across the network. It enhances possibilities for C-level learning to occur.[34]

---

[33] This is closely related to the idea of unobtrusive measures described by Webb et al. (1966).

[34] Almost four decades ago, Light and Smith (1971) detailed such an accumulating evidence strategy. While these proved formative ideas for the emergence of meta-analysis (i.e., the quantitative synthesis of research findings), Light and Smith actually cast their arguments in terms of the prospective design of a program of applied research rather than post hoc search for patterns in previously published results. It is this idea that we return to here.

Here, too, an effective compromise must be sought. Clearly, only a small number of questions can be examined at any given time and in any one place. As noted earlier, careful specification of the improvement target helps to discipline these inquiries. Tools such as the driver diagram and program improvement map assist in priority setting within this shared problem terrain. In a complementary fashion, a common inquiry protocol—the PDSA cycle—assists as well.

A Promising Tool to Structure Inquiry: The PDSA Cycle

The plan-do-study-act (PDSA) cycle is a broadly used tool in improvement research across different fields (Langley et al. 1996). Used across a network, it allows activity to occur simultaneously in different contexts, but in ways that evidence can actually accumulate.[35]

The protocol below vitalizes four core questions guiding improvement research:

1. How do we understand the presenting problem, including the organizational systems in which it is embedded?
2. What precisely are we trying to accomplish (meaning what are the targets for the improvement research)?
3. What changes might we introduce toward these ends?
4. How will we know if these changes are an improvement?

We sketch below how PDSA cycles can structure disciplined inquiries by individual participants and also function as the warp and weft of a networked improvement community (see Fig. 7.3).

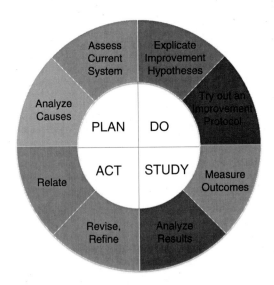

Fig. 7.3 The PDSA cycle

---

[35] See Shavelson and Towne (2002) on the role of common methods as part of a practice of disciplined inquiry.

Plan. This phase directly addresses the first of the improvement research questions: How do we understand the presenting problem and the organizational system in which it is embedded? Whenever an improvement problem comes into view, educators grasp for possible solutions. They focus in on options that seem plausible given their particular professional background, organizational role, and the standard operating procedures and norms of their respective organizations. Given that problems like the high failure rates in developmental mathematics are often complex system failures, these individual "point-of-view analyses" often come up short. To be sure, deep insights can be gained by viewing a problem deeply through a particular perspective. (By way of example, think of the microscope.) However, going deep also can blur our vision about the context that immediately surrounds the deep view and interacts with it. (By analogy, think of a wide-angle lens that locates a set of microscopes within a larger terrain.)

It is here where a networked improvement community benefits from shared tools such as program improvement maps and driver diagrams. Working with common frameworks during the planning phase encourages participants to build on and further explicate shared understandings of what otherwise might be tacit and partial explanations about the nature of a problem and the larger system in which it is embedded. The planning process creates a mechanism for participants to identify and articulate locally specific knowledge and how it fits into a larger tapestry. In doing so, it structures communicative processes, anchored now in the common language system conveyed in program improvement maps and driver diagrams that enhance network capacity to co-learn from diverse initiatives. We note that a common language framework functioned as a core organizing element in both the International Technological Semiconductor roadmap and the Linux development networks. More generally, it also has been identified as an essential characteristic of effective design communities (Norman 1988).

In addition, disciplined planning makes manifest a network narrative that all participants are researchers about practice and its improvement. As is customary in research communities, participants theorize about alternative mechanisms, plausible causes, and effects. Consequently, an explicit goal for the community is to develop a working theory of practice and its improvement. Such theory likely will entail an eclectic mix of extant practices, hunches about effective new interventions, and more basic research findings. Presumably, the working theory will be underspecified in the early stages of a community's work. The expectation is not perfection in its initial manifestation, but rather a good starting point. Through multiple PDSA cycles over time and contexts, the network advances on two meta goals: (1) specifying, refining, testing, and accumulating more effective practices and (2) simultaneously evolving better improvement theory to guide subsequent rounds of work. This developmental dynamic is represented in Fig. 7.4.

Do. In the "Do Phase," rapid trials are launched that generate evidence about both the specific practices being attempted and the improvement hypotheses that undergird them. This phase addresses improvement questions two and three, "What specifically do we hope to accomplish and what changes will we introduce toward this end?"

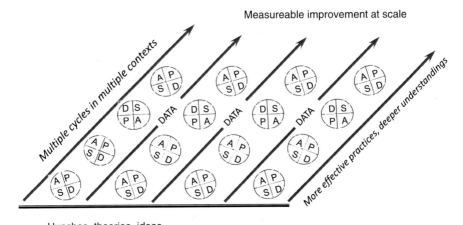

Fig. 7.4 Multiple PDSA cycles over time and across contexts

The spirit of improvement research is to get a trial quickly into the field to test improvement hypotheses. Rather than trying to solve all of the institutional problems that might need to be addressed if this proposed change were to be taken up broadly (and the endless meetings that this would likely entail), network participants embrace a spirit of rapid prototyping—try it quickly, learn from it cheaply, revise, and retry.[36] As corollary, in our Statway work, we expect, and in fact value, that each college may implement the improvement solution somewhat differently, given local system constraints. So long as these planned differences are documented and useable data about local efficacy is gathered, the network has an opportunity to build general knowledge about whether and how an intervention can be made to work under varied circumstances.

Study. It is here where the fourth improvement question is directly addressed— "How will we know if the proposed change is actually an improvement?" It is human nature to believe in the efficacy of one's work, and the field of education is replete with individual testimonials about effective programs. Improvement research, however, requires adherence to rudiments of experimental design in order to create an empirical warrant for such assertions. This is captured succinctly in the phrase (often attributed to Deming): "In God we trust; all else bring data." Each PDSA cycle must establish a plausible counterfactual and test local outcomes against it. In practice, improvement researchers often employ an interrupted time series design. An outcomes baseline is established, and subsequent performance is tracked against this baseline. Observed gains over and above the baseline provide evidence of an

---

[36] Since the Statway network begins as an innovation zone, this is the alpha development phase discussed in Bryk and Gomez (2008). To function as an innovation network has implications for selection of the initial charter members of the network, placing a premium on individuals and contexts conducive to such work.

intervention's effect. In this design, the baseline functions as the counterfactual—the outcomes we would have expected to occur absent the intervention.

As with measurement, the choice of design in improvement research is a pragmatic affair. Emphasis is afforded to nimbleness (i.e., how can we learn quickly from an individual PDSA cycle?) and practicality (i.e., how can the design of such inquiries be embedded naturally into the work life of the organization?). It is important to recognize that sturdy knowledge can accrue from a fleet of such studies, even with relatively simple designs for individual cycles of inquiry.[37] The latter especially is true when the goal is documenting large effects, and evidence of such effects can be found across multiple cycles over time and contexts. Under these circumstances, the likelihood of drawing a false generalization about improvement is greatly diminished.

In addition, it is important to remember that improvement research expects effects to vary as a function of student, staff, and organizational context characteristics. Especially when the number of concomitant factors is large and unknown, we need to rely on systematic analyses of naturally occurring variation across a network to learn about the conditions under which such variation arise.[38] A richly documented fleet of studies is an essential resource in this regard.

Act. As noted earlier, a NIC is organized around fast iterative cycles of design, engineering, and development. The idea is to test fast, fail fast and early, learn, and improve. Consequently, revision and refinement characterize the act phase. This phase also returns attention to systems thinking. While innovation development may focus on the design of some specific new tool, instructional resource, organizational role or routine, the act phase may raise new questions about how these artifacts interconnect with extant practices and local context. Getting these interconnections right can be key to achieving efficacy at scale.[39]

---

[37] To be sure, randomized trials remain the strongest design to implement in improvement research when practical. However, it is important to note that the results of randomized control are not always definitive. Weisberg (2010) documents that clinical trials can actually lead to biased conclusions when the causal effect of an intervention varies across cases (p. 23; also Weisberg et al. 2009). Not only the magnitude, but also the direction of effects may be erroneous. Since improvement research begins with an assumption of variable effects, this caution is noteworthy.

[38] For a partial example of this, see Bryk et al. (2010). Under a radical school decentralization in Chicago, significant new resources and authorities were devolved to individual schools precipitating in a natural experiment in school change and improvement. Through systematic longitudinal inquiry, the authors developed in conjunction with local leaders a working theory of school improvement, a practical measurement system to characterize changes school by school, over time, and linked this in turn to a series of value-added estimates over time, to changes in student learning. Both the working theory of practice improvement that evolved here and specific empirical evidence were taken up in continuous improvement efforts in local schools and systemwide.

[39] The conduct of improvement research documented in the *Checklist Manifesto* provides a concrete example of this. Once Gawande (2009) had established the efficacy of the checklist in his own surgical theater, the team undertook a field study that deliberately introduced the checklist into a highly varied set of healthcare settings in terms of fiscal resources, cultural norms organizing relations among physicians and nurses, and basic organizational capacities. A key design concern at this point was whether and how this routine could be integrated into practice in organizations that were quite different than the context of original development. This is a textbook case of the problem of integrative adaptivity.

Looking at this from Englebart's C-level perspective, the network aims to develop high reliability interventions consisting of good materials, technology tools, well-specified routines, support services, and so on. Rather than conceiving of scaling solely as a matter of implementing these artifacts as designed (or what some describe as "with fidelity"), the NIC also focuses on *integrative adaptivity* as a core design problem. It assumes that any new intervention subsequently will be picked up by different participants who must make it work within their particular organizational context. Therefore, C-level activity focuses explicitly on how an innovation can be made to function well in the hands of diverse individuals working under highly varied circumstances.[40] To the point, it is not good enough to know that Statway can be made to work in a few places. The network aims to build useable knowledge for the larger field.

This is another place where a fleet of studies conducted across a network of inquiry is a special resource. In contrast to a more traditional educational R&D center, a NIC opens up possibilities for harvesting the wisdom of crowds.[41] Iterative cycles occurring within each individual site naturally focus attention on how to make the intervention work in that site. Parallel activity occurring simultaneously across a network of sites creates a naturally evolving evidence base for refining designs and generalizing how an intervention can be made to work more broadly. Within each individual site, the specificity of a local context interacts with principled design of the intervention as just described.[42] Working through these transactions across a network of sites places the question of integrative adaptivity (i.e., how do I make this work in different contexts?) squarely at the center of network-level inquiry. Such learning is key to achieving efficacy and reliably at scale. It is the journey of transversing Cornfield and Tukey's dual span from data to inference.[43]

---

[40] Of note, both of the polar positions laid out earlier (translation research and action research) deflect attention away from this question. Under the translation paradigm, the aim is to standardize the treatment, and evidence on treatment variability is considered as implementation failure. The responsibility for the latter is externalized to the local context. In action research, all of the complexity and dynamism of the context are embraced, but how an innovation might effectively travel to another locale is not generally a core subject of inquiry. In contrast, this is a core inquiry goal for a NIC.

[41] See Surowiecki (2004).

[42] For an illustrative example, see how in the *Checklist Manifesto*, Gawande and colleagues systematically addressed utility of their prototype checklist by deliberately moving the checklist out to eight very different contexts. The key learning objective in this phase of the work (what we have termed beta phase inquiry) is whether this could be made to work in a very different institutional and cultural context, and if so, what would it take. This is explicit inquiry about integrative adaptivity.

[43] We note that this basic phenomenon continues in the beta phase where innovations move into new contexts. Inevitably, some accommodations may be needed to integrate the initiative into these new settings. Accomplishing this well entails an analytic practice where local conditions must intersect with the principled design of the intervention (Coburn and Stein 2010). The knowledge generated at the network level, by synthesizing learning efforts at multiple sites, is key to discerning how and the conditions necessary for the intervention to be reliably engaged in other places.

Next Big Questions

We argued in our earlier essay that educational R&D has little capacity to focus on sustained and coordinated educational problem solving. Improvement efforts abound in schools, colleges, and classrooms. Academic research grows at an accelerating pace and a large marketplace exists for commercial goods and services. But collectively, this is not adding up in ways that advance substantial improvements at scale. As an alternative, we have introduced the idea of a networked improvement community and detailed a conceptual framework for organizing the basic rules of a new approach. Next we address the question of how such a network actually comes into existence.

Evangelizing Leadership

Counter to some prevailing myths, networks engaged in collective complex product development are not self-organizing (Weber 2004). In each of the effective networks we have examined, a small number of opinion leaders played a critical role in building followership and securing moral authority for organizing the rules of the game. Each, with their own style, evangelized the vision, set goals for the collective project, persuaded others of its viability, and invited participation. For example, Berwick and colleagues crusaded the central tenets of quality improvement with an initially skeptical healthcare profession. They reframed medical complications as errors and provided hospitals with proof-cases that these could indeed be avoided. IHI was formed as an integrative context where healthcare professionals and institutions could come together to pursue this vision. Similarly, Torvalds recognized a niche for interested programmers primed to work on an open-source basis and offered an early working version of a kernel operating system as catalyst for development of the Linux community. Likewise, a cadre of Silicon Valley leaders including Noyce, Moore, Galvin, and Sporck (Schaller 2004:549) took up the mantle within their industry, arguing that cooperative efforts on a common roadmap constituted a valuable collective good in what otherwise operates as a highly competitive business environment.[44]

An Integrative Hub

In tandem with the evangelizing described above, initiating leaders also took on the role of designer as each created a hub for the network. As Goldsmith and Eggers (2004) detail: "The job of this network designer is to identify possible partners,

---

[44]This evangelizing role is now being pursued by the Statway program senior partners as they reach out to community colleges, professional associations, policy and foundation leaders, and the academic research community. Institutionally, the Carnegie Foundation seeks to draw on its reputation as a neutral broker and convener, as a resource in forming the connective tissue necessary for the Statway network to take root and grow.

bring all the relevant stakeholders to the table, analyze current in-house operations, determine and communicate to all the members the expectations of how the network will function, assemble and enmesh all the pieces of the network, devise strategies to maintain the network and finally, activate it" (2004:55). While living on the plane of ideas as in our earlier essay (Bryk and Gomez 2008), these considerations could easily remain unaddressed. As we sought to move these ideas into action, however, this hub function suddenly loomed very large.

In general, the hub's role is to function as an initiator of activity and an integrative force for the overall enterprise. When we looked across our three illustrative cases, a set of common objectives emerged: The hub aims to build field consensus on the importance of the problem and promising pathways to solutions. It seeks to catalyze network engagement, bringing more leaders and champions to the movement. It develops the initial version of the structuring agents and norms for participation. It maintains a technology core, such as a dynamic knowledge repository organized around the program improvement map and community use platform. It also provides analytic capacity to support B-level activity out in individual sites and has lead responsibilities for cross-institutional, C-level learning. Finally, it needs to secure lines of support that flow to network participants for initiation and growth.

Managing Micro–Macro Dynamics

Forming such a network also requires consideration of incentives and governance. Weber (2004) notes that the effective functioning of an intentional network requires solutions to two fundamental problems in formal organization. First at the microlevel, we need to understand why people might voluntarily allocate time and attention to such networks absent normal mechanisms of compensation. Second, at the macrolevel, we also must attend to how individuals' efforts are coordinated and sustained on developing a complex product. Absent the normal mechanisms of markets and/or hierarchical bureaucratic control, a new form of network governance must be articulated. In the early stages of operation, the hub engages in the preemptive design by establishing the initial rules of the game in accordance with the key structuring agents discussed above. Over time, however, all details are open to change and change should be expected as the network grows and evolves.

Creating Incentives

Absent a capacity to direct individuals' work through compensation, a networked improvement community must depend on alternate mechanisms for incenting participants to voluntarily allocate their time and resources to a collective project. Following Weber (2004), we argue that participation in networks is not purely altruistic. Rather, participation offers individuals many nonmonetary benefits documented in the network examples outlined here.

First, participants' ability to choose a specific microproblem to work on provides opportunities for diverse individuals to deploy their particular creative energies. Within a network, the ideas generated and the artifacts produced have a natural community of appreciation, and individuals are recognized for these contributions. The Linux community, for example, provides a forum where elegant programming solutions can be shared and are acknowledged. Contributors build a reputation within the community that is recognized on a much larger stage. Important hedonic rewards are triggered through social affiliation and the according of status. At a more instrumental level, talent that may have hidden in the workplace is brought into more public view and this increases opportunities for individual professional mobility.

Second, joining a network provides access to expertise of other participants, and this enables individuals to learn new skills. In many cases, network participation can be more efficient than going about solving local problems alone. Linux programmers, for example, report that their pursuit of network tasks actually facilitates work on their primary jobs.

Third, vibrant networks also tend to propel a shared identity among participants, anchored in a common narrative of an enlightened purpose or a common enemy. In the semiconductor industry, cooperation was catalyzed by a fear that Japan would overtake US dominance in the industry. Members of the Linux community believed that information should be free, so they banded together against their perceived enemy, which was Microsoft.

Enlivening networked improvement communities in education will require similar attention. The work structures and shared norms that we have described as fundamental to a networked improvement community depart in significant ways from the state of play in education today. Whereas engineers and software programmers are preconditioned to avoid solving the same problem twice, educators too often assume that their solutions must be invented anew in each context.[45] This means that initiating networked improvement communities will require explicit attention to incenting different kinds of thinking and behavior and to forming new norms.

Responding to these challenges entails consideration of multiple mutually reinforcing mechanisms that extend the message that cooperative participation is highly valued. The Statway network views all participants as researchers and developers. It does not reserve this status distinction only for academics from research universities. The network aims to create numerous and varied contexts where individuals' distinct expertise can come to the fore and be used and appreciated by peers. The Carnegie Foundation will bring visibility to these individuals' contributions through its print and digital media. The network needs new leaders and champions for its future growth. This means new work arenas and possible new career opportunities for at least some participants. Carnegie will use a longstanding Foundation initiative, The Carnegie Scholars of Teaching and Learning, as a formal designation to acknowl-

---

[45] It is interesting to note that these same arguments appear in the early history of the quality improvement movement in health services. Kenney's (2008) account details exchanges in this regard. There are several places in his text where one could easily exchange the words "doctors and hospitals" with "teachers and schools."

edge individuals who make major contributions and assume leadership roles. A sabbatical program offering a possible year in-residence at the Foundation represents still another mechanism for recognition. Likewise, the network seeks to incent institutional participation as well. It is important that community colleges be recognized and accorded status for their leadership. A possible elective Carnegie Classification might be used for this purpose.[46]

Evolving Governance

At present, we are focused on network initiation. Assuming participation is engaged, the ability of the network to sustain progress over time will depend on a crescent governance structure. In these forming days, the network hub is establishing a first iteration of the structuring agents. While the network is small, initiating leaders can serve as the main moderators of the community and in so doing establish norms for participation. As the network grows, so too does the time and energy required to make thoughtful decisions and justify them to the community. New structures must emerge to maintain collective agreements and sustain coherent future actions. In the cases we studied, network governance did not proceed along a preconceived path, but rather evolved over time in response to needs and conflicts that arose in the process of joint work. We expect that to happen in Statway as well. Over time, initiating structures likely will require multiple iterations of refinement and possible larger changes to accommodate network growth and movement toward becoming self-sustaining. We anticipate that tensions will need to be negotiated and accommodations made. While the final shape and organization of the network remains emergent, the clear intent is for the network governance to broaden beyond the initiating hub.

Choosing a License

In an open resource world, the license explicates the rights and responsibilities of network membership and creates ground rules for how pieces of the work are shared. It structures social transactions around intellectual property. Early in the development of Linux, Torvalds made the somewhat controversial decision to distribute the kernel code under a General Public License. At that point in the community's evolution, Torvalds single-handedly made the major decisions, but he did so with careful attention to what the community wanted, because product production depended on attracting large numbers of developers to work on the code. His license decisions were not based on any commitment to this particular type of license per se. Rather, the license was an instrument to facilitate the work of the community and scale participation.[47]

---

[46] There is a precedent in the elective community engagement classification that Carnegie established in 2005. Participation is voluntary and over 311 colleges have chosen to do so. It involves a detailed, data-based process of application and membership which has proven quite meaningful across the larger community.

[47] See Weber (2004), pp. 111–116.

Clearly, the choice of an appropriate license is key for growth of a networked R&D community. We are committed in principle to open resources and believe that all intellectual property derived by the network belongs to the network. Carnegie's role is to act as steward in this regard. The precise form of a license to deploy, however, remains an open question. We know that the license must incent the contributions of individual practitioners, researchers, and educational designers who operate in this space, but also those who bring different interests and seek different benefits from network participation. In short, a license must fit into a networked improvement community, not the other way around. A best practice is one that grows and sustains participation, focuses ongoing efforts on targeted priorities, and ultimately contributes to improvement reliably at scale.

The Work Ahead

Statway is Carnegie's first attempt to take on the integrative role of a network hub. We are working off of a set of empirically grounded hypotheses about how best to initiate and integrate a network that aims at social learning and complex product development. Through doing this, Carnegie will learn much about the essential functions of a network integrator. This chapter represents our evolving thinking to date on these matters. Our hub's first efforts have focused on creating vital connections out to colleges that afford a powerful context for innovation codevelopment. Drawing commercial partners into this work and thinking about how mutual benefit partnerships might be best structured here remain work on the horizon. Likewise, expanding engagement of the applied research community lies ahead. We have some forming ideas for initiating outreach in both of these domains, but that will be pursued in the future.

The Statway network is in an alpha or initiating phase. Its priorities now are concrete and practical. Can the hub codevelop with community colleges promising pathways for student success? Can it catalyze, sustain, and grow social participation in the charter colleges and beyond? Will it generate sufficient enthusiasm among the faculty in the initial network (including a sense of efficacy in their teaching and encouraging initial evidence on student learning) so that there is an eagerness to persist and recruit other colleagues into the work? Most important, can it vitalize both B-level and C-level learning for improvement? These are the primary concerns for evaluating alpha development in a networked improvement community.

Engaging disciplined-based research and researchers is essential throughout this work. Can emerging principles in cognitive science, for example, be translated into scalable instructional practices within Statway? Similarly, concerns about student engagement and motivation play a key role in the overall problem system. Can findings in social psychology, for example on identity development and stereotype threat, be exploited and in the process further tested here? Language and literacy issues also abound. Can researchers from these domains study and inform how the text, tasks, tests, and talk of mathematics instruction are made more productive?

These are but a few of the places where disciplinary theories meet practice and ultimately are tested and refined in the cauldron of making ideas work in action.

Assuming a successful initiation of the Statway NIC, phase II will focus on network growth. While original codevelopment efforts will continue in the initial set of college sites, a new inquiry objective moves into primary position in the beta phase. How do we make prototype interventions function reliably at scale in the hands of a more diverse faculty and working in more varied organizational contexts? Issues of institutional change come center stage and conceptual frameworks from organizational sociology and political science are key resources. Likewise as efforts scale, we also must assemble more nimble, robust and practical design and measurement strategies to continue to learn from practice and establish increasingly deep evidence warrant for the overall enterprise. Expertise in psychometrics and sociometrics becomes essential.

Subsequently, improvement becomes institutionalized in phase III. Core guidance shifts from the hub into the network that has evolved into a self-governed, professional community of practice improvement. Operating now at a very large scale, the network continues to invest in data mining strategies and other mechanisms as it seeks to continue to learn and improve from an ever-enlarging base of network level action. This is educational statistics and data analysis at large scale.

As we focus on problems of phase I network initiation, we also are attending to this developmental arc. We aim to supply a base of practical and robust artifacts, processes, work roles, and routines coupled with evidence of costs and efficacy that can be adaptively integrated by others. Likewise, we already are considering alternative strategies for the human and social resource development that will be needed in the future by others who wish to engage Statway in their particular circumstances. Further, we are moving to expand the network of academic expertise necessary to inform these developments.

Simultaneously, we also are advancing the demand side by focusing on both top and down strategies that aim to engage policy advocates, and grassroots strategies to mobilize faculty, staff, and community college leaders. From the start, we began developing for scale and see this task as both creating a supply innovation and catalyzing a demand for change. In conceptualizing scaling as a problem of collective learning, we target both supportive policy actions and seek to engage the minds and hearts of community college leaders, faculty, and staff. Ultimately, this is where scaling with efficacy will either succeed or fail in classrooms, schools, and colleges where students and educators must join together to advance learning.

In closing, we note that we have used the example of Statway to illustrate the themes of this chapter. We wish to reiterate that Statway is just one attempt to redress a larger concern—developing a more effective educational R&D infrastructure. A field is now emerging around new approaches to applied inquiry on problems of practice improvement. Each effort will entail multiple cycles of institutional design, engineering, and development. These too will follow a developmental arc, and structuring opportunities for community learning can accelerate improvement here, too. Much knowledge know-how can be gleaned from comparative analyses across multiple cases emerging in the field. Our hope is that this chapter functions as one such convening context where diverse individuals, sharing the common concern of strengthening educational R&D, might join in analysis and critique and ultimately advance a next stage in the evolution of educational improvement.

References

Bailey, T., D. W. Jeong, and S. W. Cho. 2008. Referral, enrollment, and completion in developmental education sequences in community colleges. CCRC Working Paper No. 15, Teachers College, Columbia University, New York.
Berwick, D.M. 2008. The science of improvement. *The Journal of the American Medical Association* 299(10): 1182–1184.
Boudett, K.P., E.A. City, and R.J. Murnane (eds.). 2005. *Data wise: A step-by-step guide to using assessment results to improve teaching and learning*. Cambridge: Harvard Education Press.
Bryant, M.J., K.A. Hammond, K.M. Bocian, M.F. Rettig, C.A. Miller, and R.A. Cardullo. 2008. School performance will fail to meet legislated benchmarks. *Science* 321(5897): 1781–1782.
Bryk, A.S. 2009. Support a science of performance improvement. *Phi Delta Kappan* 90(8): 597–600.
Bryk, A.S., and L.M. Gomez. 2008. Ruminations on reinventing an R&D capacity for educational improvement. In *The future of educational entrepreneurship: Possibilities of school reform*, ed. F.M. Hess, 181–206. Cambridge: Harvard Education Press.
Bryk, A.S., P.B. Sebring, E. Allensworth, S. Luppescu, and J.Q. Easton. 2010. *Organizing schools for improvement: Lessons from Chicago*. Chicago: University of Chicago Press.
Burkhardt, H., and A.H. Schoenfeld. 2003. Improving educational research: Toward a more useful, more influential, and better-funded enterprise. *Educational Researcher* 32(9): 3–14.
Campbell, D.T., and J.C. Stanley. 1963. Experimental and quasi-experimental designs for research and teaching. In *Handbook of research on teaching*, eds. N.L. Gage, 84. Chicago: Rand McNally.
Coburn, C.E., and M.K. Stein (eds.). 2010. *Research and practice in education: Building alliances, bridging the divide*. Lanham: Rowman and Littlefield Publishers.
Committee on a Strategic Education Research Partnership (SERP). 2003. Washington, DC: Strategic Education Research Partnership.
Cook, T.D., and D.T. Campbell. 1979. *Quasi-experimentation: Design and analysis issues for field settings*. Chicago: Rand McNally College Publishing Company.
Cornfield, J., and J.W. Tukey. 1956. Average values of mean squares in factorials. *Annals of Mathematical Statistics* 27: 907–949.
Cronbach, L.J. 1980. *Toward reform of program evaluation*. San Francisco: Jossey-Bass.
Cullinane, J. and U. Treisman. 2010. Improving developmental mathematics education in community colleges: A prospectus and early progress report on the Statway initiative. NCPR Working Paper, National Center for Postsecondary Research, New York.
Deming, W.E. 2000. *Out of the crisis*. Cambridge: MIT Press.
Englebart, D.C. 1992. *Toward high-performance organizations: A strategic role for groupware*. Groupware '92. San Jose: Morgan Kaufman Publishers.
Englebart, D. C. 2003. Improving our ability to improve: A call for investment in a new future. IBM Co-Evolution Symposium.
Gawande, A. 2007. *Better: A surgeon's notes on performance*. New York: Henry Holt.
Gawande, A. 2009. *Checklist manifesto: How to get things right*. New York: Metropolitan Books.
Goldsmith, S., and W.D. Eggers. 2004. *Governing by network: The new shape of the public sector*. Washington, DC: Brookings Institution Press.
Gomez, L. M., K. Gomez, and B. R. Gifford. 2010. Educational innovation with technology: A new look at scale and opportunity to learn. *Educational reform: Transforming America's*

Education through Innovation and Technology. Whistler: Aspen Institute Congressional Conference Program Papers.

Hiebert, J., R. Gallimore, and J.W. Stigler. 2002. A knowledge base for the teaching profession: What would it look like and how can we get one? *Educational Researcher* 31(5): 3–15.

Juran, J.M. 1962. *Quality control handbook*. New York: McGraw-Hill.

Kelly, G.J. 2006. Epistemology and educational research. In *The handbook of complementary methods in educational research*, eds. J.L. Green, G. Camilli, and P. Nelmore, 33–56. Mahwah: Erlbaum.

Kenney, C. 2008. *The best practice: How the new quality movement is transforming medicine*. New York: Public Affairs.

Langley, G.J., R.D. Moen, K.M. Nolan, T.W. Nolan, C.L. Norman, and L.P. Provost. 1996. *The improvement guide: A practical approach to enhancing organizational performance*. San Francisco: Jossey-Bass.

Lewin, K. 1942. Field theory of learning. *Yearbook of National Social Studies of Education* 41: 215–242.

Light, R.J., and P.V. Smith. 1971. Accumulating evidence: Procedures for resolving contradictions among different research studies. *Harvard Educational Review* 41: 429–471.

National Academy of Education. 1999. *Recommendations regarding research priorities: An advisory report to the national education research policy and priorities board*. New York: NAE.

Norman, D. 1988. *The design of everyday things*. New York: Currency Doubleday.

Paley, A.R. 2007. 'No Child' target is called out of reach. *The Washington Post*, March 14. Retrieved 1 September 2010 (http://www.washingtonpost.com/wp-dyn/content/article/2007/03/13/AR2007031301781.html).

Podolny, J.M., and K.L. Page. 1998. Network forms of organization. *Annual Review of Sociology* 24: 54–76.

Powell, W.W. 1990. Neither market nor hierarchy: Network forms of organization. *Research in Organizational Behavior* 12: 295–336.

Ruopp, R.G., S. Gal, S. Drayton, and B. Pfister. 1992. *Labnet: Toward a community of practice*. Hillsdale: Lawrence Erlbaum Associates.

Schaller, R.R. 2004. Technological innovation in the semiconductor industry: A case study of the international technology roadmap for semiconductors (ITRS). In *School of public policy*. Fairfax: George Mason University.

Schlager, M., J. Fusco, and P. Schank. 2002. Evolution of an on-line education community of practice. In *Building virtual communities: Learning and change in cyberspace*, eds. K.A. Renninger and W. Shumar. New York: Cambridge University Press.

Shavelson, R.J., and L. Towne (eds.). 2002. *Scientific research in education*. Washington, DC: National Academy Press.

Shirky, C. 2008. *The power of organizing without organizations*. New York: Penguin Press.

Surowiecki, J. 2004. *The wisdom of crowds*. New York: Anchor Books.

von Hippel, E. 2005. *Democratizing innovation*. Cambridge: The MIT Press.

Webb, E.J., D.T. Campbell, R.D. Schwartz, and L. Sechrest. 1966. *Unobtrusive measures: Nonreactive research in the social sciences*. Chicago: Rand McNally.

Weber, S. 2004. *The success of open source*. Cambridge: Harvard University Press.

Weisberg, H.I. 2010. *Bias and causation: Models and judgment for valid comparisons*. Hobokon: Wiley.

Weisberg, H.I., V.C. Hayden, and V.P. Pontes. 2009. Selection criteria and generalizability within the counterfactual framework: Explaining the paradox of antidepressant-induced suicide. *Clinical Trials* 6(2): 109–118.

Wenger, E. 1999. *Communities of practice: Learning, meaning and identity*. Cambridge: Cambridge University Press.

Chapter 8
Improving Teacher Quality: A Sociological Presage

Barbara Schneider, Erin Grogan, and Adam Maier

This chapter examines what sociology brings to studies of teacher effectiveness and why it is imperative for sociological perspectives to be a part of the discussions on teacher accountability systems, measures, and remediation. At the core of the discipline is the belief that research and scholarship should focus on those issues deeply connected to societal change (Coleman 1990; Dreeben 1994; Schneider 2003). The field of sociology of education has embraced this perspective, and scholars in this area have examined issues such as social mobility and social stratification, social organization of schools, social relationships and school reform, and opportunities for learning (Hallinan 2000a).[1]

With respect to schools, scholars have argued that the moral authority of schools resides within school personnel whose primary responsibility is the cognitive, social, and emotional development of their students (Bryk and Schneider 2002; Bryk 1988). This is not to minimize the role of the family in the process but a means to differentiate the boundaries between parent and school administrator and teacher

---

[1] *Handbook on the Sociology of Education* edited by Hallinan (2000a) provides one of the most comprehensive theoretical and empirical compendiums of the field of sociology of education. It is different from other recent anthologies in both theoretical scope and depth on understanding schools as societal institutions and what influences their organization, operation, and relationships with students, teachers, and parents both within and outside the USA.

B. Schneider (✉)
College of Education, Michigan State University, East Lansing, MI 48824, USA
e-mail: bschneid@msu.edu

E. Grogan
The New Teacher Project, Keene, NH 03431, USA
e-mail: egrogan@tntp.org

A. Maier
The New Teacher Project, Rochester Hills, MI 48307, USA
e-mail: amaier@tntp.org

responsibility (Bryk 1988). Parents and the wider community exercise control through local and state school boards that have direct responsibility for ensuring that the moral authority of schools is upheld. Traditionally, the moral authority of the schools has not directly involved the federal government. However, the passage of The No Child Left Behind Act of 2001 (NCLB 2002) substantially shifted the moral authority of schools to the federal government (Finn 2002; Ravitch 2010) and emphasized teachers' performance, minimizing the importance of the social context of schools.

NCLB greatly extended the reach of the federal government in education, altering what the purpose of education should be, when and how it should be measured, and what type of evidence should be used for its improvement (Schneider and Keesler 2007). Individual schools and teachers now are held accountable by the federal government for assuring that all public school students meet proficiency levels in reading, mathematics, and science. Schools in which a significant proportion of the student body do not make adequate yearly progress face severe financial and organizational penalties, including the firing of administrators and teachers. If over a 3-year period significant academic progress is not made by the entire student body, schools are slated for ultimate dissolution—although they could emerge as new schools operated by different public or private entities.

In this shift of power, states are delegated with enforcing new regulations that monitor public elementary and secondary schools and sanction those where student test scores fail to improve.[2] Drawing the federal and state governments into the operation of schools is significantly transforming the roles and responsibilities of school personnel—primarily teachers, who now are accountable not only to the students and their parents, but also the larger apparatus of district, state, and federal oversight provisions. Certainly, teachers have always been held accountable for the academic and social development of their students, but the major accountability function rested in the hands of the principal, teaching staff, and parent community (Ingersoll 2005). Now the process and measurement of teacher accountability have been in some sense moved from the auspices of the school to those of the state, where the criterion for teacher performance is improvement in student test scores.

This new accountability system designed to align student performance with individual teachers delves deeper into the once closed classroom by pinpointing problematic instructional situations.[3] Using standardized information to evaluate teachers and students creates something of a level playing field whereby performance is removed from localized subjective judgments that may be influenced by personal relationships. It is suggested that such systems could provide information that can be used for critical appraisal and perhaps innovation of teacher practice.

---

[2] To gain additional views on sociological perspectives on this federal educational policy, see Sadovnik et al. (2008).

[3] The reference to "closed classrooms" refers to the concept of loosely coupled systems described by Meyer and Rowan (1978).

On the other hand, accountability systems may place too much emphasis on being able to accurately measure student performance as a result of teacher performance (Ravitch 2010), encouraging cheating to raise scores (Levitt and Jacob 2003), dampening student motivation, and inhibiting flexibility in instructional practices (Coleman et al. 1997).[4]

The information typically used in state accountability systems to measure teacher effectiveness is relatively crude compared to that obtained through the intensive observational studies of schools and classrooms that have characterized research in sociology of education. Many school contextual factors, such as "teacher collegiality and relational trust" that have been shown to be critical elements for understanding changes in student performance (see Yasumoto et al. (2001) on the importance of collegiality and student achievement and Bryk and Schneider (2002) on relational trust), are missing from the discussions that currently dominate the rhetoric regarding teacher effectiveness. This lack of attention to contextual factors has jettisoned discussions of why some teachers are able to be successful with different types of students in some situations and not others (Rowan et al. 2002; Nye et al. 2004; Hanushek et al. 2005). Examining variability in social resources and its relationship to performance, whether in large organizations or smaller groups, is fundamental to the study of sociology (Dreeben 2003) yet often overlooked in present deliberations of teacher effectiveness.

Eroding Jurisdictional Authority of Teacher Professionalism

The sociological critique on teaching as a profession maintained for some time that teachers have considerable autonomy and control in their classrooms (Bidwell 2003). This view of the autonomous teacher seemed somewhat alterable by the standards movement of 1990s with states taking a stronger role in determining what should be taught in classrooms and placing a greater emphasis on testing. The standards movement focused on what students should know and be able to do and called for high-quality curricular frameworks and assessments tied to these standards. Additionally, part of the standards movement was the incorporation of professional development for teachers whose performance was directed toward meeting a defined set of standards (O'Day and Smith 1993). Despite the moves by states to enact standards, scholars were more cautious in their confidence in using standards as a mechanism to create lasting reform and to improve student performance and instruction (Swanson 2005). Researchers argued that this movement would have little impact

---

[4]The dampening of student motivation can impact both high- and low-ability students. Some may respond to the emphasis on evaluation of their teachers as an incentive to do well, whereas others may act quite differently, especially if their relationships and past performance with their teacher have been negative.

on changing the conduct of teaching, because the zone of legitimate authority remained in the hands of school administrators, leaving instruction and classroom-level decisions to teachers (Firestone 2003). Even in school systems where centralized administrators tried to revamp curricular reform, passive resistance by teachers suggested that instructional classroom practice would ultimately remain the providential domain of teachers (Hubbard et al. 2006).

What scholars did not predict was that the jurisdictional authority of teachers (i.e., those tasks which a profession claims are its authority; Abbott 1988) would become the legitimate purview of federal policymakers and would garner strong support from interest groups including philanthropic foundations.[5] Glazer (2008) suggests several reasons for this shift. His conceptualization suggests that the lack of jurisdictional authority of teachers can be linked to: (1) a shift in American's beliefs regarding what is a high-quality teacher; (2) inconsistency in teacher practice; and (3) variability in students' academic performance as evidenced by the less than stellar performance of US students compared with those in other nations, as well as the continuing achievement gap between whites and minorities, specifically blacks and Hispanics (National Center for Education Statistics 2010).[6]

Given these conditions, one serious question is whether the teaching profession can gain back its jurisdictional authority or if we will continue to see an eroding legitimate basis for teachers to act as monitors of their own professional practice. Some evidence exists to suggest that reasserting legitimacy will be difficult. First is the federal push for assessing teacher effectiveness using changes in students' test scores, which, although viewed as problematic by some scholars, has been gaining traction and legitimacy in state improvement plans. Second is continuing dissatisfaction with schools and colleges of education responsible for the training of teachers and growing federal and state interest in expanding alternative teacher training programs such as Teach for America (TFA). Third is increasing public sentiment, as evidenced by opinion polls, showing support for the notion that the slow pace of school improvement is directly linked to the quality of teachers and that the source of the problem is most likely related to the training and recruitment of teachers (Bushaw and Lopez 2010). Though often critiqued by researchers as methodologically flawed (Jacobsen 2009), polls and rankings of public schools and postsecondary institutions are used to validate public interest and establish reputational quality. Such negative public views on the quality of teaching are of concern, as they are not easily alterable without significant positive changes in student performance, especially for minority students with limited economic and social resources.

---

[5] The Gates Foundation recently has undertaken a multi-million dollar initiative to identify teacher effectiveness using primarily evidence from classroom video technology. The plan is for such information to be linked with state and other student assessment data.

[6] We have taken considerable liberty in reinterpreting Glazer's (2008) very interesting observations on the erosion of the jurisdictional authority of teachers.

Conceptions of Teacher Effectiveness

Today, teacher effectiveness typically is defined in terms of differences or variation in student achievement taking into account student background, classroom and school factors (Kane et al. 2008). The most common method for estimating teacher effects is value-added models (VAM). Employing statistical techniques that link individual teachers with student learning gains, these models estimate the unique contribution or "value added" of teachers on changes in learning outcomes net of student background characteristics (Konstantopoulos and Chung, 2011). These models have become increasingly commonplace, as federal legislation has encouraged the formulation of data systems that can move such analytic models forward.[7]

Using change in test score performance as a measure of teacher effectiveness, while important to sociological research on teaching as an occupation (Dreeben 2005; Johnson 2005) and for measuring school productivity (Bryk and Schneider 2002), rarely has been viewed as the sole unit of measurement for determining teacher success. From a sociological perspective, the contextual characteristics of the family, classroom, and school, not easily alterable by the teacher, have a significant and sustaining effect on student performance. To measure teacher effectiveness, sociological researchers have argued that assessments of occupational competence should consider organizing classrooms, establishing routines, imparting information and skills, explaining new material, changing activities, and managing the sociability among students, especially when they resist the flow of learning activities (McFarland 2004).

The major sociological thematic has been that organizational arrangements and conditions of the school and classroom play a central role in enabling and constraining efforts to improve instruction. Student performance is directly and indirectly affected by contextual factors including: curricular materials and access to technology (Roschelle et al. 2000); workplace norms, including collective responsibility for student achievement and academic press (Frank et al. 2004); and school leadership and management (McLaughlin and Talbert 2006). While these factors are fundamental to sociologists, their value is considered secondary, in both conceptual and statistical terms, by those social scientists now producing the bulk of research on teacher effectiveness. This theoretical distinction between sociologists and researchers in other social science fields is critical for measuring teacher effects, as those outside of sociology tend to conceive of the school as a singular unit that impacts all teachers in similar ways (see Koedel and Betts 2007 as an example of this approach).

In some respects, the current emphasis on evaluating the work of teachers in classrooms fits closely with earlier work by major figures in education such as John Dewey (1973) and Phillip Jackson (1968), and in sociology Robert Dreeben (1970).

---

[7]Large grants have been made to help states construct Statewide Longitudinal Data Systems (SDLS) that can link student performance with their teachers. These grants have been made to over three quarters of the 50 states to aid in the development and implementation of systems that will aid states and districts in assessing teacher effectiveness.

Scholars such as Dreeben have placed enormous value on studying life in classrooms. Although recognizing that the study of teaching is not highly valued in the discipline, Dreeben nevertheless encouraged sociologists to examine these situations to make progress in improving student achievement. Contrary to how teacher' work and assessment of their performance are being discussed today, Dreeben's interpretation of what life in classrooms is about is complex, time sensitive and not easily converted into single measurements. He argues that classrooms are historical places, and it is difficult to isolate specific classroom practices that have sustaining effects over time. Given the periodicities of classroom life, it is challenging to identify practices particularly effective for certain types of students. What works in September as a method of motivation or social control may be ineffective later in the year.

All of these conditions, Dreeben contends, speak to the value and importance of formative assessment: shorter, more time-sensitive diagnostic evaluations of student learning that can be used to guide further instruction. Formative assessment, which has considerable external validity, often is viewed as costly both in time and development (especially as it is geared to individual classrooms and student performance) by test developers, teachers, and administrative staff. Instead, policymakers, teachers, and administrators rely on yearly state standardized tests that can be more easily recorded and independently analyzed, even though such assessments are not conducive for learning or reasonable for measuring instructional practice (Dreeben 2005).

Dreeben (2005) suggests that the classroom is much like a medical facility; while a viable place for treating a disease or injury, it does not necessarily result in the improvement of health. Similarly, a classroom, while a reasonable place for study, does not necessarily result in the improvement of learning. For physicians, one of the most difficult aspects of curing diseases is getting patients to take their medicine—advice that often goes unheeded. Teachers similarly face recalcitrant students who, despite their efforts, remain unmotivated or disengaged during instruction and fail to complete assignments like homework that could enhance their academic performance. Here, Dreeben underscores the importance of norms and interpersonal relationships as central for understanding teacher effectiveness.

One of the most persistent problems in US schools has been how to motivate the kind of effort and involvement that can generate high performance among students regardless of their backgrounds. Coleman et al. (1997) in his last book, *Redesigning American Education*, also argued that the successful teacher needed to be the creator of classroom norms and relationships with their students. For Coleman, the academic performance of a student was a collective responsibility of the family, school, and the student. Such collective responsibility could be established through relational ties, which he referred to as social capital. It was the relationships formed among students, their families, and teachers which enhanced academic productivity when operating together. The teacher may bear fundamental responsibility for instruction, but responsibility for students' value-added performance is shared among the three parties directly relevant to achievement: the child, the parent, and the teacher. For example, teachers who were able to raise student scores, especially those whose scores were significantly lower than average, would be rewarded as would the parents of such children.

Recognizing the importance of teacher links with student performance, Coleman, in his redesign of American education, promotes something akin to portfolio assessment and recommends less dependency on standardized tests, which he viewed as breeding competition and invidious distinctions. This perspective is quite different than his earlier work. However, in advocating for this approach he was aware that performance measures relying on portfolio assessment can become compromised easily and promote poor performance if overly influenced by subjective interpretations and ambitious teacher input. Portfolio assessments could weaken students' motivation to excel, especially if the criteria for satisfactory performance require only a minimal level of competence. The emphasis here is on the teacher's efforts toward improving student performance, not through sanctions but through incentives.

Both Coleman and Dreeben have unique perspectives on the interrelationship between the teacher and the student, what their respective roles should be, what the nature of the instructor's job should entail, and what conditions of the workplace and family affect performance. Both place considerable value on perfecting one's skill as a teacher. But their conceptions of the academic production process are not based on a direct path from a single teacher to an individual student. Instead, they underscore the exigencies of external relationships (e.g., parents, other teachers, and administrators), time, and student motivation as major contributors to the learning process.[8]

Another way of gauging productivity, highlighted by Bryk et al. (2010) and Bryk and Schneider (2002), embeds student performance gains within the larger context of factors critical for raising school performance. This approach to understanding and measuring gains in school performance (described in Bryk et al. 2010) connects students' achievements to "the organization of a school, its day-to-day operations, including its connections to parents and community, interact with work inside classrooms to advance student learning" (Bryk et al. 2010: 48). Bryk takes into account the connections between teacher and student relationships and to a wider collective of teachers, administrators, and parents, emphasizing that it is through this collective that student learning improves. His conceptualization does not minimize the science of instruction, but rather nests it within the school, underscoring the importance of leadership, professional capacity, parent–community ties, and school climate.

This sociological emphasis on the importance of contextual relationships to learning seems at odds with current federal and state policies' focus on teacher effectiveness.

---

[8] Several sociologists of education have written extensively on teachers' work, relationships with students, the importance of teacher evaluations of students, and its impact on student learning and motivation. For this chapter, Dreeben and Coleman, two major figures in sociology of education, seem particularly relevant. Dreeben was undoubtedly the first and foremost scholar on examining teacher performance and student learning. Coleman's last book took on issues of educational reform, including teachers. Many of the ideas he outlined are being experimented with today, including teacher and family remuneration for student performance and value-added evaluation systems.

The sociological tradition views student performance as a consequence of multiple contextual factors that exist both inside and outside the classroom so that what transpires in the classroom is not divorced from but rather closely linked to the greater school community. Given the attention of current scholarship to teacher productivity as measured by test score performance, one might conclude that the role of sociology has been and is likely to continue to be diminished.

A Focus on Poor School Performance

A commonly accepted belief about US schools is that the performance of most students is mediocre at best, at least with respect to other industrialized nations. For several decades, US students have scored in the middle of industrialized nations on international mathematics and reading tests at both the elementary and secondary level (Aud et al. 2010). In urban schools, the situation is especially dire. There are some 10,781 schools that were identified as needing improvement in the 2006–2007 school year.[9] Recent results from the National Assessment of Educational Progress (NAEP) showed that the scores of US 17-year-olds were nearly the same as those of students who took the test in the early 1970s (based on 2007 NAEP results). The reading scores of 9-year-olds in 2010 were flat and those in eighth grade increased only slightly (based on 2010 scores). The scores of the 17-year-olds suggest that short-term gains in NAEP tend to decrease as students progress through school. (For further analyses of NAEP results, see National Center for Education Statistics 2010).

Even more disconcerting is that the racial and socioeconomic achievement gaps between advantaged and disadvantaged students have not changed significantly over the last decade. Differences in the achievement gap between whites and blacks have been attributed to lack of resources, especially within families and neighborhoods (Rothstein 2004; Fryer and Levitt 2006). Other scholars have turned their attention to school composition and the quality of teachers (Hanushek and Rivkin 2006).

In the past, issues of differences in achievement among racial and ethnic groups were central to work in sociology (see Hallinan 2000b). Today, many of these issues are being explored primarily by statisticians and economists (Braun et al. 2010).[10] This is not to say that any disciplinary field can or should have a monopoly on issues of public policy. However, the sociological lens tends to consider differences in achievement from a more contextual approach, emphasizing school organization, norms, and other factors. Yet this perspective receives less attention in policymaking circles, even though the importance of these factors and their relationship to

---

[9]The most recent numbers of schools needing improvement were taken from the recent report by Taylor et al. (2010).

[10]There are several sociologists who have continued to work on these issues; however, the majority of funding resources have tended to be allocated to economists.

performance has been well established. This is particularly the case when examining how teacher effectiveness is being researched today.

Since the passage of NCLB, regardless of which political party is in power, the message regarding the relationship between teacher effectiveness and student performance is decidedly different than in the past. During the previous and current administrations, interest in using state tests and other information for making important decisions, including assessing teacher effectiveness, has been growing. What is driving the educational system now and likely into the future is transparency of data, incentives for reform, and sanctions for poor performance. Large grants have been made to help the states construct Statewide Longitudinal Data Systems (SLDS) that can link student performance with their teachers.[11] The elements of these data systems (including unique student identifiers, school enrollment information, student test scores, transcript information, and mechanisms for linking students with their teachers) are designed specifically to identify teachers succeeding or struggling in efforts to improve student performance. For sociologists, this emphasis on performance and evidence has the unexpected benefits of moving social science to a more central place in the policy process and creating new conceptions of teachers' work, school organization, and the state and federal role in education. It remains to be seen whether sociologists will find opportunities to work with these rich and extensive data.

Measuring Teachers' Effectiveness

Currently one of the most popular methods for measuring teacher effectiveness is to construct a value-added model (VAM) that isolates school and teacher effects on student achievement (Sanders and Horn 1994). The primary goal of VAM is to make causal inferences between a student's test score gain and teacher performance (or a particular program or overall school effect). When measuring teacher effectiveness, analytic techniques[12] are employed to remove all relevant differences among students taught by different teachers so that individual students' academic gains can be attributed to a particular teacher. (For more technical information on VAM, see Harris and Sass 2007; Graham et al. 2009; Lockwood and McCaffrey 2009; McCaffrey and Lockwood 2008).

Value-added models are intuitively appealing, given their potential to isolate the effects of teachers from effects of other factors (such as student or neighborhood characteristics) that also are known to impact student achievement. As other measures of teacher quality, such as undergraduate institution, degree, or credentials, have proven to be poor predictors of student performance, and large scale administrative databases

---

[11] SLDS was authorized by the Educational Technical Assistance Act of 2002 and laid the groundwork for the expansion and use of data for measuring teacher effectiveness.
[12] Fixed effects or random effects models.

have become more robust, the use of a VAM approach has gained increased interest (Hanushek and Rivkin 2010; Koedel and Betts 2007). While not without strong criticisms among researchers (Rothstein 2004; Ravitch 2010), VAM has undeniably had a major influence on policymakers and researchers who now focus on using administrative data to estimate the relationship between effective teaching and the achievement gap (Braun et al. 2010; Rothstein 2009).

The appeal of VAM notwithstanding serious challenges, many of them methodological, hinders the estimation of teacher effects. VAMs often are criticized as problematic from a content side, as the standardized tests that typically provide the dependent outcomes often tap only a slice of what students know, are not necessarily sensitive to teacher instruction or curricular materials, and are subject to measurement error. Moreover, standardized tests are available only for a limited range of subject areas and grade levels, making it difficult to evaluate teacher effectiveness for those in untested grades or subjects (Harris 2009).[13] For this reason, most VAM research to date has focused on the elementary levels, where linkages of students and teachers are cleaner, rather than on the secondary grades, where the careful parsing of teachers in departmentalized settings is particularly challenging (Koedel 2009).

Perhaps the biggest issue related to the use of standardized assessments in VAM is test scaling.[14] To meet regression assumptions, test scores must be interval scaled; that is, the increase between, say, 30 and 40 is assumed to be the same as an increase between 70 and 80. However, it is not clear that this is the case with many of the assessments used in VAMs, and to relax this assumption would require sample sizes that may not be practically attainable (Braun et al. 2010; Reardon and Raudenbush 2008). There are also issues related to vertical scaling. Few states have truly vertically scaled tests, which limits justifiable comparisons of scores from different grade levels.[15]

In addition to concerns related to standardized tests, other model assumptions that underlay the precision of estimates produced from VAMs have been called into question. Some studies show that teacher effects are unstable over time (Aaronson et al. 2007; Koedel and Betts 2007; McCaffrey et al. 2009). Koedel and Betts (2007) find that teacher effects seem to differ for individual teachers (i.e., that teachers do

---

[13] Even in grades and subjects where tests are given, identifying an appropriate measure of prior achievement may be difficult. For example, if standardized tests are administered in tenth grade, but not in ninth grade, should an eighth-grade measure be used to represent prior achievement?

[14] Concerns also have been expressed with ceiling effects; on some assessments, particularly criterion referenced tests, high-performing students may have little opportunity to demonstrate gains because their proficiency levels are beyond the scale measured with the instrument (Hanushek et al. 2005; Koedel and Betts 2007; Koedel and Betts 2009). Similarly "floor effects" may hinder the accurate calculation for teachers whose students are low performing.

[15] Martineau (2006) argues that even though some states have adopted tests that are believed to be vertically scaled, "construct-shifting" occurs, especially when assessments are designed for multiple developmental ranges which also cover large content ranges. He demonstrates that when these types of vertically scaled tests are used in the estimation of teacher effects, the results are not accurate, sometimes labeling ineffective teachers effective or effective teachers ineffective.

not fall into the same performance quintiles) from year to year, although the lowest and highest performers seem relatively stable. Aaronson et al. (2007) similarly find that only 36% of teachers in the lowest performance quartile and 57% in the highest performance quartile remain in the same quartile from year to year. Goldhaber and Hansen (2010) present some conflicting evidence, showing that teacher effects remain fairly consistent over time; a teacher who produces gains one year is expected to produce them the next. They also argue that effects estimated early in a teacher's career are likely to persist after a decision about that teacher's tenure has been made.

In an era of increased demands for school and teacher accountability, VAM seems to confirm long-held beliefs that teachers matter in the success of students, having a discernable impact on achievement. Preliminary research evidence suggests that value-added estimates of teacher effectiveness can be a legitimate source of information related to teacher personnel decisions (Rivkin et al. 2005; Rockoff 2004; Kane and Staiger 2008; Goldhaber and Hansen 2010; Harris and Sass 2007). Policymakers see promise in using value-added scores in employment, promotion, compensation, and retention decisions. Further, VAMs incorporated into an annual teacher evaluation system could potentially identify teachers who are struggling; once identified, policies could be developed to offer targeted interventions to teachers who do not seem to be bringing about gains in achievement.

The research community has strong interest in testing the assumptions underlying common VAM approaches. In the real-world context of teacher evaluations, the justification for any given model must be explained to practitioners. Researchers must wrestle with developing defensible models that, in addition to being valid and reliable, also have *face* validity with the individuals who will be assessed by them. As Braun et al. (2010) state, "When used for purposes such as accountability, the choice of models needs to balance the goals of complexity and accuracy, on the one hand, and transparency, on the other" (p. 48).

Additionally, major questions remain regarding the specific contributions VAM can and should make to a comprehensive system for evaluating and compensating teachers. Few researchers have recommended that VAM be implemented as the primary measure of teacher effectiveness across all subjects and grade levels. However, it is gaining traction and states are moving toward recommending that such assessments serve as part of teacher evaluations or compensation decisions (Harris 2009; Hill 2009). Some have suggested that in addition to VAM scores, elements such as teacher portfolios documenting student work, principal evaluations, external observations, and other commonly used credentials might all form a comprehensive system used in evaluating or compensating teachers.

The VAM debate should be of major interest to sociologists. Consider the issues of high-stakes versus low-stakes accountability. Does a system in which results of performance are transparent provide an incentive for better performance? Or does it encourage individuals to resort to illegitimate means, such as cheating or teaching to the test in order to "game the system" (Levitt and Jacob 2003)? These kinds of questions seem particularly important for sociologists to consider, especially now that districts and different types of school organizations, such as charters, are using these measures for teacher accountability. Also of interest are whether schools using these measures to identify instructional problems and create professional development programs to address them are significantly altering their overall effectiveness.

Critics argue that VAM needs considerably more substantive and methodological work before it can be used either solely or in conjunction with other assessments of teacher quality (Hill 2009; Braun et al. 2010). Critically important from a sociological perspective is conceptualizing or enhancing models to account for variations in school organization and culture. Another recommendation has been to incorporate statistical procedures that make adjustments for differences between groups of students that we know are not assigned randomly to different schools, teachers, or programs. The sociological research on opportunities for learning (Sørenson and Hallinan 1977), which spearheaded later studies on tracking and course sequencing, shows explicitly how student background characteristics are related to performance independent of instruction across all school levels. Other factors such as student motivation, peer groups, and parental expectations also are associated with academic achievement, undermining the notion of randomness for estimating student fixed effects models. On the teacher side, school leadership and qualities of teachers' colleagues are present in VAM which use teacher fixed effects attributed to the teachers, whereas in sociology, these have been shown to be independent of the teacher and significantly associated with achievement gains.

Economic and statistical explanations for the exclusion of such variables suggest that results may attribute gains more to student background characteristics (e.g., race) than ones that are more contextual. However, being able to distinguish independent race and ethnicity effects from teacher effects has been fundamentally, and continues to be, of interest to sociologists. Sociology is the study of what matters for different groups. From a sociological perspective, these statistical explanations seem problematic. We know that background affects performance; sociologists are not interested in holding these factors constant but rather in understanding what measures of school characteristics impact achievement, whether they are independent or dependent of teacher characteristics. Some factors attributed to the student, such as family characteristics and expectations, are effectively hidden in student fixed effects models; similarly, school characteristics are effectively hidden in teacher fixed effects models. One message to sociologists is that it is imperative that they enter the foray of VAM before the very conditions that have defined the field become constants that are expressed as single coefficients.

From a jurisdictional authority perspective, if the criteria for assessment rest on this measure, it is easy to understand how the professional expertise of the teacher is being diminished. When thinking about other professionals, issues of malpractice are relatively hard to prove and such actions usually are brought on the basis of a single party. In proving cases of malpractice, the evidence is weighed by multiple parties and has to show beyond a reasonable doubt that the action was caused by neglect and dereliction of duty and responsibilities. Penalties often include large fines or having one's license revoked. If we take a sociological perspective to assess teacher effectiveness, what should be the evidence that warrants remediation and dismissal of teachers? Are low test scores grounds for dismissal or revoking tenure, especially for students whose schooling careers repeatedly have been unsuccessful?

Tracing the Source: Teacher Training Institutions

The position of schools and colleges of education in postsecondary institutions has had a long history of lack of status and power within the academy, and few schools have managed to continue to earn the respect of colleagues outside of education. Lack of confidence in teacher training institutions has only escalated within the last 15 years with the entrance of programs such as Teach for America (TFA) that place teachers in schools who have not gone through training in schools and colleges of education. Recent research on those who have entered teaching using alternative routes suggests that after 3 years working in schools, their performance is similar to that of those who received their training in schools and colleges of education (Boyd et al. 2006). However, the TFA trained teachers are more likely than other regularly trained teachers to leave the profession within a relatively short time in the classroom (less than 3 years). What is not clear from these recent studies is the difference in preparation for teaching in these various programs and what components affect teacher effectiveness.

If one accepts, as argued by Dreeben (2005) and Abbott (1988), that jurisdictional authority is obtained through the acquisition of specific knowledge and skills, these types of questions seem critical to sociologists not only with respect to teachers but other professionals as well. There have been steps to bring teacher licensure more in line with other professions through the establishment of a National Board Certification (NBC) process (see Darling-Hammond 2009). Studies on the effectiveness of certification seem relatively limited in number and not consistent in results. The lack of uniformity with respect to the impact of NBC points again to the problems of trying to isolate specific effects tied to individual performance that are nested within a larger context. It is rather disheartening that sociologists are not part of these studies, as few researchers are considering the relationship between different teacher training programs and whether they can be linked to academic performance taking into account variations in student race and ethnicity or developmental periods. Also absent from much of this literature is the value of norms and the ability of teachers to motive and facilitate student learning.

When sociologists have entered the area of teacher certification, their impact has been considerable. Here, the work of Ingersoll (2003) is especially relevant, as he showed the relationships between student learning and teacher expertise. His work had an enormous impact and significantly changed requirements so that the problem of teaching out of field is not the issue it was a decade ago. Some of the most interesting work being undertaken by sociologists on teaching is that by Downey (Downey et al. 2004, 2008), who using large scale databases has directly confronted the teacher effectiveness problem. Downey has investigated the summer learning loss for low-income and minority students and estimated what the likely student gain should be during the regular academic year. Results show that teacher effects on learning are much greater than assumed for low-income and minority students. These types of studies that change the conversation and methodology should be part of the sociological approach to teacher effectiveness.

Sociologists have been at the forefront of using large scale databases to research issues of social stratification, access to learning opportunities, and educational attainment. Few younger scholars are pursuing issues of teacher effectiveness, yet the issues of school and context and their impact are central to the field. Teachers often choose where they want to teach and when forced to change buildings seek new positions. It is difficult to distinguish statistically between those effects that are related to the teacher and those of the classroom, school, or neighborhood. Given the importance of these issues, sociologists can and should be researching them.

Steps for the Future

Of course, there are other issues that sociologists could examine with the potential to change the discussion on teacher effectiveness. For example, rather than looking at whether a teacher was trained in a school or college of education or Teach for America, we could think hard about the criteria for hiring teachers. What would happen if teachers had to demonstrate how they perform with a group of students similar to those in the potential school, by submitting videos of their classroom performance or teaching a class—a practice common among hiring college professors and professionals in a wide variety of fields. This is but one example of the portfolio of evidence that could be submitted to a group making hiring decisions, including interviews with teachers at and above and below their grade level. Similarly, there should be cautions and perhaps guidelines for late hires when there are extenuating circumstances.

Instead of just looking at test score gains, another proactive strategy that sociology of education could advance would be paying closer attention to early warning signs of struggling teachers. Research indicates that teachers who have difficulty with classroom management and tend to place inordinate blame on parents and students often are dissatisfied with their careers. Career satisfaction is a major topic of sociological inquiry and sociologists could and should be making a greater contribution to this issue. Other topics which sociologists have and should continue to research as indicators of teacher effectiveness include time devoted to class instruction, alignment of curriculum with instruction, student motivation and engagement, personal beliefs about students' math and science abilities, and low expectations for certain immigrant, racial, and ethnic groups. These factors may be referred to as symptomatic, although not necessarily unalterable, problems that affect student performance. It is unclear that VAM could perform a similar diagnostic function.

VAM can offer important information about a particular aspect of teacher performance but education involves more than a test score gain, especially if that gain is something akin to a fraction of a standard deviation. Properly used VAM could assist in the identification of struggling teachers, but one would have to be clear that effectively masked characteristics of teachers and students are always operating in classrooms. In response to economic constraints facing many districts, schools may increase the numbers of courses taught online and by multiple teachers making it difficult to isolate the individual effect of a teacher. The very circumstances of testing could also impact calculation of teacher effectiveness, though it is not captured in the score. For example, due to budgetary concerns, some school districts eliminated as much as a week of instructional time in the 2009–2010 academic year, and high school students expecting to take end of year high school exams were given earlier than expected, with only one day's notice to students and their teachers. These end-of-course exams are high-stakes assessments for individual students, their teachers, and schools.

Economists do seem to regard teacher effectiveness as an important area of study. There is a message here for sociologists of education. Studies of teachers and how they structure opportunities for learning in their classrooms and schools are a legitimate and critical area of study. If one had to presage what sociologists should be involved in with respect to the future, it surely would be working with state data and their economist colleagues. It is not that sociologists should take over where economists currently are, but rather that they need to work together, using VAM for identification purposes and augmenting large scale studies with observational representative samples, allowing more of the organizational, leadership, and social characteristics of schools and teachers to be examined. Sociologists should focus their efforts on adding value to value-added models in order to learn more about teacher effectiveness and student learning.

References

Aaronson, D., L. Barrow, and W. Sander. 2007. Teachers and student achievement in Chicago public schools. *Journal of Labor Economics* 25: 95–135.

Abbott, A. 1988. *The system of professions*. Chicago: University of Chicago Press.

Aud, S., W. Hussar, M. Planty, T. Snyder, K. Bianco, M. Fox, et al. 2010. *The condition of education 2010 (NCES 2010–028)*. Washington, DC: National Center for Education Statistics.

Bidwell, C.E. 2003. Analyzing schools as organizations: Long-term permanence and short-term change. *Sociology of Education* 74(Special Issue): 100–114.

Boyd, D., P. Grossman, H. Lankford, S. Loeb, and J. Wyckoff. 2006. How changes in entry requirements alter the teacher workforce and affect student achievement. *Education Finance and Policy* 1: 176–216.

Braun, H., N. Chudowsky, and J. Koenig. 2010. *Getting value out of value-added: Report of a workshop*. Washington, DC: National Academies Press.

Bryk, A.S. 1988. Musings on the moral life of schools. *American Journal of Education* 96: 256–290.

Bryk, A.S., and B. Schneider. 2002. *Trust in schools: A core resource for improvement*. New York: Russell Sage Foundation.

Bryk, A.S., P.B. Sebring, E. Allensworth, S. Luppescu, and J.Q. Easton. 2010. *Organizing schools for improvement: Lessons from Chicago*. Chicago: University of Chicago Press.

Bushaw, W. J., and S. J. Lopez. 2010. *A Time for Change: The 42nd Annual Phi Delta Kappa/Gallup Poll of the Public's Attitudes Toward the Public Schools*. Retrieved from http://www.pdkintl.org/kappan/docs/2010_Poll_Report.pdf.

Coleman, J.S. 1990. *Foundations of social theory*. Cambridge: Harvard University Press.

Coleman, J.S., B. Schneider, S. Plank, K. Schiller, R. Shouse, and H. Wang. 1997. *Redesigning American Education*. Boulder: Westview Press.

Darling-Hammond, L. 2009. Teacher preparation and teacher learning: A changing policy landscape. In *Handbook of education policy research*, eds. Gary Sykes, Barbara Schneider, and David Plank, 613–636. New York: Routledge.

Dewey, J. 1973. *The philosophy of John Dewey*. Chicago: The University of Chicago Press.

Downey, D.B., P.T. von Hippel, and B.A. Broh. 2004. Are schools the great equalizer? Cognitive inequality during the summer months and the school year. *American Sociological Review* 69: 613–635.

Downey, D.B., P.T. von Hippel, and M. Hughes. 2008. Are 'Failing' schools really failing? Using seasonal comparison to evaluate school effectiveness. *Sociology of Education* 81: 242–270.

Dreeben, R. 1970. *The nature of teaching: Schools and the work of teachers*. Glenview: Scott Foresman.

Dreeben, R. 1994. The sociology of education: Its development in the United States. *Research in Sociology of Education and Socialization* 10: 53–70.

Dreeben, R. 2003. Classrooms and Politics. In *Stability and change in American education: Structure, process, and outcomes*, eds. M. Hallinan, A. Gamoran, W. Kubitschek, and T. Loveless, 229–249. Clinton Corners: Eliot Werner Publications.

Dreeben, R. 2005. Teaching and the competence of occupations. In *The social organization of schooling*, eds. L. Hedges and B. Schneider, 51–71. New York: Russell Sage Foundation.

Finn, C.E. 2002, April. What ails U.S. high schools? How should they be reformed? Is there a Federal Role? Paper presented at *Preparing America's Future: The High School Symposium*, Washington, DC.

Firestone, W.A. 2003. The governance of teaching and standards-based reform from the 1970s to the new millennium. In *Stability and change in American education: Structure, process, and outcomes*, eds. M. Hallinan, A. Gamoran, W. Kubitschek, and T. Loveless, 153–170. Clinton Corners: Eliot Werner Publications.

Frank, K.A., Y. Zhao, and K. Borman. 2004. Social capital and the diffusion of innovations within organizations: The case of computer technology in schools. *Sociology of Education* 77: 148–171.

Fryer, R.G., and S.D. Levitt. 2006. The black-white test score gap through third grade. *American Law and Economics Review* 8: 249–281.

Glazer, J.L. 2008. Educational professionalism: An inside-out view. *American Journal of Education* 114: 169–189.

Goldhaber, D., and M. Hansen. 2010. *Assessing the potential of using value-added estimates of teacher job performance for making tenure decisions*. Working Paper 31. Washington, DC: National Center for Analysis of Longitudinal Data in Education Research.

Graham, S.E., J.D. Singer, and J.B. Willett. 2009. Longitudinal data analysis. In *Handbook of quantitative methods in psychology*, eds. A. Maydeu-Olivares and R. Millsap. Thousand Oaks: Sage.

Hallinan, M.T. (ed.). 2000a. *Handbook of the sociology of education*. New York: Plenum.

Hallinan, M.T. 2000b. On the linkage between sociology of race and ethnicity and sociology of education. In *Handbook of the sociology of education*, ed. M. Hallinan, 65–84. New York: Plenum.

Hanushek, E., and S. Rivkin. 2010, January. Generalizations about using value-added measures of teacher quality. Paper presented at *The Annual Meeting of the American Economic Association*, Atlanta.

Hanushek, E.A., and S.G. Rivkin. 2006, October. *School quality and the black-white achievement gap*. NBER Working Paper No. W12651. Cambridge: National Bureau of Economic Research.

Hanushek, E. A., J. F. Kain, D. M. O'Brien, and S. G. Rivkin. 2005. *The market for teacher quality*. NBER Working Paper No. w11154. Cambridge: National Bureau of Economic Research.

Harris, D.N. 2009. Teacher value-added: Don't end the search before it starts. *Journal of Policy Analysis and Management* 28: 693–699. 709–711.

Harris, D., and T. Sass. 2007. What makes a good teacher and who can tell? Paper presented at *The Summer Workshop of the National Bureau for Economic Research*, Cambridge.

Hill, H. 2009. Evaluating value-added models: A validity argument approach. *Journal of Policy Analysis and Management* 28: 700–709. 711–712.

Hubbard, L., H. Mehan, and M.K. Stein. 2006. *Reform as learning: School reform, organizational culture, and community politics in San Diego*. New York: Routledge.

Ingersoll, R.M. 2003. *Out-of-field teaching and the limits of teacher policy: A research report.* Seattle: Center for the Study of Teaching and Policy.
Ingersoll, R.M. 2005. The problem of underqualified teachers: A sociological perspective. *Sociology of Education* 78: 175–178.
Jackson, P. 1968. *Life in classrooms.* New York: Holt, Rinehart and Winston.
Jacobsen, R. 2009. The voice of the people in education policy. In *Handbook of education policy research,* eds. Gary Sykes, Barbara Schneider, and David Plank, 307–318. New York: Routledge.
Johnson, S. M. 2005. Supporting and retaining the next generation of teachers. Paper prepared for *The National Education Association Visiting Scholars Series,* Washington, DC.
Kane, T.J., and D. Staiger. 2008. *Estimating teacher impacts on student achievement: An experimental evaluation.* NBER Working Paper No. w14607. Cambridge: National Bureau of Economic Research.
Kane, T.J., J.E. Rockoff, and D.O. Staiger. 2008. What does teacher certification tell us about teacher effectiveness? Evidence from New York City. *Economics of Education Review* 27: 615–631.
Koedel, C. 2009. An empirical analysis of teacher spillover effects in secondary school. *Economics of Education Review* 28: 682–692.
Koedel, C., and J. Betts. 2007. *Re-examining the role of teacher quality in the educational production function.* Working Paper 0708. Columbia: University of Missouri, Department of Economics.
Koedel, C., and J. Betts. 2009. *Value-added to what? How a ceiling in the testing instrument influences value-added estimation.* NBER Working Paper No. W14778. Cambridge: National Bureau of Economic Research.
Konstantopoulos, S., and V. Chung. 2011. The persistence of teacher effects in elementary grades. *American Educational Research Journal* 48: 361–386.
Levitt, B.A., and S.D. Jacob. 2003. Rotten apples: An investigation of the prevalence and predictors of teacher cheating. *The Quarterly Journal of Economics* 118: 843–877.
Lockwood, J., and D. McCaffrey. 2009. Exploring student-teacher interactions in longitudinal achievement data. *Education Finance and Policy* 4: 439–467.
Martineau, J. 2006. Distorting value added: The use of longitudinal, vertically scaled student achievement data for growth-based, value-added accountability. *Journal of Educational and Behavioral Statistics* 31: 35–62.
McCaffrey, D., and J. Lockwood. 2008, November. Value-added models: Analytic issues. Paper presented at *The National Research Council and the National Academy of Education, Board on Testing and Accountability Workshop on Value-Added Modeling,* Washington, DC.
McCaffrey, D., T. Sass, J. Lockwood, and K. Mihaly. 2009. The intertemporal variability of teacher effect estimates. *Education Finance and Policy* 4: 572–606.
McFarland, D.A. 2004. Resistance as a social drama: A study of change-oriented encounters. *American Journal of Sociology* 109: 1249–1318.
McLaughlin, M.W., and J.E. Talbert. 2006. *Building school-based teacher learning communities: Professional strategies to improve student achievement.* New York: Teachers College Press.
Meyer, J.W., and B. Rowan. 1978. The structure of educational organizations. In *Organizations and environments,* eds. M. W. Meyer and Associates, 78–109. San Francisco: Jossey Bass.
National Center for Education Statistics. 2010. *National assessment of educational progress: The nation's report card.* Retrieved from http://nces.ed.gov/nationsreportcard/.
No Child Left Behind (NCLB). 2002. Act of 2001, Pub. L. No. 107–110, § 115, Stat. 1425.
Nye, B., S. Konstantopoulos, and L.V. Hedges. 2004. How large are teacher effects? *Educational Evaluation and Policy Analysis* 26: 237–257.
O'Day, J., and M. Smith. 1993. Systemic reform and educational opportunity. In *Designing coherent policy: Improving the system,* ed. S. Fuhrman, 250–312. San Francisco: Jossey-Bass.
Ravitch, D. 2010. *The death and life of the great American school system: How testing and choice are undermining education.* New York: Basic Books.
Reardon, S., and S. Raudenbush. 2008, April. Assumptions of value-added models for estimating school effects. Paper presented at *The National Conference on Value-Added Modeling,* Madison, WI.

Rivkin, S.G., E.A. Hanushek, and J.F. Kain. 2005. Teachers, schools, and academic achievement. *Econometrica* 73: 417–458.

Rockoff, J. 2004. The impact of individual teachers on student achievement: Evidence from panel data. *The American Economic Review* 94: 247–252.

Roschelle, J.M., R.D. Pea, C.M. Hoadley, D.N. Gordin, and B.M. Means. 2000. Changing how and what children learn in school with computer-based technologies. *The Future of Children* 10: 76–101.

Rothstein, R. 2004. *Class and schools: Using social, economic, and educational reform to close the black-white achievement gap*. Washington, DC: Economic Policy Institute.

Rothstein, J. 2009. Student sorting and bias in value-added estimation: Selection on observables and unobservables. *Education Finance and Policy* 4: 537–571.

Rowan, B., R. Correnti, and R. Miller. 2002. *What Large-Scale Survey Research Tells Us About Teacher Effects on Student Achievement: Insights from the Prospects Study of Elementary Schools*, CPRE Research Report Series RR051. Philadelphia: University of Pennsylvania, Graduate School of Education.

Sadovnik, A.R., J. O'Day, G. Bohrnstedt, and K. Borman (eds.). 2008. *No Child Left Behind and the reduction of the achievement gap: Sociological perspectives on federal educational policy*. New York: Routledge.

Sanders, W., and S. Horn. 1994. The Tennessee Value-Added Assessment System (TVAAS): Mixed-model methodology in educational assessment. *Journal of Personnel Evaluation in Education* 8: 299–311.

Schneider, B. 2003. Sociology of education: An overview of the field at the turn of the twenty-first century. In *Stability and change in American Education: Structure, process, and outcomes*, eds. M.T. Hallinan, A. Gamoran, W. Kubitschek, and T. Loveless, 193–226. Clinton Corners: Eliot Werner Publications.

Schneider, B., and V.A. Keesler. 2007. School reform 2007: Transforming education into a scientific enterprise. *Annual Review of Sociology* 33: 197–217.

Sørenson, A.B., and M.T. Hallinan. 1977. A reconceptualization of school effects. *Sociology of Education* 50: 273–289.

Swanson, E.F. 2005. Anchors of the community: Community schools in Chicago. *New Directions for Youth Development* 107: 55–64.

Taylor, J., B. Stecher, J. O'Day, S. Naftel, and K.C. Le Floch. 2010. State and local implementation of the no child left behind act, Vol. IX—Accountability under NCLB: Final Report. Washington, DC: U.S. Department of Education.

Yasumoto, J.Y., K. Uekawa, and C.E. Bidwell. 2001. The collegial focus and student achievement. *Sociology of Education* 74: 181–209.

Chapter 9
Perfectionist Dreams and Hidden Stratification: Is Perfection the Enemy of the Good?

James E. Rosenbaum, Janet E. Rosenbaum, and Jennifer L. Stephan

Research on stratification in schools has proven to be a powerful way to understand the mechanisms that contribute to social stratification. These studies describe mobility patterns within institutions (Alexander et al. 1978; Sørensen 1977); identify institutional procedures that shape stratification outcomes (Deil-Amen and DeLuca 2010; Hallinan 1994); and reveal how institutional actors implement procedures that create stratification barriers, sometimes in spite of actors' good intentions (Gamoran and Berends 1987). Such analyses not only describe fine-grained stratification mechanisms, but also identify how and why they are created.

The conceptual model for much of this research has been the status attainment model, which identifies a wide variety of factors that influence attainment. Students' educational expectations are central to the model, both as an initial outcome, and as an important influence on attainment. The status attainment model assumes that there is variation in students' expectations. It also assumes that prior achievement influences students' expectations because society presents realistic information to guide students' educational plans based on achievement requirements. Further sociological research suggests that providing information is not sufficient and that additional social mechanisms are necessary. Gatekeeping processes are encouraged by high school guidance counselors (Cicourel and Kitsuse 1963), and cooling-out processes are implemented by community college advisors (Clark 1960). These may be considered hard and soft versions of the same kinds of processes that direct students away

---

J.E. Rosenbaum (✉) • J.L. Stephan
Institute for Policy Research, Northwestern University,
Evanston, IL 60208, USA
e-mail: j-rosenbaum@northwestern.edu; j-stephan@northwestern.edu

J.E. Rosenbaum
University of Maryland Population Center, University of Maryland,
College Park, MD 20742, USA
e-mail: janet@post.harvard.edu

from plans considered highly unrealistic. This body of research was developed in the 1960s, but much has changed since then. We propose that these three processes are not functioning as they once did. In contrast, some recent research suggests that counselors often deplore such actions and advise students quite differently today (Krei et al. 1997). Indeed, prior research may have contributed to these changes.

This chapter considers a new well-intentioned perspective that has transformed the operations of these institutions. The new approach is more complex and the resulting stratification is harder to see than earlier approaches and is an improvement over gatekeeping and cooling-out practices that often were highly biased and placed unnecessary limits on disadvantaged groups. However, there may be unintended consequences to these improvements. Although guidance counselors' optimism is hard to criticize, these new practices create hidden stratification by indirectly encouraging low-achieving students to pursue pathways with a low likelihood of payoffs, depleting limited financial and social capital, particularly for disadvantaged youth. The problems with these new practices are hard to see because we want to believe in them. They encourage youth to raise their expectations, and the resulting stratification does not appear immediately. Idealistic counseling practices are likely to create failures and contribute to stratified educational and occupational outcomes.

These idealistic practices arise from the perfectionist model: adults pose high ideals for adolescents, giving them advice and information designed to encourage the pursuit of those ideals. Alternative goals that fall short of perfectionist ideals either are not discussed or are disparaged to avoid inadvertently encouraging youth to depart from the perfectionist ideal. Discussing alternatives as plausible options is viewed as encouragement of those options with the potential to decrease a student's dedication to pursue the ideals. In some cases, adults withhold information and even present incorrect information (Rosenbaum 2001). Given a strong social consensus on the desirability of the ideal, institutional staff may be criticized or even fired for offering any options short of the ideal. In effect, the perfectionist model is not only optimistic and encouraging; it creates a normative consensus that refuses to tolerate any other options short of the ideal.

The perfectionist model can help determine the elements of this new approach that create barriers and undermine the desired goals. Originally described in studies of the sexual abstinence movement (Rosenbaum 2009; Rosenbaum et al. 2010), we use this model to identify comparable features in the BA-for-all movement, which encourages all high school graduates to seek bachelor degrees. In both cases, perfectionist advice poses high ideals, leading students to commit to lofty goals. Yet, it also leads to high rates of predictable failures and precludes considering realistic back-up options, thus making failure more damaging than if students had back-up options. Moreover, perfectionism is not limited to the education field; it springs from deeper roots in our society.

We do not advocate the abandonment of high goals; however, there should be an awareness of limitations in perfectionist models and the importance of more complex advice, multiple options, and back-up plans. Students should aim high but also be aware of these strategies and the probabilities of achieving them. Low-achieving students can consider safer options by earning certificates and degrees along the way in the event that plans to earn a BA do not materialize, as is often the case for students with poor grades in high school. While the perfectionist strategy of withholding information about realistic probabilities and future requirements succeeds in encouraging high aspirations, it conceals useful information that could enable youth to take constructive actions to achieve some goals with a high likelihood. Withholding information about alternative degrees with fewer academic demands and shorter timetables may support students' dreams, but if accompanied by 80% failure rates, it is not a kindness. Viewing current practices through the lens of the perfectionist model, we can see hidden stratification mechanisms that simultaneously give hope while limiting opportunities.

Perfectionist ideals deserve some credit for the enormous progress in college access. Over the last 40 years, high school seniors increased their educational plans, and high schools actively supported these plans. The increase in college attendance is in part due to the reduction in barriers to college access. Community colleges have experienced a fivefold increase in enrollment (Rosenbaum et al. 2006) by offering low cost, proximity, flexible hours, diverse offerings, and dedicated staff. Almost half of all college students attend community colleges. However, rapid changes in college attendance and college programs create confusion and a need for information and advice, particularly for first-generation college students. The perfectionist impulse to withhold discouraging information may do unintended harm.

This chapter aims to identify some of the elements of the BA-for-all movement that are potentially harmful. By seeing the perfectionist dynamic in the abstinence movement, we can better understand how our own ideals distort reality in three ways: posing oversimplified goals, withholding key information, and advocating actions that lead to predictable failures.

We propose that stratification processes no longer function as they once did. First, contrary to the status attainment model that assumed high school seniors would have diverse levels of educational plans, the perfectionist model suggests that society encourages a narrow course of action. It exaggerates the value of BA degrees and downplays the value of associate degrees. Second, contrary to the gatekeeping model, high schools following the perfectionist model do not engage in gatekeeping and allow everyone to pursue high goals. Third, contrary to the cooling-out model, colleges following the perfectionist model often do not temper students' ambitious plans.

In addition to the review of prior findings, this chapter brings new research to bear on these issues. The new findings come from interviews with high school students, and community college students, graduates, and staff, and are reported extensively in research by Rosenbaum et al. (2010). Ninety high school seniors were interviewed, randomly selected from six high schools with different ethnic and SES composition in the Chicago area. Also interviewed were 78 administrators and faculty and 86 students at 7 community colleges and 2 private occupational colleges in California and Illinois. We have collected surveys from over 2,000 students at these colleges. These data persistently find a systematic absence of certain key information in ways that prevent students from considering alternatives to BA goals and prevent them from anticipating predictable obstacles. Even if one chooses to reject our model, these data along with prior findings raise baffling questions about why key information is not more readily available.

This model has implications for educators and sociologists. Awareness of these features may help educators design better advising on the high school to college transition—advising that identifies multiple goals, crucial information that students need to know, and specific advice tailored to individual situations and preferences that is more likely to lead to successful outcomes.

It also can help researchers examine our own perfectionist assumptions and whether we are failing to consider hidden forms of stratification. It suggests that sociological analyses can play a constructive role in informing institutional actors. We propose three kinds of sociological analyses that could inform practitioners and policymakers about the stratification implications of their well-intentioned actions and suggest more complex goals and procedures that would be more candid and possibly lead to better outcomes.

The Perfectionist Model

Social movements often create representations of society (social constructions) that limit our views of reality. The perfectionist model describes the way some social movements attempt to implement perfectionist goals in spite of serious constraints. The sexual abstinence movement is a good example because it provides a clear and distinctive perspective with clear steps to implement its ideals.

As described in prior work (Rosenbaum 2006, 2009), the abstinence movement presents a desirable goal (Government Accountability Office 2006). Preventing teenagers from engaging in sexual activity too early is a goal that most parents endorse. The movement is perfectionist in that it advocates that young people can conform perfectly to the abstinence ideal. Indeed, it is successful in motivating youth to state these intentions publicly, often in large meetings.

Three important features of the perfectionist abstinence movement raise concerns (Bearman and Bruckner 2005; Rosenbaum 2006, 2009). First, the perfectionist model oversimplifies the stated goals to encourage a narrow course of action. In that case, it advocates total abstinence from sexual relations before marriage. Unlike traditional comprehensive sex education curricula, which recognize that about half of high school students have engaged in sexual activity (e.g., Eaton et al. 2008), the abstinence movement sets a perfectionist standard for teen sexual behavior. Federal abstinence-only policy requires teaching that premarital abstinence is the only "expected standard, and that any other behavior is likely to have harmful psychological and physical effects" (2008:3). This precludes discussion of safe sex and disease except in the context of their failures (Government Accountability Office 2006). A Sunday school teacher confided to one of the authors that, although he hears students discussing alternative practices, he would be asked to resign if he candidly discussed alternatives with them, even outside of class, a sentiment common among school sex educators (Luker 2006).

Second, abstinence programs withhold information about less than perfectionist goals, realistic probabilities, and alternative procedures for attaining desirable goals. Proponents of the abstinence movement believe that providing information about alternatives creates an implicit endorsement. Moreover, proponents argue against schools providing information about sex, contending that parents can do this better (Rosenbaum and Weathersbee 2009). Evidence suggests that few parents teach about vital areas such as disease prevention (2009), many parents have incorrect information (Eisenberg et al. 2004), parents overestimate how much information they give to their adolescents (Miller et al. 1998; Rosenbaum et al. 2007; Newcomer and Udry 1985), and they underestimate their adolescent's activity (Bylund et al. 2005). If they do not obtain information in school, students in devout environments may rely on information from their peers that likely is deficient and omits vital details (2009). As a result, adolescents do not learn about alternatives, including safe methods to prevent pregnancy and life-threatening disease.

Third, the movement ignores failures and alternatives. Advocates are convinced of the validity of the model and are happy with adolescents' highly visible optimism. Despite strong evidence to the contrary, failures are denied, and alternatives are not discussed (Rosenbaum and Weathersbee 2009). Although evangelical Protestant denominations endorse premarital abstinence as the only standard, 82.8% of women raised in evangelical Protestant denominations fail to meet that standard (Chandra et al. 2005). Despite having been shown ineffective in a congressionally commissioned evaluation (Trenholm et al. 2008), evidence of failures is not sufficient to alter policy, and abstinence education again was funded by Congress in the 2010 Health Reform Bill. Perfectionist movements are content to advocate well-intentioned goals; they do not ask how these goals affect their members.

The BA-for-All Movement

While the BA-for-all movement differs from the abstinence movement in some ways, it has many of the same attributes as the perfectionist model, namely, oversimplified goals, withheld information, and denial of failures. We see this perfectionist model operating in three components of the BA-for-all movement: idealization of the BA degree, open admissions policies without warnings, and stigma-free remediation.

Idealization of the BA Degree

Contrary to the status attainment model, which assumes that high school seniors would have diverse levels of educational plans, the perfectionist model suggests that society encourages a narrow course of action, exaggerates the value of this action, and understates the value of midlevel attainment. Students have been taught the value of the BA degree. Over recent decades, the proportion of high school students planning to earn BA degrees has steadily increased (Schneider and Stevenson 1999). As a result, high school seniors' educational plans, which showed great variation in the status attainment model research of the 1960s, now have little variation. In a 2004 national sample, 89% of high school graduates reported plans to earn a BA and another 6.5% planned to attend college but did not expect to graduate from a 4-year college (author's calculations from the Educational Longitudinal Survey [ELS]). Many of the other students reported that they did not know their plans. Less than 1% of high school graduates plans not to attend college. In other words, while high school graduates' plans used to be a variable, now 89% plan to earn bachelor degrees. Contrary to the assumption in the status attainment model that society would provide realistic information to guide student plans, the perfectionist model suggests that society encourages a narrow course of action, it exaggerates the value of this action and does not encourage midlevel attainment.

In particular, we find evidence that society encourages the oversimplified, idealized goal that everyone should strive for a BA degree. Public service ads, educational reform literature, and guidance counselors' advice provide a consistent message that BA degrees have a million-dollar payoff in lifetime earnings (Rosenbaum 2001; Smith 2009). This message is simple and powerful. BA degrees are the traditional degree goal, and now they are the most common degree goal of students.

In interviews, many students attribute their BA goal to earnings with some students reporting that they expect a million-dollar payoff (Rosenbaum et al. 2010). Some economists discuss the overestimation of payoffs from college degrees (Avery and Kane 2004), but this is not likely to be recognized by the public. While the payoff may be accurate, on average, it is oversimplified and incomplete. It encourages a single goal and prevents students from considering other options, including other degrees that may have a higher probability of success.

Indeed, the message is oversimplified. While the million-dollar payoff seems to promise a fixed amount, earnings vary greatly within educational levels, and there is substantial overlap in earnings' distributions at different educational levels. While median earnings of BA recipients are higher than those with AA recipients, 25% of those holding a BA have earnings below the median earnings of AA recipients, with some falling below earnings of the top 25% of high school graduates (Baum and Ma 2009).

Moreover, the average earnings' payoff does not reflect the lower earnings of groups of students. We can predict who will be in the bottom quartile. Even among graduates with bachelor degrees, those who had low grades in high school tend to earn less than those who received higher grades (Rosenbaum 2001). Similarly, students who attend less selective colleges or choose nontechnical majors also receive lower earnings, even if they have bachelor degrees (Grubb 1996; Carnevale 2009). However, some majors do receive a large financial advantage from a BA degree. The median income for students in health-related fields was higher than the 75th percentile for all other fields (Jacobson and Mokher 2009). Students rarely are told this, and some low-achieving students believe a bachelor degree will guarantee the million-dollar payoff even if they only do the minimum necessary to graduate (Rosenbaum et al. 2010).

While we usually assume BA recipients receive better earnings because they secure jobs that demand better skills, many BA graduates have jobs that do not use their college-level skills (Mittelhauser 1998; Barton 2008). Many find jobs in pink-collar or low-skilled clerical work, especially if they attend less selective colleges. Conducting a regression discontinuity analysis, Hoekstra (2009) showed that, among students with very similar achievement, BA recipients from state colleges receive substantially lower earnings than those who obtained degrees from the state's flagship university.

These numbers are not surprising. Many people with jobs that require a BA (e.g., teachers, social workers) are paid less than many with jobs that require an AA (e.g., computer specialists, engineering technicians, mechanics, heating/air conditioner repairers, dental and medical assistants). In addition, well-paying jobs are likely to have increasing employment demand over the next 6 years, according to the Bureau of Labor Statistics (Sommers 2009). Moreover, the BA payoff may have declined in recent years (Di Meglio 2010).

Recent research indicates that earnings are not the only indicator of success, and indeed it may indicate undesirable jobs (Redline and Rosenbaum 2010). While the million-dollar payoff message implies that earnings should be the primary criterion for choosing education and occupations, economic theory recognizes that high pay is sometimes offered to offset disagreeable job conditions. Practitioners who place students in jobs are well aware of these issues. In a recent study of private occupational colleges, job placement staff reported that they urge graduates to avoid the highest paid jobs (2010). These job placement staff are responsible for helping their students find good jobs, yet they discourage graduates from taking the highest paid jobs. They report that the highest paid jobs often have serious disadvantages; they tend to be dirty, demanding, and dangerous. Importantly, they are also often dead-end jobs, which do not lead to long-term earnings' payoffs or are deceptive, promising high commissions that rarely occur. Instead, placement staff urge graduates to take jobs that use relevant skills learned in college and provide job training as well as future promotions. Although these reports are about the BA degree labor market, we suspect these concerns are more general. They are particularly noteworthy because they suggest that a focus on high pay in starting jobs may be self-defeating in that high starting pay may not lead to long-term earnings' payoffs.

Following the perfectionist model, some community college counselors discourage associate degrees because they lead to settling for an inferior degree, diverting students from seeking a BA (Rosenbaum et al. 2010). In fact, many of the students who complete degrees go on to obtain bachelor or other higher degrees. In the National Educational Longitudinal Survey of the high school class of 1992, 803 students earned an associate degree by 2000 (according to official transcripts). Of these degree recipients, 78% received further education after earning an associate degree and 34% earned a bachelor degree (Stephan 2010). Moreover, this may underestimate actual degree completion.

As part of a larger study (Rosenbaum et al. 2010), we conducted interviews with a random sample of 80 community college graduates 7 years after they obtained degrees. This survey finds a similar pattern of further education. While this sample is of uncertain generalizability, it is one of the few sources that allows a 7-year follow-up after the degree and focuses on applied degrees in occupational fields, such as health, business, and technical programs, that often are assumed to be dead-end degrees. In this sample of 80 applied degree recipients from community colleges, 54% received further education and 35% earned a bachelor or higher degree. Compared with the national percentages, the local sample shows fewer students pursuing further education, but almost the same proportion receiving BA or higher degrees. In both samples, less than half terminate their education after completing a degree. Indeed, 6% of our local respondents earned master degrees within 7 years of completing an applied degree.

Despite perfectionism, associate degrees are not always seen as inferior to BAs. Applied associate of science degrees (AAS) degrees have become more common over the last several decades, and they today are a formal requirement for certain skilled jobs. A study of AAS graduates revealed that some BA graduates returned to community college to earn an AAS degree (Rosenbaum et al. 2010). These BA graduates disliked their jobs or could not get a job that used their skills. Some students wanted jobs that were more satisfying or allowed them to help other people. Others wanted more technical or practical skills. One reported that a degree in radiography leads to higher paid jobs than her previous teaching job. These individuals clearly did not believe that BA graduates obtain better jobs than AAS degree graduates. Although further research is needed, it seems to indicate that our preconceptions are too simple.

In summary, the million-dollar payoff message that idealizes the BA degree is compelling, and it may be the best way to command students' attention, but this simple message is incomplete and too narrow. The million-dollar payoff makes a compelling message, but it provides vague, insufficient, and sometimes misleading guidance for helping students make good career choices. Failing to clarify and elaborate this message can lead to serious problems for students.

Open Admissions Without Warnings

Many high school guidance counselors used to be gatekeepers, discouraging low-achieving students from attending college (Cicourel and Kitsuse 1963; Rosenbaum 1976). Sociological research identified this process and was perhaps responsible for giving it a poor reputation, although no one will regret a reduction in the old biased system. While some counselors still may practice gatekeeping, many high school guidance counselors report that they do not like the concept and do not practice it (Rosenbaum 2001).

Open admission policies at community colleges are one reason that counselors do not have to discourage anyone from attending college. Since the 1960s, enrollment at 4-year colleges doubled, enrollment at community colleges has increased fivefold, and open admissions policies allow access for almost anyone. Today, nearly half of all new college students attend community colleges, and high school counselors can promise all students that they can attend college. Unlike prior counselors, today's counselors do not have to discourage low-achieving students from enrolling in college.

However, like the perfectionist model, counselors avoid discouraging students by presenting an oversimplified understanding of open admissions. Counselors say that students can enter college even with low achievement records, but they rarely warn students of the probabilities of completing a degree (Rosenbaum 2001). Research indicates that students who enter community colleges with poor high school grades have a low chance of successful degree completion (Stephan et al. 2009).

In interviews with 90 high school students from four urban and two suburban high schools (Rosenbaum et al. 2010), we found that high school students rarely know about remedial classes. Few students realize that low achievers cannot enter college credit classes or certain programs (2010). Avoiding these details keeps students optimistic and encourages their college plans. However, it may give insufficient information for students' decisions.

Counselors also can withhold information. When a guidance counselor asked in an interview, "Who am I to burst their bubble?," she was denying responsibility for a task that others assume is part of the counselor's job (Rosenbaum 2001). Advising a senior with a D-average who wants to apply to Harvard, another counselor reported that he recommended the student to first attend the local community college and transfer to Harvard later. We assume the counselor meant to keep the student's dreams alive, but did not expect that Harvard would be an option (2001).

Although low-achieving students can enter college, their low probability of degree completion has been documented in recent research. In a national longitudinal survey, degree-planning high school seniors who had poor grades (Cs or lower) had less than a 20% chance of completing any degree in the 10 years after high school (Rosenbaum 2001). More recent research using administrative data in Florida shows remarkably similar results. For students with a C average in high school, 82% earned no credential in the 11 years after high school, almost the same proportion as in the national study (Jacobson and Mokher 2009). Open admissions policies offer a second opportunity for the nearly 20% who succeed. However, the vast majority of low-achieving students fail to attain any degree, and many do not earn a single college credit (2001).

Although these examples seem to blame counselors for following the perfectionist model, often they do not have a choice. Counselors face three kinds of structural influences that limit their actions. First, they cannot obtain authoritative information about their graduates' college outcomes. Institutional graduation-rate data on colleges rarely are provided, and these gross numbers may not apply to their school's graduates since several high schools usually feed into the same community college.

Second, counselors do not have enough time to discuss with students the consequences of various college choices. Even if counselors had good information, their many noncounseling duties mean that most spend less than 20% of their time on counseling (Moles 1991; Parsad et al. 2003; McDonough 1997). The average student/counselor ratio is large, 284:1 (2003), and prevents counselors from devoting much time to any particular student.

Third, and most important, the perfectionist model limits what counselors can say. Perfectionist norms imposed by parents and principals prevent them from providing candid information. Many counselors report that they receive complaints from parents and principals when they inform students that certain colleges are not likely to admit them. Some counselors report they would lose their job if they gave such advice (Rosenbaum 2001), and similar comments are reported in a more recent study (Rosenbaum et al. 2010). Just as sex education teachers are not free to give candid advice, counselors similarly are constrained by perfectionist norms that they may believe are misleading. In both cases, these norms create ethical dilemmas. Unfortunately, the perfectionist model limits information in ways that prevent youth from making informed choices about their options.

Like the million-dollar payoff, open admissions is true but incomplete. Many crucial details are not presented. Open admissions admits students into classes in college buildings, but not necessarily into college-credit classes, and noncredit classes (e.g., basic skills, remedial, and vocational) do not lead to degrees. The details of open admissions are unclear: Counselors do not mention them and perhaps do not know about them. These details are not easily available or understandable on college websites and in catalogs. When counselors have doubts, they believe they cannot voice them.

Unfortunately, the perfectionist model not only misleads high school seniors about their future prospects, it also prevents students from taking the right actions in high school. When encouraged to attend college despite low achievement, students infer that college is a place where low achievement does not matter. Just as they managed to graduate from high school with minimal efforts, they expect to do the same in college.

In the recent study of 90 seniors in urban and suburban public schools, we find that some students report they can enter community college even with an easy senior year (Rosenbaum et al. 2010). Seniors report that they do not need to take difficult courses (such as math and sciences), work hard in class, or think about college in advance. Senior year can be a time to rest before thinking seriously about college. These reports are consistent with findings from national surveys. Although most high school seniors plan to obtain a BA degree, many do not take demanding courses to prepare themselves for college-level coursework (National Commission on the High School Senior Year 2001). Moreover, many seniors do very little homework (Deluca and Rosenbaum 2001).

While some critics observe these patterns and blame students for refusing to prepare for college, this criticism assumes that students know they are not prepared for college, that students know what they need to do to prepare for college, and that they refuse to take those steps. These assumptions are probably wrong since high school students rarely are given good information about these issues. The perfectionist model may shield students from this knowledge, keeping them optimistic, but preventing them from knowing that they should take steps to prepare for their BA plans.

Indeed, students often are given misleading information, possibly due to the perfectionist model. For instance, some states require exit exams to certify mastery in order to graduate from high school, yet the standards for these exams vary. Many states are concerned that low pass rates will lead to political criticism, and, therefore these tests usually certify mastery far below the 12th grade level. Consequently, after passing these exams, many students fail the college placement exams 3 months later. They understandably are surprised to learn that high school competency does not indicate college readiness.

Students cannot be blamed for refusing to prepare for college when educators do not inform them of what is required. The perfectionist advice that low-achieving students can attend college seems to tell students they are prepared, and high school competency exams appear to support that message. Researchers suggest that students could be better informed if they took college placement tests early in their senior year, or if high school competency exams indicated college readiness levels, even if those levels were not required for graduation (Rosenbaum 2001; Kirst and Venezia 2004). However, only a few small programs have been created along these lines (Long and Riley 2007). Until such steps are taken, students may believe they are prepared for college, and may not see any reason to take difficult courses that would reduce college costs and their timetables. A simpler first step would be to make students aware of the limits of open admissions that allow access to college, but not to college-credit courses. Unfortunately, our perfectionist ideals prevent this message from being communicated.

Community College: Warming Up and Stigma-Free Remediation

Just as high school counselors encourage everyone to attend college, some community college staff also follow the perfectionist model by encouraging all students to enter traditional BA transfer programs. Community colleges also offer a variety of certificates and degrees (Associate of Arts, Associate of Sciences, Associate of Applied Sciences, Associate of General Studies, etc.) other than BA transfer programs. Many of these have fewer requirements and shorter timetables than BAs, but can lead to desirable job conditions and sometimes better pay. Nonetheless, some community colleges focus only on BA degrees, particularly for traditional college students under the age of 22 (Rosenbaum et al. 2010). Unfortunately, this ambitious goal conflicts with some students' poor academic skills. Since half of high school graduates have less than tenth grade achievement (Murnane and Levy 1996), many are not prepared for college credit classes.

The mismatch between student college attainment goals and academic readiness has two logical responses: lower the goals or raise student achievement. Community college counselors engage in cooling out, that is, dampening students' ambitious plans and convincing them to consider lesser goals (Clark 1960). However, just as gatekeeping became less common in high school, cooling out is now less common in community college. Following the perfectionist model, advisers often "warm up" students' plans, encouraging students with sub-BA plans to seek higher degrees, particularly BA degrees (Rosenbaum et al. 2006). Analyses of national survey data (Beginning Postsecondary Survey [BPS]) find that many students raise their expectations after entering community college. Indeed, among students who began at community college, "warm ups" (from associate and certificate goals to BA goals) "make up a higher percentage of all community college beginners than cool outs" (2006:46). Examining this issue more closely, a study of seven community colleges found that many students report that faculty and advisers strongly encourage warming up their degree plans (2006:63–64).

Of course, since many students' academic achievement is too low for college credit classes, remedial courses are used to bring achievement up to the level required by transfer programs. Over two thirds of community college students are directed into such remedial courses (Bailey 2009), and in some urban areas, the rate is over 90% (Rosenbaum et al. 2006). Remedial classes do not give credit toward a college degree, but rather are high school level courses to bring students up to college level so they can enter transfer programs, if students successfully complete them. Unfortunately, many students do not (2006).

Recent research indicates that, consistent with the perfectionist model, community college staff avoid discouraging students who are placed in remedial courses. Contrary to the old stigmatized image of remedial courses, colleges offer stigma-free remediation. Catalogs and staff do not use the term remedial, they use the euphemism, "developmental" (Rosenbaum 2006:73). Faculty and counselors "communicate their high expectations of students in order to combat their students' tendency to lack academic self-confidence," and they tell students that developmental courses are "a positive and necessary step in fulfilling their ultimate goals" (2006:73–74). Moreover, they also withhold key information about remedial courses.

Withholding Information About Placements

To protect students from stigma and discouragement, college advisors often withhold information. All entering students with degree goals must take a placement test to determine whether they can enter college-credit courses or must take remedial courses, and if so, how many and for how long. In other words, this test determines how long it will take to qualify for college-credit courses, and how long their degree plans will be delayed.

We find that community college staff say very little about the placement test, the scores students receive, and implications for degree timetables (Rosenbaum 2006:82). Moreover, there is little discussion about the test results. Students merely are told what courses they should take based on the results (Rosenbaum et al. 2010). In addition, because college staff, catalogs, and websites downplay the placement test, students rarely anticipate this test before arriving at college.

In a 2010 survey of community college students in Illinois and California (Rosenbaum et al. 2010), most students were not aware that they would be taking this test when they entered college. As a result, they did not use their senior year to prepare, and only 26% reported that they refreshed their knowledge before the test, which was taken after a long summer vacation (2010). Since poor scores on the test cause college to take more time and money, it provides a strong incentive to work hard in senior year and review in tested subjects, but the incentive is ineffective because most students do not know about it.

College staff also tell students very little about remedial courses (Rosenbaum et al. 2010). Colleges not only remove the stigma about remedial, they also remove clarity. College staff, catalogs, and websites are unclear as to whether taking remedial courses will earn college credits or prolong degree timetables. These classes that are several levels below college credit classes can add one or more terms of remedial study before students can enroll in college credit classes; however, community colleges can make it difficult for students to understand this process.

As a result, students rarely comprehend the implications of remedial courses. Many students believe that a 2-year degree will take 2 years; however, it averages 3.5 years in some community colleges, even for full-time students (Rosenbaum et al. 2006). Moreover, after counselors have advised a set of remedial courses, students could infer how long their degree will be delayed if counselors explained their remedial placements. Research indicates that most students do not understand that remedial courses are noncredit and delay degree completion (Rosenbaum et al. 2006). Given student confusion about the meaning of remedial, researchers cannot trust the validity of students' reports of being in remedial courses. Thus, alternative methods are necessary. In a survey conducted in seven community colleges, students were asked if they had taken any of a list of courses, all of which were remedial. Of students reporting they had taken any of these courses, 39% wrongly believed these courses counted toward their degree, and another 35% said they were not sure (2006:84). In other words, over 70% of students were wrong or not sure about these courses.

More seriously, remedial coursework is related strongly to degree outcomes, but students do not realize it. In a national survey (BPS), as the number of remedial subjects increases from 0 to 3 or more, students' perceived chances of achieving degree goals barely change (increasing from 90.7% to 91.0%, Rosenbaum et al. 2006:85). However, in the same data, as the number of remedial courses went from 0 to 3 or more, students' degree completion severely declined (from 26.6% to 15.3%). Moreover, this relationship remains large and significant in logistic regressions that control for individual attributes.

Denying Failure in Remedial Classes

Finally, and perhaps most importantly, college staff rarely warn students about the low success rate of remedial coursework. While research evidence is mixed about the remedial impact on students near the cutoff score, there is overwhelming evidence that students who have many deficiencies in several subjects often fail to complete the remedial sequence and frequently drop out of college without completing a degree (Bailey et al. 2010).

In an important recent study of the Achieving the Dream program, researchers found that only "46% of students referred to reading remediation and 33% of those referred to math remediation completed their sequence" (Bailey et al. 2010:259). For students referred to the lowest level remedial courses, completion rates are much lower (29% in reading and 17% in math). The authors replicated these findings in national data (NELS). Although community college staff avoid cooling out, they do so by telling students that remedial courses are a pathway into transfer programs; however, they do not say that while remedial courses work well for 17% of students who are low math achievers, the other 83% do not complete the remedial sequence. This pathway turns into a dead end for the vast majority of students.

Unseen Options

Are students handicapped for pursuing these high goals initially? Although students who fail in courses they find too challenging could return to a more realistic curriculum, this would require adequate time and resources. Many students have limited financial capital—limited savings, limited financial aid from Pell and state grants, limited amounts of earnings, and limited social capital. Even when parents or partners are willing to sacrifice to support a student's studies, they too have limits, particularly when they see college failures and degrees taking longer than expected. Students who drop out of college, especially disadvantaged students who have little financial and social capital, run the risk of depleting their resources.

Research supports this inference. Of beginning students in community colleges, 42% left in the first year, 50% of these return, and more than half of those who return leave before receiving a credential (Horn 1999). In sum, three quarters of dropouts do not return, or they return and leave again without earning a degree. Of course, while a 5-year time span may not be long enough, 5 years is a meaningful time span, and the three quarters who left are increasingly unlikely to return in later years.

Even success is a step down for those who planned to obtain a BA degree: 27.4% of those who returned received a credential (less than 14% of all first-year dropouts). These are split evenly between certificates and degrees, often in occupational programs (Horn 1999). If students had not received perfectionist advice, and initially had chosen a certificate or degree program that generally require lower academic skills, they would have earned the same credential in a shorter period of time, and many of the three quarters who dropped out might have completed one of these programs. In addition, that accomplishment could have given them confidence, practical skills, potentially better jobs while in college, and experiences to inform their career choices. An associate degree also could have been the first step to a bachelor degree, and 35% might be expected to do that. If students were informed about both options and their likely implications, they could choose the one that best fits their needs. As long as BA ideals justify withholding information, students cannot make informed choices.

Unfortunately, by focusing only on BA transfer, the perfectionist model may prevent students from considering other goals. Those with low academic achievement are told that remedial courses are the way to gain access to college credit classes, but they are not warned that this approach rarely is successful. Researchers also focus on the perfectionist model. While many studies examine remedial course outcomes (see Bailey et al. 2010 for a review), we are not aware of any that uses placement test results to inform and advise a student's program and degree choices. Researchers and practitioners should continue to explore ways to improve remedial courses, but the meager attention given to alternatives to pursuing a BA degree is surprising.

Other options do exist that require less remedial coursework. Community colleges offer certificates and applied degrees in a variety of occupational fields, many of which require lower academic achievement in one or more subjects. Students with academic deficiencies would need fewer remedial courses to enter these programs, and the programs would take less time, thus reducing the likelihood that unforeseen obstacles might interrupt their college plans.

Placement tests provide a profile of students' strong and weak areas of knowledge. Although these scores rarely are explained to students, if they were, students could use them to consider programs with faster degree timetables. Program options other than BA transfer might be chosen, particularly if students have limited time for college or if they are at high risk of having college interrupted by work or family demands. Since different degrees and programs have various academic prerequisites, students with low scores in writing might choose an occupational program with lower prerequisites in writing (e.g., computer networking) and students with low scores in math might choose a program with lower prerequisites in math (e.g., medical coding, court reporting). These occupations are in strong demand and offer desirable job conditions and decent pay. Yet placement test results rarely are used to assist students' choice of programs (Rosenbaum et al. 2010).

Adding Realistic Options to Perfectionist Ones

The perfectionist model prevents researchers and policymakers from considering goals other than BA transfer. In a study showing poor completion rates from low-level remedial placements (Bailey et al. 2010), the authors speculate that the placements might be justified since these students received more academic instruction, even if they do not complete the remedial sequence. While that justification might appeal to college staff, it might not satisfy students. One of the students interviewed in the study commented, "but that wasn't my purpose" (Rosenbaum et al. 2006).

Most students enter community college to improve their job prospects, and to do so quickly (Rosenbaum et al. 2006). That may be more true for low-achieving students who generally have acquired a distaste for schooling, but have been persuaded that community college will improve their labor market prospects. Raising their academic skills by small increments through remedial courses is not likely to improve job outcomes—only credentials can do that (Marcotte et al. 2005).

Indeed, recent research results "suggest that it is feasible for students to increase their earnings substantially by completing the courses needed to obtain a certificate" (Jacobson and Mokher 2009:2).

Unlike the perfectionist model in community colleges, private occupational colleges show that another approach is possible. While the private sector has some colleges with dubious and even fraudulent practices (Government Accountability Office 2010), it also includes some that have devised innovative and effective procedures. These colleges recognize the serious constraints that can interrupt the college careers of disadvantaged students. Although these colleges do encourage students to seek BA degrees, they also match students with appropriate occupational programs based on students' interests and achievements. They encourage a BA pathway that includes a series of credentials along the way, and they devise procedures to prevent mistakes and failures (Rosenbaum et al. 2006). In addition, private occupational colleges often hire job placement staff whose job is to place students in desirable jobs requiring midlevel skills. Many students are not aware of these types of jobs, and these colleges inform them of these options. As they attain each credential along the way, students become increasingly confident that they will attain their occupational goals, and that confidence keeps students motivated and willing to sacrifice to complete their degrees (2006).

These procedures seem to have benefits. Analyses of national longitudinal data (NELS) find that private occupational colleges have higher degree-completion rates than community colleges (56% and 37%, respectively), although both kinds of colleges enroll similar students. Private occupational colleges enroll slightly more low-achieving and low-SES students, and propensity-matched students have 20–24% higher degree completion rates at these colleges than at public 2-year colleges (Stephan and Rosenbaum 2009).

Community colleges could implement similar private occupational college practices; however, the perfectionist model is a serious impediment. Community colleges encourage students to create unrealistic goals that often result in dropping out of the remedial sequence and leaving college, with no degree and often no credits. In contrast, many private occupational colleges advise students to pursue careers in realistic and desirable jobs requiring midlevel skills (e.g., computer networking, business, medical technology, etc.). These jobs are in high demand, with good working conditions, and decent annual earnings ($40,000–$90,000). Many community colleges offer similar occupational programs, but they discourage young adults from taking them. Many college catalogs classify these as adult programs that new high school graduates may infer do not apply to them (Rosenbaum et al. 2010).

The practice of cooling out is misleading about the way higher education actually works. Cooling out refers to the ways counselors may encourage students to reduce their plans, sometimes in subtle ways (Clark 1960). In fact, however, counselors who do the opposite—allow low-achieving students to set unrealistically high goals and avoid mentioning more realistic jobs with desirable attributes—also are misleading students, as some counselors confess privately (Rosenbaum 2001). The harm will come later when many students fail and they lack the time, funds, or confidence to return to college for an applied degree with fewer academic requirements.

In contrast, when occupational colleges cool students' unrealistic dreams, they are adding lower interim goals, but not replacing their BA plans. They advise students about degree ladders that lead to bachelor degrees, as well as certificates and associate degrees along the way. These colleges also offer advising and job placement services that will make these outcomes more likely to happen.

Conclusion

Perfection may be an enemy of the good. Sociologists of education have used the perfectionist model to represent the BA-for-all movement. This chapter examines whether the model provides a helpful conceptualization of the path from high school to higher education. Four limitations of the perfectionist model are identified. First, the model poses degree choices as mutually exclusive, whereas in reality students can pursue more than one degree at the same time or sequentially. Second, it regards backup options as negative, but they can reduce risks and lead to good jobs, degree ladders, and student confidence. Third, it regards attaining a BA as the preferred outcome, although sub-baccalaureate degrees have some advantages, especially if time is limited (and they don't rule out BA degrees). Fourth, it encourages remedial courses over occupational courses, although they could be taken together or in sequence (Rosenbaum et al. 2006:191).

In effect, the perfectionist model has unintended consequences. It leads to hidden stratification because it encourages low-achieving students to pursue pathways with a low chance of payoffs, while failing to mention realistic backup options that could lead to good jobs with fewer prerequisites. The perfectionist model presents high goals and strong encouragement, but negative consequences are not mentioned. This avoids discouragement, but gives insufficient information to students to help them decide the best way to achieve favorable outcomes.

The perfectionist model projects an ideal image of society and provides a positive goal. However, it implicitly disparages midlevel attainments, thus suggesting that high goals are the only ones worth seeking, which inevitably can create disappointment. The perfectionist model disparages all but the top jobs. Urging 100% of adolescents to aspire to the top 20% of jobs makes most youth feel like failures.

In addition to disparaging many desirable jobs, the perfectionist model discourages the less demanding and time-consuming degrees that lead to these jobs and shows no concern about helping students find realistic careers. The perfectionist model encourages counselors to advise low-achieving students to enroll in remedial course sequences that only 17% will complete, and colleges offer no warnings and no procedures to offer other alternatives before students drop out.

Remarkably, the perfectionist model prevents counselors from facing these outcomes. Much like the abstinence movement that ignores 80% failure rates, the BA-for-all movement ignores failures that are sometimes of similar magnitude. Even if planning to attain a BA degree, low-achieving students can earn certificates and associate degrees along the way, just in case they fail at their BA plans, as 80%

do (Rosenbaum 2001). Many counselors following the perfectionist model believe that they are acting to accomplish societal ideals; however, perfectionism can make it difficult to face actual outcomes.

Accountability provides an alternate point of view. Unlike perfectionism's focus on ideal goals, accountability focuses on actual outcomes and makes those outcomes visible. Yet accountability may not be sufficient to fix the problems. Even if accountability forces colleges to focus on outcomes, that may not allow counselors to feel comfortable advising students to get degrees other than BA degrees. Indeed, most accountability reformers continue to focus on the traditional BA degree as the only criterion for success. Accountability reformers criticize colleges for poor rates of BA completion and remedial programs for low success rates (Education Trust 2010). However, there is no discussion of alternate degree goals or alternate pathways to the degrees. Accountability reformers criticize colleges for ignoring outcomes, but reformers do not seem interested in criticizing the perfectionist model.

The perfectionist model also has implications for sociological research. It requires that as researchers, we examine our own perfectionist assumptions, and consider whether we are failing to examine hidden forms of stratification. While it is useful to assess the causal impact of remedial coursework on marginal students near the cutoff score. The Bailey et al. (2010) study points to the importance of studying very low-achieving students, and alternative pathways such students could take other than remedial pathways that lead to failure.

Sociological analyses can play a constructive role in informing institutional actors, especially advisors whose duties require such information. We propose three kinds of sociological analyses that could inform practitioners and policymakers about the stratification implications of their well-intentioned actions, and suggest more complex goals and procedures that would be more candid, realistic, and lead to better outcomes.

First, sociologists can identify the probabilities of various outcomes associated with particular pathways for different kinds of students. This is the accountability approach, and this is where sociological research designs can be useful. Transparency about placement tests and remedial courses will help (Stephan and Rosenbaum 2009). However, transparency requires specific information about outcomes that rarely are studied now.

Social stratification models can be useful for providing the requisite information. Colleges can systematically analyze the full range of possible program options for various groups of students, and what outcomes occur for each. Random assignment to programs cannot be done, but analytic methods that compare outcomes for comparable students (such as propensity matching) can provide useful information (Stephan et al. 2009). In some cases, success rates are so low that inferences can be made. Students in the lowest level of remedial math need to be aware of the 17% success rate associated with this choice, so they can consider backup options. Systematic research can have a real impact.

Indeed, many counselors may suspect failure, but in the absence of systematic information, they cannot be sure. Research could have a powerful influence by confirming their suspicions, and such research can free them to give authoritative advice with confidence. Colleges correctly assert that simple graduation-rate percentages do not adjust for students' goals, motivation, or prior achievement. The most appropriate statistics require multivariate analysis, which is almost never done. Roderick and colleagues' (2006, 2008) studies of Chicago public schools (CPS) are a noteworthy exception. After Roderick reported that a particular college had a graduation rate under 30% for students with A averages in high school (2006:81), a CPS principal prohibited the college's recruiter from entering his school (Roderick, personal communication 2008). Researchers could play a powerful role in informing high school staff about their graduates' college outcomes, which could improve students' incentives in high school and improve their college choices.

However, accountability is not sufficient. It responds to these results largely by blaming colleges for low success rates. Facing accountability pressures to improve graduation rates, colleges may lower their standards or turn away disadvantaged students if they fear that they will have difficulty graduating these students. Clearly something more is needed.

Second, sociological analysis suggests that colleges should promote a broader conception of desirable jobs and degrees than promoted by the perfectionist model. Although they are not self-conscious about the process, community colleges create a social construction of career options, which identifies various choices, their desirability, and the pathways leading to them. While the perfectionist model focuses only on the BA degree and related occupations, reality offers a much wider variety of desirable jobs and pathways to those jobs. Just as placement staff focus on jobs which use graduates' skills and offer training and advancement opportunities (Redline and Rosenbaum 2010), sociological analysis could examine the various ways different colleges portray career options and the pathways to them. In addition, career advice may vary by types of college staff, with general college counselors offering different advice than occupational faculty, many of whom have strong labor-market contacts. This would include qualitative research on the ways programs describe career paths in initial orientation meetings, class content, and career advising at the end of the program.

Third, sociology suggests that colleges can create institutional procedures that include more transparency and dependable opportunities for a variety of desirable outcomes. For instance, colleges can build stronger degree ladders. Like tracking reforms that allow lower track students to advance into upper tracks through new institutional options (summer or after-school programs), college programs can be designed that offer alternate pathways to upward mobility. Indeed, like tracking reforms, new degree ladders can be created that construct explicit institutional procedures for advancing—through certificates, associate degrees, and bachelor degrees with a high probability of success. This requires clearly articulated pathways and procedures that reduce the possibility of mistakes as well as student information systems that quickly detect mistakes and correct them. Today, applied associate degrees can lead to applied bachelor degrees, an option that barely existed a decade ago (Bragg, Townsend, and Ruud 2009). Based on sociological research findings like those in our prior research (Rosenbaum et al. 2006), a national reform group (Complete College America 2010) has over 20 governors signed on to an agenda of reforms to improve college completion, and a grassroots organization has begun working with community colleges to implement similar reforms (Women Employed). Colleges can design institutional procedures to make students aware of these options, to make these degree ladders more transparent, and to provide supports so that students can get short-term applied associate degrees and then continue on to applied bachelor degrees.

Community colleges have gone to great lengths to provide access to new students from disadvantaged backgrounds. But students still face constraints and can benefit from new options and procedures. If colleges are going to make open access effective, they need to provide nontraditional institutional procedures to serve these students. Recognizing the limits of traditional perfectionist ideals is the first step to taking such actions.

Acknowledgments The authors thank the Spencer Foundation, the William and Melinda Gates Foundation, the Institute for Policy Research at Northwestern University, and Johns Hopkins Bloomberg School of Public Health for support of this research. While these institutions do not necessarily endorse our views, they support the dissemination of research to improve understanding and policy efforts. We also thank Karl Alexander, Paul Barton, David Bills, George Bohrnstedt, Amy Foran, Josh Jarrett, Melvin Kohn, Annette Lareau, Ann Person, Julie Redline, and Pam Schuetz for thoughtful suggestions on an earlier version.

References

Alexander, Karl L., Martha Cook, and Edward L. McDill. 1978. Curriculum tracking and educational stratification. *American Sociological Review* 43(1): 7–66.

Avery, Christopher, and Thomas Kane. 2004. Student perceptions of college opportunities. In *College choices: The economics of where to go, when to go, and how to pay for it*, ed. C.M. Hoxby, 355–394. Cambridge: National Bureau of Economic Research.

Bailey, Thomas. 2009. Addressing the needs of underprepared students. *CCRC Currents*. New York City: Teachers College, April.

Bailey, Thomas, Dong Wook Jeong, and Sung-Woo Cho. 2010. Referral, enrollment, and completion in developmental education sequences in community colleges. *Economics of Education Review* 29: 255–270.

Barton, Paul. 2008. *Windows on achievement and inequality*. Princeton: Educational Testing Service.

Baum, Sandy, and Jennifer Ma. 2009. *Education pays*. Princeton: College Board.

Bearman, Peter S., and Hannah Bruckner. 2005. After the promise: The consequences of adolescent virginity pledges. *Journal of Adolescent Health* 36(4): 271–278.

Bragg, Debra, Barbara K. Townsend, and Collin M. Ruud. 2009. *The adult learner and applied baccalaureate: Emerging lessons for state and local implementation*. Office of Community College Research and Leadership, University of Illinois.

Bylund, C.L., R.S. Imes, and L.A. Baxter. 2005. Accuracy of parents' perceptions of their college student children's health and health risk behaviors. *Journal of American College Health* 54: 31–37.

Carnevale, Anthony. 2009. Postsecondary education goes to work. Working Paper, Center on Education and the Workforce, Georgetown University.

Chandra, A., G.M. Martinez, W.D. Mosher, J.C. Abma, and J. Jones. 2002. Fertility, family planning and reproductive health of U.S. women: Data from the 2002 National Survey of Family Growth. *Vital Health Statistics* 23(80): 1–160.

Cicourel, Aaron V., and John I. Kitsuse. 1963. *The educational decision-makers*. Indianapolis: Bobbs Merrill.
Clark, Burton. 1960. The 'cooling out' function in higher education. *American Journal of Sociology* 65: 569–576.
Complete College America. 2010. *Freedom to fail*. Zionsville: Complete College America.
Deil-Amen, Regina, and Stefanie DeLuca. 2010. The underserved third: How our educational structures populate an educational underclass. *Journal of Education for Students Placed at Risk* 15: 1–24.
Deluca, Stefanie, and J. Rosenbaum. 2001. Individual agency and the life course: Do low-SES students get less long-term payoff for their school efforts? *Sociological Focus* 24(4): 357–376.
Di Meglio, Francesca. 2010. College: Big investment, paltry return. *Businessweek* June 29.
Eaton, Danice K., Laura Kann, Steve Kinchen, Shari Shanklin, James Ross, Joseph Hawkins, William A. Harris, Richard Lowry, Tim McManus, David Chyen, Connie Lim, Nancy D. Brener, and Howell Wechsler. 2008. Youth risk behavior surveillance—United States, 2007. *Mortality and Morbidity Weekly Report* 57(SS04): 1–131.
Education, Trust. 2010. *Opportunity adrift: Our flagship universities are straying from their public mission*. Retrieved 1 November 2010, http://www.edtrust.org/dc/resources/publications/higher-education.
Eisenberg, M.E., L.H. Bearinger, R.E. Sieving, C. Swain, and M.D. Resnick. 2004. Parents' beliefs about condoms and oral contraceptives: Are they medically accurate? *Perspectives on Sexual and Reproductive Health* 36(2): 50–57.
Gamoran, Adam, and Mark Berends. 1987. The effects of stratification in secondary schools: Synthesis of survey and ethnographic research. *Review of Education Research* 57(4): 415–435.
Government Accountability Office. 2006. *Abstinence education: Efforts to assess the accuracy and effectiveness of federally-funded programs*. Tech. Report GAO-07-87. Washington, DC: Government Accountability Office.
Government Accountability Office. 2010. *For-profit colleges: Undercover testing finds college encouraged fraud and engaged in deceptive and questionable marketing practices*. Tech. Report GAO-10-948T. Washington, DC: Government Accountability Office. Retrieved 2 November 2010, http://www.gao.gov/new.items/d10948t.pdft.
Grubb, W.N. 1996. *Working in the middle: Strengthening education and training for the mid-skilled labor force*. San Francisco: Jossey-Bass.
Hallinan, Maureen T. 1994. Tracking: From theory to practice. *Sociology of Education* 67(April): 79–91.
Hoekstra, M. 2009. The effect of attending the flagship state university on earnings: A discontinuity-based approach. *Review of Economics and Statistics* 91(4): 717–724.
Horn, Laura. 1999. *Stopouts or stayouts? Undergraduates who leave college in their first year*. NCES 1999–087. Washington, DC: U.S. Department of Education.
Jacobson, Louis, and Christine Mokher. 2009. *Pathways to boosting the earnings of low-income students by increasing their educational attainment*. Retrieved 10 November 2010, www.hudson.org/files/publications/Gates%2001–07.pdf.
Kirst, Michael, and Andrea Venezia. 2004. *From high school to college*. San Francisco: Jossey Bass.
Krei, Melinda, James E. Rosenbaum, and Shazia Miller. 1997. What role should counselors have? In *Advances in educational policy*, vol. 3, ed. Kenneth K. Wong, 79–92. Greenwood: JAI Press.
Long, Bridget Terry, and Erin K. Riley. 2007. Sending signals to students: The role of early placement testing in improving academic preparation. In *Minding the gap*, eds. Nancy Hoffman, Joel Vargas, Andrea Venezia, and Marc Miller, 105–112. Cambridge: Harvard Education Press.
Luker, Kristin. 2006. *When sex goes to school*. New York: W. W. Norton.
Marcotte, David, Thomas Bailey, Carey Borkowski, and N. Gregory Kienzel. 2005. The returns of a community college education. *Educational Evaluation and Policy Analysis* 27: 157–175.
McDonough, P.M. 1997. *Choosing colleges: How social class and schools structure opportunity*. Albany: State University of New York Press.

Miller, K.S., B.A. Kotchick, S. Dorsey, R. Forehand, and A.Y. Ham. 1998. Family communication about sex: What are parents saying and are their adolescents listening? *Family Planning Perspectives* 30: 218–222.

Mittelhauser, Mark. 1998. Outlook for college graduates, 1996–2006. Bureau of Labor Statistics, Federal Consumer Information Center. Washington, DC: U.S. Department of Labor. Retrieved October 27, 2010, www.Pueblo.gsa.gov/cic_text/employ/3college/3college.htm (accessed September 28, 2005).

Moles, O.C. 1991. Guidance programs in American high schools: A descriptive portrait. *School Counselor* 38(3): 163–177.

Murnane, Richard J., and Frank Levy. 1996. *Teaching the new basic skills*. New York: The Free Press.

National Commission on the High School Senior Year. 2001. Student transitions: The senior year of high school: Briefing paper. Retrieved October 20, 2010, www.wtcsystem.edu/pk16/goals/pdf/student_transitions.pdf.

Newcomer, Susan F., and J.R. Udry. 1985. Parent-child communication and adolescent sexual behavior. *Family Planning Perspectives* 17: 169–174.

Parsad, B., D. Alexander, E. Farris, and L. Hudson. 2003. *High school guidance counseling*. National Center for Education Statistics. No. NCES 2003-015. Washington, DC: U.S. Department of Education.

Redline, Julie, and James Rosenbaum. 2010. Institutional job placement: Can it avoid reproducing social inequalities? *Teachers College Record* 112(3).

Roderick, M. 2008. Personal communication to James Rosenbaum, May, 2008.

Roderick, Melissa, Jenny Nagaaoka, and Elaine Allensworth. 2006. *From high school to the future: A first look at Chicago public school graduates college enrollment, college preparation, and graduation from four-year colleges*. Chicago: Consortium on Chicago School Research.

Roderick, M., J. Nagaoka, V. Coca, and E. Moeller. 2008. *From high school to the future: Potholes in the road to college*. Chicago: Consortium on Chicago School Research.

Rosenbaum, James. 1976. *Making inequality*. New York: Wiley.

Rosenbaum, James. 2001. *Beyond college-for-all*. New York: Russell Sage Foundation Press.

Rosenbaum, Janet E. 2006. Reborn a virgin: Adolescents' retracting of virginity pledges and sexual histories. *American Journal of Public Health* 96(6): 1098–1103.

Rosenbaum, Janet E. 2009. Patient teenagers? A comparison of the sexual behavior of virginity pledgers and matched non-pledgers. *Pediatrics* 123: e110–e120.

Rosenbaum, Janet, and Byron Weathersbee. 2009. True love waits: Do Southern Baptists? Premarital sexual behavior among newly married Southern Baptist Sunday school students. Presented at *The Annual Meeting of the American Sociological Association*, August, San Francisco.

Rosenbaum, James, Regina Deil-Amen, and Ann Person. 2006. *After admission: From college access to college success*. New York: Russell Sage Foundation Press.

Rosenbaum, Janet, Marc Elliott, David Kanouse, and Mark Schuster. 2007. A comparison of parents' and adolescents' ratings of parent-initiated sex education. Presented at *The Society of Adolescent Health and Medicine Meeting*, March, Denver.

Rosenbaum, James, Pam Schuetz, and Amy Foran. 2010. How students make college plans and ways schools and colleges could help. Working Paper, Institute for Policy Research, Northwestern University.

Schneider, Barbara, and David Stevenson. 1999. *The ambitious generation*. New Haven: Yale University Press.

Smith, Lisa. 2009. Invest in yourself with a college education. *Forbes Magazine*. Retrieved November 8, 2010, http://www.investopedia.com/articles/younginvestors/06/investineducation.asp.

Sommers, Dixie. 2009. National labor market projections for community college students. *New Directions for Community Colleges* 146: 33–52.

Sørensen, Aage. 1977. The structure of inequality and the process of attainment. *American Sociological Review* 42(6): 965–978.

Stephan, Jennifer. 2010. Is an associate's degree a dead end? Institute for Policy Research, Northwestern University. Unpublished analyses, National Educational Longitudinal Survey.

Stephan, Jennifer L., and James E. Rosenbaum. 2009. Permeability and transparency in the high school-college transition. In *AERA handbook on education policy research*, eds. D. Plank, G. Sykes, and B. Schneider, 928–941. Washington, DC: American Educational Research Association.

Stephan, Jennifer L., James E. Rosenbaum, and Ann E. Person. 2009. Stratification in college entry and completion. *Social Science Research* 38(3): 572–593.

Trenholm, Christopher, Barbara Devaney, Kenneth Fortson, Melissa Clark, Lisa Quay Bridgespan, and Justin Wheeler. 2008. Impacts of abstinence education on teen sexual activity, risk of pregnancy, and risk of sexually transmitted diseases. *Journal of Policy Analysis and Management* 27(2): 255–276.

Chapter 10
Changing Family, Changing Education

Laura Hamilton, Regina Werum*, Lala Carr Steelman, and Brian Powell

When it comes to education, family matters. Scholars from a number of different theoretical perspectives have demonstrated various ways in which family either impedes or facilitates educational growth and attainment. The classic status attainment paradigm, for example, incorporates educational attainment of parents, parental encouragement, and parental aspirations as key precursors to educational and occupational outcomes (Blau and Duncan 1967; Sewell and Hauser 1975). Various theories of capital investments—be they human capital, cultural capital, social capital, or economic capital—are predicated on the premise that parental investments in children are critical means by which familial advantages and disadvantages are replicated across generations (Becker 1964, 1981; Bourdieu and Passeron 1977; DiMaggio 1982; Coleman 1988; Steelman and Powell 1991; Schneider and Coleman 1993; Lareau 2003).

Given this legacy, virtually all scholars interested in educational outcomes are presumably cognizant of the important role that parents play in their offspring's

---

*This chapter is partly based on work conducted while the second author served at the National Science Foundation.

L. Hamilton (✉)
School of Social Sciences, Humanities and Arts, University of California-Merced, Merced, CA 95343, USA
e-mail: lhamilton2@ucmerced.edu

R. Werum
Department of Sociology, Emory University, Atlanta, GA 30322, USA
e-mail: rwerum@emory.edu

L.C. Steelman
Department of Sociology, University of South Carolina, Columbia, SC 29208, USA
e-mail: steelman@sc.edu

B. Powell
Indiana University, Bloomington, IN 47405, USA
e-mail: powell@indiana.edu

educational chances. Some sociologists of education—in particular those who study educational policy and educational structure—may be troubled by this conclusion. By definition, the greater the role that parents play, the lesser the role that schools play. Indeed, one reason Coleman and colleagues' (1966) classic report on educational opportunity is so compelling is because it demonstrated just how powerful parental influence is: Family background overshadowed the effect of school factors. In fact, one might contend that it is difficult to isolate the impact of schooling in the absence of knowledge about family structure and experiences. One of the main challenges that scholars of education must attend to is the incorporation of insights from those who study family to better understand how schools can work most effectively (Schneider and Coleman 1993).

Scholars of family and education face yet another challenge, however. All too often research on families (not only in the field of education) presumes a particular, normative image. This image corresponds with what Smith (1993) characterizes as the Standard North American Family (SNAF). This prototypical family is composed of a married mother and father and their biological children, in which specified gender roles, marriage, heterosexual relationships, and, implicitly, monoracial relations are privileged. The SNAF often acts as a yardstick against which other family arrangements are judged, most often as less effective families or not as families at all. This idealized conception of family is insensitive to and unrealistic about the growing number of children living in other familial forms—for example, single-parent families and stepfamilies, families with older parents, same-sex families, adoptive families, and interracial families—both in the USA and other nations. As a consequence, current educational scholarship lags behind the dramatic changes in sociodemographic profiles of families.

In this chapter, we identify recent developments that connect family change with schooling. While we cannot exhaustively cover all scholarship that moves in this direction, we have chosen some areas in which new lines of research are currently under development. Our purpose is threefold. First, we briefly discuss various theoretical approaches through which scholars have viewed family structure effects in education. Next, we report what existing and cutting-edge research has to say about how the changing shape and diversity of families affect children's educational outcomes. While seemingly disparate, many of the changes we discuss next are interconnected—both by the larger macroforces that set them into motion and in how they challenge existing research on the intersection of family and education. Our final goal is to use the review of literature to glean theoretical insights into how family structure shapes children's educational outcomes. We also point to challenges that scholars may face in conducting future research and identify efforts that hold the most promise.

Theoretical Approaches to Family Structure Effects

The question of how, and through what processes, family structure influences children's educational experiences has been approached from many different angles. One group of studies highlights the direct influence of family structure, in which family structure itself matters. This approach is premised on the idea that traditional family structures are intrinsically more effective than others, thereby providing some children with an educational advantage. Within the subfield of sociology of education—and, arguably, within sociology more broadly—this approach has increasingly been challenged. Despite these challenges, however, this perspective continues to be visible in scholarly debates, public discourse, and public policy.

Both sociological and evolutionary theories posit direct effects of family structure on children's welfare. Sociological studies argue that growing up without two biological parents is linked to a broad array of disadvantages for children (Popenoe 1999; Amato 2005). Cherlin and Furstenberg (1994) argue that departing from the traditional nuclear family gives rise to ambiguities in how children and parents should behave. These ambiguities result in difficulties in family functioning that shape, among other things, children's educational outcomes.

Parallel theories from the evolutionary sciences also have been imported into educational research. Kin selection theory argues that parental investment is a form of reproductive survival, in which parents—especially mothers—invest more in their biological offspring (Buss 1995; Salmon 2005). This genetic link is embedded in traditional family structure and is at the core of the advantages that these children are expected to experience. Biblarz and Raftery (1999), for example, apply evolutionary theories to predict that children from two-biological-parent families will attain higher levels of education than children from single-mother families, who in turn will attain higher levels of education than children from single-father and stepparent families.

A second but more indirect approach to the study of the effect of family structure on children's outcomes focuses primarily on characteristics associated with family structure. This approach has grown largely out of work challenging the pathology of matriarchy in which children in single-mother households are seen as victims of a damaging family structure. Downey (1994) and Biblarz and Raftery (1999) have emphasized the importance of recognizing that often it is not family structure per se, but associated characteristics—such as high levels of unemployment, lower income, and less occupational prestige—that make certain family structures less educationally advantageous for children. Indeed, they find that once factors such as these are taken into account, children from single-mother households have similar levels of educational success as those in more traditional structures.

A third line of theoretical reasoning, the most nascent of the three, emphasizes how context shapes the educational effects of family structure. Like the approach just discussed, it is focused on indirect effects of family structure; yet, a contextual approach recognizes that the characteristics associated with family forms will change depending on the social, legal, economic, and political climate. Steelman et al. (2002), for example, discuss how even the most seemingly established patterns associated with family structure—such as the negative effect of increasing sibship size on parental investment (Downey 2001; Conley 2004; Conley and Glauber 2006; but see Guo and VanWey 1999; Rodgers et al. 2000)—are moderated by social policy, including educational policy. Much of the work in this direction is therefore cross national and comparative (Pong 1997a, b; Park 2008; Xu 2008). However, some research has suggested that positive educational effects of certain nontraditional family forms in the USA are a compensatory response to cultural devaluation (Hamilton et al. 2007).

Next, we discuss five developing changes in family structure, notably, increases in (1) single-parent and stepparent families, (2) families with older parents, (3) same-sex families, (4) adoptive families, and (5) multiracial families. We present the extant literature on each, as well as addressing theoretical perspectives that have been used to understand how they shape children's educational welfare. In the conclusion, we use this evidence to assess which perspectives provide the most fruitful way of thinking about the role that family structure plays in creating educational advantage and disadvantage.

Single-Parent Families and Stepfamilies

Increases in cohabitation, divorce, and nonmarital childbearing are key features of a major demographic transition that began in the USA during the 1960s (McLanahan 2004). These changes are at the heart of a major shift in American family structure: Conservative estimates suggest that well over half of all children will spend some of their childhood apart from at least one biological parent (McLanahan and Sandefur 1994). Indeed, current census data suggest that 26% of all American children under the age of 18 in 2009 were living in single-parent families (Kreider 2008). The number of children living in stepfamilies is more difficult to deduce, given definitional issues in most national data. Estimates of the percentage of children under the age of 18 living in a stepfamily often fall in the 8–20% range, depending on whether or not marriage is a definitional requirement (Fields 2001; Stewart 2007).

Of all the changes in family structure discussed in this chapter, the educational scholarship on single-parent families and stepfamilies is among the most developed. As McLanahan and Sandefur (1994) conclude, children in single-parent families experience an educational disadvantage when compared to children in families with two, married biological parents. For example, they note that children from single-parent families are twice as likely to drop out of high school, are less likely to attend college, and are less likely to graduate from college than students in families with two biological parents. Other scholars have reached similar conclusions (Astone and McLanahan 1991; Zill 1996; Pong 1997b; Pong and Ju 2000). Interestingly, the disparity between single- and two-parent families is greatest for white children, for whom the advantage of being white is intricately intertwined with the advantage of being from a family with two married parents. This finding is consistent with more recent research showing that black children's academic achievement takes only a small or negligible setback when they are in single-parent families (Battle and Coates 2004; Wu and Qi 2006).

As Stewart (2007) reports, more than two decades of research on children in stepfamilies also suggests that they do not perform as well as children in married, two-biological-parent families. They have lower GPAs, worse attendance records, higher high school drop-out rates, and receive fewer years of total education overall.

Like children in single-parent families (Dawson 1991; McLanahan and Sandefur 1994), these children also are more likely to experience behavioral and health issues that impact their ability to achieve in school. However, of the two family types, children in stepfamilies have more problems in school, perhaps due to the greater number of disruptive family transitions (Stewart 2007).

It is important to note that while disparities exist between children from single-parent families and stepfamilies and those in married, two-biological-parent families, they are small and highly situational. Amato and Keith (1991) found significantly worse academic outcomes for children in divorced and remarried households; however, in later work, Amato (1994) assessed the lifetime costs (including educational) of divorce on children. He found that while these costs remain, they are small, and there is considerable overlap between children who experienced parental divorce and those who did not. In addition, the impact of divorce or remarriage is profoundly shaped by situational factors, such as contact with the noncustodial biological parent and conflict surrounding the divorce.

Scholars posit various explanations for these findings. Explanations often focus on characteristics associated with family types that make parental investment difficult. As McLanahan (2004) indicates, single-parent families and stepfamilies are most common among already disadvantaged families. These families often lack the educational resources—such as money or time to spend with children—that biological, married parents often provide. Downey (1994) and Biblarz and Raftery (1999) argue that the poor performance of single-mother households can be attributed largely to a lack of economic resources, whereas in single-father households, a lack of interpersonal resources (e.g., helping with schoolwork) has a similar result. Similarly, research suggests that stepfamilies do not invest as heavily in their children as do biological parents with respect to both economic and interpersonal resources (Anderson et al. 1999; Zvoch 1999). Moreover, these studies show that the least privileged families are most likely to experience a family transition that educationally disadvantages children while more privileged families are likely to experience a transition that provides more resources for children. This finding suggests ways in which changes in family structure may exacerbate patterns of class and race-based educational inequalities.

One interesting difference between research on single-parent families and stepfamilies is the explanation posited for these resource disparities. Research on stepfamilies often calls attention to problems with the family structure itself. Sociologists have tended to see stepfamilies as incomplete institutions, that is, family structures hampered by the absence of clear roles for parents and children (Cherlin 1978; Cherlin and Furstenberg 1994). For evolutionary theorists, low levels of parental investment in stepfamilies present evidence of genetic selection whereby stepparents are disinclined to invest resources in nonkin (Buss 1995; Daly and Wilson 1998). This explanation, however, is challenged by research on adoptive families, as we discuss next (Hamilton et al. 2007), and suggests a need to move beyond holding structure itself responsible.

Scholarship on the educational achievement of children in single-parent families provides a model in this regard. It often focuses on the context in which these families are placed, rather than on the families themselves. In fact, research indicates that the economic hardships that result from divorce help to explain a considerable amount of the difference between children from single-parent and those from two-biological-married-parent families (McLanahan and Sandefur 1994). Research from an international perspective further highlights the tendency to see single-parent families as a victim of social policy rather than pathology. Scholarship has shown that in other European and Western countries, performance gaps between children reared in two-parent versus one-parent families are reduced (Hampden-Thompson and Pong 2005; Pong et al. 2003). Furthermore, in several large Asian countries, such as China, South Korea, Hong Kong, Thailand, and Indonesia, the negative effect of single parenthood is negligible or even reversed (Park 2007, 2008; Xu et al. 2008).

These patterns suggest that social policy plays an important role in moderating the effects of family/parent composition on children's educational outcomes. They suggest that future efforts might be directed to parsing out the effects of the context in which families are embedded—either at the macrolevel with social or economic policy, or at a more microlevel with situational factors (Amato 1994)—from those of the family structure. This approach will result in a better understanding of how educational disadvantage experienced by children in single-parent families and stepfamilies can be reduced and even mitigated.

Families with Older Parents

The major demographic transition that began in the 1960s also included several other features, most notably a rising age at marriage and delayed childbirth (McLanahan 2004). These characteristics are not just limited to the USA, but also have been occurring in most industrialized, Western nations. For instance, in 1970, the median age at marriage was 20.8 for women (23.2 for men), and the average age of first-time mothers was 21.4. By 2006, the median age at marriage had risen to 25.5 for women (27.5 for men), with mothers' first-time births at age 25 (Census Bureau 2009; Mathews and Hamilton 2009). In this regard, the USA may be considered somewhat behind, having the lowest age at first birth compared to peer countries (Mathews and Hamilton 2009). The increase in births among older, predominately more privileged married women comes in sharp contrast to patterns of younger, nonmarital births among the least privileged (McLanahan 2004).

Like other changes in family, the shift in the average age of parents represents a change in the composition of family—and is thus considered to be a structural change with educational consequences for children. Extending classic resource allocation arguments, Mare and Tzeng (1989) and Powell et al. (2006) suggest that children benefit from being born to older parents. Both maternal and paternal ages are linked positively to a broad array of educational benefits, including financial, cultural, and interactional resources, as well as educational expectations (Powell et al. 2006). The patterns are evident both at the bivariate level and with the addition of sociodemographic controls. These findings are important, as parental investments have consistently been linked to higher educational attainment (Blau and Duncan 1967; Sewell and Hauser 1975; Coleman 1988; Alexander et al. 1997).

Indeed, considerable research suggests that children born to older parents perform better in school. For instance, Spieker et al. (1999) find that school-related problem behaviors are negatively related to maternal age at birth. Similarly, an older body of research suggests that children born to teen mothers are at a greater risk for low academic performance than those born to older mothers (Brooks-Gunn and Furstenberg 1986). These results also have been corroborated internationally. A longitudinal study of Canadian adolescents shows that being born to a mother under the age of 18 has a long-term, negative effect on math performance (Dahinten et al. 2007). The influence of parental age is perhaps most clear in Kalmijn and Kraaykamp's (2005) comparative historical study, looking at the educational outcomes of siblings born to the same mother in the Netherlands. They find that children born when mothers are younger are distinctly disadvantaged, as increasing maternal age is positively and directly related to children's educational attainment.

Several explanations for the educational benefits provided by older parents have been offered. Some contend that older parents may simply be more mature, having time to develop the preference structure, values, networks, goals, and experiences that assist in parental investment well before becoming parents themselves (Heuvel 1988; Mirowsky and Ross 1992). Others note that older parents tend to be further along in their careers, have larger incomes, are more economically stable, and thus have more financial resources to spare (Featherman and Spenner 1988; Ross and Mirowsky 1999). This is likely in part a result of selectivity. The effects of maternal age on children's academic achievement are largely indirect, being strongly determined by the mother's personal and family background (Geronimus et al. 1994; Levine et al. 2001).

Selectivity may occur through an intergenerational transmission of wealth as well as class-based understandings of the life course. More privileged individuals often receive the parental financial support and socialization necessary to postpone the typical markers of adulthood—such as full-time employment, marriage, and childbearing—for academic and career development (Furstenberg et al. 2004). By the time these individuals bear children, they have had several additional years to build credentials and skills that translate into economic rewards. In fact, some have argued that young adulthood is a new, class-based life stage that sets privileged and nonprivileged youth on entirely different life trajectories. The more privileged show evidence of later childbearing and considerable financial security, while the less privileged have less financial security and early childbearing (Osgood et al. 2004). These disparate trajectories have consequences for the educational fates of children in future generations. Flint (1997) finds that individuals who received parental financial support necessary to attend college (a hallmark of the young adult life stage) were better situated and more inclined to do so for their own offspring.

McLanahan (2004) aptly describes the different experiences of privileged and less privileged children as diverging destinies. While the more harmful results of demographic shifts are largely concentrated among minority and poor youth, the beneficial aspects—such as older parental age and the concentration of marriage among the highly educated (Goldstein and Kenney 2001)—are likely to have a positive impact on privileged youth. She suggests that this bifurcation in how family structures are changing is apt to widen existing educational disparities. Future research needs to examine further how race and class-based patterns in shifting family structures differentially influence the educational fates of youth.

Same-Sex Families

As Rosenfeld (2007, 2010) documents, the development of a young adult life stage in which youth are increasingly independent of families and communities of origin has played a large role in the rise of same-sex couples. He argues that in the post-1960s, parents lost much of their ability to exert control over the mating choices of their children. As youths became more geographically mobile, urban, and disconnected from their hometowns, it was easier to evade and challenge social norms that prohibited nontraditional unions. He concludes that same-sex couples, much like interracial couples, have been on the rise. According to the 2000 Census data, roughly 1% of all US couples are same sex—a figure that has risen in the past decade.

Despite their growing visibility, particularly in certain geographic and urban locations, same-sex couples and, in particular, same-sex parents still face considerable social stigma and discrimination. In many states, for example, same-sex families have no access to legal marriage and face difficulties adopting. In addition, Americans' attitudes, while changing, are still largely conservative. Powell et al. (2010) report that in 2006, less than three fifths (58.9%) of Americans considered a gay couple with children to be a family, and a slightly higher number (61.4%) considered a lesbian couple with children to be a family. When compared to the 99.4% who saw a heterosexual married couple with children as a family (or even the 81.4% who saw an unmarried couple with children as family), the disparities become obvious. Even the law continues to reflect this preference for heterosexual parents. For example, in upholding Washington state law's ban on same-sex marriage, Justice Barbara A. Madsen wrote: "Limiting marriage to opposite-sex couples, furthers procreation essential to the survival of the human race, and *furthers the well-being of children by encouraging families where children are reared in homes headed by the children's biological parents*" (emphasis added) (*Andersen v. King County* 2006: 6). The claim that children are better off living with their biological father and mother has been a predominant argument used by opponents of same-sex marriage and same-sex adoption.

Theories about how same-sex parenthood affects the well-being of children on a variety of measures—including educational performance—abound. Some theorists posit a deficit model, in which same-sex families, like stepfamilies, do not have essential components for children's success (e.g., parents of both genders by virtue of their structure [Wardle 1997]). Most sociological scholarship, however, points to the social and legal context in which same-sex families exist. Lack of access to the full set of legal and economic benefits accompanying marriage may decrease the educational resources available to children of same-sex parents. Others, however, have observed that parenthood is more difficult for same-sex parents to achieve, and is the result of explicit choice, such as artificial insemination, surrogacy, adoption, or a partner who already has children (Stacey 2006). The high level of difficulty and intention involved in becoming a parent may better equip these individuals to parent in ways that facilitate academic achievement.

Despite the multiple, and often competing, assumptions about how children of same-sex parents compare to children in other family structures, it has been difficult to obtain sufficient data to test these conjectures. As Meezan and Rauch (2005) argue, research has been constrained by small sample sizes, difficulty in identifying gay and lesbian couples within existing datasets, and considerable heterogeneity within same-sex families. Given these challenges, it has been difficult to make informed statements about the experiences of children of same-sex couples.

As a whole, however, evidence is beginning to accumulate showing that children of gay and lesbian couples look largely like children of heterosexual couples. A number of small studies suggest that children of same-sex parents show no additional behavioral, emotional, or mental health issues compared to families with a different structure. In addition, same-sex parents show high levels of parenting skills and interaction with children. Recent comprehensive reviews on this topic may be found in Stacey and Biblarz (2001) and Biblarz and Stacey (2010). In short, there is minimal evidence to suggest that these children are particularly disadvantaged when it comes to factors that may shape school performance. However, these studies are limited by small, nonrepresentative samples.

On this front, Rosenfeld (2010) recently has made considerable progress. In a creative use of Census data, he examined how the children of same-sex parents compare to others in rates of grade retention. Higher rates of grade retention indicate lower levels of progress through school, whereas lower rates of grade retention indicate normal progress through schooling. Rosenfeld found that the educational advantage of children in families with two heterosexual married parents can be explained by a higher socioeconomic status in comparison to same-sex families. Once controls are added, no significant difference remains between children in these traditional family structures as compared to children with same-sex parents.

Rosenfeld's (2010) research provides the strongest evidence to date that same-sex families do not harm children's educational progress. In fact, his work, in combination with previous research, suggests that these families may provide benefits over other family forms. In addition, his approach suggests promise in solving some of the difficult data challenges surrounding the study of how nontraditional family forms influence students' educational outcomes.

Adoptive Families

Since the 1980s, adoption has become increasingly common. While no official counts of adoption exist, best estimates suggest that around 4% of Americans are adopted and half of these have been adopted by nonrelatives (Fisher 2003). These statistics suggest one of the difficulties in studying adoptive families. As with same-sex families, adoptive families are formed in a variety of ways. Relative adoptions occur through extended family and increasingly with grandparents. Most nonrelative adoptions are domestic, and can also occur through foster arrangements. By 2004, international adoptions comprised as much as 25% of all nonrelative adoptions, although this number is likely to decrease due to stricter legal conventions both within the USA and internationally (Hollinger 2004; Vandivere et al. 2007).

Relative and nonrelative adoptions involve two different sets of parents. Relative adopters have lower levels of education and income and are more likely to be black. Their adoptive children tend to remain in situations close to those at birth. In contrast, nonrelative adopters are typically well educated, with at least some college education, have higher levels of income, are older, and are predominately white. Among this group, international adopters are the most privileged, likely because of the exceptional cost and difficulty involved (Vandivere et al. 2007). Children who are adopted internationally end up in vastly different situations (e.g., in different countries, cultures, and families with greater family resources) than they would have otherwise.

Differences in parental income, race, and age, along with variation in the circumstances of adoption, suggest the difficulties in drawing conclusions about adoptive families as a whole. Since samples tend to be small, researchers often combine them and also may include other nonbiological family structures. This approach is likely to yield negative educational outcomes. Case et al. (2001) find that when combined with stepchildren, adoptive and foster children receive, on average, 1 year less of education than biological children. A reliance on clinical populations, in which adoptive parents have sought help for their children's social, educational, or emotional issues, also hinders research. These populations, not surprisingly, have higher levels of problem behaviors, school related and otherwise (Versluis-den Bieman and Verhulst 1995; Bimmel et al. 2003).

Currently, the most effective way to investigate the educational effects of adoptive family structure may be to isolate a specific type of adoptive family in nationally representative data. In their investigation of how adoptive family structure shapes the parents' provision of educational resources, Hamilton et al. (2007) use inferential techniques to locate nonrelative adopters in a nationally representative sample of first graders. Analyses of these data show that in basic group comparisons, adoptive parents invest more resources in their children than does any other family type. Some of this advantage can be accounted for by the better education, higher income, and the older age of these parents. However, even with controls taken into consideration, an adoptive advantage over most other family structures remains. Nonrelative adopters invest at least as many resources in their children as two biological parents do.

These findings are important, as they contradict both sociological and evolutionary theories that emphasize the inadequacy of nontraditional family structures. Nonrelative adoptive families provide the strongest test possible, as there are no biological ties between parents and children. For sociological theories that privilege traditional family structures over less traditional ones (Cherlin 1978; Cherlin and Furstenberg 1994; Popenoe 1999), these patterns question the assumption that two biological parents are a necessary precondition for a highly functioning family—or in this case, one that can provide children with educational advantages. For evolutionary theories (Buss 1995; Salmon 2005), such findings counter the notion that biology alone dictates parental investment in children's educational resources.

Hamilton et al. (2007) point to a contextual mechanism to account for their findings. They argue that adoptive families invest at high levels because they are actively compensating for many of the social, legal, and circumstantial conditions under which nonrelative adoption occurs. Like same-sex parents, adoptive parents face a long and costly path to parenthood (Kirk 1984). This struggle, in combination with social norms that privilege blood relations, may motivate adoptive parents to fulfill all the requirements of good parents (Hartman and Laird 1990; Bartholet 1993). In addition, adoptive parents may be socialized to pour more time, money, and effort into their children. This is partly to counter negative media coverage on adoptive children and parental awareness of detrimental conditions prior to adoption that may lead to a heightened awareness of potential educational problems (Miall 1996; Waggenspack 1998; Priel et al. 2000).

Outside of clinical populations, research on the effects of adoptive family structures on educational attainment is limited. Perhaps the best basis of comparison for these children is with what life would have been like if they had not been adopted. In a review of the literature, Hoksbergen (1999) suggests that adoption improves children's emotional and intellectual well-being beyond that of those who remain in institutions or are re-placed with their biological families. Similarly, in supplementary analyses, Hamilton et al. (2007) argue that without adoptive parental resources, adoptive children would have even lower test scores. Such findings indicate that adoptive families help to erode the barriers to achievement that adoptive children face. Indeed, despite earlier educational struggles, Feigelman (1997) shows that by adulthood, adoptive youth look most like children of two-biological parents with respect to their educational attainment.

Multiracial Families

The rise of multiracial families in which multiple races are represented among parents and children is linked to the same shifts in youth independence that generated increases in same-sex families (Rosenfeld 2007). At the same time, important legal changes, such as the Supreme Court decision (*Loving v. Virginia* 1967) that rendered so-called antimiscegenation laws unconstitutional, paved the way for interracial couples (Moran 2001). In addition, military and economic factors have played a significant role in shaping the overall level of intermarriage. So-called war brides from several Asian countries with US military involvement have increased the number and visibility of interracial marriages. Selective immigration laws have brought educated elites from India and China, as well as unskilled laborers from Central America. These women have married into the US population, increasing the number of interracial families (Jacobs and Labov 2002; Donato et al. 2008).

Current estimates suggest that, as of 2000, about 7% of American couples were interracial—a number that is almost certain to rise. Indeed, a historical perspective suggests that we will see sharp increases over the next 50 years. Since 1960, there has been a fivefold increase in black–white married couples, and a tenfold increase in Asian–white married couples. Since 1970, Hispanic–non-Hispanic marriages have tripled (Rosenfeld and Kim 2005). As a result of increased interracial coupling, the number of multiracial children has been growing rapidly, comprising about 4% of all children (Radina and Cooney 2000; Cheng 2004). By 2050, demographic predictions indicate that over one fifth of all Americans will identify as multiracial (Lee and Bean 2004).

The educational experiences of multiracial youth arguably represent one of the most critical frontiers for research at the intersection of education and family. Race has long been one of the central mechanisms through which family transmits advantage or disadvantage to children (Coleman et al. 1966; Fejgin 1995; Kao and Thompson 2003; Roscigno and Ainsworth-Darnell 1999). In multiracial families, educational decisions and processes are filtered through more than one set of racial traditions and statuses (Herring 1992; Radina and Cooney 2000). Given that so many youth will be living in multiracial families in the near future, it is essential to understand what the consequences of this shift will be for the educational outcomes of youth (Kao 1999).

Current research on the topic is limited, but growing rapidly. One of the challenges has been to understand variation in educational processes and outcomes among the various sex and race compositions of interracial couples, such as a black father and white mother household versus an Asian mother and white father household. In this regard, Cheng and Powell (2007) explore how biracial families are different from or similar to monoracial families in the transmission of a broad range of educational resources. They find that biracial families, with the exception of black father and white mother families, provide an educational advantage in comparison to corresponding monoracial families, particularly with regard to cultural and economic resources. Cheng and Powell (2007) attribute this pattern to a compensatory mechanism, similar to that operating among adoptive families. However, they also show that the advantage of biracial families does not extend to social and interactional resources. The authors interpret this as evidence of social and structural constraints for which biracial families simply cannot compensate. For example, they may find it harder to form extrafamilial social ties due to the social stigma that multiracial families continue to encounter.

The question of educational outcomes for multiracial youth remains more open. Cheng (2004) shows that, at kindergarten age, multiracial children actually outperform monoracial peers academically, due in part to greater educational resources. This performance edge gradually disappears and, in fact, reverses itself by the time multiracial children reach adolescence. Cheng (2004) speculates that this reversal is related to school and peer group racial composition, as well as a potentially hostile school climate and a generally unsupportive cultural environment (Aschaffenburg and Maas 1997; Cheng and Klugman 2010). While being bi- or multiracial in a society that values binary racial classification can produce temporary academic setbacks, multiracial adolescents also compensate by creating more expansive social support networks that may benefit their future achievement and attainment trajectories (Cheng and Lively 2009).

Much work remains to be done on the educational experiences of multiracial youth. Given the complex and multi-veiling processes that both benefit and potentially harm these youth, it is important to sort through their long-term consequences. For instance, we know very little about how multiracial children fare in postsecondary education and as adults. The inclusion of multiracial racial categorization options that started in the 2000 Census offers considerable potential for future research, and may help to solve some of the data issues that have plagued research on this topic, as with many of the changes in family structure.

Conclusion

The diversity of families is growing. Sociologists of education have recognized this change and have moved beyond the normative image of the SNAF to recognize the multiplicity of family shapes, sizes, forms, and compositions (Smith 1993). Still, we contend that sociologists of education and sociologists in general need to direct more attention to understanding ways that the changing face of American families shapes the educational futures and overall well-being of youth. This chapter reports extant theory and research on how several kinds of family structure influence the transmission of family advantages and disadvantages to children and shape children's academic performance.

One goal of this chapter is to use this cutting-edge research on new family forms to assess how well extant theoretical approaches explain the way family structure shapes educational policy. Much of the evidence being marshaled by sociologists of education vigorously challenges a deficit model of family structure in which the educational benefits children receive, or the struggles they face, are blamed on the direct functioning of structures themselves, either as social forms or in a larger evolutionary sense. While the researchers find clear links between certain family structure and educational advantage or disadvantage, it is too facile of a response to blame the functioning of these families themselves.

Instead, we found evidence for both characteristics and contextual approaches, each of which focuses on indirect effects of family structure. Some family contexts that seem to provide children with an advantage are rooted in the higher socioeconomic status of parents (i.e., older parents and adoptive parents), whereas children who receive fewer benefits via family structure (i.e., single-parent families, stepfamilies, and same-sex families) are often living in less privileged contexts. In addition, the social climate in which families exist matters. In several nontraditional family forms, parents may work hard to compensate for the presumed disadvantages of the children or the difficulties of growing up in a world that views the SNAF as an ideal family type. In several cases, most notably adoptive, same-sex, and multiracial families, they appear to be largely successful. Still there are limits. Multiracial families, for example, simply cannot will away the social stigma that makes the formation of extrafamilial ties that may be instrumental for academic success more difficult.

Taken together, the sociological evidence continues to weaken the dominance of traditional views of how family structure is linked to educational attainment. Much of the past theoretical edifice is built in the legacy of SNAF as a dominant cultural image and in a time when families were more homogenous than they are today. Leading family scholars now question the wisdom of upholding the traditional American family as the yardstick by which all others are infavorably measured (Cherlin 1999; Biblarz and Stacey 2010). A more insightful approach, and one that has been embraced increasingly by sociologists of education, is to consider first the contextual features families need in order to succeed in helping their children through the educational system. They may then examine how such factors as social support, economic stability, social acceptance as a family, and legal rights with regard to partners and children vary among existing family structures.

The complexity of the patterns reported in this chapter also suggests that we have many gaps to fill, implying that a great deal of work lies ahead. For example, we know a great deal about parental allocation of valuable educational resources and how they influence children's education. But this is only part of the process. We also must attempt to explain how students are actually influenced by these resources, as well as by the social, economic, and legal contexts in which families exist. Determinants of postsecondary achievement and attainment, in many cases, have not received the empirical attention that they warrant.

This is in large part a data issue. Many of the family structures discussed here are not specified on most national surveys, and only recently have some larger datasets recognized multiple racial categories. While nationally representative data often oversample smaller populations (e.g., African Americans), this step has not yet been taken for nontraditional families (Cheng and Powell 2005). As a result, small sample sizes limit research on nontraditional family forms. One response has been to focus on studying these family forms through qualitative methods alone. However, while qualitative research yields valuable insights, it is limited in identifying generalizable patterns.

We argue that there are two necessary responses to the data challenges that research on the intersection of family and education increasingly will face. The first is to exert influence to ensure that the inclusion of more diverse family forms is included explicitly in nationally representative datasets that focus on educational outcomes. However, as some of the scholarship described here suggests, it is not sufficient to wait for better data to be collected. Rosenfeld (2010) solved a particularly difficult case—namely, that of children in same-sex families—by relying on admittedly limited Census data on educational success of youths. Similarly, Hamilton et al. (2007) used inferential techniques to locate nonrelative adoptive children that were explicitly identified. In fact, there are a variety of methods through which scholars can deal with small sample sizes typical of nontraditional family forms (Cheng and Powell 2005).

When it comes to education, families matter. This statement applies not only to families that correspond with traditional conceptualizations of family. Education scholars already have made great progress in understanding the role that a broad array of families assumes in passing on educational advantages and disadvantages across generations. As American families continue to change and diversify, education scholars should be vigilant in assessing and, when the evidence calls for it, dismantling the assumptions embedded in the notion of the Standard North American Family.

References

Alexander, Karl L., Doris R. Entwisle, and Carrie S. Horsey. 1997. From first grade forward: Early foundations of high school dropout. *Sociology of Education* 70: 87–107.
Amato, Paul R. 1994. Life-span adjustment of children to their parents' divorce. *The Future of Children* 4: 143–164.
Amato, Paul R. 2005. The impact of family formation change on the cognitive, social, and emotional well-being of the next generation. *The Future of Children* 15: 75–96.
Amato, Paul R., and Bruce Keith. 1991. Parental divorce and adult well-being: A meta-analysis. *Journal of Marriage and the Family* 53: 43–58.
Andersen v. King County, 138 P. 3d, 963, 969 (Wash. 2006).
Anderson, Kermyt G., Hillard Kaplan, and Jane Lancaster. 1999. Paternal care by genetic fathers and stepfathers I: Reports from Albuquerque Men. *Evolution and Human Behavior* 20: 405–431.
Aschaffenburg, Karen, and Ineke Maas. 1997. Cultural and educational careers: The dynamics of social reproduction. *American Sociological Review* 62: 573–587.
Astone, Nan M., and Sara S. McLanahan. 1991. Family structure, parental practices, and high school completion. *American Sociological Review* 56: 309–320.
Bartholet, Elizabeth. 1993. *Family bonds: Adoption and the politics of parenting*. New York: Houghton Mifflin.
Battle, Juan, and Deborah Coates. 2004. Father-only and mother-only, single-parent family status of black girls and achievement in grade twelve and at two-years post high school. *Journal of Negro Education* 73: 392–407.
Becker, Gary S. 1964. *Human capital*. New York: Columbia University Press for the National Bureau of Economic Research.
Becker, Gary S. 1981. *A treatise of the family*. Cambridge: Harvard University Press.
Biblarz, Timothy J., and Adrian E. Raftery. 1999. Family structure, educational attainment, and socioeconomic success: Rethinking the 'pathology of matriarchy'. *American Journal of Sociology* 105: 321–365.
Biblarz, Timothy J., and Judith Stacey. 2010. How does gender of parents matter? *Journal of Marriage and Family* 72: 3–22.
Bimmel, Nicole, Femmie Juffer, Marinus H. van IJzendoorn, and Marian J. Bakermans-Kranenburg. 2003. Problem behavior of internationally adopted adolescents: A review and meta-analysis. *Harvard Review of Psychiatry* 11: 64–77.
Blau, Peter, and Otis Dudley Duncan. 1967. *The American occupational structure*. New York: Wiley.
Bourdieu, Pierre, and Jean Passeron. 1977. *Reproduction in education, society and culture*. London: Sage.
Brooks-Gunn, J., and Frank F. Furstenberg Jr. 1986. The children of adolescent mothers: Physical, academic, and psychological outcomes. *Developmental Review* 6: 224–251.
Buss, David M. 1995. Evolutionary psychology: A new paradigm for psychological science. *Psychological Inquiry* 6: 1–30.
Case, Anne, I-Fen Lin, and Sara McLanahan. 2001. Educational attainment of siblings in stepfamilies. *Evolution and Human Behavior* 22: 269–289.
Census Bureau. 2009. *Estimated median age at first marriage, by sex: 1890 to the present*. Retrieved November 9, 2010, http://www.census.gov/population/socdemo/hh-fam/ms2.csv.

Cheng, Simon, and Joshua Klugman. 2010. School and racial composition and biracial adolescents' school attachment. *Sociological Quarterly* 51: 150–178.

Cheng, Simon, and Kathryn Lively. 2009. Multiracial self-identification and adolescent outcomes: A social psychological approach to the marginal man theory. *Social Forces* 88: 61–98.

Cheng, Simon, and Brian Powell. 2005. Small samples, big challenges: Studying atypical family forms. *Journal of Family and Marriage* 67: 926–935.

Cheng, Simon, and Brian Powell. 2007. Under and beyond constraints: Resource allocation to young children from biracial families. *American Journal of Sociology* 112: 1044–1094.

Cheng, Simon. 2004. Standing in the middle of interracial relations: The educational experiences of children from multiracial backgrounds. PhD dissertation, Indiana University, Bloomington, IN.

Cherlin, Andrew J. 1978. Remarriage as an incomplete institution. *American Journal of Sociology* 84: 634–650.

Cherlin, Andrew J. 1999. Going to extremes: Family structure, children's well-being, and social science. *Demography* 36: 421–428.

Cherlin, Andrew J., and Frank F. Furstenberg Jr. 1994. Stepfamilies in the United States: A reconsideration. *Annual Review of Sociology* 20: 359–381.

Coleman, James S. 1988. Social capital in the creation of human capital. *American Journal of Sociology* 94: 95–120.

Coleman, James S., Ernest Q. Campbell, Carol J. Hobson, James McPartland, Alexander M. Mood, Frederic D. Weinfield, and Robert L. York. 1966. *Equality of opportunity*. Washington, DC: Government Printing Office.

Conley, Dalton. 2004. *The pecking order: A bold new look at how family and society determine who we become*. New York: Pantheon.

Conley, Dalton, and Rebecca Glauber. 2006. Parental educational investment and children's academic risk: Estimates of the impact of sibship size and birth order from exogenous variation in fertility. *Journal of Human Resources* XLI: 727–737.

Dahinten, Susan, Jennifer Shapka, and J. Douglas Willms. 2007. Adolescent children of adolescent mothers: The impact of family functioning on trajectories of development. *Journal of Youth and Adolescence* 36: 195–212.

Daly, Martin, and Margo I. Wilson. 1998. *The truth about Cinderella: A Darwinian view of parental love*. New Haven: Yale University Press.

Dawson, Deborah A. 1991. Family structure and children's health and well-being: Data from the 1988 national health interview survey. *Journal of Marriage and the Family* 53: 573–584.

DiMaggio, Paul. 1982. Cultural capital and school success: The impact of status culture participation on the grades of U.S. High School Students. *American Sociological Review* 47: 189–201.

Donato, Katharine, Chizuko Wakabayashi, Shirin Hakimzadeh, and Amada Armenta. 2008. Shifts in the employment conditions of Mexican migrant men and women: The effect of U.S. Immigration Policy. *Work and Occupations* 35: 462–495.

Downey, Douglas B. 1994. The school performance of children from single-mother and single-father families: Economic or interpersonal deprivation. *Journal of Family Issues* 15: 129–147.

Downey, Douglas B. 2001. Number of siblings and intellectual development: The resource dilution explanation. *American Psychologist* 56: 497–504.

Featherman, David L., and Kenneth I. Spenner. 1988. Class and the socialization of children: Constancy, change, or irrelevancy? In *Child development in life-span perspective*, eds. E. Mavis Hetherington, Richard M. Lerner and Marion Perlmutter, 67–90. Hillsdale: Lawrence Erlbaum Associates.

Feigelman, William. 1997. Adopted adults: Comparisons with persons raised in conventional families. *Marriage and Family Review* 25: 199–223.

Fejgin, Naomi. 1995. Factors contributing to the academic excellence of American Jewish and Asian Students. *Sociology of Education* 68: 18–30.

Fields, Jason. 2001. Living arrangements of children: 1996. *Current Population Reports*, April, 70–74.

Fisher, Allen P. 2003. Still 'Not Quite as Good as Having Your Own'? Toward a sociology of adoption. *Annual Review of Sociology* 29: 335–361.

Flint, Thomas A. 1997. Intergenerational effects of paying for college. *Research in Higher Education* 38: 313–344.

Furstenberg, Frank, Sheela Kennedy, Vonnie C. McCloyd, Ruben Rumbaut, and Richard A. Settersten. 2004. Growing up is harder to do. *Contexts* 3: 33–41.

Geronimus, Arline, Sanders Korenman, and Marianne Hillemeier. 1994. Does young maternal age adversely affect child development? Evidence from cousin comparisons in the United States. *Population and Development Review* 20: 585–609.

Goldstein, Joshua R., and Catherine T. Kenney. 2001. Marriage delayed or marriage forgone? New cohort forecasts of first marriage for women. *American Sociological Review* 66: 506–519.

Guo, Guang, and Leah K. VanWey. 1999. Sibship size and intellectual development: Is the relationship causal? *American Sociological Review* 64: 169–187.

Hamilton, Laura, Simon Cheng, and Brian Powell. 2007. Adoptive parentism, adaptive parents: Evaluation the importance of biological ties for parental investment. *American Sociological Review* 72: 95–116.

Hampden-Thompson, Gillian, and Suet-Ling Pong. 2005. Does family policy environment moderate the effect of single-parenthood on children's academic achievement? A study of 14 European countries. *Journal of Comparative Family Studies* 36: 227–248.

Hartman, Ann, and Joan Laird. 1990. Family treatment after adoption: Common themes. In *The psychology of adoption*, eds. D. Brodzinsky and M. Schechter, 139–221. New York: Oxford University Press.

Herring, Roger D. 1992. Biracial children: An increasing concern for elementary and middle school counselors. *Elementary School Guidance and Counseling* 27: 123–130.

Heuvel, Andrey Vanden. 1988. The timing of parenthood and intergenerational relations. *Journal of Marriage and the Family* 50: 483–491.

Hoksbergen, Rene A.C. 1999. The importance of adoption for nurturing and enhancing the emotional and intellectual potential of children. *Adoption Quarterly* 3: 29–41.

Hollinger, Joan. 2004. Intercountry adoption: Forecasts and forebodings. *Adoption Quarterly* 8: 41–60.

Jacobs, Jerry, and Teresa Labov. 2002. Gender differentials in intermarriage among sixteen race and ethnic groups. *Sociological Forum* 17: 621–646.

Kalmijn, Matthijs, and Gerbert Kraaykamp. 2005. Late or later? A sibling analysis of the effect of maternal age on children's schooling. *Social Science Research* 34: 634–650.

Kao, Grace. 1999. Racial identity and academic performance: An examination of Biracial Asian and African American Youth. *Journal of Asian Americans Studies* 2: 223–249.

Kao, Grace, and Jennifer S. Thompson. 2003. Racial and ethnic stratification in educational achievement and attainment. *Annual Review of Sociology* 29: 417–442.

Kirk, David. 1984. *Shared fate: A theory and method of adoptive relationships*. Port-Angeles: Ben-Simon.

Kreider, Rose M. 2008. Living arrangements of children: 2004. *Current Population Reports*, February, 70–114.

Lareau, Anette. 2003. *Unequal childhoods: Class, race and family life*. Berkeley: University of California Press.

Lee, Jennifer, and Frank D. Bean. 2004. America's changing color lines: Race/ethnicity, immigration and multiracial identification. *Annual Review of Sociology* 30: 221–242.

Levine, Judith, Harold Pollack, and Maureen Comfort. 2001. Academic and behavioral outcomes among the children of young mothers. *Journal of Marriage and the Family* 63: 355–369.

Loving v. Virginia, 388 U.S. 1 (1967).

Mare, Robert, and Meei-Shenn Tzeng. 1989. Fathers' ages and the social stratification of sons. *American Journal of Sociology* 95: 108–131.

Mathews, T.J., and Brady Hamilton. 2009. *Delayed childbearing: More women are having their first child later in life*. U.S Department of Health and Human Services. Centers for Disease Control and Prevention. Retrieved November 5, 2010, http://www.cdc.gov/nchs/data/databriefs/db21.pdf.

McLanahan, Sara. 2004. Diverging destinies: How children are faring under the second demographic transition. *Demography* 41: 607–627.

McLanahan, Sara, and Gary D. Sandefur. 1994. *Growing up with a single parent: What hurts, what helps*. Cambridge: Harvard University Press.

Meezan, Williams, and Jonathan Rauch. 2005. Gay marriage, same-sex parenting, and America's children. *The Future of Children* 15: 97–115.

Miall, Charlene E. 1996. The social construction of adoption: Clinical and community perspectives. *Family Relations* 45: 309–317.

Mirowsky, John, and Catherine E. Ross. 1992. Age and depression. *Journal of Health and Social Behavior* 33: 198–207.

Moran, Rachel. 2001. *Interracial intimacy: The regulation of race and romance*. Chicago: University of Chicago Press.

Osgood, D. Wayne, Gretchen Ruth, Jacquelynne S. Eccles, Janis E. Jacobs, and Bonnie L. Barber. 2004. Six paths to adulthood: Fast starters, parents without careers, educated partners, educated singles, working singles, and slow starters. In *On the frontier of adulthood: Theory, research, and public policy*, eds. Richard A. Settersten, Frank F. Furstenberg, and Ruben G. Rumbaut, 320–355. Chicago: University of Chicago Press.

Park, Hyunjoon. 2007. Single parenthood and children's reading performance in Asia. *Journal of Marriage and Family* 69: 863–888.

Park, Hyunjoon. 2008. public policy and the effect of sibship size on educational achievement: A comparative study of 20 countries. *Social Science Research* 37: 874–887.

Pong, Suet-Ling. 1997a. Sibship size and educational attainment in Peninsular Malaysia. *Sociological Perspectives* 40: 227–242.

Pong, Suet-Ling. 1997b. Family structure, social context, and eighth-grade math and reading achievement. *Journal of Marriage and Family* 59: 734–746.

Pong, Suet-ling, and Dong-Beom Ju. 2000. The effects of change in family structure and income on dropping out of middle and high school. *Journal of Family Issues* 21: 147–169.

Pong, Suet-Ling, Jaap Dronkers, and Gillian Hamden-Thompson. 2003. Family policies and children's school achievement in single-versus two-parent families. *Journal of Marriage and Family* 65: 681–699.

Popenoe, David. 1999. Can the nuclear family be revived? *Society* 36: 28–30.

Powell, Brian, Lala Carr Steelman, and Robert Carini. 2006. Advancing age, advantaged youth: parental age and the transmission of resources to children. *Social Forces* 84: 1359–1390.

Powell, Brian, Catherine Bolzendahl, Claudia Geist, and Lala Carr Steelman. 2010. *Counted out: Same-sex relations and Americans' definitions of family*. New York: Russell Sage Foundation.

Priel, Beatriz, Sigal Melamed-Hass, Avi Besser, and Bela Kantor. 2000. Adjustment among adopted children: The role of maternal self-reflectiveness. *Family Relations* 49: 389–396.

Radina, Elise, and Teresa Cooney. 2000. Relationship quality between multiracial adolescents and their biological parents. *American Journal of Orthopsychiatry* 70: 445–454.

Rodgers, Joseph Lee, H.Harrington Cleveland, Edwin van den Oord, and David C. Rowe. 2000. Resolving the debate over birth order, family size, and intelligence. *American Psychologist* 55: 599–612.

Roscigno, Vincent J., and James W. Ainsworth-Darnell. 1999. Race, cultural capital, and educational resources: Persistent inequalities and achievement returns. *Sociology of Education* 72: 158–178.

Rosenfeld, Michael. 2007. *The age of independence: Interracial unions, same-sex unions, and the changing American family*. Cambridge: Harvard University Press.

Rosenfeld, Michael. 2010. Nontraditional families and childhood progress through school. *Demography* 74: 755–775.

Rosenfeld, Michael, and Byung-Soo Kim. 2005. The independence of young adults and the rise of interracial and same-sex unions. *American Sociological Review* 70: 541–562.

Ross, Catherine E., and John Mirowsky. 1999. Parental divorce, life-course disruption, and adult depression. *Journal of Marriage and the Family* 61: 1034–1045.

Salmon, Catherine. 2005. Parental investment and parent-offspring conflict. In *The handbook of evolutionary psychology*, ed. David M. Buss, 506–527. Hoboken: Wiley.

Schneider, Barbara, and James Coleman (eds.). 1993. *Parents, their children and schools*. Boulder: Westview Press.

Sewell, William, and Robert Hauser. 1975. *Education, occupation and earnings: Achievement in the early career*. New York: Academic Press.

Smith, Dorothy E. 1993. The Standard North American Family: SNAF as an ideological code. *Journal of Family Issues* 14: 50–65.

Spieker, Susan, Nancy Larson, Steven Lewis, Thomas Keller, and Lewayne Gilchrist. 1999. Developmental trajectories of disruptive behavior problems in preschool children of adolescent mothers. *Child Development* 70: 443–459.

Stacey, Judith. 2006. Gay parenthood and the decline of paternity as we knew it. *Sexualities* 9: 27–55.

Stacey, Judith, and Timothy J. Biblarz. 2001. (How) Does the sexual orientation of parents matter? *American Sociological Review* 66: 159–183.

Steelman, Lala Carr, and Brian Powell. 1991. Sponsoring the next generation: Parental willingness to pay for higher education. *American Journal of Sociology* 96: 1505–1529.

Steelman, Lala Carr, Brian Powell, Regina Werum, and Scott Carter. 2002. Reconsidering the effects of sibling configuration: Recent advances and challenges. *Annual Review of Sociology* 28: 243–269.

Stewart, Susan D. 2007. *Brave new stepfamilies: Diverse paths toward stepfamily living*. Thousand Oaks: Sage Publications.

Vandivere, Sharon, Karin Malm, and Laura Radel. 2007. *Adoption USA: A chartbook based on the 2007 National Survey of Adoptive Parents*. U.S. Department of Health and Human Services.

Versluis-den Bieman, Herma, and Frank Verhulst. 1995. Self-reported and parent-reported problems in adolescent international adoptees. *Journal of Child Psychology and Psychiatry and Allied Disciplines* 36: 1411–1428.

Waggenspack, Beth M. 1998. The symbolic crisis of adoption: Popular media's agenda setting. *Adoption Quarterly* 1: 57–82.

Wardle, Lynn D. 1997. The potential impact of homosexual parenting on children. *University of Illinois Law Review* 1997: 833–920.

Wu, Fang, and Sen Qi. 2006. Longitudinal effects of parenting on children's academic achievement in African American Families. *Journal of Negro Education* 75: 415–429.

Xu, Jun. 2008. Public policy and the effect of sibship size on educational achievement: A comparative study of 20 countries. *Social Science Research* 37: 874–887.

Xu, Anqi, Jiehai Zhang, and Yan R. Xia. 2008. Impacts of parents' divorce on Chinese children: A model with academic performance as a mediator. *Marriage and Family Review* 42: 91–119.

Zill, Nicholas. 1996. Family change and student achievement: What we have learned, what it means for schools? In *Family-school links: How do they affect educational outcomes?* eds. Alan Booth and Judy F. Dunn, 139–174. Hillsdale: Lawrence Erlbaum Associates.

Zvoch, Keith. 1999. Family type and investment in education: A comparison of genetic and stepparent families. *Evolution and Human Behavior* 20: 453–464.

Part II
Essays by Social Scientists and Educators

Chapter 11
Creating Our Future: Some Challenges for American Precollegiate Education

George W. Bohrnstedt

As we move into this new decade, it may be useful to consider some of the challenges that face the American education system if all students (especially students of color and students raised in poverty) are to leave high school not only career and college ready, but also prepared to take on the roles of participating citizens at the community, state, and national levels—goals many Americans hold for their children. Without claiming to be exhaustive, I focus on four challenges we face in reaching these goals, listed in order of importance. The challenges are:

- Closing minority–majority achievement gaps
- Implementing at-scale quality early childhood education programs
- Implementing quality summer school programs for children in need
- Educating the whole child

The Challenge of Closing Minority–Majority Achievement Gaps

The reason achievement gaps are important is because they translate into long-term achievement outcomes. For example, according to the National Center for Education Statistics, in 2008, the status dropout rates for blacks, Hispanics, and whites were roughly, 10%, 18%, and 5%, respectively, where status dropout rate is defined as the percentage of 16–24-year-olds who are not enrolled in school and have not earned a high school credential. We continue to have persistent achievement gaps between blacks and whites and between Hispanic and whites at the elementary and middle

---

G.W. Bohrnstedt (✉)
American Institutes for Research, Washington, DC 20007, USA
e-mail: GBohrnstedt@air.org

school levels. Figuring out how to close achievement gaps is going to become even more important given the projected growth of the Hispanic population in the coming decades (Tienda, this volume).

Black–White Achievement Gaps

Significant gains have been made in the scores of both 9- and 13-year-old blacks in reading and mathematics over the past several decades as determined by the National Assessment for Educational Progress (NAEP) Long-Term Trend study, and that is very good news. But the picture is more distressing when one looks at the size and persistence of the achievement gaps between blacks and whites. Even though the achievement of blacks has increased over time, the achievement of whites has increased as well. There was significant achievement gap closing in the 1970s for black students, probably due to compensatory education and the Great Society programs. Since the mid-1980s, the gap in black–white achievement has been reduced for some grades and subject areas, the gap remains unchanged in others, and in some cases has actually increased.

For 9-year-olds, the black–white reading gap has closed from 32 points in 1984 to 24 points in 2008—a reduction of just under a quarter of a standard deviation (the standard deviation for 9-year-olds in reading in 2008 was 37 NAEP points). For 13-year-olds, the black–white reading gap has closed from 26 points in 1984 to 21 points in 2008 which is a 0.13 standard deviation reduction (the standard deviation in reading for 13-year-olds was 48 NAEP points in 2008). The black–white mathematics gap for 9-year-olds in 2008 was 26 points—about the same as the 25-point gap that existed in 1986. The gap for 13-year-olds was 28 points in 2008, which is four points *larger* than the 24-point gap in 1986.

Another way to examine the achievement gap is to look at the size of the current gap in standard deviation units. The current black–white gaps in reading are .65 and .55 standard deviations for 9- and 13-year-olds, respectively. The black–white gaps in mathematics are larger—.76 and .80 standard deviations for 9- and 13-year-olds respectively. To summarize, the mathematics gap is larger than the reading gap even though considerable progress has been made in achievement gains in mathematics by black students in recent years.

Hispanic–White Achievement Gaps

As is the case for black students, there have been significant gains over the past several decades for Hispanic students in NAEP reading and mathematics. This, too, is good news. Significant Hispanic–white gaps remain, again because of gains in performance made by white students. The Hispanic–white reading gap for 9-year-olds has closed from 31 points in 1984 to 21 points in 2008—a significant .27 standard deviation move towards closing the reading gap. However, for 13-year-olds, the reading achievement gap increased from 23 points in 1984 to 26 points in 2008. In standard deviation units, the current Hispanic–white gaps in reading are .57 and .68 for 9- and 13-year-olds. The Hispanic–white mathematics gap for 9-year-olds was 21 points in 1986, compared to a 16-point gap in 2008—a .15 standard deviation gap reduction. However, the gap for 13-year-olds was 19 points in 1986 compared to a 23-point gap in 2008—a 4-point increase. In standard deviation units, the current Hispanic–white gaps in reading are .57 and .68 for 9- and 13-year-olds, respectively, and the comparable gaps in mathematics are .47 and .66 standard deviations. That is, the size of the reading and mathematics gaps are about the same.

Going back to the 1966 Coleman Report, we know that the ability of schools to close achievement gaps has been limited. This does not mean that we should discontinue our current efforts to improve our schools, especially those in urban areas where the schools are disproportionately populated with poor, minority children. But the schools can do only so much. Among the many efforts that have been tried, we cannot overemphasize what has been learned from the work of sociological researchers such as Robert Slavin and George Farkas, that is, the importance of intense reading instruction in early grades.

The problem of gaps is a deep societal one with deep historical roots involving both social class and discrimination. As a result, gaps begin to show up before formal schooling begins. We know, for example, that children of poverty (many of whom are blacks and Hispanics) start kindergarten well behind Asian and white students, and they never catch up by the completion of secondary school. For example, recent research in Miami-Dade County shows that at the age of four, children who are raised in poverty are 18 months behind for their age group, and these differences persist. Similarly, data from the national Early Childhood Longitudinal Study shows that black children start kindergarten more than a standard deviation behind white students in vocabulary as well as .64 and .40 standard deviations behind in mathematics and reading respectively. Hispanic students are slightly further behind in mathematics and reading—.72 and .43 standard deviations.

The roles that poverty and discrimination play in minority–majority achievement gaps are important research areas in which sociologists of education should have a greater investment. In this regard, we need further investigation along the lines of William J. Wilson's work that tries to disaggregate the roles of income, wealth, and culture as they play out for the achievement of blacks as well as for Hispanics. We also need sociologists of education to better research how the family mediates this relationship, including the impacts of family structure, language spoken in the family, interactions within the family, and socialization styles.

The Challenge of Implementing Effective Early Childhood Education Programs at Scale

We know from interventions using random assignment designs that high quality early childhood programs have significant short- and long-term effects on school performance. The High Scope Perry Preschool Project, begun in 1962 in Ypsilanti,

Michigan, was designed to provide quality preschool education for 3- and 4-year-old, low-income black students who were judged to be at high risk of not graduating from high school. The study was a randomized controlled trial where 64 children were assigned to the treatment group and 64 to the control group. All the teachers in the program were certified and had at least a bachelor degree. Most of the children participated for 2 years and the others for 1 year. Classes met each weekday for two-and-a-half hours. Some of the short- and long-term outcomes for the treatment group as contrasted to the control group are as follows: The high school graduation rate for those in the treatment group was 65% compared to 45%, and those in the treatment group spent 1.3 years less on average in special education services. Those in the treatment group had a much lower rate of out-of-wedlock births, and a 16% lower rate of arrest for violent crime, than the controls. At age 40, they were 26% less likely to have received government assistance.

The Abecedarian project involved 111 North Carolina infants born between 1972 and 1977. The overwhelming majority of the participants were black (98%) and poor. Random assignment was used in the Abecedarian program as well. Unlike most preschool programs, which begin at age 3–5, the Abecedarian project began in infancy (many as young as 4 months old) and continued until the children were of school age. The follow-up results are very impressive. Those in the program showed an increase of 1.8 grade levels in reading achievement and 1.3 grade levels in math achievement compared to those not in the program. Importantly, enhanced language development is credited with being most important in accounting for these cognitive gains. In the long-term follow-up, a much higher percentage of those in the program were enrolled in school at age 21 (42% versus 20% for those not in the program), and eventually a much higher percentage had skilled jobs (36% versus 14%).

Another preschool program, and one with a larger sample size, that has been shown to have both short- and long-term positive educational effects (15 and 19 years later) is the Chicago Child-Parent Centers (CPC) program, initiated in 1967 to serve poor, largely black families not being served by Head Start or other similar programs. Evaluations using a quasi-experimental design have shown that program participants (N=1,150) compared to nonparticipants (N=389) arrived at kindergarten scoring 3 months further advanced on a measure of cognitive readiness, were less likely to be retained in grade, and were less likely to need remedial or special education services; and when they did need such services, they were likely to use fewer of them. They also scored higher on mathematics and reading achievement through grade six. Long-term follow-ups showed the continuing impact of the program. Program participants at age 23–24 were more likely than nonparticipants to have completed high school and to have attended a 4-year college.

I have not recommended the federally funded Head Start program because the results continue to be mixed to negative in terms of impact. For example, the most recent federally funded evaluation found effects for both 3- and 4-year-olds on several outcomes measures, but none of the effects carried through to kindergarten or first grade.

Given the evidence that high quality early childhood programs can have an impact on helping to close if not eliminate achievement gaps, the challenge is how to replicate projects such as Perry Preschool, Abecedarian, and CPC on a large scale with the same effects as these relatively small model programs have shown. We have one example of implementation of early childhood education at scale in the state of Oklahoma, which has made universal preschool available to all of the state's 4-year-olds. A recent study showed significant gains in both vocabulary and math skills for those who participated in the program compared to those who had missed the cut-off age for program participation. While children of all sociodemographic backgrounds showed gains, the impact was greatest for children of low-income households—an important finding with clear implications for closing minority–majority achievement gaps for children arriving at kindergarten.

The Annie E. Casey Foundation website reports that roughly 60% of children age 3–5 in the USA are enrolled in nursery school, preschool, or kindergarten. However, there is considerable unevenness in the curriculum as well as teacher quality in these programs. Part of the success of the model early childhood programs just described is related to quality curricula, well-trained teachers, and involved parents. These programs also take into account the context in which these children are raised—often one of multi-generational poverty. To deal with these contextual issues, quality programs also should provide parent training and involvement, family services (e.g., health services), as well as nutritional meals—features sometimes referred to as wrap-around services. Because of these important program elements, there are substantial costs associated with the development of quality early childhood education programs. However, there are even greater costs for not enacting such programs, since they have been shown not only to reduce achievement gaps, but also to reduce negative long-term outcomes such as mental health problems, and problems with the law—both of which incur important societal costs.

Before taking these programs to scale, however, it is important to test them further using one or more large multisite randomized trials. While these model early childhood programs have shown that they can work in what are called efficacy trials in health research, we also need research that shows they will work in more typical, real-life environments. In this regard, we know that context plays a significant role in whether and how interventions work. But we need more research on the ways context matters in the scaling up of early childhood programs. We also need to understand the social and organizational factors that affect the quality of implementation of the interventions. In all these areas, sociologists of education could make useful research contributions to the understanding of successful versus unsuccessful scaling up of early childhood programs.

The Challenge of Implementing Quality Summer School Programs for At-Risk Children

The emphasis given to early childhood programs is not meant to suggest that they are a panacea, which, if implemented, will entirely solve the issue of achievement gaps. We know, for example, that the amount of learning loss that occurs during summers affects elementary students from lower socioeconomic families more than it does those from wealthier families. Indeed, research shows that students from wealthier families actually gain in learning over the summer. The work of sociologist Karl Alexander and his colleagues at Johns Hopkins University suggest that two thirds of the black–white achievement gap at grade nine can be accounted for by the summer loss that occurs in the elementary years.

These findings indicate the importance of summer school, modified school calendars, or year-round schools as a way to guard against summer unlearning. The research evidence for the effects of modified school calendars and year-round schooling is mixed, and parents, children, and teachers all have reasons not to embrace these alternatives. However, the evidence for the effectiveness of summer school has been shown in a meta-analysis by Harris Cooper and his colleagues at Duke University where they examined data from 93 evaluations of summer school. The results suggested that summer programs that focused on remedial, accelerated, or enriched learning have a positive impact on learning.

Sociological research needs to be done before taking summer school for at-risk children to scale. First, we need more research on what accounts for how sustained the effects of summer school are. Second, we must examine the leadership and organizational factors that influence the effectiveness of summer school programs. Third, we need research on factors associated with who benefits from summer school, aside from the obvious cases where students must retake courses they failed. This research is important since we know that summer loss is a problem for many if not most low-income children, not just those who require remedial education because of course failure. Fourth, we need research on how to encourage students to attend summer school. For example, can a district mandate summer school for all children below a certain income level? Probably not, but states and districts might encourage attendance using direct mailings to parents as well as using the local media to alert them to the opportunity for summer school for students from low-income families. Understanding what works and what does not and with which parents is another research opportunity. Fifth is the question of what should be taught in summer school. Students likely need a combination of review and enrichment, but more research is needed to determine what curricula best stop summer loss. Finally, interventions devised to stop summer learning loss should be evaluated carefully for their cost-effectiveness.

The Challenge of Educating the Whole Child

Clearly, academics must be the core emphasis in our schools. But we sometimes seem to forget that schools have our children during a period when incredible physical, emotional, social, and cognitive changes are occurring. Because of this, there has been a growing concern about students' social and emotional learning (SEL) as well as their academic development. The goal is to develop social and emotional as well as academic competencies starting at an early age as a way to produce well-rounded children, since these skills will be important not only for success in school, but across the lifespan. Roger Weissberg and his colleagues at the Center for Academic, Social, and Emotional Learning (CASEL) at the University of Illinois-Chicago have done experimental research showing the power of social and emotional learning. It can lead not only to safer learning environments for children, but also to their creating and developing self- and social-awareness, self-management skills, relational skills, and responsible decision making—skills necessary for success both in school and society. CASEL conducted an analysis of 213 intervention studies which showed that SEL not only significantly improved social and emotional skills and other positive behaviors, but also resulted in an 11-percentile-point average gain on standardized achievement assessments for those in the intervention as compared to the control condition.

An example of another type of SEL intervention is captured by the work of Sheppard Kellam and colleagues. For some time, they have been doing experimental interventions in grade one in the Baltimore school system to improve classroom management. Boys who were in first-grade classrooms that used the Good Behavior Game (GBG) had more positive outcomes than those who did not participate in the game in the short, moderate, and long runs. Over 15 years later, boys who were in GBG had less drug dependence, were less likely to need school and mental health services, and were less likely to have been in trouble with the law. Moreover, they were more likely to have graduated from high school than those who had not been in GBG in the first grade. Importantly, the effects were greatest for those boys who in the first grade had the strongest aggressive tendencies. Similarly impressive findings are associated with two other SEL programs—the Seattle Social Development Project and Promoting Alternative Thinking Strategies.

Finally, some children and their families need even more help. Many disadvantaged children come from backgrounds where not only are their academic, social, and emotional needs not being met, but neither are their health and mental health needs. They also often lack supportive mentors to help them understand what is required to become college and/or career ready. Many of these children need academic, social, health, and mental health services of the kind provided in model early childhood intervention programs. It is encouraging that the Obama Administration has seen the value of these programs and has invited applications for funding for them through the Promise Neighborhood grants program.

An example of a districtwide effort is *Say Yes to Education* which just completed its first year of operation in the Syracuse City School District. *Say Yes* schools will not only be carefully monitoring the academic progress of each student each year, but also will be monitoring their social, emotional, and health progress as well. Students are being provided with the academic, emotional, and health supports to stay on track to graduate. They also are being provided with counseling about finances that are available to them for college as well as help in getting through the application process. An incentive being provided to help students stay on track is the promise of free college tuition at any one of over 25 colleges and universities if they can meet the admission requirements.

To summarize, our view of education has to move beyond academics. We need to focus as well on the social and emotional development our children will need if they are to become well-rounded individuals. More research on the effectiveness of these programs at scale is needed, even though the evidence thus far has been promising. For example, the cost effectiveness of these programs would be increased if we knew more about which elements are the most and the least effective, especially the school-related program elements. Is peer mentoring as effective as higher cost tutoring? What is the cost effectiveness of after school and summer school programs, and are there ways they might be more effective by better monitoring the needs of students across their early school years and building programs around these needs? These are the types of questions for which sociologists of education could help provide needed research.

Despite the fact that these are difficult economic times, the federal government is making choices for investment, and education has fared well. It is important that this money not be squandered. Expenditures in research and program development should be informed by the critical challenges that face education and in areas with a good chance of improving the educational, developmental, and social skills of our children. We need to determine what the highest priority challenges are and how we might meet them. Sociologists of education have much to contribute by conducting research in these areas.

Chapter 12
Some Potential Contributions of Social Psychology to Public Education in the Face of the Current Disinvestment in Education

Karen S. Cook

In a recently published commentary on the state of funding for education in California, Wendy Brown (2010:3) argues that "California's disinvestment in education not only entrenches and deepens inequalities, not only breaks the promise of opportunity for every able student, not only chokes the engine of invention and achievement that built California's twentieth century glory, it destroys the fundament of democracy itself—an educated citizenry capable of thoughtful analysis and informed judgment." She is not the only person worried about the consequences of the general disinvestment in education currently occurring across the nation as states and local communities struggle to balance tight budgets in the aftermath of the worst economic recession in US history in terms of its magnitude and its persistent, lingering effects on the economy. Faced with tough choices, citizens and their representatives seem to be backing away from the challenges confronting educational institutions at all levels, especially those in the public sector that rely heavily on public financing. Given the depth of the recession, it does not appear likely that private funding will be able to close the gap. Brown captures succinctly the reasons we should all be losing sleep over the state of education in the nation. And, those affected exist not only in the K–12 schools, but on either ends of the spectrum—in preschools and in our institutions of higher education, as funding for all of these programs is cut.

Education has been and continues to be the primary route to success under most economic conditions. Public education in the United States over the past century has fueled not only the economy and the labor market, but also the emergence of entrepreneurial activities and innovation, key drivers of growth. Educators and citizens alike should worry about the persistent high school dropout rates disproportionately

---

K.S. Cook (✉)
Department of Sociology, Stanford University, Stanford, CA 94305-2047, USA
e-mail: kcook@stanford.edu

distributed among those who could benefit from obtaining further schooling to move them out of poverty or urban ghettos. These teenagers rarely, if ever, subsequently finish and go on to obtain higher education. And, the consequences for the communities in which we live often include higher crime rates, high rates of unemployment, increased drug use, and the need for related social services, as well as increased pressures on nonprofits and local governmental agencies to fill the void and to help mitigate the negative effects of these factors.

With respect to higher education, according to College Board statistics, the United States ranks only twelfth worldwide in terms of the share of young adults 25–34 with postsecondary degrees (about 40% compared to 55% in Canada). It is generally feared that this will be the first generation of young adults in the United States who are not better educated than their parents (de Vise, Daniel 2010). These numbers should serve as a wake-up call not only to academics, but also to practitioners, politicians, and parents, not to mention the public. The problems are multiple. Clearly, an important step is to mobilize academics and policymakers, teachers, school administrators, and parents to find solutions to the most pressing concerns. What can be done to provide adequate funding for schooling, in particular in areas underserved by existing educational institutions? What are the most promising programs for keeping young people in school, helping them complete high school and granting them access to community colleges, universities, or technical training programs and apprenticeships that put them on paths to employment opportunities? And, at the school level what can be done to energize teachers and motivate students to make the most of their educational programs? How can we replicate successful programs and manage the politics of implementation? How can we create student success and sustain their commitment to education?

As a social psychologist, I am particularly concerned about matters of self-esteem, performance expectations, skill development, stereotype threat, and teacher–student as well as peer group interactions and their consequences. Research in various fields could be brought to bear more effectively on matters of education if we can determine how to move promising research findings more quickly into the policy arena or at least to experimental and demonstration projects. Richeson (along with Shih et al. 1999, 2002), Walton and Cohen (2003), and others are conducting research demonstrating that fairly simple measures can be taken to short circuit what Claude Steele refers to as *stereotype threat*—the lowering of self-expectations for performance of those who experience this type of threat. An example is the stereotypical expectation that girls may not do as well as boys at math, or that blacks may not do as well as whites on certain standardized tests. Simple demonstrations in a variety of experiments in many performance domains (see Steele 2010) indicate that in various situations, the threat to performance can be mitigated by altering the information provided to students prior to test taking or engaging in other forms of behavior required for performance or skill evaluation. Other interventions may also reduce stereotype threats and positively impact the performance of students (as well as other categories of individuals) under various situations.

An important aspect of Steele's findings is that often when stereotype threat is experienced, limitations on performance are self-imposed. That is, internalized beliefs and the stress created in performance settings interfere with a person doing his/her best. This type of threat does not need to be triggered by others in the situation (and their potentially prejudiced beliefs); it can be triggered simply by cues in the environment as von Hippel (2010) points out in his recent review of Steele's book. Such cues can be quite subtle. They can come from the relative numbers of actors in one's subgroup when compared to a majority group (e.g., being the only woman trying out for the soccer team or being the only black student in the classroom taking the weekly math quiz). Other types of environmental cues can be embedded in text instructions, parental or teacher expectations, however subtly conveyed, or in the school or organizational context—such as pictures representing the class or the work group, or practice and training materials in which minority images are not present or they are stereotypic in presentation. Who is on the cover of the training manual, for example? Or, which employees or children are chosen to represent their firm or school in public settings?

Von Hippel (2010:1469) notes that in the original demonstration of the effect of stereotype threat, Steele and Aronson (1995:797) report results suggesting that African Americans perform more poorly on a difficult verbal test if they are asked to indicate their race before taking the test, activating stereotype threat in the setting. Similar results are indicated in Shih, Pittinsky, and Ambady's (1999) research on Asian American females who do better on a math test when initially indicating their race alone, but less well when simply reporting their gender before being tested. The fact that stereotype threat is internalized and affects individuals in spite of efforts to bolster self-esteem in other ways makes this type of social psychological process difficult to mitigate. Given that it is embedded in society and in the social relations individuals experience on a daily basis, efforts to ameliorate its effects need to be managed carefully. While some research indicates that such effects in performance settings can be reduced given the proper framing of the experience, long-standing research concerning discrimination and its everyday effects (see, for example, Williams 1999) shows that persistent educational efforts will be required to alter the fundamental basis for the internalization of the actual experiences of daily discrimination and stereotyping. Fortunately, recent research gives hope that in some situations relatively simple interventions can mitigate the effects of stereotype threat. For example, Cohen et al. (2006) demonstrate that some interventions in classrooms may reduce the impact of such threats in a sustained fashion (von Hippel 2010).

We need further research into how schools and educational institutions more broadly can take advantage of this and related research to improve their effectiveness in the facilitation of skill development and learning in all students including those who fall into these different categories. Steele's findings and those of his collaborators and former students are significant and have wide-ranging implications for education. Establishing an environment in which diversity is appreciated and managed well, enhancing the sense of belonging for all, and increasing the trust levels among those in the setting (teachers, parents, students, administrators, staff, and local community members) are important elements in creating a positive educational experience and a renewed commitment to education in general. Too many seem to have relegated these problems to others to solve.

Social psychologists who study the fundamental nature of self-conceptions more broadly and how they are developed also might have much to contribute to educational institutions. Thoits (1999, 2005, 2011) has written extensively on the self and identity issues. While much of her work has focused on those diagnosed with mental illnesses and what factors inhibit or facilitate positive images for self as well as for others with whom they interact in work settings and in their personal lives, some of the ideas she has developed have clear relevance for other types of spoiled identities. In classrooms in which children with various learning differences and disabilities have been mainstreamed, Thoits' research has potential application even though her focus has been on adult populations. She also does research on emotions and emotion displays that violate social norms of appropriateness, another topic that has potential application in classrooms in many settings. Finally, she deals with the unequal social distribution of stress experiences and how various coping strategies and social support help moderate the negative impact of such stressors.

What would be helpful would be the more rapid dissemination of significant findings in the social sciences and in the field of education as well as widespread discussion of their implications and implementation in our schools. Steele's work is only one example of the type of research that has made its way from the academy to our schools. There are many more studies with potential implications for our educational institutions that may never extend beyond the covers of the journals in which they are published and often buried. Thoits' work, for example, has not been mined for its relevance in educational settings (and she recently won the ASA sponsored Cooley Mead Award for her career contributions to social psychology).

We need to shorten the time from "lab to bench" as they say in the health sciences. The walls between academia and our public schools and colleges should be lowered. Academics should be more open to and rewarded for making their research findings more readily and rapidly available to potential practitioners. Furthermore, educators in our schools and administrative buildings outside of the academy should be more open to experimentation and quick application of promising approaches. This may be occurring in some parts of the world, but it would seem that in the United States, scholars outside of our schools of education have not been as engaged as they could be in solving what are some of the most pressing educational problems facing us. It appears that years and years of efforts to reform schools and curricula have not yet had the hoped for impact. And, politics seems to have invaded the curricular and personnel decisions that school boards and administrators frequently have to make.

Perhaps, it is time to consider more bold experiments with American educational institutions. Private management of public schools is only one such experiment and the jury is still out on this experiment in several major cities in the United States. Allowing teachers and administrators to experiment broadly with newly developed alternative forms of instruction, with new types of technology, an increased use of volunteer help (from the recently retired as well as the currently unemployed), extended school hours, before- and after-school enrichment programs in the community or on school grounds, more effective technical and apprenticeship programs for talented high school and middle school students—some of whom may be destined to drop out of regular schooling—and many other potentially good steps forward. We (as researchers and educators) should be collaborating to produce the most innovative educational experiences we can provide to our preschoolers, K–12 students, community college and university students, as well as those seeking new forms of skill development at later stages of life. It is not clear that our best universities and colleges are leading the way.

In addition, bringing our research concerning the production of collective or public goods to bear on solutions to some of these problems could engage sociologists of education, as well as social psychologists, economists, and political scientists. Coming up with new forms of assessment, program evaluation, and methods for motivating creativity could engage psychologists and clinicians. Team building is needed; turf wars should end. Above all, the right kind of leadership clearly is required—new visions, new ideas, and, most important, entirely new efforts to reform what is not working and reward what is. Should we create a new national dialogue about educational reform? Can we do this at the local level? I can think of no other more pressing problem than the education of our future citizens, not only so that they can become productive members of society, but also to become educated citizens and sophisticated political consumers as the safeguarding of our future democratic institutions demands.

References

Brown, Wendy. 2010. Commentary: Without quality public education, there is no future for democracy. *The California Journal of Politics and Policy* 2(1): 1–3.
Cohen, G.L., J. Garcia, N. Apfel, and A. Master. 2006. Reducing the racial achievement gap: A social-psychological intervention. *Science* 313: 1307.
de Vise, Daniel. 2010. The U.S. goes from leading to lagging in young college graduates. *Washington Post* (online version), July 22.
Shih, M., T.L. Pittinsky, and N. Ambady. 1999. Stereotype susceptibility: Identity salience and shifts in quantitative performance. *Psychological Science* 10: 80.
Shih, M., N. Ambady, J.A. Richeson, K. Fujita, and H.M. Gray. 2002. Stereotype performance boosts: The impact of self-relevance and the manner of stereotype activation. *Journal of Personality and Social Psychology* 83: 638–647.
Steele, Claude M. 2010. *Whistling Vivaldi: And other clues to how stereotypes affect us*. New York: W. W. Norton and Co.
Steele, Claude M., and J. Aronson. 1995. Stereotype threat and the intellectual test performance of African-Americans. *Journal of Personality and Social Psychology* 69: 797.
Thoits, Peggy A. 1999. Self, identity, stress, and mental health. In *Handbook of the sociology of mental health*, eds. Carol S. Aneshensel and Jo C. Phelan, 345–368. New York: Kluwer Academic/Plenum.
Thoits, Peggy A. 2005. Differential labeling of mental illness by social status: A new look at an old problem. *Journal of Health and Social Behavior* 46(1): 102–119.
Thoits, Peggy. 2011. Cooley Mead Award address. *Social Psychology Quarterly*.
Von Hippel, William. 2010. Performance sapped by stereotypes. *Science* 329: 1469–1470.
Walton, G.M., and G.L. Cohen. 2003. Stereotype lift. *Journal of Experimental Social Psychology* 39: 456–467.
Williams, D.R. 1999. Race, socioeconomic status, and health: The added effects of racism and discrimination. *Annals of the New York Academy of Sciences* 896: 173–188.

Chapter 13
From Data to Actionable Evidence: How Sociologists Can Drive School Reform

Paul Goren and Emily Krone

More raw data on schools exist today than at any other time in history. States and districts are using these data to make a wide range of high-stakes decisions, from which schools to close, to which teachers to fire, to which students to promote. Yet, despite the magnitude of data on education, policymakers, practitioners, parents, politicians, journalists, and other stakeholders lack crucial information about what actually takes place in schools and actionable evidence about how to improve them. To redress this shortage, sociologists and other education researchers must find new ways to organize, conceptualize—and move beyond—the mountains of data that threaten to overwhelm schools.

Over the past two decades, an accountability movement has swept through the US public education system, placing a new emphasis on student outcomes and generating a profusion of new facts and figures on schools. The largest driver of this proliferation of public data was the 2001 reauthorization of the Elementary and Secondary Education Act. Renamed "No Child Left Behind," the federal law holds all schools accountable for reaching certain measurable goals and for publicly reporting key metrics such as graduation and attendance rates and the percentage of students passing standardized tests. Schools must disaggregate the data for particular groups, including racial and ethnic minorities, students with special learning needs, English language learners, and students from low-income families. Without question, disaggregation was a positive development for the education field, which for too long camouflaged the struggles of certain groups with the achievement of others.

The move successfully changed the conversation from "all students can learn" to "here is what we know about the learning of all students." Nevertheless, the increased emphasis on test score data also has had a reductive effect, narrowing the complex

P. Goren (✉) • E. Krone
Consortium on Chicago School Research, University of Chicago Urban Education Institute, Chicago, IL 60637, USA
e-mail: pgoren@uchicago.edu; ekrone@uchicago.edu

activities of teaching, learning, and schooling to an isolated grade on a single test at a specific moment in time. To be sure, test score data are necessary for purposes of accountability—but they are not sufficient. A comprehensive accountability system must include measures that move beyond test scores. Sociologists of education can contribute by producing indicators that are rigorously validated, reliably measurable, and empirically linked to desired outcomes such as college graduation, gainful employment, and productive citizenship.

Most other fields are rife with these types of indicators. A corporation's annual report, for example, provides a wealth of data designed to illuminate the company's short- and long-term prospects. The medical field has developed hundreds, if not thousands, of health indicators, from blood pressure to body mass index. Even our pastimes boast more effective indicators than our schools. Baseball teams with statistical measures of success and failure, some of which border on the absurdly specific: batting average, on-base percentage, walks, strikeouts, how a hitter performs against left-handed pitchers on games played in the rain after 5:00 p.m. All of these data points combine to form a reasonably accurate portrait of a player, allowing managers to make data-driven decisions in nearly every conceivable situation.

Developing more robust indicators of student and school success will go a long way toward providing the public with objective information on school performance and holding schools accountable for improvement. But sociologists and other education researchers must not stop there, for even a robust accountability system that incorporates multiple indicators of success or failure still falls short of providing practitioners with the kind of actionable evidence they need. To drive improvement, rather than simply hold schools accountable for improvement, a complementary array of indicators on teachers, principals, classrooms, and schools is required. Practitioners and others concerned with improving the quality of public education need to know which policies, procedures, and organizational structures lead to improvement, as well as how to measure those policies, procedures, and organizational structures. In other words, they must move past data and data-based decisions and on to evidence and evidence-based solutions. Again, sociologists have a crucial role to play in developing this type of evidence.

A recent book by researchers at the Consortium on Chicago School Research at the University of Chicago Urban Education Institute illustrates the power of focusing on the search for evidence-based solutions in education. *Organizing Schools for Improvement: Lessons from Chicago* (Bryk et al. 2010) provides empirical evidence for why students in 100 public elementary schools in Chicago managed to improve substantially in reading and math over a 7-year period, while students in another 100 schools did not.

By matching multiple years of survey data from students and teachers with a massive longitudinal data set of student outcomes, the authors were able to pinpoint a set of practices that promote school improvement. These practices—which the researchers call the Essential Supports—are school leadership, professional capacity, parent–community ties, student-centered learning climate, and instructional guidance. Schools that measured strong in three of the five supports were at least ten times more likely than schools with just one or two strengths to achieve substantial gains

13 From Data to Actionable Evidence: How Sociologists Can Drive School Reform

in reading and math. Moreover, a sustained weakness in just one of these areas nearly guaranteed stagnation.

The practical applications of this evidence are clear. Each essential support comprises a number of core indicators, providing practitioners with fine-grained information about crucial levers for improvement. In other words, teachers and school leaders now have evidence of the inputs that drive desired outputs. Moreover, the essential supports provide a conceptual framework that helps prioritize and systematize the hard work of school reform.

Such evidence becomes even more powerful when paired with a tool that helps make the conceptual framework tangible for practitioners. In Chicago, schools receive survey reports organized around the Essential Supports that show how teachers and students answered questions about their school. Principals can use the information to see how their school stacks up on the Essential Supports relative to other comparable schools, create improvement plans, and support professional development goals. Importantly, because the Essential Supports are known to drive improvement, the survey results can also serve as a sort of leading indicator of test score gains—crucial for schools looking to gauge the progress of new initiatives or judge whether they are on the right track.

The process around building the Essential Supports—from raw data to actionable evidence to conceptual framework to evidence-based tool—clearly illustrates the data-to-practice pipeline at work at the Chicago Consortium. It is a pipeline that moves schools past simple accountability and past the simple rhetoric that all children can learn and places them on the path to continuous improvement.

More sociologists can contribute to this crucial data-to-practice pipeline by duplicating some of the factors that characterize the Chicago Consortium. Researchers at the Chicago Consortium are able to bridge the gap between research and practice because they have unfettered access to data about all students in Chicago Public Schools; true independence that prevents the district from limiting findings or transparency; a long-term commitment to studying critical problems over time in a single location; and a primary emphasis on outreach and collaboration so that research informs practice and practice, in turn, informs subsequent research.

At no other time in history have states and districts been so poised to benefit from research organizations like the Chicago Consortia. Race to the Top and other competitive education grants established by the Obama administration have turned the entire nation into a laboratory of reform. From New York to Florida to Hawaii, states are revamping teacher evaluation and training; implementing common national standards and tests to gauge students' mastery of the standards; creating statewide data systems to track progress; and developing new strategies for turning around the nation's lowest-performing schools. A Consortium-like entity in every state—or, more ambitiously, in every district in every state—would significantly extend the benefits of the federal competition by allowing districts and states to evaluate and understand these reforms and determine how to bring the most successful of them to scale.

Sociologists of education are uniquely positioned to contribute to these consortia because of their training and experience unpacking the complex relationships between institutions and individuals. Their expertise is especially critical given the current and at times myopic emphasis on the role that individual actors play in school improvement. Many reformers, for example, have placed enormous stress on improving teacher quality and have campaigned aggressively to tie teacher evaluations to student test scores. Meanwhile, they neglect or discount the role that the larger school community plays in determining each teacher's success. Sociologists of education can help broaden the reform conversation by focusing on conceptual frameworks and evidence-based tools that take into account the wide range of factors that contribute to pressing problems of practice.

To participate in this important endeavor, however, more sociologists of education must move beyond the role of disinterested critic and become active participants in school reform. To be sure, there is a critical role for sociologists who wrestle solely with issues of race or class or structural determinism. But there also is a real, urgent need for sociologists of education willing to provide practitioners with actionable evidence for improvement, evidence that will help make the reality of the nation's public schools match the hope and promise we have ascribed to them. The time to act is now, before the work of sociologists becomes the work of historians.

Reference

Bryk, Anthony S., Penny Bender Sebring, Elaine Allensworth, Stuart Luppescu, and John Q. Easton. 2010. *Organizing schools for improvement: Lessons from Chicago*. Chicago: University of Chicago Press.

Chapter 14
Grasping the Past to Inform the Present

Patricia Albjerg Graham

Understanding the present often involves a grasp of the past. Our present concern about the inadequate academic achievement of many American youth focuses upon their race, poverty, temperament, teachers, family, and culture. Today, we hold the institution that encompasses them all, their schools, largely responsible for their poor performance. Has this always been so, and if not, why blame schools now?

Schools have a long and largely honorable history in America. We provided schooling for more children for more years than any other country in the world in much of the nineteenth and most of the twentieth century. We were proud of our enrollment data. However, we did not look at what they learned. Neither were we much concerned about extensive school learning for all, only for some. We were proud that our nation prospered economically and internationally during this time, and we asked the schools to deal with our most intransigent social and moral problem, racial segregation. In short, we expected schools to assimilate the immigrants in the early twentieth century, to assist in children's social adjustment in the middle years of the twentieth century and later to provide access to special programs (desegregation, gifted and talented, enriched Title I activities for the poor, bilingual). Only by the end of the twentieth century did we emerge with the most audacious objective of all: universal academic achievement.

Academic achievement for all emerged as a slogan that challenged reality. We had always assumed normal distributions with half above the mean and half below it. Typically, we permitted some students below the mean to pass, but we did not expect them or their less successful brethren to achieve. Staying in school involved much more than academic learning and adopting other traits—fair play, hard work, honesty, respect, cooperation, punctuality, regularity — was reason enough to remain

P.A. Graham (✉)
Harvard Graduate School of Education, Harvard University, Cambridge, MA 02138, USA
e-mail: patricia_graham@harvard.edu

enrolled until one's midteens. Democratic citizenship required them to do so, we argued, even more than an understanding of square root. John Dewey explained the necessity of education, broadly defined, in *Democracy and Education* (1916), a tome that many cited but few understood. Others argued that schools should enhance the wit and the character of the young.

By the last two decades of the twentieth century, our assessment of our schools became gloomy. We held schools responsible for producing a workforce that had difficulty competing with European and Asian manufacturers, although when the economy improved, management took the credit, not better prepared workers. Colleges blamed schools for sending them graduates who could not pass college-level courses without remediation. And, then, test scores became public.

Schools always have tested their students, but on the whole these results were not revealed publicly. When IQs were first measured in schools before World War II, they were kept secret from parents and certainly from children. Teachers in midcentury reviewed comprehensive records with a student's IQ from age seven and assumed that if it were low (many were, due to the cultural bias of old IQ tests), the teacher could be excused if the child failed to learn. Many did, and the pact was sealed. The teacher taught youngsters who wanted to learn, and the rest were socially promoted since holding them back a grade was thought to be harmful to their psyches, often of greater concern than their intellects.

Testing was a twentieth-century growth industry. From its rudimentary beginnings in early twentieth century French mental asylums through its first widespread use in World War I in the United States to separate potential officers from soldiers, testing caught the attention of the emerging profession of psychologists who made it their tool. By the middle of the twentieth century, both aptitude and achievement tests entered classrooms, but like the IQ tests, the results were not widely disseminated. Only with the passage of the first broad federal aid to education, the Elementary and Secondary Education Act of 1965, did Senator Wayne Morse of Oregon, a former professor, along with Senator Robert F. Kennedy of New York insist that a nationwide test be developed, the National Assessment of Educational Progress (NAEP). But it was decades before its results were released, initially only by region and eventually by state. Privacy lingered.

Within the last two decades, however, testing has come into its own and as a public matter. It is the original metric. The term, *metric*, has become widely utilized as quantitative methodologies have come into the ascendancy in many aspects of American life, including education. The simplicity of a single score to define a youngster's knowledge of a broad subject entranced us. With the removal of the most egregious cultural bias of old tests, we have come to believe that our new, improved instruments are objective. Furthermore, since we have concluded that the goal of schools is academic achievement for all, an alien notion to earlier generations, we have a simple means of determining whether our schools are fulfilling their task: pupils' test scores.

Inevitably, we learned that not all children do well on these tests. To no one's surprise, though to the regret of many, children from low-income families and from families of color generally do less well than children of affluent white families.

A prime benefit of public testing is to make these differences clear so that they can no longer be hidden and ignored. Remedy now appears urgent.

Researchers find it easy to work with test scores. Many calculations can be made using them. What researchers have found much more elusive, however, is identifying the changes schools can make in order to help more children flourish, including mastery of more academic material.

We have few metrics for making children flourish. Nor do we have many metrics for what makes a good school. We even have difficulty discussing what the purpose of schooling is in America since we have over time asked the schools to concentrate on different issues. Today's emphasis, academic achievement for all, is a novelty in the history of American schools.

These are not new questions. More than 30 years ago when I was the Director of the National Institute of Education, then the federal government's educational research agency, our two primary research questions were: (1) How do we increase equity in education, meaning reducing the predictive value of race, class, and gender for academic achievement, and (2) what makes a good school? Some good work resulted from these studies, but the questions are still unresolved.

During the last half of the twentieth century, leading historians and sociologists (James Coleman, Lawrence Cremin, Christopher Jencks) stressed the limited role that schooling played, relative to the "many agencies that educate" (Cremin's phrase), in influencing young people. Our metrics were excellent for demonstrating that family, community, and cultural conditions influenced academic achievement more than schooling did. Daniel Patrick Moynihan, a sometime academic (his original Harvard tenure was at the Graduate School of Education) and better known public figure, provided us with masses of statistical material documenting poverty figures and the family patterns of black families, which included substantial incidence of single-parent families. Neither poverty nor single-parent families correlated with academic success.

Leading schools of education recognized the intellectual significance of these findings. Since family was found to be a more important predictor of academic and economic success than schooling, these schools of education in elite universities dramatically reduced their preparation of students for careers in schools. In fact, Christopher Jencks sought to title his 1972 volume *The Limits of Schooling*. His co-authors and publisher talked him out of it, and it became *Inequality*. Some universities already had eliminated their schools of education (Yale, Johns Hopkins, Duke), which had prepared many excellent teachers. Others seriously considered such action (Berkeley, Stanford, Harvard), and Chicago subsequently did. Other leading schools of education dropped or minimized teacher and administrative preparation programs and in the late 1960s and 1970s turned their attention to behavioral and social science research related to education. Unlike their older colleagues, new professorial appointments were unlikely to have teaching experience in schools but rather to have earned a Ph.D. in a discipline whose methodology, often but not exclusively quantitative, they now applied to educational issues.

National concern about education, encapsulated in the brief 1983 *A Nation at Risk* report, refocused attention on schools as principal providers of children's education.

Currently, we have rejected the analytically accurate observation of the importance of family and community as educators brought to us by historians and sociologists who favored an emphasis upon schools. Schools are subject to policy manipulation, something that is difficult to undertake with families or adolescent culture. Under the rubric of "academic achievement for all," we now expect or at least, hope, that the school will take care of this extraordinary task. It does not seem likely that the school can do this alone, though improvements are possible.

Beginning in the late 1980s and 1990s, research in schools of education, social science departments, and think tanks shifted to issues of schooling: first, to governance issues, then to preparation of teachers and administrators, and finally to making schools more effective in preparing the future workforce. The latter has put pressure on schools, whose academic success with the bottom third of their students previously functioned below the public radar. While many suburban schools still contend with getting more graduates into prestigious colleges (more Advanced Placement courses, more leadership activities), the focus is now upon students with low academic achievement as measured by tests. This task is a novelty and not one for which most professors are well prepared to assist.

The initial efforts have been primarily policy ones, a category of scholarship that emerged relatively recently in education. Before the 1960s, schools of education focused on learning theory, classroom management, administration, methods of teaching specific subjects, and reading. In addition, most believed that some foundation work was necessary, such as history or philosophy of education or other disciplines (sociology, political science, economics) applied to education. These were intended to give a perspective on education and its role in a society. With the Elementary and Secondary Education Act of 1965 and the resulting Title I funding came educational policy, and the foundations fields began to disappear in favor of studies of policy—its formulation, implementation, and ultimately its evaluation. These questions have occupied many professors and address their strengths in research design and methodologies. The standards movement and testing enthusiasms all result from this policy emphasis. Essentially the policy motif was "we can set standards, then, we can test whether they have been met." Lost were questions about purpose of education, why we engage in education, and what contribution we expect education to make to society. Lost also was much serious inquiry into how reluctant or recalcitrant students might become engaged with their studies.

The difficulty, of course, (as most sentient adults would have anticipated) occurs when learning as measured by tests is inadequate. What to do now? Most faculty, particularly those in Research I universities, have little direct experience as adults with either schools or with students who do badly academically and especially with schools filled with low-performing students. Their expertise (for which they get tenure) is principally for their demonstrated research productivity. This expertise, important as it is to the academy, does not prepare them adequately for the present challenge: improving educational practice, primarily in schools populated largely by students who are not scoring well on tests. Metrics for this task are obscure.

In an age when responsible research requires metrics, this is a complication. For example, are test scores, very handy metrics, actually indicative of academic achievement? Probably not, but what are better metrics for that ineffable concept? What are metrics for, an innovative idea or technique, or for the conditions that stimulate them? Too often, we go with the metrics we have rather than seek evidence, including new metrics and other sources of insight that will enhance educational practice and lead to its improvement.

Thus, this vexing problem, raising the academic achievement of youngsters, many of whose homes and neighborhoods are not conducive to scholarly success, is profoundly difficult for the educational research community. Their research designs are not applicable, and their metrics while often helpful in demonstrating the problem are less helpful in solving it. Furthermore, the purpose of schooling is inevitably narrowed by using standardized tests as the only measure of a school's success. Finally, if the heart of the matter is the culture of these children, a culture largely unknown to many of the researchers, then another obstacle asserts itself. Our brethren in social and cultural anthropology of an earlier era may be helpful here, though many of us do not recognize our ignorance of American youngsters as being as deep as our ignorance of the Trobriand Islanders. Without deeper understandings of what we are studying and of our own lacunae, beneficial scholarship will be difficult.

Anthony Bryk and his co-authors in *Organizing Schools for Improvement* (2009) cite John Kotsakis, who was a wise leader of the Chicago Teachers Union and an admired colleague of many of us. Kotsakis described school improvement as analogous to baking a cake. Many steps must be precisely taken in the correct order and under the right conditions for the cake to emerge from the oven as a delicacy. Both metrics and art are involved, but above all, one must recognize and implement the many steps accurately and in the proper sequence.

One critical lack in enhancing school improvement now is agreement on what purpose the school serves. Is it only academic achievement or are we still interested in the schools' promotion of democratic citizenship, a function they previously undertook explicitly? With recent excesses in our economy and the actions of some graduates of our most eminent schools to enhance their earnings at considerable risk to others, democratic citizenship might need a little bolstering among the high scorers on achievement tests. Without clarity of purpose of the enterprise, we do not know what kind of cake to bake. Once there is agreement that increasing academic achievement as well as fostering positive characteristics needed by a democracy, we can decide on the kind of cake we want: yellow, spice, chocolate, marble, or something else. Then, we can undertake the baking process. But for many with low academic achievement, as well as those whose academic achievement may be adequate but whose qualities of character are weak, we need dramatically better understandings of how to bake Kotsakis' cake. That will require more imaginative research than we have currently.

As an historian, I have viewed sociologists as those who deal with contemporary dilemmas that my fellow historians have identified in the past. Some issues genuinely are new, but most have roots that intrigue historians. Today, I would offer to sociologists of education three general areas of inquiry.

First, John Dewey published *Democracy and Education* in 1916. Does it have meaning for us in the United States today, and if so, what is it? How does a society that considers itself a democracy best prepare its children educationally? What is the role of schooling, and how can it be improved? What are the roles of the youngsters' environments in nurturing education, and how can they be improved? Is learning by doing really an effective mode of instruction and for what kinds of learning? Are there unique educational needs of a democracy that totalitarian nations do not require? If so, what are they?

Second, if we accept that the goal of schooling is to nurture and enhance the wit and character of the young, what are the most effective means of nurturing wit? What are the characteristics of school environments that foster children's intellectual development and curiosity? How do we make these optimal environments more widespread? What do we know about increasing children's enthusiasm for academic learning? How do we get them in the mood to learn? Do tests as we now know them measure wit accurately? What kinds of instruments might do better?

Third, if wit is the domain schools presently focus upon, what is their role in enhancing character? Is there an effective pedagogy for this? Or is this the ultimate case of learning by doing? Is the student who wants to win at all costs reminded that rules must be followed? Are teamwork and cooperation valued as much as showmanship? Are similar punishments given to rich and poor for the same infractions of rules? Recent examples of high achievers in many extremely competitive environments, including Congress, financial institutions, and large corporations, reveal significant lapses not in their own undoubtedly high test scores but in understanding responsibility for others, a vital attribute of character in leaders. When expected to calculate risk, do they have greater tolerance for risk to others than to themselves, and if so, is that honorable in a leader? How do we address that question, especially in our most prestigious academic institutions where many of these individuals were enrolled?

Thus, I leave to the sociologists' investigation the profound issue of our time: How can education contribute to our democracy by nurturing and enhancing the wit and character of our youth?

References

Bryk, Anthony S., Penny B. Sebring, Elaine Allensworth, Stuart Luppescu, and John Q. Easton. 2009. *Organizing schools for improvement: Lessons from Chicago.* Chicago: University of Chicago Press.

Dewey, John. 1916. *Democracy and education: An introduction to the philosophy of education.* New York: The Free Press.

Jencks, Christopher, Marshall Smith, Henry Acland, Mary Jo Bane, David Cohen, Herbert Gintis, Barbara Heyns, and Stephan Michelson. 1972. *Inequality: A reassessment of the effect of family and schooling in America.* New York: Basic Books.

National Commission on Excellence in Education (NCEE). 1983. *A nation at risk: The imperative for educational reform.* Washington, DC: U.S. Department of Education, Government Printing Office.

Chapter 15
Reforming General Education and Diffusing Reform

Daniel J. Myers

The challenges facing educational systems, and those conducting research with the intent to improve them, are many. This essay though, is limited to two problems that cross many levels of education and bookend educational research. The first is the foundational input to the understanding and practice of education (and thus of educational research as well), namely, how we define the core purpose of general education. The second problem is concerned not with inputs, but the output and impact of our research—how it comes to be consumed (or more likely not consumed) by practitioners of the art of teaching.

My perspective on these challenges is informed by three interlocking experiences. First, I am a sociologist who, although having only a glancing engagement in the sociology of education literature, has been learning and working in the field of education most of my life. Second, and more recently, I have spent less time in the classroom and the better part of a decade in administration, taking on a broader responsibility for the functioning and well-being of the educational apparatus. Third, a different kind of experience, although no less pivotal to my thinking, has been my service as president of the board of a small, deliberately inventive Montessori school. Each of these roles has invited, even demanded, increasing reflection on the systems of education, how they are changing, and what we need to know as researchers and practitioners to improve them. As disparate as these experiences are, they have produced several observations about the state of education that apply across all types and levels of educational institutions. The problems of defining the purpose of general education and disseminating educational research are acute, and my sense of urgency has grown with each of my encounters with these segments of the educational system.

D.J. Myers (✉)
Department of Sociology, University of Notre Dame, Notre Dame, IN 46556, USA
e-mail: Daniel.J.Myers.33@nd.edu

The first issue is a fundamental driver of almost all educational efforts: What core accomplishments are we trying to attain as educators? The notion of general education varies by level and perhaps is articulated most formally by the university-level liberal arts requirements, but the driving notion of preparing students with the cognitive tools and moral judgment to be active, productive citizens is the central role of education from the moment formal schooling begins. Much has been written about this purpose, both opinion and research, but I will focus here on one particular strain of thinking about general education as a route forward.

Second, education is a field in which research has clear, practical implications and purposes. It is not enough to develop and support theory; one must also disseminate and induce practical application of what has been discovered. The second issue, then, concerns the penetration of what we have learned as researchers into the actual structure of the educational system and the performance of teaching. What obstacles slow the translation of new knowledge into systemic intervention and how can we increase the rate of diffusion?

The Purpose of General Education

As many observers of our educational system have lamented, the aims of general education always seem to be narrowing: budget cuts threaten art, music, and sports at primary and secondary levels; test content constricts course coverage across all levels; and the idea of university-level liberal arts education is thwarted for the purpose of preparing students for specific vocational tracks. Critics who fear the loss of good preparation for adult life, beyond merely succeeding in a specific job, voice their concerns to an often sympathetic audience. Indeed, many educators agree that students are becoming too specialized too early, too enamored with credentialing, and too instrumentally driven in defining the purpose of education. But, at the same time, these educators seem to continue replicating the structures that not only produced this trend, but are accelerating it at a breathtaking pace.

While our ability to produce general education is changing, how that is happening and to what degree are questions that need clear answers. After all, educational pundits can find any trend they wish using anecdote and opinion, but we need to know the actual trends, the real *whys*, and of course, the *hows*, if we are going to arrest deterioration and track our systems toward desired outcomes. But before that lies a larger core problem: We do not have anything remotely resembling consensus on the desired outcome. What should be the aim of general education? What educational experiences arm students for the demands of the twenty-first century? Even if we constrict ourselves to higher education, the variety of definitions and aims of general education are many, such as basic information everyone needs to function as a citizen, simple variety in coursework as an end in itself, exposure to a range of disciplines, and perhaps the most common, learning how to think. And, even those who agree on one of those broad aims cannot agree on what specifically we need to know, or what it might mean to know how to think.

But in the end, these differences matter little because the de facto outcome of any definition of general education is a requirement that students take a collection of disciplinary courses—a distribution requirement that does not necessitate coherence or thematic connection. These courses rarely build upon one another, they often can be taken in any sequence, in any year, and frequently they become unconnected, segmented data that students temporarily memorize. If learning to learn, exposure to a range of ideas, or acquisition of critical knowledge for citizenry occurs, it generally happens by accident. We assume a set of courses will produce some of this, but there is no design, no theory, no systematic practice of developing those habits of mind that we claim are the paramount outcomes of our efforts, and thus we are left only with hope that any of our desired outcomes will result. We need to think harder about what we are trying to do and what is demanded of students in our changing world. We need to design and adhere to a curriculum that meets those needs, and we need to assess our efforts.

I cannot hope to address the complexity of general education in one short essay, but, based on my experiences across a wide variety of educational situations, I can offer one example of an orientation that could be the basis of an alternative educational design. It is neither well-developed sufficiently to be considered a theory or specific enough to be called a hypothesis, but it points toward steps that can be constructed deliberately and assessed competitively against existing practice. We need to systematically reduce the emphasis both on disciplinary identification and on educational success being defined as exposure to disciplinary subsets of information. Learning facts of any kind—sociological, mathematical, and so on—is becoming passé. The irony of the age of information is that teaching information becomes less important. Why then, should teaching be organized around transmitting this disciplinarily bound information? Arithmetic is a pointed example. How often do people mentally perform arithmetic in their daily and work lives? Beyond calculating restaurant tips and counting change from the cashier, basic arithmetic was made obsolete by the hand-held calculator years ago—and now the cash register, spreadsheet, and specialized software do it all for us. We do need to understand the concepts of addition and multiplication—but beyond that, easy access to a data base of sum and products takes care of the rest.

Rather, I propose a shift of the fundamentals of a class and curriculum from being about *what* to being about *how*—and not just one how, but multiple integrated *hows*. In the information age, the primary skill is not retaining information but rather sets of skills used to manage our encounters with information. How do we find relevant information? How do we collect it, organize it, and judge it? How do we process it into a coherent set of thoughts that can be used for the task at hand? How do we present it effectively to other people? These are the key tasks that should define a general education curriculum. The natural science curriculum is ubiquitous from elementary school through the university. Is the purpose of these requirements to ensure that students memorize physics equations and are able to recite elements in the periodic table? Or, is it to understand and appreciate the scientific method—a way of gathering, processing, and assessing information? I posit that it should be the latter—and this claim can be evaluated by assessing the students' varying educational experiences and their success both in school and after graduation. If the evidence shows that building this kind of conceptual apparatus proves more beneficial than learning facts and information, then perhaps a satisfying educational reform could transpire.

Dissemination

Or could it? A researcher's positive assessment of a new technique or orientation hardly guarantees that it will be adopted, as was recently reinforced for me in several conversations with educational researchers. In those discussions, I came to understand that the vast majority of educational and cognitive psychologists focused on learning would agree with the intuitions about general education expressed in this essay. That reaction induced me to think further about the research process and reminded me that dissemination is an essential part of a complete research project. It is not enough to find satisfying answers to questions that animate our own interest, but, especially in a field like education where there is a clear praxis imperative, the knowledge produced in our investigation should be translated into on-the-ground changes.

Dissemination, however, turns out to be a difficult step. Penetrating the day-to-day practice of teaching and the structure of education is apparently more difficult than conducting the research in the first place. As an educational administrator, I have read many polemics on the state of the liberal arts and general education—but these books rarely engage actual educational research. Likewise, I have served on many committees concerned with curriculum reform at all levels of education and have never heard a mention of educational research or had a committee even consider consulting educational researchers when adjusting requirements and curriculum.

The problem is not unique to educational research, of course. Any field that has an active applied side confronts the challenge of making the leap from the basic research to application (and back again as well), but the education community has a special need to connect research and practice, and perhaps a special set of resources to accomplish it. After all, the field of education is fundamentally engaged with this very task—enabling others to learn, judge, incorporate, and use new knowledge. Researchers should be able, therefore, to propose routes of educating practitioners about their discoveries, make attempts to ignite these diffusion mechanisms, and evaluate the success of these attempts. An important step would be to consult the existing literature about diffusion. Based on Everett Roger's (2003) classic diffusion of innovations ideas, a large literature has developed analyzing the spread of social phenomena ranging from hybrid corn to protest tactics to new communication technology to terrorism. Roger's ideas can be put to work in the applied educational arena to tap communication and influence networks in an attempt to spread the word and induce adoption of new educational practices. To induce such work, the research system should demand that researchers embed theory-based dissemination into their research processes. Grant proposals should include not merely a dissemination *plan*, but a substantial method of *assessing* the dissemination as well, and funding agencies should be enthusiastic and demanding about dissemination. Such efforts would not only increase the real-world impact of research, but also would improve the research, as data from implementation attempts can be cycled back into the research process to condition theory and new studies.

In preparing this essay, I have been struck by the disconnect between researchers, on the one hand, and policymakers and practitioners on the other. The questions raised here about general education deserve to be answered—but not just behind the closed doors of research journals and what can seem to be arcane statistical maneuvering. Practitioners have a responsibility to reach out to educational research, but even more so, researchers have a responsibility to ensure that their findings end up mattering in practice. Failure to do so leaves the research process incomplete, and the disposition of important decisions, such as what to do about general education, in the hands of the systematically uninformed.

Reference

Rogers, Everett. 2003. *Diffusion of innovations*, 5th ed. New York: Free Press.

Chapter 16
The Rise and Fall of Civic Education in American Schools

Sandra Day O'Connor

Early in its history, the American experiment in self-government had its fair share of skeptics. Many believed that our society's heterogeneity and geographic expansiveness were insurmountable barriers to self-rule. Thomas Jefferson, James Madison, John Adams, and other founding fathers believed that the answer to this skepticism was public education. In the preamble to his 1779 bill for free schools in Virginia, Thomas Jefferson argued for public education as a way to preserve self-rule. With knowledge of the experiences of other societies, Americans could identify and defeat would-be tyrants. Jefferson further asserted that people need to be educated so that Americans can draw from the widest possible pool of citizens to find wise and honest lawmakers. And since educating citizens would benefit society at large, he reasoned, all should share the cost of this education (Jefferson 1905).

Benjamin Rush and Noah Webster also were advocates of public education as a means of strengthening a republican form of government. Rush argued that in order to teach youth how to fulfill the "new class of duties" required of every citizen of our new government, students should be "directed frequently to attend the courts of justice, where he will have the best opportunities of acquiring habits of arranging and comparing his ideas by observing the secretion of truth in the examination of witnesses and where he will hear the laws of the state explained" (1806:18). Webster believed that bad legislative decisions rarely result from bad intentions, but rather "generally proceed from ignorance either in the [legislators] themselves, or in their constituents." Thus, "the more generally knowledge is diffused among the substantial yeomanry, the more perfect will be the laws of a republican state" (Webster 1790:25).

Our public schools were founded with this same mission of educating students to become informed citizens. In the antebellum period (1789–1849), reformers such as Horace Mann led the common school movement, building systems of free and

S.D. O'Connor
Supreme Court of the United States, Washington, DC 20543, USA

compulsory public education across the country. Rapid social change, precipitated by accelerating economic growth, urbanization, industrialization, and immigration, cultivated a sense of urgency for the movement. Responding to growing class strife, which the reformers saw as a threat to the founders' republican vision, Mann wrote that common education was the great equalizer that would help unify and promote understanding between rich and poor, immigrant and native. Additionally, common schools would provide a fair opportunity for all to gain the education necessary to participate actively in government. Mann argued that citizens of our republic must "understand something of the true nature and functions of the government under which they live." Mann went on to conclude that, without a citizenry educated in the roles and responsibilities of the different branches of government, a republic is merely a "political solecism" (1848:8).

The movement's lasting achievement lives on to this day; free public education has been enacted in every state. Today, 40 state constitutions mention the importance of civic literacy among students, and 13 state constitutions explicitly point to civic education as the primary purpose of schools. In the past few decades, however, civic education has declined. A multitude of factors led to this downturn, including a loss of faith in traditional government institutions and our leaders in the wake of the Vietnam war and the Watergate scandal, the difficulty reconciling heterogeneity and diversity in the American population with the ethnocentric values that formed the foundation of early civic education, and inadequate preparation of teachers in civics, political thought, and government. No Child Left Behind and other recent educational initiatives have unintentionally contributed to the lessening focus on civic education by placing an emphasis on federal funding and testing in the schools for reading, math, and science. Teachers feel pressured to focus on teaching the subjects that are tested under this legislation at the expense of other subjects such as civics and history. Whereas students in the 1960s commonly took as many as three classes in government and civics, many students' only exposure to civics today comes through a one-semester government class in high school. Only 29 states require students to take a civics or government course for high school graduation.

National assessment tests demonstrate the effects of this lapse in civic education. On the last nationwide civics assessment, administered in 2006, more than two thirds of students scored below proficiency. Not even a third of eighth graders surveyed could identify the historical purpose of the Declaration of Independence. Less than a fifth of high school seniors could explain how citizen participation benefits democracy (O'Connor and Hamilton 2008:A12). Equally troubling is the major civic achievement gap between poor, minority, and immigrant youth and middle-class, white, and native-born youth. From the fourth grade to the twelfth grade, African American, Hispanic, and disadvantaged students score significantly worse on the National Assessment of Educational Progress (NAEP) civics test than their white, Asian, and middle-class counterparts. In addition to the civic knowledge gap, poor and minority students are disadvantaged in learning the skills that they need for effective civic engagement, such as leadership and communication. Often these skills are learned in the workplace and voluntary associations. But poor and minority youth often fail to benefit from these opportunities because they are more likely to have lower-status jobs and less likely to participate in voluntary associations. Unfortunately, these same populations are those who are likely to face the most civic problems. Poor students contend with issues such as crime at a higher rate than their middle-class counterparts. When it comes to civic education, our schools' failures are especially stark in communities most in need of effective civic engagement.

An entire generation of American young people who were not taught civics has now grown up, and our neglect of civics education has impacted both their knowledge of and trust in the federal government. Only 39% of Americans can name all three branches of government, let alone adequately explain what each branch does. Surveys show that approximately 75% of the public cannot distinguish the role of a judge from that of a legislator. They believe that judges are politicians in robes and should be controlled by popular opinion. Forty percent think the Constitution permits the President to ignore a Supreme Court ruling if he believes that doing so will protect the country from harm (Jamieson and Hennessy 2007).

There is a direct correlation between an individual's civic knowledge and higher levels of "political participation, expression of democratic values including toleration, stable political attitudes, and adoption of enlightened self-interest" (Levinson 2007:8). It is therefore unsurprising that "[b]y almost every measure, Americans' direct engagement in politics and government has fallen steadily and sharply over the last generation" (Putnam 1995:68) and that the victims of the civic achievement gap show the most troubling lack of participation in the political process. In the 2004 presidential election, the voting rate of members of families with an income of less than $15,000 was almost half the voting rate of people in families with an income of over $75,000 (45–80%). This disparity extends to other levels of civic participation as well, including involvement in political campaigns, membership on organizational boards, participation in protests, and communication with political representatives about specific issues. The success of any democratic system depends on the participation of a cross section of its citizens. Aristotle stated that "[i]f liberty and equality, as is thought by some, are chiefly to be found in a democracy, they will be attained when all persons alike share in the government to the utmost." To create a society that is truly governed by the people, we must ensure that all American citizens have the knowledge and tools to participate in democratic government.

The Need for a New Approach to Civic Education

In spite of the decline in civic education, Americans today still believe in the civic mission of public schools. In 1996, when a poll asked people's opinions on the most important purpose of schools after providing a basic education, "prepar[ing] students to be responsible citizens" was considered "very important" by more people than any other goal (Elam et al. 1996:55). Eighty-four percent of teachers agreed with this assessment (Quigley 1999:1425–50). We cannot, however, continue to teach civics the way it was taught throughout the nineteenth and twentieth centuries.

Our civics and history courses of the past may have been sufficiently extensive, but they often provided a one-sided view, failing to adequately address the kinds of controversy and conflict that citizens must understand and effectively confront. Although diverse viewpoints and controversial topics have to some extent been incorporated into current civics curricula, all too often, today's students continue to describe civics and social studies as dull and boring and rate it as one of their least favorite subjects. Civics is an active subject—it is about engaging in political or other processes to accomplish results. However, civics courses often do not focus on helping students develop a thoughtful understanding of our political history and their role in the functioning of our republican government. Rather, schools attempt to teach civics by having students memorize facts and read textbooks, some as long as 844 pages (*Save a Tree per Year Using E-Textbooks,* 2007). Instead of continuing with this method of teaching civics, we must create new approaches to engage the twenty-first century student. We need curricula that present information in a problem-based and interactive way and in the context of relevant issues.

To understand how to make civic education relevant to today's students, we should look to the ways in which youth are engaging in civic life. Recent trends for civic engagement among young people are encouraging. The 2008 presidential election saw a higher percentage of youth aged 18–29 voting than any election since 1972, when 18-year-olds were first guaranteed the right to vote. In 2009, 36% of college freshman surveyed by UCLA's Higher Education Research Institute said that keeping up with politics was a "very important" or "essential" life goal. Further, a third of incoming first-year students indicated that there was a very good chance that they would engage civically by either participating in community service or volunteering during college. This number represents an increase of 82% in less than 20 years (Pryor et al. 2010).

Part of this increase may be due to pressing world events that make government decisions seem more consequential than those of prior decades. In addition, politicians, policymakers, and entertainers are learning to engage young people using the language and tools of their generation. Today's students are encouraged to use new technologies to design their own networks for civic engagement. For example, in the 2008 election, two thirds of Internet users under the age of 30 had a social networking profile, and half of them used social networking sites to get information and share their views about politics or the campaigns (Rainie and Smith 2008). As the first generation of digital natives, today's youth have demonstrated the potential of digital media for civic education, political organizing, and civic decision making.

Some educators have seized on the renewed interest of youth in civics and politics to convey the information that students will need to make responsible choices and informed decisions as citizens. In one program, high school government teachers combined a semester of traditional classroom curriculum with a second semester in which students worked in teams on service projects at county administrative offices. Teams worked to determine whether curbside recycling was a good policy for their community, to identify jobs that could be performed by persons incarcerated for less than a 90-day period, and to develop a five-year plan for the local fire department. In support of their proposals, the students collected input from residents via phone surveys, projected costs of their projects, wrote reports on their findings, and presented those findings at formal hearings before county government officials. After participating in these sorts of experiential learning, students have reported increased enthusiasm about their own responsibility to engage in civic activity, feelings that they could effect real change, and greater knowledge about the mechanisms for getting involved in decision making in their communities (Westheimer and Kahne 2004:237–269).

The key contribution of these programs is providing students with the opportunity to learn about civic processes by participating in them. To be effective, twenty-first-century civic education must not only be hands-on; it must also help students navigate multiplying sources of information, evaluate it for its objectivity and reliability, and apply it in new contexts. The Internet offers endless civic opportunities. Online tools allow citizens to gather information and communicate their preferences directly to each other and to government entities. Nevertheless, it can be difficult to distinguish good information from bad information and to learn how to communicate effectively. Students need guidance about how to navigate these new pathways for civic engagement. Otherwise, their participation will be at best ineffective and at worst counterproductive.

The mixed quality of news media and the sheer volume of information available make it even more important that students have good civic education so that they can understand and evaluate the information they receive. Studies have shown that the effect of biased information is compounded by the fact that people's political affiliations affect how they process unreliable information. In one study, 56% of Democrats initially disapproved of John Roberts' nomination to the Supreme Court. After viewing a false ad attacking Roberts as a supporter of violent anti-abortion groups, this number rose to 80%. Even after viewing a refutation of the ad by abortion-rights supporters and being informed that the ad had been withdrawn, 72% of participating Democrats still disapproved of Roberts' nomination. Among Republicans surveyed, disapproval of Roberts rose after viewing the ad but dropped back to the initial level after the ad was debunked. The misinformation, then, was more likely to have a lasting result on those predisposed to agree with it (Vedantam 2008).

That citizens are likely to be affected by misinformation based on their initial political leanings, and that they may continue to be affected even after they receive accurate information suggests an emotional, rather than a logical response. Too often, we see the results of such emotional responses in our news media, where one-sided partisan commentary often eclipses objective reporting. To reverse this trend, students must learn how to discuss and debate the difficult issues our society faces in a rational and respectful way. A citizen is a more effective decision maker if she is able to recognize the arguments on all sides of an issue and respond logically rather than emotionally.

Determined to help address the crisis we face in civic education, I assembled a team of experts at Georgetown Law and Arizona State University to develop a free, interactive, online civics curriculum called iCivics (www.icivics.org). Our goal is to create civics learning portals for teachers and students that include online games, social networking, and other pathways to civic participation. We are using problem-based approaches to facilitate student exploration of government responses and solutions to pressing issues. In iCivics activities, students use persuasive and informed arguments to effect change in games and simulations and can then take these skills into the real world.

Our hope is that the activities are engaging enough to bridge the gap between classroom time and out-of-classroom time. A recent study found that children spend 40 hours per week using media, whether it is computers, television, video games, or music. That is more time than they spend in school or with their parents (Roberts et al. 2005). If we capture just a little bit of that time to get students thinking about government and civic engagement, it will be a big step in the right direction. To do this, we are leveraging the synthesis between teens' interest in Internet gaming and the potential of games in civic learning. A recent study found that "[t]eens with the most (top 25%) civic gaming experiences are more likely to report interest and engagement in civic and political activities than teens with the fewest (bottom 25%)" (Lenhart et al. 2008:vi). This finding is potentially very powerful since 97% of teenagers ages 12–17 play some kind of computer, web, portable, or console games. iCivics uses games to allow students to experience civic processes and to connect civic learning to real-world engagement through avenues for action and discussion.

Civic education must be understood, at its root, as education for informed participation in government and society. The goal is for students to have the knowledge to understand the political history of our nation, appreciate different perspectives, craft their own informed opinions, and gain the skills to persuasively advocate their views in the public sphere. This combination of outcomes will motivate students to participate and to lead so that self-rule can be continued and perfected. We have a long way to go to rejuvenate our nation's commitment to educating active citizens. To do so, we must commit to a new curricular approach that will make civic education more relevant and engaging. I believe this new approach will encourage policymakers to once again view civic education as a central mission of American education and bring robust civics requirements back into our nation's classrooms.

Acknowledgments The author would like to thank Gretchen Blauvelt-Marquez and Abigail Taylor for their excellent assistance with this chapter.

References

Elam, Stanely, Lowell C. Rose, and Alec M. Gallup. 1996. The 28th annual Phi Delta Kappa/Gallup poll of the public's attitudes toward the public schools. *Phi Delta Kappan* 78(1): 41–59.

Jamieson, Kathleen Hall, and Michael Hennessy. 2007. Public understanding of and support for the courts: Survey results. *Georgetown Law Journal* 95: 899–902.

Jefferson, Thomas. 1905. A bill for the more general diffusion of knowledge. In *The works of Thomas Jefferson*, vol. 2, ed. Ford Paul Leicester, 414–426. New York/London: G.P. Putnam's Sons. Retrieved from Online Library of Liberty on August 10, 2010.

Lenhart, Amanda, Joseph Kahne, Ellen Middaugh, Alexandra Rankin Macgill, Chris Evans, and Jessica Vitak. 2008. *Teens, video games, and civics*. Washington, DC: Pew Internet & American Life Project. Retrieved August 10, 2010. http://www.pewinternet.org/~/media// Files/Reports/2008/PIP_Teens_Games_and_Civics_Report_FINAL.pdf.

Levinson, Meira. 2007. *The Civic Achievement Gap.* CIRCLE Working Paper 51, CIRCLE: The Center for Information and Research on Civic Learning and Engagement. Retrieved August 10, 2010. http://www.civicyouth.org/ PopUps/ WorkingPapers/WP51Levinson.pdf.

Mann, Horace. 1848. *Twelfth Annual Report to the Secretary of the Massachusetts State Board of Education.* Retrieved August 10, 2010. http://americanhistory.unomaha.edu/countDownload.php?resource_file=true&ID=159&filename=Horace+Mann+Twelfth+Report+to+MA+Board+of+Education+1848.rtf.

O'Connor, Sandra Day, and Lee H. Hamilton. 2008. Schools must teach rudiments of self-government. *New Jersey Record*, November 14, A12.

Pryor, John H., Sylvia Hurtado, Linda DeAngelo, Laura Palucki Blake, and Serge Tran. 2010. *The American freshman: National norms fall 2009.* Los Angeles: Higher Education Research Institute, UCLA.

Putnam, Robert D. 1995. Bowling alone: America's declining social capital. *Journal of Democracy* 6(1): 65–78.

Quigley, Charles N. 1999. Civic education: Recent history, current status, and the future. *Albany Law Review* 62: 1425–1450.

Rainie, Lee, and Aaron Smith. 2008. *The internet and the 2008 election.* Washington, DC: Pew Research Center. Retrieved August 10, 2010. http://www.pewinternet.org/~/media//Files/Reports/2008/PIP_2008_election.pdf.

Roberts, Donald F., Ulla G. Foehr, and Victoria Rideout. 2005. *Generation M: Media in the Lives of 8–18 year-olds.* Menlo Park: The Henry J. Kaiser Family Foundation. Retrieved August 10, 2010. http://www.kff.org/ entmedia/upload/Generation-M-Media-in-the-Lives-of-8–18 -Year-olds-Report.pdf.

Rush, Benjamin. 1806. Of the mode of education proper in a republic. In *Essays, literary, moral and philosophical*, 2nd ed, 6–20. Philadelphia: Thomas and William Bradford.

Save a Tree Per Year Using E-Textbooks. 2007. *Café Scribe.* Retrieved August 10, 2010. http://www.cafescribe.com/index.php?option=com_content&task=view&id=210&Itemid=127.

Vedantam, Shankar. 2008. The power of political misinformation. *The Washington Post*, September 15, A06.

Webster, Noah. 1790. On the education of youth in America. In *A collection of essays and fugitive writings on moral, historical, political and literary subjects*, 1–37. Boston: I. Thomas and E.T. Andrews.

Westheimer, Joel, and Joseph Kahne. 2004. What kind of citizen? The politics of educating for democracy. *American Educational Research Journal* 41: 237–269.

Chapter 17
Improving Grades: Urban Public Schools, Racial and Socioeconomic Segregation, and the Promise of Innovation

James M. Quane and William Julius Wilson

Increasingly, public schools have student populations that are overwhelmingly minority, disproportionately poor, and more likely to drop out or have below grade-level skills in academic performance (Orfield and Gordon 2001). The path to this juncture has been well chronicled in the vast literature on urban education, which describes decades of racial and socioeconomic shifts in neighborhood composition, misguided policies, ill-informed intervention strategies, blatant neglect, and well-intentioned but ultimately unsuccessful attempts to compensate for past indifferences. Going forward, we face the prospect of a trove of innovations and policies that address the academic attainment of minority youth who are overrepresented in poorly performing urban public schools. Whether these efforts will have a fundamental impact on the school outcomes of poor urban Americans or will register as just another piecemeal approach to system change is unclear. Ultimately, however, the likelihood of success will depend in large part on a coordinated approach to change, one that addresses the root causes of inequality, including socioeconomic and residential segregation as well as the disconnect between the out-of-school and academic experiences of urban, minority families.

To help motivate additional research on these complex relationships, we explore some key issues for sociologists to consider in the coming decade. In particular, we call attention to the continuing role of economic and social disparities that contribute to the academic divide between whites and students of color. Some of these inequities originated far beyond the front doors or district boundaries of urban schools, but their impact on public education has been substantial and research can help to expand on these associations. As such, demographic shifts, changes in the safety net that bolsters low-income families against instability, as well as the recent

---

J.M. Quane (✉) • W.J. Wilson
John F. Kennedy School of Government, Harvard University, Cambridge, MA 02138, USA
e-mail: james_quane@harvard.edu

economic collapse are factors that have a strong bearing on the academic attainment of children and youth. Finally, many of these contextual forces collide in urban neighborhoods. How residents experience and interpret these realities is another critical area for social science research to explore.

Neighborhood Context and the Economic and Social Vulnerability of Urban Black Families

There are strong indications that the decline in the spatial concentration of chronic poverty in metropolitan areas that Jargowsky (2003) observed was curtailed or reversed by the recent economic collapse. What is gaining momentum is a rise in the physical and social isolation of chronically poor blacks and to a lesser, but unacceptable degree, impoverished Hispanics in disadvantaged neighborhoods (Orfield and Gordon 2001). In addition, persistent exclusionary patterns of school enrollment and neighborhood residence among whites and non-poor families contribute to the ongoing racial segregation of blacks in these areas. The result is that public schools in predominantly minority districts will likely continue to experience the same racial and socioeconomic disparities, inadequate allocation of resources, and unacceptable educational outcomes that have defined the experiences of inner-city students for several decades. To begin to address these issues, research should first and foremost help resolve some fundamental questions concerning the measurement of the racial, ethnic, and socioeconomic makeup of public schools as well the ability to accurately assess drop-out rates, school attendance, grade completion, and other basic benchmarks of school performance. Though No Child Left Behind (NCLB) increased attention on the achievement gap, school districts came up with inventive ways of reporting enhanced performance levels without actually improving students' abilities. Researchers urgently need to address these inconsistencies to ensure that even rudimentary evaluations are completed with a basic degree of rigor.

Beyond that, research should address the cumulative effects of concentrated poverty on student outcomes. Emerging research sheds new light on the debilitating effects of multigenerational residence in high poverty neighborhoods. Looking at the residential patterns of a nationally representative sample of black and white families, Sharkey (2008) convincingly demonstrates that not only are low-income blacks much more likely to reside in the poorest quartile of urban neighborhoods, but the chances that their children will live in similarly disadvantaged areas as adults are considerably greater. Building on a vast literature, which provides convincing evidences of the debilitating consequences of poverty for children, these studies find that a pronounced effect on cognitive impairment is still evident even among children of parents who relocated to better neighborhoods before their children were born (Sampson et al. 2008; Sharkey and Elwert 2010). Moreover, the most acute effects on development, in terms of decreased reading and verbal abilities, were found among second generation children who reside in severely disadvantaged neighborhoods (Sampson et al. 2008; Sharkey and Elwert 2010).

Education research has long considered socioeconomic background and family characteristics as important predictors of the black–white academic achievement gap (for reviews see Wells et al. 2005; Hallinan 2001), but this recent research on the durable effects of neighborhood contexts introduces a structural explanation that is often omitted from analyses to date. Studies that consider the cumulative concentration or legacy effects of poor neighborhoods have deeper implications than the status attainment literature has revealed to date, and researchers should be alert to these implications.

Low-Income Family Stability and Children's Learning

Despite its challenges, the public school system is perhaps the only major public policy initiative that is operating at scale with low-income youth in disadvantaged neighborhoods across the country. Similar to public housing developments, public schools in many inner-city districts have undergone enormous changes in the past 30 years to adjust to the changing demographics and socioeconomic profile and constituent needs of the people they serve. Preparing students for the transition to the twenty-first century workforce raises numerous challenges and it is fair to say that the burden on public schools is even greater in economically depressed metropolitan areas.

Over the years, schools incorporated additional services and courses as an adjunct to their central mission in order to compensate for inadequate local economies and social services. In the 1990s, these pressures were somewhat offset by a healthy labor market for unskilled and semiskilled workers, as well as an expansion in supports for low-income working families, including the Earned Income Tax Credit (EITC), income disregards for working families in subsidized housing, and the expansion in coverage for the Child Health Insurance Program (CHIP) (Blank and Ellwood 2001). Many of these policies helped assuage the effects of welfare reform, which in 1996 introduced life-time term limits on the receipt of welfare. No doubt, the additional work and family supports as well as employment opportunities helped to keep many low-income households stable during their transition off the welfare rolls.

Today, however, low-income inner-city families face a different reality, which is likely to have repercussions in the classroom. Confronting unemployment rates that far outpace national averages and the reality that they have exhausted their life-time allotment of welfare benefits, many households in poor urban neighborhoods are approaching or experiencing a crisis. For some of these families, home foreclosures and job layoffs have increased with alarming rates. Resilient low-income families may be able to buffer their children against the negative consequences of isolated setback or short-term economic hardship. However, the sharp economic downturn is likely to result in increased instability. A focus on early warning signs among families clustered in poor school districts, such as elevated rates of school truancy or tardiness, children's mental and physical health issues, and sharp decreases in rates of homework completion, might help to direct needed assistance. But the cumulative ecological and household effects on students' abilities are probably the most serious. Building on the neighborhood contexts literature, researchers should consider carefully how work disruptions, inconsistent employment schedules, and other household uncertainties, including the availability of cash and noncash benefits, cluster among families in poor neighborhoods. These problems can have important spillover effects on students' ability to stay focused and attentive in school, and ultimately their likelihood of dropping out altogether.

Other Community Supports and Family Engagement

Attention to the structural and household conditions that shape the out-of-classroom experience therefore provides an important context for understanding the academic attainment of low-income students. Indeed, efforts to link the school performance of pupils with the social, economic, and physical conditions of their neighborhoods are a central component of the Harlem Children's Zone (HCZ) and Promise Neighborhoods initiative, which is patterned after the HCZ. This approach is not without its detractors, especially those who argue that the value is not justified by its price tag and the lack of documented evidence of effectiveness to date. However, extant literature points to some theoretical frameworks that can help researchers understand how such multifaceted initiatives may make a difference in students' lives, especially in light of the other adversities that inner-city families of resource-deficient neighborhoods must confront.

In his work on the segregation of minority students in chronically poor neighborhoods, James Coleman (1988) argued that organizations such as public schools provide an important milieu for the acquisition and reinforcement of positive social norms. Indeed, as argued earlier, schools may be one of the few remaining formal institutions in poor neighborhoods. The erosion of other institutions in many inner-city neighborhoods is a troubling development. Research by Sampson and his colleagues (Sampson and Raudenbush1997; Morenoff et al. 2001) suggests that neighborhood organizations are important venues for the generation of trust and social obligation among residents and ultimately can play an important role in mediating the relationship between neighborhood disadvantage and residents' well-being.

Work by Bryk and Schneider (2002) raises the possibility that trust in the school system shapes low-income parents' interactions with administrators and teachers. For poor adults who may have little prior exposure to educational institutions, developing a sense of trust is sometimes complicated by a host of cultural and socioeconomic dynamics. Poor parents, for example, are more likely to defer to school officials when it comes to decisions about the academic enrichment of their children.

However, attempts to socialize students may be considered outside the school's purview and regarded with suspicion. For their part, teachers may favor the professional deference and broad discretion allotted to them by low-income parents, but also criticize their lack of responsiveness to teachers' periodic efforts to engage them. Neckerman's (2007) historical analysis of Chicago's public school system documents the cleavages in relational trust among low-income minority parents and educators. Her research reveals that eroding trust in inner-city neighborhoods beset by decades of disinvestment filtered into the classroom and negatively impacted teacher/student interactions. Accordingly, researchers should be alert to the possibility that initiatives attempting to instill a sense of cooperation and mutual understanding among parents and school staff in poor inner-city neighborhoods may succeed in directly counteracting the distrust that hampers consensus building. Indeed, efforts that foster improvements in the social organization of chronically disadvantaged neighborhoods may provide the capacity for change and yield the dividends that observers say are critical to the ultimate success of the Promise Neighborhood approach. The following research question might be tested in this regard: Do efforts to promote social capital in resource depleted neighborhoods with low rates of social organization help to generate collective efficacy, which in turn contributes to the academic attainment of the children and youth who reside in these neighborhoods?

Furthermore, sociologists should assess theories that undergird alternative approaches to parental involvement in schools. One distinction that observers make about so-called paternalistic schools—ones that are highly prescriptive and closely regulate students' behavior—is that they often operate to counteract what they consider to be inadequate family norms and attempt to replace them with traditional middle-class values. This approach is in sharp contrast to the family-engagement model, which provides for a more inclusive role for low-income parents. A fertile area for empirical investigation is the systematic comparison of paternalistic and family-engagement oriented programs.

Understanding Caregivers' Considerations

In some regards, policymakers' emphasis on increased school options—for example, charter schools, magnet schools, and public school choice—appears to be in line with the need to better incorporate low-income families into the decision making about their children's education. However, it is not clear how low-income parents weigh the pros and cons of school choice or whether they even feel comfortable having to make these critical decisions in the first place. Lewis and Nakagawa's (1995) study of school decentralization in Chicago found considerable support among inner-city parents for their neighborhood schools, even though many of these institutions were of inferior quality. Echoing previous studies on why low-income urban families select informal child care arrangements provided by relatives or friends over more structured and developmentally enriching institutional arrangements, this research suggests that schooling decisions may not be based on the same concerns that school choice policymakers presuppose. Likewise, in a recent study of the impact of the Moving to Opportunity (MTO) program, which moved low-income families from areas of concentrated poverty to mixed-income neighborhoods, researchers point to the "cultural logic" that parents draw on when selecting a school (Briggs et al. 2010:233). For many of these parents, safety considerations, allegiance to a neighborhood, work schedules, and other household obligations were among the major factors that motivated school selection, not academic quality. This is not to say that academic quality does not matter for these caregivers. Rather, it suggests that other pressing concerns take precedence and research should not only discover and elaborate on these factors, but also consider ways to address these concerns from a policy perspective.

A troubling implication for parents who are unable to navigate the myriad options available to them is that their children may be unwittingly harmed. Parents with lower education and income are less likely to participate in important decisions about their children's education, and children in these families already may be concentrated in the lowest performing or ineffective schools. Presented with sound alternatives, resourceful and informed parents may decide to move their children to schools that promise higher graduation rates. Accordingly, more research comparing families who actively pursue better educational options for their children with those that do not is needed. Among the latter, especially those who have the option to transfer their children to other schools, such research may shed additional light on their circumstances, including critical insights into the constraints they face in making such difficult decisions. For example, some of these parents may decide to keep their children in a poor performing school because they feel that the disruptions associated with relocation may have a more adverse effect on their educational outcomes. To address this and related possibilities, researchers might examine the test results of students who transferred to other schools or who were affected by school closure or district consolidation and compare them to students who remained in poor performing schools.

Undergirding considerations about decision making among low-income families in poor neighborhoods are questions concerning economic opportunities. For many of these parents, who themselves have been completely disconnected from an increasingly specialized labor market, the danger is that society will continue to shift the burden onto them to make important decisions about their children's future. Whether it is choosing among a number of schooling options, picking an appropriate child care facility, or urging their child to obtain a high school diploma or GED, low-income parents are likely to draw on their own realities to inform their conclusions. Among low-income families of color, these realities are infused with a sense of despondence arising from their own limited circumstances that may unwittingly but understandably lead them to make decisions that can further impair their children's chances of escaping poverty as adults. How to provide viable opportunities for minority families in urban neighborhoods is a laudable goal, but research can ensure that the desires and best interests of families and children are well represented in the process.

Conclusion

In sum, sociologists researching urban school reform, which takes into consideration the structural and cultural impediments to student success, can help advance policy initiatives aimed at dismantling barriers to educational opportunity for students of color. In particular, we advocate for research that reflects the inherent interconnectedness among families, neighborhoods, and the macroeconomic forces that shape their daily experiences. In addition to quantitative and qualitative studies that situate student achievement within the physical and social contexts of schools and the neighborhoods they operate in, this line or research calls for more holistic theoretical frameworks, which advance our conceptual understanding of how disadvantaged youth engage with school. While the public school system bears considerable responsibility for helping to prepare youth for a successful transition to adulthood, its chances for success are seriously diminished in communities where academic achievement is not enhanced by other experiences, including cumulative experiences. By drawing attention to all of the developmental domains that children and youth occupy, the research community can foster a deeper understanding of what real reform would entail and what we need to do to accomplish it.

Acknowledgments We thank Maureen T. Hallinan and Jessica Houston Su for comments on an earlier draft of this chapter.

References

Blank, Rebecca M., and David T. Ellwood. 2001. *The Clinton Legacy for America's Poor*. NBER Working Paper 8437. Cambridge: National Bureau of Economic Research.
Briggs, Xavier de Souze, Susan J. Popkin, and John Goering. 2010. *Moving to opportunity: The story of an American experiment to fight ghetto poverty*. New York: Oxford University Press.
Bryk, Anthony S., and Barbara Schneider. 2002. *Trust in schools: A core resource for improvement*. New York: Russell Sage.
Coleman, James. 1988. Social capital in the creation of human capital. *American Journal of Sociology* 94: S95–S120.
Hallinan, Maureen T. 2001. Sociological perspectives on black-white inequalities in American schooling. *Sociology of Education* 74: 50–70.
Jargowsky, Paul A. 2003. *Stunning progress, hidden problems: The dramatic decline of concentrated poverty in the 1990s. Living cities census series, Center on urban and metropolitan studies*. Washington, DC: The Brookings Institution.
Lewis, Dan A., and Nakagawa Kathryn. 1995. *Race and educational reform in the American metropolis: A study of school decentralization*. Albany: SUNY Press.
Morenoff, Jeffrey, Robert Sampson, and Stephan Raudenbush. 2001. Neighborhood inequality, collective efficacy, and the spatial dynamics of homicide. *Criminology* 39: 517–560.
Neckerman, Kathryn M. 2007. *Schools betrayed: Roots of failure in inner-city education*. Chicago: The University of Chicago Press.
Orfield, Gary, and Nora Gordon. 2001. *Schools more separate: consequences of a decade of resegregation. New Research Findings*. Cambridge: The Civil Rights Project, Harvard University.
Sampson, Robert, Stephan Raudenbush, and Felton Earls. 1997. Neighborhoods and violent crime: A multilevel study of collective efficacy. *Science* 277: 918–924.

Sampson, Robert J., Patrick Sharkey, and Stephan W. Raudenbush. 2008. Durable effects of concentrated disadvantage on verbal ability among African-American children. *Proceedings of the National Academy of Sciences* 105: 845–853.

Sharkey, Patrick. 2008. The intergenerational transmission of context. *American Journal of Sociology* 113: 931–969.

Sharkey, Patrick, and Felix Elwert. 2010. *The Legacy of Disadvantage: Multigenerational Neighborhood Effects on Cognitive Ability*. CDE WP 2010–06. Center for Demography and Ecology, University of Wisconsin-Madison.

Wells, Amy S., Jennifer J. Holme, Anita J. Revilla, and Awo K. Atanda. 2005. How society failed school desegregation policy: Looking past the schools to understand them. *Review of Research in Education* 28: 47–99.

Chapter 18
Policymaking and Research

Diane Ravitch

Since 2001, when Congress passed the No Child Left Behind legislation, education research has moved to center stage in battles about policymaking. That law used the phrase *research based* more than 100 times, although much that was mandated by the law had no basis in research. Never has there been more attention to research, nor more controversy about research findings, nor greater need for research, nor greater willingness to make consequential policy decisions without regard to any research. In the past decade, policymakers have forged ahead in their decision making, relying on intuition and on policy briefs prepared by interest groups and partisan think tanks as if they were research. By *research*, I refer here to studies that are peer reviewed and that have been prepared by independent scholars who are not dependent on funding by organizations with a specific agenda.

The NCLB law included many assumptions that were either unfounded or that relied on hunches. It assumed that a statewide accountability system would produce higher achievement. It assumed that higher test scores were by themselves a proxy for higher achievement. It ignored the possibility that a regime reliant on incentives and sanctions would produce test score inflation, teaching to the test, a narrowed curriculum, cheating, and a variety of other undesirable behaviors that raised scores but did not improve education.

The federal law included specific remedies that Congress believed would improve schools, even though these remedies had no basis in research. Thus, Congress decreed that schools must enable 100% of their students to achieve proficiency and that those unable to make "adequate yearly progress" over a sustained period of time would be required to change their governance to: become charter schools, be taken over by the state, fire the staff, close the school, or to restructure. The research on these legislated goals and remedies was meager, and in no case sufficiently robust

---

D. Ravitch (✉)
New York University, Southold, NY 11971, USA
e-mail: gardendr@gmail.com

to support federal legislation that affected every public school in the nation. Federal legislation often—one might even say customarily—precedes the findings of educational researchers, but it is unusual to see policymakers pass a law that invokes the authority of educational research so assuredly without referring to research to validate its own premises.

NCLB was but a prelude to an even more vigorous bout of federal policymaking that occurred after the election of Barack Obama. Determined to reform the nation's schools, the administration received an unprecedented $5 billion for this purpose from Congress as part of the economic recovery program of 2009. Of this amount, $4.3 billion funded a program called Race to the Top (RTTT). This program assumed that the best lever for reform was competition. Most states, experiencing severe financial problems, responded eagerly to the competition for federal funding, which was especially enticing in light of the large sums available to the winning states. The Obama administration won its wager that states would change their laws and adopt policies favored by the administration, but the policies themselves had little or no evidence, whether from research or demonstration, to validate them.

Thus, RTTT awarded points in the competition to states that removed obstacles to creating more privately managed charter schools, although the one consistent finding of research showed that the quality of such schools varies dramatically. And, points were awarded to states willing to evaluate teachers in relation to their students' test scores, although research showed that such evaluations were rife with problems, such as instability of teacher effects, nonrandom assignment of students to teachers, and the likely negative consequences of attaching additional stakes to tests.

As the administration forged ahead with its plan for reauthorization of the Elementary and Secondary Education Act, it claimed that its policies were research based, but they were not. It continued to wager that accountability would motivate significant improvement, despite 8 years of NCLB, in which gains on the National Assessment of Educational Progress were modest or nonexistent. It asserted that merit pay would improve teaching, despite inconclusive research evidence and the likely racheting up of the negative consequences of high-stakes testing. It supported the expansion of privately managed charter schools, despite evidence that the charter sector was likely to produce as many bad schools as good ones and despite the risk posed by privatization to the very concept of public education. It maintained the NCLB menu of sanctions for low-performing schools—closing them, firing the staff, turning them into charters, and so on—despite the manifest failure of such policies in the previous decade.

At the same time, conflicts over research spilled over into the mass media, where some researchers took their findings to the court of public opinion, rather than peer reviewers. Pundits and politicians discussed the latest study or think tank brief and discovered that they could find a study to support whatever they wanted to do.

In a perfect world, policymakers would not impose their hunches and ideology on the nation's schools without evidence of the likely consequences. This is not a perfect world, so researchers must defend the importance of evidence; insist that studies funded by advocacy groups are not the same as research; and explain to policymakers, in clear and concise language, how to tell the difference between research and advocacy.

There are many challenging topics for education researchers today. Now is the time to launch longitudinal studies that track the life course of students who have been subject to the current high-stakes testing regime through graduation and beyond. The pressure to produce higher scores and higher graduation rates raises pertinent questions about the validity of both. Some states have been gaming the system (witness the collapse of state scores in New York in 2010 after Daniel Koretz and Jennifer Jennings determined that they were set so low as to be without meaning; Medina 2010). Now is a good time to probe the very concept of proficiency, which allows officials to manipulate scores, adjusting them up or down to produce the desired results. Now is the time to investigate whether graduation rates have been artificially inflated by credit recovery and other stratagems that enable students to graduate despite failing required courses. It is also a good time to investigate the persistence rates of high school graduates in 2-year and 4-year colleges, as a way of determining the quality of their preparation. The emphasis on high-stakes testing has opened up so many avenues for gaming the system and inflating results that there are many research topics that bear further investigation.

Another fruitful field for study is the role of private money in advancing the agenda of privatization through charters and vouchers. Scholars have only scratched the surface in studying the influence of private money in education policymaking. The foundations that have spent the most money to shape public policy are ripe for study, including the Gates Foundation, the Broad Foundation, and the Walton Family Foundation. Scholars have been slow to examine their programs, their assumptions, and their goals. Janelle Scott at Berkeley is among the few who have studied the role of foundations in the policy process, but to date no one has looked closely at the role of advocacy groups that represent Wall Street titans, like Democrats for Education Reform and its spin-off Education Reform Now. As the national agenda increasingly reflects the views of major foundations and well-funded advocacy groups, scholars must examine the interconnections between government policymakers and these organizations, as well as the policies that they advance and the extent to which these policies are research based.

There has never been a better time to demonstrate the relevance and importance of research in the shaping of education policy.

Reference

Medina, Jennifer. 2010. State's exams became easier to pass, education officials say. *The New York Times*, July 19. Retrieved August 9, 2010. http://www.nytimes.com/2010/07/20/nyregion/20tests.html?_r=1&scp=1&sq=Daniel%20Koretz&st=cse.

Chapter 19
Sociology for the Future Historian

William Reese

Imagine it is 2050, and you are nearing retirement. You are a historian, mostly interested in the history of education generally and public schools specifically. You finally feel enough distance from the passions of the first two decades of the twenty-first century to consider writing about it. You have waited this long for good reasons. Your mentors in graduate school always insisted that you should never write about your own time and place. Let journalists and social scientists, concerned with the here-and-now, do their job and you do yours. A historian's job is to understand the past, not the present. The passing of time will provide perspective.

Historians often depend upon documents to help reconstruct the past. You want to answer some basic questions about the nature of public schools in the years between Barack Obama's election as president in 2008 and the dozen years that followed. Happily, you discover that sociologists of education during that period studied many of the topics in which you are most interested. Their scholarship is now history: sitting in hard copies on the shelves or in the latest digital form, found in dissertations, professional journals, and many types of publications. A preliminary search in an electronic card catalogue and *Sociological Abstracts* has unearthed titles of research completed in the 2010s that seem especially promising. What did sociologists once study that a historian in 2050 might find especially valuable?

Here is a partial list of the kinds of topics and concerns sociologists attended to that help us understand the world of public schools as they once existed. Sociologists in the early twenty-first century believed that schools are social institutions. As in earlier periods of history, schools during and after the Obama years were shaped by the actions of a multiplicity of governmental and nongovernmental agencies. The federal government expanded its authority in school policy thanks to the liberalism of the Great Society in the 1960s and the bipartisan enthusiasm for raising standards

---

W. Reese (✉)
History of Education, University of Wisconsin, Madison, WI, USA
e-mail: wjreese@wisc.edu

in the decades that followed. Did that trend continue after 2010? Did the role of the federal government expand its authority in educational policy? In what precise ways? If state and local agencies that traditionally controlled different aspects of schooling weakened, what social, economic, and political trends helped shape the changing role of different levels of government in educational policy?

Some of the best sociological studies from the 2010s also identified and analyzed the broad social forces that helped make schools such familiar yet contentious places in the early twenty-first century. They help explain large-scale changes that had huge effects on schools: how, for example, the global economy undermined America's industrial sectors and intensified demands for school improvement, which generally meant widespread support for higher academic standards. Other traditional goals for schools—civic education, for example, or support for the creative arts—seemed to recede in importance. Which interest groups such as fundamentalists and patriots in Texas and liberals in certain communities shaped what children studied at school?

Among the most useful sociological studies generated in the 2010s will be those that help explain how society viewed schools during a time of dramatic economic, social, and political change. Why were so many policymakers at the time convinced that schools should face more market competition, in the form of vouchers, charter schools, and other innovations, especially when Western banking practices and markets had failed miserably, as revealed during the Great Recession? What social or professional groups favored or opposed these reforms? Why did philanthropic foundations spend millions of dollars on various school reforms, which usually attempted to weaken teachers unions, emphasized accountability, and imposed change from outside the normal political process? These initiatives seemed most evident in cities. Why did urban mayors and other elected officials often welcome these initiatives? Had public schools in cities, as some critics feared in 2010, become mostly schools for the least advantaged, impoverished masses? Did movements to privatize public schools in cities improve academic achievement? Did charter schools effectively reform urban schooling? The scholarship conducted by sociologists in the 2010s will help answer these questions.

By the early twenty-first century, the main justification for having schools seemed to be economic, specifically to create a more productive, competitive workforce. Hopefully, sociological studies from the Obama and post-Obama years can help verify if that is an accurate depiction of the past. In addition, anyone living through that period remembers that No Child Left Behind was headline news and the source of considerable angst among the teaching profession. It is now refreshing to see, in a preliminary search of *Sociological Abstracts,* that scholars after 2010 critically examined how the proliferation of standardized testing shaped everyday life for teachers and pupils. How testing influenced the nature of the teaching profession, classroom pedagogy, and school organization attracted some of the best sociological minds. They not only studied whether scores rose or fell among various groups of students but also assessed how testing shaped instruction and classroom dynamics. There is, of course, a venerable tradition of research on the sociology of teaching. Some class scholarship, such as Waller's (1932), was written before test scores became the central measure of school effectiveness. After 2010, however, a strong cadre of sociologists closely examined the nature of teaching and the lives of teachers, including their backgrounds, working conditions, and other factors. Historians of education in 2050 will find these studies invaluable.

If the titles of the books and articles written by sociologists in the 2010s are any guide, historians will understand more clearly how teachers and schools responded to the spread of standardized, high-stakes testing. Without these studies, historians will be unable to answer related questions about the social life of schools. Sociologists will enlighten the future historian by answering the following questions: Did school systems after 2010 substantially reduce instructional time in certain subjects in the liberal arts and humanities that were not tested frequently? Subjects such as art and music, and history and geography, for example, were once a venerable part of an academic course of study. Which subjects were diminished in value or squeezed out of the curriculum? Which states and local districts, hard pressed for financial resources, altered their methods of teacher evaluation and compensation to receive money from the Race to the Top program initiated during the Obama years? Did teachers, facing evaluation systems linking merit reviews to student scores, increasingly "teach to the test," as once was commonly feared by critics of testing? What were the unintended consequences of testing? Is it true that high-stakes tests narrowed the curriculum even within tested subjects, including mathematics, since important topics within the subject were not tested? Did drill, the bane of progressive educators for generations, become even more entrenched, as teachers tried to improve test scores in the favored subjects? Was enhanced testing a passing phase or did it become more pervasive after 2010?

Sociologists have long studied the effects of race, ethnicity, and social class in schools. *Sociological Abstracts* and the electronic card catalogue indicate that interest in these topics was undiminished in the 2010s. This is good news for future historians of education. Sociologists, for example, will help them understand how the children of immigrants shaped school cultures. Student populations became increasingly diverse in the early decades of the twenty-first century, thanks to massive immigration from Mexico and Central America as well as from the Pacific Rim. Which regions of the nation were most affected by these changes? Did schools respond to new populations of students by altering teaching styles, curriculum, and language instruction? How did changing student populations influence patterns of academic achievement in different types of school systems, specifically in rural, urban, and suburban districts? Had a national curriculum, once the dream of some reformers, finally been imposed on America's vast network of public schools? Did students, increasingly the children of immigrants, improve the ranking of America's schools in international examinations?

Historians of education always have drawn upon descriptions of schools written during the time period they are studying. Happily, sociologists after 2010 continued to examine the many ways that particular social groups shaped and were shaped by schools; during the Obama and post-Obama era, some sociologists, for example, published case studies of individual schools or school systems that explored the role of racism and segregation in education; others focused on the impact of poverty and other variables on student performance. Had sociologists helped pinpoint the relative power of different family variables on schools? How did poverty or gender affect scholastic achievement? Did racial and class segregation widen or lessen in America's tens of thousands of school districts? How well were children's schools funded in different neighborhoods, regions, and school districts?

Finally, the most perceptive sociologists of the 2010s addressed how well citizens reconciled two seemingly incompatible goals: the effort to make schools more socially inclusive but also more academically rigorous. How well did schools promote equality and excellence? How did educators, policymakers, and citizens define equality and excellence? For example, how well did schools respond to federal mandates, which began in the 1970s, to provide special-needs children with a quality education, and to the growing public mandate after *A Nation at Risk* (1983) to upgrade standards? Did children once labeled at-risk for failure receive more effective, higher quality instruction? How commonly were special-needs pupils mainstreamed? Were different labels devised to describe these children, and after 2010 were they included more frequently in the testing pool?

By addressing some of the basic issues that shaped school policy during the Obama and post-Obama era, sociologists will make the task of the historian much easier. By 2050, sociological studies completed decades before will be part of the historical record, invaluable to anyone concerned with understanding schools in an earlier era. This scholarship will better enable historians to understand the vital issues that once shaped schools, including the impact of standardized testing on curriculum and pedagogy, the social forces that influenced school practices in various settings, and the relative power of federal authority in local educational decision making. This scholarship not only will enable policymakers to understand more clearly how schools function as social institutions but also strengthen the quality of scholarship in historical studies of education.

References

National Commission on Excellence in Education (NCEE). 1983. *A nation at risk: The imperative for educational reform.* Washington, DC: U.S. Department of Education, Government Printing Office.

Waller, Willard Walter. 1932. *The sociology of teaching.* New York: Wiley.

Chapter 20
How the Sociology of Education Can Help Us Better Understand Religion and Morality

Christian Smith

What might the sociology of education contribute to our broader understanding of crucial issues related to schools and education, viewed from the perspective of someone, like me, who is not directly involved in that field but still interested in these matters? Much of my own research in recent years has focused in the sociology of religion and morality, and I bring those concerns to the present question. When I survey the sociology of education, it seems to me that the field could improve its research in at least four significant areas.

First, more research is needed on explicit and implicit *moral education* in school settings of various kinds. Supreme Court rulings prohibit the direct teaching of comprehensive normative worldviews in public schools. But a strictly amoral education is literally impossible. Schools in fact teach morality and moral reasoning of one kind or another, one way or another. That is unavoidable. The only question is *what* about morality is taught and how *well* it is taught. Furthermore, over the long run, any functioning democracy and humanistic society requires at least minimum shared cultural understandings of how to sort out moral choices and disagreements, as well as a substantive body of shared moral beliefs and values as references for those choice and debate processes.

My own research on contemporary teenagers and emerging adults (Smith and Denton 2005; Smith and Snell 2009; Smith et al. 2011) finds that the moral reasoning skills of most young people are profoundly underdeveloped, in some cases almost non-existent. At the same time, most youth venture a variety of moralistic claims and judgments. Lacking the ability to explain the reasons behind their own moral views, youth and emerging adults can quickly dissolve into moral relativism. Tolerance of moral differences (within widely set non-negotiable

C. Smith (✉)
Department of Sociology, University of Notre Dame, Notre Dame, IN 46556, USA
e-mail: chris.smith@nd.edu

bounds) is a virtue in a pluralistic society. But absolute moral relativism is impossible, sociologically and otherwise (Smith 2003).

How might schools play into forming the moral realities I have observed? Many American youth I have interviewed report that the major "strategy" employed by their school authorities for dealing with moral issues, especially those involving disagreement and potential conflict, is outright avoidance. "We just don't go there," is the recurrent practice and message. Sometimes, when it comes to things like cheating, students also report to me that their teachers simply look the other way. That is problematic. In a pluralistic society, schools need to function as institutions that teach students not how to evade moral quandaries and conflicts and hide compromised behavior, but how to engage, process, and adequately resolve moral difficulties. In this sense, schools I think are failing to equip our youth with the cognitive and relational tools they need to negotiate real life in our increasingly pluralistic society and world.

Yet I also suspect that the facts cannot be quite as simple as reported by those I have interviewed. So, there is much more we might learn from good studies of the overt and tacit moral education that is promulgated in various ways in different kinds of schools. What moral beliefs are students learning about and how are they learning them? How consistent or in tension are schools' various moral messages? How might this vary by the social class of students' families and therefore school districts? How does de facto moral education at school relate to what students are taught at home, in religious congregations, in the media, or other sites? And how do students actually combine and negotiate these inputs for the living of their own lives? Studies of these sorts could capitalize upon now-budding work in the sociology of morality and contribute a great deal of value to our discipline and culture more broadly.

In my view, methodologically, much of that research will require in-depth ethnographies to identify not only the manifest but also the hidden curricula of schools and classrooms, when it comes to assumptions, modeling, and teaching about what in life is right and wrong, good and bad, just and unjust, and so on. Such studies, I suspect, could tell us a great deal about not only school culture and processes, but also about the important moral challenges and dilemmas facing our society more broadly.

Second, and somewhat related, the sociology of education has the opportunity to contribute much more to our understanding of the relationship between students' schooling lives and their *religious lives*. I understand that many in the sociology of education have historically focused on "hard-outcome" matters, like identifying variables that shape educational aspirations and achievement, outcomes of tracking, the educational effects of inequality, and so on—all of which is valuable. But schooling can have many kinds of consequences in people's lives beyond mere grades, test scores, career achievement, and so on. One of them may be people's religious lives.

After many decades of the then-dominant secularization theory training social scientists during the mid-twentieth century to virtually ignore religion, we have learned from many events in recent decades that religion is actually not going away with modernization, at least anytime soon, and that it therefore needs to be better understood. Part of that better understanding ought to come from how religion relates to schooling and education. How might experiences in school form students' religious lives in different ways? How may the personal religious faith and practices of teachers influence their professional teaching? How might religion affect relations to schooling and shape educational aspirations and achievement? How might religious beliefs reinforce what is taught in school, and not simply—as with recurrent controversies over evolution and creationism, which draw so much attention—conflict with them?

Such matters are increasingly important in schools and school systems populated by religiously diverse students and families. How, for example, does schooling interact with religious faith and practice when Catholics, evangelicals, Muslims, Jews, pagans, members of other religious faiths, and non-religious people are being educated together? How do school cultures, organizations, and educational and extra-curricular activities accommodate or resist those differences? And how, in turn, does that affect the students and perhaps their families and communities over the long run? There is much more of value that we could learn in response to these questions, which could help to bridge the sociology of education to other fields, including immigration, race and ethnicity, culture, and, of course, religion.

Third, the sociology of education simply needs to do a better job of understanding *conservative Protestant schools* and religiously motivated *home schooling* as institutions and cultures. We all know that a lot of educating happens outside of the public school system. But I, for one, am not impressed with the current sociological accounts of the character of that education. Some of the literature on conservative Protestant schools is dated and, in some cases, I think at least somewhat misrepresents the phenomena in question. Some of the literature on home schooling makes valuable contributions, but also often fails to represent some of the diversity and complexities and more recent developments in that movement, which need better understanding.

In particular, more than a little—though not all—of sociological analyses of conservative Protestant schools and home schooling seem stuck in the rut of incessantly viewing them through the lens of the threat of the political Christian Right. Jerry Falwell and Pat Robertson still haunt some of these inquiries. Christian-Right politics may indeed be one dimension of the issue in question, but hardly the most important. Future studies need to better explore and understand conservative Protestant schools and religiously motivated home schooling for what they as phenomena actually are themselves, understood first on their own terms, and not by bringing political fears and imposing sociological theories upon them that diminish our understanding. A bit of the anthropologist's cultural relativism could help here. Research needs especially to be sensitive to the diversity, complexities, ambiguities, and internal tensions and ambivalences of kinds of schools and schooling families that comprise these private religious sectors of education. Much of the extant literature can give the impression of a monolithic uniformity, which is false.

Fourth, the sociology of education could do more to investigate the larger consequences of the *demise of Catholic schooling*, particularly in urban neighborhoods. The dramatic transformation of American Catholicism itself in the latter half of the twentieth century and other forces have resulted in a recent significant weakening of the Catholic primary and secondary school system in the USA, relative to its institutional condition earlier in the twentieth century. According to Brinig and Garnett, for example, "More than 1,600 Catholic elementary and secondary schools, most of them located in urban neighborhoods, have closed during the last two decades. The Archdiocese of Chicago alone…has closed 148 schools since 1984" (2010a: 889).

Partisans of secular public schooling may cheer this news. But early, exploratory research on their effects suggests that the closing of Catholic schools has negative consequences for neighborhoods and children's education opportunities (Brinig and Garnett 2010a, b; Meyer 2007; Baker and Riordan 1998). Scholars may hold various normative positions about the best or most just system of schooling in a pluralistic society. But the consequences of the weakening of the Catholic schooling system appear to matter sociologically and practically, and so they deserve further sociological investigation. Here again, scholars in the sociology of education researching this topic could partner with and build valuable bridges to researchers in other fields, such as urban sociology, criminology, religion, law, and family.

These four suggestions are of course only a few out of myriad possibilities that scholars in the sociology of education might consider as avenues for potentially expanding the breadth, complexity, relevance, and attraction of their field. But from my perspective, and those of many colleagues I know in my regular fields of study, these would be much welcomed and appreciated research programs for sociologists of education to undertake in the future.

References

Baker, David P., and Cornelius Riordan. 1998. The Eliting of the common American Catholic school and the national education crisis. *Phi Delta Kappan* 80: 16–23.

Brinig, Margaret, and Nicole Stelle Garnett. 2010a. Catholic schools, urban neighborhoods, and education reform. *Notre Dame Law Review* 85(3): 887–954.

Brinig, Margaret, and Nicole Stelle Garnett. 2010b. Catholic Schools and Broken Windows. Unpublished paper.

Meyer, Peter. 2007. Can Catholic schools be saved? *Education Next* 7(2): 12–20.

Smith, Christian. 2003. *Moral, believing animals: Human personhood and culture*. Oxford: Oxford University Press.

Smith, Christian, Kari Christoffersen, Patricia Snell Herzog, and Hilary Davidson. 2011. *Lost in transition: The dark side of emerging adulthood*. New York: Oxford University Press.

Smith, Christian, and Melinda Lundquist Denton. 2005. *Soul searching: The religious and spiritual lives of American Teenagers*. New York: Oxford University Press.

Smith, Christian, and Patricia Snell. 2009. *Souls in transition: The religious and spiritual lives of young adults*. New York: Oxford University Press.

Chapter 21
Thoughts on Reform and the Sociology of Education: Toward Active Engagement

Marshall S. Smith

My background is in policy analysis, practice, and methodology, and I have some familiarity with cognitive theory and technology. In this paper, I focus on two areas important to the sociology of education: understanding change and measurement, methodology, and inference. Some of my comments may appear critical of the strength of the profession of the sociology of education, but they are not meant to be. This academic discipline has a rich and powerful history and has had a profound impact on our understanding of education from Durkheim's observations on the education system as mirroring society to the early Coleman reports that do little to counteract that view, to the social mobility literature, the work on desegregation, school structure and school culture, and on the ways that education systems, institutions, and organizations at all levels behave. If I ask for more, it is only to honor the reality that the profession is strong enough to respond.

Understanding Change

Many research studies in educational sociology are descriptive—they are studies of the present or the past. To an extent, this characteristic is embedded in the choice of a measure for an independent variable in a regression equation. Though this practice may be changing, sociologists often choose the percent of variance explained in their data or a standardized regression coefficient to describe an existing or past relationship. In contrast, economists select the unstandardized regression coefficient as a way to estimate what might be if the world were changed. Of course both

---

M.S. Smith (✉)
Carnegie Foundation for the Advancement of Teaching, Stanford, CA 94305, USA
e-mail: mike.marshallsmith@gmail.com

disciplines rely substantially on the past to understand the present or the future. Economists predict most of the time by changing the mixtures of inputs, but only a few alter the relationships among the inputs or add new inputs building on a theory of what the production functions of the future might be.

Without question, understanding the past is useful for understanding the future. Yet the greatest challenges for schools and schooling in the USA right now are to change and improve in order to meet societal conditions that are quite different from the past. The stable, dependable, not particularly effective, and segregated schools and schools systems of the 1950s have been buffeted by many events. These include Sputnik, the Coleman report(s), the Great Society, school desegregation, inclusionary practices, effective schools, *A Nation at Risk,* substantial immigration, standards-based reforms, charter schools, test-based accountability, an increased role for the federal government, serious budget crises, greater understanding of how children learn and how to effectively teach, and technology. Yet, except for the attention now paid to students with disabilities and greater variation in ethnicity, in most other regards the schools appear very similar to what they were 50 years ago even though their clients are exposed to a dramatically different out-of-school environment.

Some call this stability and predictability, if not excellence and excitement. Others call it calcification or rigidity. Whichever is the case, one result is that many Americans are uncomfortable with many of our current schools and are frustrated with our collective lack of will and/or knowledge and resources to change them in ways that better fit the needs of our nation's children.

One problem of educational change is particularly evident. For over 40 years, we have known that a substantial percentage of children from low-income families go to school in settings with many other students from similar circumstances, with less experienced teachers and often fewer other resources than students from higher income families. This is particularly true for children from low-income African American and Hispanic American families. We also have known that in the lowest achieving 10–20% of schools, the children learn substantially less than children do in other settings, that they are less likely to graduate from high school or go to college, and that these schools are more likely to have high percentages of African American and Hispanic American students. How our nation substantially improves these schools and thereby reduces and eventually eliminates the yawning gaps in achievement and attainment is a deep and glaring problem that we have not solved. We think we know what good schools look like and what poor schools look like but we have not figured out how to take a poor school and make it a good school. Perhaps the schools should continue to look the same way they are now and just do a much better job. Or perhaps the change should be more dramatic. Either way our understanding of the mechanisms for change are lacking. In order to address this challenge, we need a deeper understanding of how schools as organizations behave and change and how school systems can be structured and given incentives to stimulate, support, and sustain the change.

A second problem of change also has been around for 40 or more years but has become glaring only in the past 15 years. Unlike education, almost every other domestic and international sector has successfully adopted and adapted information technology (IT) to improve its efficiency and productivity. To be sure, IT is used extensively in the back offices of schools, districts, and states. Marginal improvements are common, such as somewhat better record keeping, automated phone calls for absenteeism, and bookkeeping. But the improvement in quality and efficiency is still modest and it is not surprising to see extensive paperwork supplementing payroll or other standard processes. Legacy machines, outdated software, and low-paid programmers are commonplace. Almost all districts have IT departments while sharing or moving to cloud computing is rare.

The same situation is true for teaching and learning. The classroom is particularly hard to penetrate. Students in many classrooms have computers in the back of the room or have access to computer labs. In some classrooms, the computers and a smart board provide both teacher and students with greater opportunities to create interactive settings and to demonstrate ideas in ways that were not possible without these materials. However, observers note that computers often are used only as search machines and the technology built into smart boards typically is underused, leading to their acting as an expensive blackboard. Relatively few classrooms and schools make extensive and creative use of technology to teach, support, and extend the curriculum.

Christensen, Horn, and Johnson (2008) make the case that online courses will spur a major change in teaching and learning. They argue that this form of disruptive innovation first enters an institution or industry by taking on a marginal role that is overlooked or tolerated by the rest of the industry. In this case, they argue that online learning can get its foot in the door by entering schools with marginal courses like Advanced Placement and credit recovery, where there is substantial need but few teachers who will be required to change their typical patterns of work. They predict increasingly rapid growth in the use of online courses, spreading from the marginal courses to the mainstream curriculum within the next few years. While there is considerable evidence to support the effectiveness of online learning, many observers doubt the accuracy of the predictions about the penetration into the basic curriculum of high schools, much less middle schools. They base their skepticism on the past history of school reform. The change question then is how to understand and create the conditions in the back offices of the education system and in the classroom to make powerful and appropriate use of technology to support the education system and especially teaching and learning. What are the incentives or circumstances that facilitate the adoption of technologies that have promise of reducing costs and increasing productivity in all parts of the system? Is this problem common to government organizations or is it more deeply rooted in K–12 and higher education institutions, and if so, why? Are there differences among schools and districts in adoption and usage patterns and why?

A third, age-old problem in the USA is how to successfully implement serious systemwide reform. One impediment is the size and multilayered nature of the system where policy is often created near the top and implemented at the bottom after going through layers of government that modify, alter, distort, and reinterpret the nature and even the purpose of the policy. And, unlike school systems in other developed nations, the core policies are established largely by political bodies and non-educators (Congress, state legislatures, state and school education boards), rather than education professionals. This results often in reforms comprised of layers of compromised legislation and regulations that end up bearing little relationship to the original design and barely reflecting any theory that may have driven the initial impetus for the reform.

Moreover, at the federal and state level, there generally is little capacity and no driving interest in insuring that the policies and rules are implemented in ways that lead to improved practice. Most federal and state actions in the guise of implementation support are simply exercises in compliance. In defense of committed federal and state employees, they often do not act this way out of choice. These activities are reinforced by legislative language and regulation as well as by agencies and departments like the Government Accountability Office that focus largely on compliance, in part because they do not have the expertise in the profession to make legitimate judgments about quality and intent.

Finally, in many state and local school systems, there are few effective mechanisms and practices for quality control and systematic improvement. As a consequence, it is practically impossible to implement even modest systemic change successfully. The upshot is that often local systems and schools make conforming adjustments to comply and otherwise absorb the new reforms into their ongoing daily practices.

There are important counter examples. Some kinds of change are more easily adopted and should be implemented. But, they do not guarantee success in the classroom. The Gates Foundation launched programs that resulted in the creation of a large number of small high schools. In 1994, the federal government launched a program to provide incentives to states to create laws to support charter schools. During the 1970s and 1980s, a substantial number of states instituted laws that changed the distribution of education dollars to be more equitable within the states. Each one of these reforms was successful. Yet, small high schools alone did not result in changed behavior that increased achievement and attainment nor did adopting state charter laws, although it did lead to more charter schools. The finance equalization efforts by the states did change resource distributions to become more equitable but there was little noticeable effect on achievement and, over time, many of the states regressed in degree of fairness of resource distribution.

I think of these three examples as technical and linear policies. Deep and lasting change in complex organizations like school systems and classrooms is not linear. Technical and cookie-cutter methodologies will not suffice. Complex environments and complex change require methodologies that permit, support, and sustain adaptive responses in different environments. Moreover, in order to reach and change classroom practice and student achievement, the theory must be robust and the implementation sustained.

Yet, even though our school systems are designed to resist change, and even under the best conditions pose great challenges to change, as a nation we seem devoted to reform. The research challenge is one of understanding complex organizational change—the practical question is whether there are approaches (including methodologies) to successfully implement school, state, and national/federal systemic change that would both accomplish the aims of the reforms and provide the flexibility for state and local authorities to adapt the reforms to meet the context of their jurisdiction. Like change in the schools and the use of technology in schools, this is in no way a new problem.

We all have ideas about each of these three problem areas—to some extent, of course, they are the same problem. I don't think the solution resides in eliminating the teacher unions and/or school and state boards of education or the role of Congress, though each may be dysfunctional in some circumstances. Nor do I think we will be successful by mandating regulatory structures that focus on getting teachers to work harder—most teachers already work hard. And, we don't seem able to depend on charter schools having the magic elixir, though some charter management organizations have made substantial strides and should be studied by sociological researchers.

Let me suggest three components to help address these problems of change. The first is better theoretical models and different forms of methodology. In short, we need to begin to study change and improvement by participating with it in the field, rather than by passively observing it. Studies should be guided by theory and use methodologies appropriate for complex environments. Such methodologies require active involvement in the environment. The challenge is to propel and understand change in adaptive environments. This requires models and methodologies that embrace adaptation. Such methodologies typically use feedback loops and on-time intervention strategies.

In the initial stages for research and for ongoing evaluation, the rapid prototyping in the tool development literature and developmental evaluation in the evaluation literature provide some beginning ways to think about new methodologies. Bryk and Gomez's (2008) recent paper on developmental research and rapid prototyping describes the general outlines of such a research approach, and the work on improving remedial education in community colleges being carried out at The Carnegie Foundation for the Advancement of Teaching is a good example of one such research project.

Research is one thing but the challenge of implementing new policy in a thoughtful way is quite another. For this challenge, the practice of continuous improvement (CI) processes in school systems like Long Beach Unified and Garden Grove in California are intriguing. CI is an ongoing effort to improve products, services, or processes. These efforts can seek incremental improvement over time or breakthrough improvement all at once. Delivery processes are constantly evaluated and improved in the light of their efficiency, effectiveness and flexibility. Long Beach Unified and Garden Grove are good examples of school systems that are thoughtful, deliberate, and evidence based. Their goals are clear and they execute them as best they can while being open to examine change suggested from within or without the school system.

Perhaps, continuous improvement processes is a silver bullet for education systems. The education research on this is slight as is our understanding about how to go about changing a typical school system into one that embraces and implements continuous improvement processes. Is there a methodology that would facilitate such an implementation? What are the environmental conditions that would enable a system to be created? These are areas where more work by sociologists of education is desperately needed.

A second component has to do with deepening our theoretical understanding of how change interventions work. Most interventions have a variety of components. Some of these components are causal mechanisms that form the core of the intervention and are necessary in all environments. Others are potentially replaceable—they may facilitate the causal drivers or even be necessary in some environments. Figuring out which is which requires a theory robust enough to separate core causal drivers from other parts of an intervention. Such middle-range theory provides insights into strategies for going to scale and for implementing the intervention in different contexts.

Finally, the third component necessary to improve educational practice and student outcomes in a systematic and systemic fashion calls for an integration of social and organizational theory with a deep understanding of the critical psychological and cognitive factors to facilitate and engage learning behavior in students. Dramatically changing the effectiveness of very poorly performing low-income schools, for example, probably requires changes in culture, curricula and instruction, as well as structure and organization.

Measurement, Methods, and Inference

Theory and methodology are at the heart of scientific disciplines. An understanding of change in various settings will require the development, testing, and application of theory. The quality of the theory will often be determined by the tools, the methodologies of the discipline. In the following, I suggest three advances that might be made in the methodologies of education sociology.

My first point is that it is not uncommon for two or more studies that explore a relationship, such as that between class size and academic achievement, to arrive at quite different estimates of the size of the relationship between the same concepts even though they use the same statistical methodology. This variation occurs even when the researchers control for background and context variables by using measures such as social class.

The variation can be due to a variety of reasons. Different studies may be carried out with different populations or in different contexts where the relationships between the independent and dependent variables are truly different. Or the studies may not have been executed perfectly which introduces error. Or the measures themselves may not be entirely reliable which introduces more error. These and other sources may bias the results.

There is, however, another source of variation that arises where the biases are potentially far more systematic and which, over time, could be substantially reduced. The measures of the dependent and independent variables are often different from one another across the various studies. For example, there are many ways of measuring class size and particular teacher characteristics as well as substantial differences among measures of achievement and attainment. Moreover, background and other context variables in the various studies may range from a single measure of poverty such as free or reduced lunch to multiple sophisticated measures of social class.

The lack of consistency among the studies in one or more of the control, independent, and dependent variables makes it impossible to determine whether the differences in results are due to systematic differences in the definitions and/or composition of the variables, to systematic differences among populations or context, or to random error. Of course, we expect each source that is present to make some contribution to the overall error term. Often, however, even in the context of understanding that these issues confound results, some researchers ignore the differences and proceed with a literature review or meta-analysis and report conclusions that ignore some or all of the inconsistencies in the context and in the measurement of similarly named constructs.

Such practices create serious problems in the accumulation of knowledge and thereby developing theory by legitimating results of meta-analytic and other reviews that are problematic and may be systematically biased. In particular, selection rules in most meta-analytic studies focus on the design and statistical methodology and often ignore systematic variation in the way that various important constructs are defined. Although it does not solve the problem of varying context, one practice that might ameliorate some of these problems would be for members of the profession to adopt common and theoretically grounded definitions and develop common variables for the most important and widely used constructs in the sociology of education, including constructs such as socioeconomic status and class size. Each selected construct could have multiple common variables, each theoretically defined and benchmarked against one another.

Over time, researchers would be expected to use one of the alternative measures in appropriate situations, when at all possible. When there is good reason not to use one of the selected alternative measures, a researcher might create a new measure. The expectation in this situation could be that the researcher would show how their new measure related to at least one of the standard measures so that some baseline understanding of the differences would be recorded. One possible result of this approach is that methodological practice gradually would move to a point where the systemic error introduced by varying measures would be reduced substantially.

A danger in taking such a step is that locking into a common measure may be worse for the science than continuing with multiple definitions. This concern was raised repeatedly in a recent National Research Council workshop that considered this issue. It can be alleviated if a few important steps are taken. The first step would be the selection of a few clear definitions for common variables for each construct. The definitions would include rules for measurement and construction and would have to be solidly based in objective theory. Second, there would need to be studies that examine the relationships among the few selected variables. This would provide the foundation for researchers to select among the possible alternatives to be used in a particular study and provide ways of understanding differences in the way the variables behaved. Third, as mentioned earlier, there would be no penalty for constructing a new version of the construct, as long as researchers provided a theoretical rational and did their best to indicate how the new version related to one or more of the standardized variables.

I am not suggesting that all or even any constructs integral to sociological theory be standardized. I am pointing out that there is an important alternative to the unsystematic fashion for constructing variables that is common practice. One might begin by standardizing two or three constructs and judge whether the approach is worthwhile. It would be wise to focus initially on the dependent variable to clarify what we are trying to explain. The ultimate goal might be defined as to enhance the capacity of scholars to advance knowledge by providing a mechanism to aggregate and build on prior research and to be able to explain differences among studies within the field and to the public.

Secondly, we need to develop analytic and data management procedures for massive amounts of data including network data. Practically infinite memory and the rapidly increasing speed of computing have made it potentially possible for scientists to construct and reconstruct several models directed at better understanding relationships among many variables in large masses of data. A recent National Science Foundation report on cyberlearning (2008) explores these issues. In addition, information flows from ubiquitous state and local education data systems and across a variety of electronic and human networks, such as Twitter and Facebook, and has the potential to generate huge volumes of data that may be used to model human and organizational social activity.

Developing a better understanding of Twitter and Facebook spontaneous networks, such as those that formed in very short periods of time in government protests in Iran and Egypt, might give us a deeper understanding of the ways that these social tools can be used in learning. We are aware of the power and utility of small networks such as those formed for lesson planning in Japan and for groups of students studying together in colleges all over the world. But there are much larger interactive networks also used for educational purposes, and they are appearing on the internet in many forms. Our need to better understand the social structure and functioning of these networks for social and educational purposes is evident to all parents and grandparents. In the education sphere, the use of networks will increase exponentially as the use of technology expands to deliver traditional and nontraditional educational content in a variety of contexts. The exploration of these data will allow researchers to ask new questions in new ways and to develop new theories about individual, peer-related, and institutional behaviors. The resources are essentially untapped, and the field lacks a coherent set of analytic tools and practices.

Third, we need to avoid simple errors in inference and reporting. A common statement in the press is that because countries or states have higher than average percentages of a particular school characteristic (x) and higher than average student achievement (y), then (x) is a mechanism that helps to cause (y). Apart from the problem of confusing correlation and causation, this kind of statement makes the assumption that the aggregate relationship seen at the state level must hold at the school level. This form of ecological or aggregation fallacy is standard fare in many US education

Table 21.1 NAEP fourth grade reading scale scores and population percentage (in parentheses)

	1994	2002	2009	Total gain (1994–2009)
Total U.S. Public	212	217	220	+8
White	222 (71)	227 (60)	229 (54)	+7
Black	184 (18)	198 (18)	204 (16)	+20
Hispanic	186 (7)	199 (17)	204 (21)	+18
Asian	217 (3)	223 (4)	234 (5)	+17

Table 21.2 NAEP fourth grade mathematics scale scores

	1992	2003	2009	Total gain
Total U.S. Public	219	234	239	+20
White	237	243	248	+11
Black	192	216	222	+30
Hispanic	201	221	227	+26
Asian	231	246	255	+24

discussions. Another concern is the frequently made leap from an N of one or even a few to a false generalization that is without bounds, such as some of the rhetoric around the *Harlem Children's Zone*. Also common are exaggerated claims by reputable sources about the impact of particular policies.

One of the more common and frequently heard erroneous claims is that the total NAEP national gains demonstrate that schools are not improving. Tables 21.1 and 21.2 address those claims. The Tables contain data from fourth grade reading and mathematics for the Main NAEP with the national public school sample. Using scale scores and 10–11 points as a rough rule of thumb for the equivalent of a grade level, the national average in reading has increased between 1994 and 2009 by 8 points or roughly three quarters of a grade level—this is a modest but real gain. Whites have gained 7 points, roughly two thirds of a grade level. However, the three minority groups with large enough samples to be examined gained between 1.5 and 1.9 grade levels each. In mathematics the national average gain is 20 scale points or roughly 1.8 grade levels—all three minority groups substantially exceed that level and whites gained 11 points or one grade level.

In support of the claims of small gains, it is possible to point out that the national average gain for reading does not seem very large, a cause for concern. But, surprisingly the subgroup gains in reading are in three of the four instances considerably larger than the national gains. Indeed, even though the minority groups have smaller percentages of the population than whites, the sum of the parts would seem to be greater than the whole. The reason for this, of course, is that the composition of the population has changed over the past 15–20 years, which has an effect on the total population score but not on the scores of the subgroups. In particular, the percentage of whites dropped from 71 to 54 and the percentage of Hispanics increased from 7 to 18 over the 15-year period (see the percentages in parentheses next to the Reading scale scores of the four subgroups). The effect of this on the average total US gains in fourth grade reading is substantial because Hispanics as a group score considerably lower than whites. Even though the Hispanic gains are large, the overall shift in population reduces the total US population-gain score by 4 points. Without the change, the total population score would be an estimated 12 points rather than the 8 points displayed in the table. This effect is called Simpson's paradox.

Typically, the NAEP national mean score is used as the measure of most interest to the press, practitioners, and politicians. Yet, as suggested above, the NAEP national gains may be thought of as a function of two factors, the national gain attributed to the gains of the subgroups which may be estimated as 12 points and the gain due to changes in population which is −4 points for a total +8 points. Because of changes in the demography, not changes in the schools, the total scores are lower than they might have been if the demography had not changed. In analyzing these results, we must recognize that gains that might be attributed to the schools are the gains of the subgroups. These gains are not confounded with ethnicity changes in demography. For both reading and mathematics, for the minority subgroups, these gains are substantial, representing one to two grade levels of improvement over the 15–17 years in time.

On the other hand, we have real national average gains. The question is what does the national-gain statistic mean? I think of this gain as representing a change in the national level of human capital—insofar as academic assessments can be thought of as providing crude estimates of human capital. The subgroup scores then are an estimate, albeit partial, of the effects of schools on student achievement. Beaton and Chromy (2007) carry out a similar analysis using the longitudinal NAEP data, which are based on a somewhat different assessment.

Looked at this way, the picture of school achievement improvements is considerably less gloomy than the press and many politicians would have us believe.

There are many reasons why journalists and politicians make such errors in interpretation—the alternative is not understood, is more complex, and, in some cases, the incorrect interpretation is more alarming, newsworthy and politically correct. Simple errors of inference thus become accepted fact.

We should be concerned about these errors of inference because they frequently are repeated and cited by reputable people and in scholarly journals. Sociologists of education need to address such concerns in the future.

Most of this essay is about the need for sociologists of education to conduct research that actively engages them in trying to both understand and influence change and the future. This is a different role than many have been trained for and is, perhaps, less comfortable than their way of conducting research. But, in order to understand how to change complex institutions and practices, it may be necessary to be involved in the change. An important and typically ignored way to improve and extend the discipline is to actively experiment with new and different ways of carrying out studies, new approaches to measurement, and new strategies for increasing the quality and speed of accumulating knowledge. The ultimate goal in this complex process is to develop robust theories, test them in the field, refine them, and then repeat the feedback loop fairly rapidly in single and multiple sites. The result is that knowledge grows and practice improves.

Acknowledgments Special thanks go to the Spencer Foundation for their support and to George Bohrnstedt for his thoughtful comments and suggestions on earlier drafts of this paper.

References

Beaton, A., and J. Chromy. 2007. Partitioning NAEP Trend Data. Commissioned by the NAEP Validity Studies Panel. AIR, Washington, DC.
Bryk, A., and L. Gomez. 2008. Ruminations on reinventing an R&D capacity for educational improvement. IREPP Working Paper No. 2008-05, Institute for Research on Education Policy and Practice, Stanford.
Christensen, C.M., M. Horn, and C.W. Johnson. 2008. *Disrupting class: How disruptive innovation will change the way the world learns*. New York: McGraw-Hill.
Report of the National Science Foundation Task Force on Cyberlearning. 2008. Fostering learning in the networked world: The cyberlearning opportunity and challenge, p. 59.

Chapter 22
How Would We Know If Public Colleges and Universities Are Productive?

Teresa A. Sullivan

A profound ideological divide over the proper role of government has been part of the political scene in the various states for decades. These polarized views have become more prominent nationally in the aftermath of the economic stimulus packages that responded to the Great Recession and of the proposed regulation of major industries, such as health insurance and financial services. The proponents of limited government argue that private enterprise has been forced to downsize to remain more competitive, with the result that corporations increasingly emphasize efficiency and productivity. The problem, these proponents claim, is that there is no incentive for government to emphasize efficiency and productivity. "Starving the beast," or sharply limiting taxation, is the proposed solution to Big Government. And the public universities, particularly the public research universities, are in the cross-hairs of the critics.

While some observers believe that there might be ways to turn back the clock and restore public funding for public higher education, I am skeptical that this will be a successful strategy. I argue here that higher education researchers need to turn their attention to the issues of higher education productivity simply because if the educational community does not do it, then others are likely to enforce productivity initiatives that could compromise academic quality. The conceptual problem, of course, is that efficiency and productivity make sense in the context of producing widgets and are much harder to define and measure when the output is the education of individuals.

T.A. Sullivan (✉)
University of Virginia, Charlottesville, VA 22904, USA
e-mail: terry.sullivan@virginia.edu

Why Public Universities?

American higher education has many fine private institutions, and they receive both taxpayer funds and the benefit of foregone tax revenues. Besides direct subsidies, private institutions benefit in the form of student financial aid (federal and state), taxpayer credits for tuition and tax deductions for charitable and educational contributions, research grants, and sometimes direct subsidies (Mundel et al. 2007). I concentrate here on the public universities, however, because of their great significance within the United States. If we concentrate on the Carnegie "high" and "very high" research universities, these public institutions educate 85% of the undergraduates and 70% of the graduate students in the United States, and they perform 62% of the federally funded research (McPherson, Gobstein, and Shulenburger 2010:27). Most of the growth in higher education enrollment has taken place in these universities. The national capacity to educate depends critically upon their well-being.

The public universities are more reliant than the private institutions on taxpayer aid, albeit aid that has been declining steadily. In the 1990–1991 recession, there was a round of cuts in higher education that was not restored in the economic recovery. One reason for this stagnation was the increased cost of Medicaid to the states, a cost that is unlikely to be rolled back any time soon (Kane and Orszag 2003). One group of experienced administrators has claimed:

> Today, the state side of the partnership is failing. Public institutions of higher education are gravely threatened. State support of public universities, on a per student basis, has been declining for over two decades; it was at the lowest level in 25 years even before the current economic crisis. As the global recession has deepened, declining tax revenues have driven state after state to further reduce appropriations for higher education, with cuts ranging as high as 20% to 30%, threatening to cripple many of the nation's leading state universities and erode their world-class quality. (Courant, Duderstadt, and Goldenberg 2010)

And even though the public research universities have raised tuition, the increased revenue has just barely offset the legislative cuts, while the number of students served has continued to increase. Real educational expenditures per student at the Carnegie-class high and very high research public universities have remained essentially constant, increasing at a compounded annual rate of 0.9% between 1987 and 2007 (McPherson, Gobstein, and Shulenburger 2010:17).

Why Productivity?

Economists define productivity as the ratio of the value of outputs to the value of inputs. If the ratio increases, then productivity has increased. Increased productivity is historically associated with economic growth and development, although great leaps in productivity (such as the Industrial Revolution) have also been associated with social upheaval and displacement. In the current American political climate, productivity is also being used as a proxy for wise stewardship of both public funds (appropriations) and private funds (tuition).

In either the primary or the secondary industrial sectors, output is relatively easy to measure: bushels of corn, tons of coal mined, number of gallons of oil refined, number of cars produced, and so on. In the service sector, productivity is much harder to measure. In the university, output is especially difficult to determine. One reason is that the university is jointly producing multiple "products": semester credit hours completed, degrees earned, patients receiving care, research publications produced, patents earned, and many others. Even if one limits the discussion to a single output such as semester credit hours, however, it is hard to assume that credit hours are somehow homogeneous in the way that we assume metric tons of steel or bushels of wheat are basically interchangeable.

One might know the cost of a semester credit hour in terms of tuition or, more rarely, in terms of total cost, but the value of the semester credit hour will vary depending on subject, level, degree of motivation of the student, and degree of skill and care of the instructor. Should we count equally the major who worked very hard and earned the highest possible grade and the bored nonmajor who skipped class on most days and barely passed? Does it matter if the professor who taught the semester credit hours was at the top of her game and routinely challenged her students to think more critically? Or is it the same if the professor used yellowed notes from years back and handed out blanket A's?

Quality control measures are fairly weak, as anyone who teaches the second course in a two-semester sequence can verify. And yet no one dismisses quality as an important issue in higher education. Diploma mills can be quite productive in terms of the number of degrees produced, and yet that productivity is not thought to reflect any true value. This judgment is summed up in the comment that such a diploma "is not worth the paper it is printed on."

Two measures that often are used as productivity measures are the freshman retention rate and the 4-year or 6-year graduation rate. The freshman retention rate is the proportion of newly entering first-year students who return in good standing for their second year. The graduation rate is the proportion of first-time, full-time entering first-year students who graduate with a degree within 4 (or 6) years. Both of these measures have shortcomings that render their use problematic. Notably, both measures seem to assume that a student's departure from a class or from an institution signals something negative about the schooling experience rather than some problem from within the rest of the student's life space (e.g., family, health, or financial issues). In fact, because of the association of social class with all of these competing reasons, one spurious way to increase the "productivity" of an institution is to select students on the basis of SES.

Similar criticisms can be made of both the input and the output indicators for most of the productivity measures that have been proposed in the academy. It is time for sociologists—who have excelled in measuring things that are hard to measure—to turn their expertise to thinking through indicators that are valid, reliable, and comparable across institutions. Researchers in many subfields of sociology, such as survey methods and demography, have developed remarkably clever and useful proxies for measures that are inherently difficult. This is a subject area ripe for such developments.

Getting Started

Standardization is a generalizable tactic often used to enhance comparability. Hospital death rates, for example, are routinely adjusted for case-mix, or how ill on average the patients in the hospital are. A higher death rate in a teaching hospital could thus be understood in the context that the most complex medical cases had been referred there, with more patients in danger of dying and harder to treat. A refinement of the graduation rate that might make some sense would be to compute the rate separately by economic background—or perhaps, report separately the success of Pell grantees. In effect, such a calculation would adjust for the complex circumstances of lower-income students (or alternatively, quantify the advantage of wealthier students).

A standardized graduation rate could be developed to adjust for the case-mix of students with varying needs, both financial and academic. An open-admissions urban university would then be expected to have a lower graduation rate than a selective, residential institution. There are two ways to develop such a measure.

The overall graduation rate at an institution could be conceptualized as the weighted average of the graduation rates for a set of strata, with the strata exhaustively classifying the students. The strata could be defined in various ways. Examples might be ranges of parental income, or ranges of high school grade point averages. Then it is possible to model what the graduation rate would be if the student composition were different. The commuter school could show not only its current graduation rate, but also what its graduation rate would be with a different mix of high-risk students. In effect, this second, standardized graduation rate would be similar to the hospitals' use of mortality rates that are adjusted for case-mix. The standardized graduation rate adjusts for serving more high-risk students.

Graduation rates are also flawed by the large numbers of students who are lost from the calculation. The rate omits students who begin summer or spring, who are part time, or who transfer. Some simple ratios could be developed to address this problem. One example is the ratio of the number of graduates in a year n divided by the number of first-time students in year $n-4$. A ratio greater than 1.0 would indicate a school serving more transfer or part-time students, the very students typically dropped from the graduation rate.

Another more complex concept from demography is summarizing the risk of event over a long period of time, contingent upon the occurrence of other events. For example, a table of working life summarizes the risk at every age that a person will retire or die, two risks that are known to rise with age. A life table technique adapted to graduation rates could use the risk that a person who had accumulated a certain level of credits would graduate—a risk that obviously rises with more credits completed and yet never reaches a probability of 1.0. Such a technique would have the advantage that it could be used even if a student were part time, an intermittent attendee, or a transfer student—cases that are all currently dropped from the calculation of graduation rates. What will be necessary is that the measures be calculable from available data in time series and not based on one-shot investigations.

What is important is that the research community take this task upon itself, and not wait for politicians to impose a set of measures on them. Required standardized tests for graduates are one solution that is often proposed (APLU n.d.) Some states already have required metrics to compare institutions with one another (State of Texas n.d.) If sociologists of education take issue with such metrics, they must also suggest replacement metrics. The failure to take the challenge seriously becomes validation for the critics' mistrust of public institutions.

References

APLU. n.d. *Voluntary system of accountability program.* Retrieved June 28, 2010, http://www.voluntarysystem.org/index.cfm.
Courant, Paul N., James J. Duderstadt, and Edie N. Goldenberg. 2010. Needed: A national strategy to preserve public universities. *The Chronicle of Higher Education,* January 3. Retrieved June 28, 2010, http://chronicle.com/article/A-Plan-to-Save-Americas-Pu/63358/.
Kane, Thomas J., and Peter R. Orszag. 2003. Higher education spending: The role of medicaid and the business cycle. *Brookings Institution Policy Brief* #124, September. Retrieved June 28, 2010, http://www.brookings.edu/papers/2003/09useconomics_kane.aspx.
McPherson, Peter, Howard J. Gobstein, and David E. Shulenburger. 2010. *Forging a foundation for the future: Keeping public research universities strong.* APLU. Retrieved June 28, 2010, http://www.aplu.org/NetCommunity/Document.Doc?id=2263.
Mundel, David, Elaine Maag, Kim Reuben, and Loise Dickson Rice. 2007. *Subsidizing higher education through tax and spending programs.* Brookings Institution, May. Retrieved June 28, 2010, http://www.brookings.edu/papers/2007/05education_maag.aspx.
State of Texas. Texas Higher Education Coordinating Board. n.d. *Higher education accountability system.* Retrieved June 28, 2010, http://www.txhighereddata.org/Interactive/Accountability/.

Chapter 23
Hispanics and US Schools: Problems, Puzzles, and Possibilities

Marta Tienda

In 2003, the US Census Bureau announced that Hispanics surpassed blacks as the largest US minority group. If this historic milestone is prologue to the future, its social significance is an unfolding, yet uncertain narrative, with the main chapters being scripted in the schools. That fertility, not immigration, currently drives Hispanic population growth has two important implications for US schools and the future contours of educational stratification. First, the youthful age structure of Hispanics will keep demand for education high. Second, four decades of mass migration from Latin America set in motion an unprecedented generational transition that will define the contours of social inequality, depending greatly on the educational attainments of the swelling second generation. In this essay I argue that the success of US schools in closing achievement gaps will determine not only the pace of Hispanic social mobility, but also whether the nation garners a productivity boost by harnessing the Hispanic demographic dividend.

To make my case, I first provide a thumbnail sketch of recent educational trends, spotlighting higher education because of its importance for labor market success. In the interest of parsimony, I do not dwell on differences among Hispanic national origin groups; instead, I emphasize comparisons by nativity because these are particularly salient for understanding the contemporary and future contours of Hispanic educational inequality. After discussing three puzzles and elaborating future research needs to address each, the final section elaborates the potential economic significance of the Hispanic generational transition.

M. Tienda (✉)
Office of Population Research, Princeton University, Princeton, NJ 08544, USA
e-mail: tienda@princeton.edu

Problems in the Pipeline

In a recent report issued by the Educational Testing Service (Tienda 2009), I showed that Hispanics have made remarkable educational gains since 1980, even as disparities between them and other demographic groups widened. In fact, most of Hispanics' educational progress has occurred at the secondary level, and particularly among the foreign born. For example, the 22%-point gap in 1980 high school graduation rates between US-born Hispanics and whites was reduced by more than half over the next 25 years, mainly due to the larger shares of Hispanics earning high school diplomas. Less progress was made among the foreign born, however. Roughly 50% of foreign-born Hispanics aged 25–34 held high school diplomas in 2006, compared with 83% of US-born Hispanics, 86% of blacks, and 94% of non-Hispanic whites. The stagnation of Hispanics' high school graduation rate largely reflects the downward pull from low-skill Latin American immigrants since 1980, which includes many young adults who never attended US schools.

Trends in Hispanics' postsecondary attainment are more worrisome because persisting gaps are not confined to the foreign born. Table 23.1 shows the widening college enrollment gap over the past quarter century, a period when the wage returns to higher education rose appreciably. In 1980, 30% of Hispanic high school graduates ages 18–24 enrolled in college, compared with 28% and 32%, respectively, of blacks and whites. A quarter century later, the Hispanic college enrollment rate rose to 36%, versus 39% for blacks and 44% whites. Thus, not only did African Americans surpass Hispanics in their college enrollment, but the Hispanic–white enrollment gap also rose from two to eight percentage points (Tienda 2009).

Conditional on college enrollment, Hispanics' postsecondary graduation rate also rose over the last 25 years or so, but less than the rate for whites. Thus, even as Hispanic college graduation rates reach an historic high, gaps between them and majority whites remained unchanged for the native born and widened for the foreign born. In 2006, white adults ages 25–34 were almost twice as likely as comparably aged US-born Hispanics, and over three times as likely as foreign-born Hispanics, to graduate from college. Clearly, unskilled Latin American immigration cannot account for the persisting disparities for the US born.

The National Center for Public Policy and Higher Education (2005) portrayed the bleak Hispanic educational pipeline based on a hypothetical ninth grade cohort. Only 53% graduate from high school within 4 years, and a meager 27% attend college immediately after high school. Of the original cohort, 10% graduate within

Table 23.1 College enrollment rates of high school graduates ages 19–24 by race and Hispanic origin, 1980–2006

	1980	1990	2000	2006
White	32	40	44	47
Black	28	33	39	42
Hispanic	30	29	36	36

Source: 2007 *Digest of education statistics*, Table 195

6 years of beginning college. Among the key factors invoked to explain Hispanics' low attainment levels are low parental education and lack of fluency in English, but many researchers also point to their disproportionate representation in ethnically segregated, under-resourced schools. Each of these circumstances raises an important puzzle that warrants further investigation.

Persisting Puzzles: Legacies of Segregation or Institutionalized Discrimination?

The landmark *Brown v. Board of Education* (1954) Supreme Court decision, which struck down racist Jim Crow laws, is widely celebrated for eliminating *de jure*, if not *de facto* school segregation. The decision's applicability to Hispanics, and Mexicans in particular, was unclear because their racial status was ambiguous from a legal standpoint. In fact, *Méndez v. Westminster School District* (1947), not *Brown*, was the first federal case to rule that separate schools are not equal. At that time, California state law sanctioned segregation by requiring Native Americans, Japanese, Chinese, and Mongolians to attend separate public schools, but made no mention of Mexicans. By claiming that Mexicans are white, local authorities throughout California systematically denied them equal protection under the law by routinely invoking language barriers and low cognitive ability to justify their relegation to separate and distinctly inferior schools. Similar practices of "blind" segregation were prevalent in Texas, where officials used language, surname, and physical appearance as race proxies to assign white and Mexican children to schools of differing quality.

Although less notorious than *Brown*, *Hernández v. Texas* (1954) outlawed the "blind" segregation practices used by public officials to exclude Mexicans from jury duty and to deny them civil rights. By the mid-1950s, the majority of Texas Mexicans were US born, yet language barriers were used to justify their systematic exclusion from civic offices and to reinforce school and job segregation. Whether coincidental or not, *Hernández* was argued immediately after *Brown*, and the decision is filed just before *Brown* in the US Supreme Court Reporter volume. Its profound sociological significance is its explicit acknowledgement that race is a social construction based on perceptions, beliefs, and prejudices. In designating Mexicans as "a class apart" that warranted access to equal protection, the *Hernández* decision also broadened the interpretation of the equal protection clause of the Fourteenth Amendment to the US Constitution.

Méndez and *Hernández* originated in the two states with the largest Hispanic populations, both in the 1950s when Hispanics comprised less than 4% of US residents and today, when their population share surpasses 15%. Aguirre (2005) argues that, *Méndez* played a pivotal role in the eventual success of the *Brown* litigation. Supreme Court Chief Justice Earl Warren was governor of California when the *Méndez* decision was rendered, which apparently sensitized him to the egregious inequities endured by minority groups under his watch. Among the most striking parallels between the *Méndez* and *Brown* decisions that Aguirre (2005) outlines are references about: (1) the civic benefits of ethnic co-mingling (*Méndez*) versus claims that exposure to diverse cultural values is a compelling state interest (*Brown*); (2) how segregation limits exposure to English (*Méndez*) versus that it retards mental development (*Brown*); (3) how segregation fosters antagonism and suggests inferiority (*Méndez*), subsequently reformulated to acknowledge that segregation designated the Negro group as inferior (*Brown*); and (5) that separate schools do not serve equal protection (*Méndez*) versus the explicit claim that separate facilities are inherently unequal (*Brown*).

Notwithstanding these five broad parallels between the core elements of the *Méndez* and *Brown* decisions, a major difference is the continued racial ambivalence of Mexicans, which consequently permitted, and in some instances appears to have institutionalized blind segregation well into the twenty-first century. That is, because language has remained a powerful instrument of social exclusion in the schools, both the *Méndez* and *Hernández* decisions are highly relevant for understanding contemporary educational inequalities between Hispanics and whites.

Three puzzles related to the circumstances that provoked the original lawsuits (language, segregation, and social class) warrant further research to determine whether current inequities are legacies of past traditions or represent new, subtle forms of social exclusion. These include: the disproportionate representation of native-born children among English language learners; the rising school segregation of Hispanic students; and the weaker ability of college-educated Hispanic parents to confer their status advantages to their offspring compared with their white counterparts. I elaborate on each with a focus on future research opportunities.

English Language Learners and Academic Achievement

No Child Left Behind (NCLB) imposed new, if imprecise, accountability standards for schools. Title I requires English language learners to be included in state assessments of reading, language arts, and math, thus initially raising new barriers for students not yet proficient in English. NCLB also requires states to administer English language proficiency tests annually to students whose first language is not English. These provisions are designed to generate benchmarks for assessing progress both in English proficiency and academic subjects.

In principle, school accountability for educational progress is a positive development; however, NCLB initially worked to the disadvantage of schools that serve large numbers of limited English-proficient students. Separate reporting of testing results for limited English proficiency (LEP) students not only focused a spotlight on their achievement gaps, but also increased the number of schools that failed to meet yearly progress benchmarks.

There exists a general presumption that the majority of LEP students are foreign born, but data indicate otherwise. The Urban Institute claims that 75% of elementary school students classified as LEP, and over half of LEP students enrolled in grades 6–12 are US born. If reports that large numbers of LEP students fail to achieve minimal academic standards implicate immigration, it does not explain why three quarters of LEP students are US born. Because they begin their education in English, US-born school children should not need special English language services, and certainly not on a prolonged basis, even if their parents are foreign born or lack fluency in English. It is puzzling, therefore, that the majority of long-term English language learners (ELLS) are native-born citizens, many of them residing in states that passed English Only Laws.

Language is frequently invoked as a reason for the underperformance of Hispanics today, just as it was in Texas and California during the 1950s, raising the possibility that blind segregation based on English proficiency operates to thwart the academic achievement of all Hispanic students, just as it did in Texas and California before the *Méndez* and *Hernández* decisions. State education agencies use home language surveys, teacher observation, teacher interviews, and parent information for classifying LEP students, but these criteria are applied inconsistently across states and even across districts *within* states. Over half of state education agencies also use student records, grades, informal assessments, and referrals to classify students as limited English proficient. Some of these criteria are objective, but many are highly subjective. Using student records and "informal assessments" to classify children often results in misclassification due to unverified assumptions about the extent to which a second language is used in the home, by whom, and for what purposes. Furthermore, student records may reveal deficiencies accumulated over time due to poor instruction, not lack of English proficiency.

To address whether and in what ways blind segregation contributes to the Hispanic achievement gap, future research should first address the influence of LEP designation in producing achievement gaps, particularly for US-born children who begin their scholastic instruction in English. Even more important is the need for a longitudinal study that compares the achievement of native-born LEP students who are exposed to different English language interventions. If designation as LEP status is the contemporary version of blind segregation in a post-*Méndez* and *Hernández* world, then it is conceivable that the achievement gap has been manufactured via the remedial approach to language arts for Hispanic youth, which likely compounds their failure to master academic subjects. In addition, how students are initially classified as limited English proficient, especially those who begin their US education in primary school, warrants systematic evaluation.

I hypothesize that Hispanic students who are not compelled to sit in remedial classes from first grade forward will advance academically faster than their statistical counterparts who are placed in classrooms for non-native speakers, particularly if they begin their US schooling in the primary grades. Furthermore, given the legal precedents acknowledging that language segregation reproduced academic underachievement, it is also critical to investigate the complicity of schools and their administrators in generating Hispanic–white education gaps by accepting earmarked funds based on the number of students designated as limited English proficient. Addressing whether targeted funding for LEP students has become a pernicious incentive to subsidize school budgets also warrants systematic empirical investigation either to prove or refute the panoply of anecdotes about how schools hold back proficient students in order to qualify for Title I funds.

Resegregation and Achievement

A second, puzzle, which is related to the concentration of Hispanic students in remedial English instruction programs, concerns the resegregation of public schools during the post-Civil Rights period. There is ample social science and legal evidence that school segregation, particularly in the context of concentrated poverty, poses formidable barriers to academic success. Therefore, the rising levels of Hispanic school segregation since school districts were allowed to end their court-ordered segregation plans bode ill for Hispanic students. In 2000, for example, Hispanic students disproportionately attended segregated schools where over half of the student body qualified for free or reduced lunch. Nearly 40% of Hispanic students attend high schools where over half of entering ninth graders graduate in 4 years.

These trends raise an important question about the social forces through which segregation fosters academic (under) achievement, and in particular whether the contemporary mechanisms are similar to those prevalent during the first half of the twentieth century. The resegregation of Hispanic students is puzzling because this trend coincides with an unprecedented geographic dispersal beginning in the late 1980s and continuing through the first decade of the twenty-first century. That recent immigrants and their families were major players in the residential dispersal provides a unique research opportunity to evaluate *the process* of school segregation and its association with academic achievement. Several research questions suggest themselves.

First, how does segregation of Hispanic students differ in the traditional and nontraditional destinations? Second, is the association between segregation and academic performance similar in the new and traditional destinations and if not, how does it differ? Third, to what extent is segregation the product of covert mechanisms, such as those used in California and Texas during the pre-Civil Rights period, and what role does language play in academic tracking of Hispanic students in the schools that are unaccustomed to serving ethnically distinct populations?

As the *Méndez* and *Hernández* decisions revealed, blind segregation is an effective social exclusion mechanism; moreover, it is often more difficult to combat than overt discrimination. Therefore, future research should consider not only differences in the assignment of Hispanic students across schools to evaluate how segregation promotes underachievement, but also *within* schools via academic tracking and assignment to remedial language arts courses. Finally, determining whether and how Hispanics may be differentially impacted by the charter school movement and the proliferation of voucher programs warrants further investigation to determine whether these developments aggravate or attenuate unequal participation of Hispanics in underperforming schools.

Unequal Mobility or Institutionalized Discrimination?

Most research about the Hispanic–white achievement addresses the K–12 experience, but given the growing importance of postsecondary education for labor market success, there is rising research interest in postsecondary outcomes. Most studies of college gaps, whether focused on enrollment, persistence, or completion, emphasize differences in family background as core explanatory factors. This body of evidence presumes that if Hispanic parents' educational attainment were comparable to that of whites, their postsecondary achievement gaps would be nonexistent. An implicit assumption is that the *rate of mobility* is uniform between Hispanic and white parents of similar education.

Using four longitudinal surveys, Alon and her colleagues (2010) show that parental educational attainment explains only part of the Hispanic–white college enrollment gap, and that college-educated Hispanic parents are handicapped in their ability to confer status advantages to their offspring. Moreover, this handicap is not limited to the foreign born. The authors were unable to explain why this should be so, but given the broad implications of their result for the mobility prospects of the fastest growing population segment, their claim warrants further verification and explanation of the underlying mechanisms.

Several tenable hypotheses should be subjected to empirical scrutiny. First, it is conceivable that college-educated Hispanic parents have lower stocks of social capital, either because they attended less selective universities with weak alumni networks, or because they received their education abroad. Second, as a process, college orientation begins well before high school, and admissibility to a selective postsecondary institution hinges on the sequencing of key courses in math and science in the middle grades as well as preparation for the PSAT and SAT examinations. It is plausible that the lower educational transmission rates of college-educated Hispanic parents reflect their lack of knowledge about these core antecedents of postsecondary admission. Furthermore, if the offspring of Hispanic college-educated parents attend high schools that have lower college-going traditions compared with college-educated white parents, this may also contribute to the unequal ability of Hispanic parents to transmit their status advantage to their children. A third possibility is that admissions officers discriminate against Hispanic students that allegedly have the class advantages of their parents in favor of low-income students who are eligible for federal financial aid. Adjudicating among these alternative hypotheses is likely to generate more policy-relevant evidence compared with past studies showing that Hispanic parents average less education than all other demographic groups except, perhaps, Native Americans.

Promise and Possibility: Why Everyone Should Care

Despite improvements in educational levels, recent trends are worrisome because they occur in the context of widening disparities at the postsecondary level. Demography is not destiny, but the burgeoning Hispanic school-age population represents a formidable risk for the nation if the achievement gap is allowed to continue down its current path. Because the majority of the Hispanic second generation currently is enrolled in school, as a group it offers the nation a unique opportunity to reap a demographic dividend – that is, a productivity boost enabled by a youthful age structure. At a time of rising global competition with both developed and developing nations (especially China and India, but also Brazil), the United States can ill afford to under invest in human capital.

That Hispanics are coming of age in an aging society further underscores the urgency of closing Hispanic–white educational achievement gaps, which is the responsibility of the education system. As the predominantly white baby boom generation approaches retirement, it is in the national interest to educate the students who will replace them in the labor market. Schools will play a major part in determining not only the shape of ethnic stratification, but also whether the nation will retain its economic status on the world stage. Finally, it bears emphasizing that future research in educational stratification will be better served by asking what new insights about how schools operate and about intergenerational transmission processes emerge from studying Hispanics, rather than confining themselves to conventional questions about how Hispanics differ from other groups.

References

Aguirre, Frederick P. 2005. *Mendez v. Westminster School District*: How it affected *Brown v. Board of Education*. *Journal of Hispanic Higher Education* 7(4): 321–332.

Alon, Sigal, Thurston Domina, and Marta Tienda. 2010. Stymied mobility or temporary lull? The puzzle of lagging Hispanic college degree attainment. *Social Forces* 88(4): 1807–1832.

Brown v. Board of Education of Topeka, 347 U.S. 483 (1954).

Hernandez v. Texas, 347 U.S. 475 (1954).

Mendez v. Westminster School District, 161 F.2d 774 (9th Cir. 1947).

National Center for Public Policy and Higher Education. 2005. *Income of U.S. workforce projected to decline if education doesn't improve*. Policy Alert. National Center for Public Policy and Higher Education.

Tienda, Marta. 2009. *Hispanicity and educational inequality: Risks, opportunities and the nation's future*. 25th Tomás Rivera Lecture. Princeton: Educational Testing Service.

Index

A
A2i software, 116
Ability grouping, 112, 114, 115, 117, 118
Abstinence programs, 185
Academic
    achievement, 18–20, 23, 24, 43, 45, 53, 55, 93, 127, 192, 195, 208, 211, 213, 245–249, 267, 271, 278, 279, 290, 306–308
    attainment, 265, 266, 268, 269
    intelligence, 18–20, 23, 27, 30
    performance, 17, 19, 40, 41, 112, 114, 118, 166, 168, 211, 217, 265, 308
    preparation, 23, 247, 248
    productivity, 168
Accountability system, 163–165, 242, 273
Achievement
    gap(s), 46, 55, 115, 118, 166, 170, 172, 227–232, 258, 259, 266, 268, 303, 306, 307, 309, 310
    trajectories, 119, 120
Adequate yearly progress, 164, 273
Admission policies, 188
Adolescent social structure, 94
Adolescents, 41, 94, 127, 182, 185, 197, 211, 217
African American, 64–66, 69, 74, 75, 218, 237, 258, 286, 304
Algorithm, 4, 116
Alpha trials, 128
Alternate degrees, 198
American
    educational system, 38, 39
    higher education, 13, 54, 298
    schools, 61, 65, 247, 257–262
Amoral education, 281
Aptitude-treatment interaction, 115, 116
Archdiocese of Chicago, 284
Asian American, 237
Assessment, 5, 18, 38. 111, 116, 117, 122, 132, 134, 137, 140, 148, 165–170, 172–174, 177, 228, 233, 239, 246, 254, 258, 259, 274, 294, 306, 307
Assessment tests, 258
Associate degrees, 183, 187, 188, 194, 197, 199, 200
Attainment research, 94, 97
Augmentation, 91–92, 95–97

B
Bachelor degree, 25, 182, 186–188, 194, 197, 199, 200, 230
BA-for-all movement, 182, 183, 185–191, 197
Barriers
    normative, 213
    political, 113
Behavioral
    data, 4, 104
    dynamics, 92
Beta investigations, 128
Broad Foundation, 275
Budget crises, 286
Busing, 54, 61–64, 66, 68–70, 72, 73, 76

C
Carnegie Foundation for the Advancement of Teaching, 127, 132, 289
Catholic schooling, 283, 284
Causal modeling, 16
Cell phones, 87, 102, 103
Certificate programs, 194

Change interventions, 290
Charter schools, 3, 269, 273, 274, 278, 286, 288, 289, 308
Child Health Insurance Program (CHIP), 267
Christian-Right politics, 283
Citizenship, 15, 242, 246, 249
Civic
  achievement gap, 258, 259
  education, 257–262, 278
  engagement, 258–262
  literacy, 258
  participation, 259, 261
Civil Rights, 56, 58, 64–66, 69–71, 75, 77, 78, 305, 308
Class size, 290, 291
Classroom
  organization, 4
  pedagogy, 278
  practice, 166, 168, 288
Cognition, 14, 18–21, 23, 101, 118, 158
Cognitive development, 20–21, 24, 28
Cognitive function, 13, 14, 16, 19, 20, 24
Collective action, 87, 130, 138, 156, 158, 168
College
  credit, 189–193, 195
  enrollment gap, 304, 309
  graduation, 129, 242, 304
  placement tests, 191
  readiness, 191
Common school movement, 257
Community college, 127–129, 131, 133, 134, 138–140, 144, 146, 148, 155, 158–160, 181, 183, 187–196, 199, 200, 236, 239, 289
Comparative studies, 2, 3, 41
Competency exams, 191
Conceptual frameworks, 145, 155, 160, 243, 244
Conservative Protestant schools, 283
Consortium on Chicago School Research, 138, 242
Continuous improvement, 134, 144, 146–148, 153, 243, 289
Cooling out, 181–183, 191, 194, 196
Coping strategies, 130
Course taking, 99, 138
Creationism, 283
Crime rates, 236
Cultural consciousness, 87
Culture, 6, 7, 11–31, 58, 59, 64, 69, 100, 174, 229, 245, 248, 249, 279, 282, 283, 285, 290

Curricular differentiation, 41
Curricular reform, 166
Curriculum, 3, 14, 21–24, 27, 41, 54, 99, 132, 139, 140, 176, 231, 253, 254, 260, 261, 273, 279, 287
Cyber-bullying, 88

D

Data-based decisions, 117, 242
Data management procedures, 292
Data-to-practice pipeline, 243
Degree attainment, 11, 24
Degree completion, 187–189, 193, 196
Democracy, 11, 235, 246, 249, 250, 258, 259, 281
Democratic citizenship, 246, 249
Democratic government, 259
Democrats for Education Reform, 275
Demographic change, 42
Dependent variables, 91, 92, 285, 290–292
Desegregation, 3, 54, 59, 61–73, 76, 77, 285, 286
Design-Educational Engineering and Development (DEED), 128
Detracking, 113
Developmental mathematics, 127, 133, 134, 138, 151
Diagnosis and instructional response, 115–118, 122
Differential teacher effects, 119–121, 123
Differentiation, 4, 41, 46, 99, 112–114, 118
Diffusion, 12, 87, 252, 254
Digital media, 94, 157, 260
Disaggregation, 241
Discrimination, 67, 68, 77, 212, 229, 237, 305–309
Disinvestment in education, 235–239
Dissemination, 238, 254–255
Dropout rates, 208, 227, 235, 266
Dropouts, 194, 227, 235
Drug use, 93, 236
Dyadic modeling, 103

E

Economic background, 38, 118, 267, 300
Economics, 2, 3, 6, 12, 14, 15, 17, 18, 22, 24, 28, 30, 38, 40, 42, 118, 166, 174, 176, 187, 205, 207, 209–212, 215, 216, 218, 234, 235, 247, 248, 258, 265,–268, 270, 274, 278, 297, 298, 300, 303, 310
Educational
  achievement, 3, 7, 11, 17, 30, 46, 209, 310

Index

attainment(s), 12, 16–18, 29, 40, 44–46, 99, 176, 205, 211, 215, 218, 303, 309
expectations, 40, 41, 181, 210
inequality, 44, 73, 303
institutions, 42, 235–237, 251, 268
meritocracy, 30
outcomes, 3, 40, 43, 46, 205–208, 210, 213, 214, 216, 218, 266, 270
policy, 1–7, 15, 42, 54, 57–62, 78, 164, 206, 207, 217, 248, 278
reform, 5, 56, 169, 186, 239, 254
research, 1, 4, 5, 7, 30–31, 88, 91, 127–129, 132, 207, 247, 249, 251, 254, 255, 274
stratification, 29–30, 43, 303, 310
theory, 2, 7
trends, 303
Education for All Handicapped Children Act, 59
Education policymaking, 275
Education reform, 55, 56, 63, 275
Education Reform Now, 275
Education revolution, 2, 11–20, 22–30
Education structure, 24, 215, 217
Effective schools, 286
Elementary and Secondary Education Act (ESEA), 59, 241, 246, 248, 274
Empirical reality, 88, 89
Empty spaces, 53–79
Endogenous network processes, 92
English language learners (ELLS), 241, 306–307
English language proficiency tests, 306
Environmental cues, 237
Equal Educational Opportunities Act, 68–70
Equal protection clause, 71
Essential Supports, 242, 243
Ethnicity, 4, 122, 174, 175, 279, 283, 286, 294
Evidence-based solutions, 242
Evidence-based tools, 243, 244
Evolution, 2, 7, 93, 137, 158, 161, 283
Expectations, 6, 17, 28, 37, 40, 41, 43, 112, 123, 131, 144, 151, 156, 174, 176, 181, 182, 192, 210, 236, 237, 291

F
Facebook, 87, 135, 292
Failure rates, 133, 139, 151, 183, 197
Family characteristics, 174, 267

Family structure, 6, 7, 39, 206–210, 212–214, 217, 218, 229
Federal government, 60, 63, 71, 164, 234, 247, 259, 277, 278, 286, 288
Finance equalization, 68, 288
Financial services, 297
Flexible skill grouping, 117
Formative assessment, 117, 168
Fourteenth Amendment, 305
Four-year graduation rate, 299
Free public education, 258
Freshman retention rate, 299

G
Gaming the system, 275
Gatekeeper, 20, 43, 188
Gates Foundation, 127, 166, 200, 275, 288
Gender, 16, 26, 29, 44, 45, 78, 94, 135, 137, 206, 212, 219, 237, 247, 280
General education, 251–255, 277
Global economy, 278
Global society, 1, 2, 7, 35, 36, 42
Globalization, 2, 26, 36, 37, 42, 45
Governmental agencies, 236, 277
Grade completion, 266
Grades, 12, 19, 20, 23, 96, 103, 119, 172, 183, 186, 189, 228, 229, 264–271, 282, 306, 307, 309
Graduation rates, 6, 129, 133, 199, 270, 275, 300, 304
Great Recession, 278, 297
Great Society, 228, 277, 286
Guidance counselors, 6, 181, 182, 186, 188

H
Harlem Children's Zone (HCZ), 268
Health insurance, 57, 267, 297
Hierarchical linear modeling, 88
High school
  counselor, 191
  dropout rates, 235
  graduation rates, 304
Higher education productivity, 297
High-stakes testing, 274, 275, 279
Hispanic, 65, 66, 166, 216, 227–229, 258, 266, 286, 293, 294, 303–310
  generational transition, 303
  social mobility, 303
Historians, 244, 247–249, 277, 279, 280

Home schooling, 283
Homework completion, 268
Homogeneous subsets, 112

I
iCivics, 261, 262
Ideals, 182–184, 191, 194, 198, 200
Identity, 91, 157, 159, 238
Immigration, 45, 46, 215, 258, 279, 283, 286, 303, 304, 306
Immigration policies, 45
Inclusionary practices, 286
Independent variables, 290
Inequality, 41, 42, 44, 55, 58, 60–63, 65–67, 71–73, 76, 77, 111–114, 118, 121–123, 247, 265, 282, 303
Inference, 19, 147, 149, 154, 171, 194, 198, 285, 290–294
Inferential methods, 88
Information technology, 286–287
Institutional
 differentiation, 99
 influences on education, 6
 discrimination, 305–306, 308–309
 politics, 56, 57, 62
 procedures, 181, 199, 200
Instructional
 activities, 116
 design, 115
 diagnosis, 118
 differentiation, 4, 41, 46, 99, 112–114, 118
 strategies, 117
Integration, 36, 42, 46, 47, 63, 65, 68, 69, 78, 88, 142, 290
Interaction between research and practice, 4
Interconnected systems, 88
Interdependency, 88, 89, 92, 97
Interdependent data sets, 89
Intergenerational mobility, 16, 17, 95
International research, 36–42, 47, 114
Internet, 89, 102, 260–262, 292
Inter-societal research, 39

J
Jobs, 11, 12, 22, 25–28, 157, 187, 188, 194, 196, 197, 199, 230, 259, 260

L
Language barriers, 305
Latin American immigration, 304

Learning, 1, 2, 4–7, 14, 15, 20–23, 41, 43, 61, 87, 89, 104, 111–123, 127, 129, 131–135, 137, 138, 141, 143–149, 153, 154, 156, 157, 159, 160, 163, 167–169, 173, 175–177, 231–233, 237, 238, 241, 242, 245, 248, 250–254, 258, 260–262, 267, 282, 287, 290, 292
 opportunities, 2, 3, 38, 40, 43, 44, 53, 59, 61, 63, 64, 68–71, 76–78, 94, 96, 98, 99, 111, 114–115, 118, 141, 143, 145, 147, 157, 160, 163, 171, 174, 176, 177, 183, 199, 236, 257, 258, 261, 267, 270, 284, 287, 306
 theories, 1, 15, 18, 35, 36, 39, 41, 42, 46, 47, 56, 93, 97, 98, 115, 130, 160, 205, 207, 208, 212, 214, 215, 269, 283, 294
Learning by doing, 250
Limited English proficiency (LEP), 306, 307
Linked-in, 87
Longitudinal achievement data, 120

M
Mass education, 11–13, 17, 37
Mass media, 26, 274
Master degrees, 188
Measurement, 147–149, 153, 160, 164, 167, 168, 266, 285, 290–295
Mental health, 25, 213, 231, 233
Mental illnesses, 238
Methodological individualism, 101, 102
Methodology, 88, 120, 134, 175, 247, 285, 289–291
Methods, 1, 3, 17, 21, 88–94, 101, 103, 104, 142, 146, 150, 171, 193, 198, 218, 239, 240, 279, 290–295
Metrics, 96, 160, 241, 247–249, 301
Mexican American, 66, 67, 77
Million-dollar payoff, 186–188, 190
Misinformation, 261
Mobility patterns, 181
Models, 1, 3, 5, 29, 46, 56, 88, 89, 91–98, 103, 104, 119–121, 167, 171, 173, 174, 182, 198, 289, 292
Moral
 authority, 64, 155, 163, 164
 education, 281, 282
 relativism, 281, 282
Morality, 281–284
Moving to Opportunity (MTO) program, 270

Index

N
National Assessment of Educational Progress (NAEP), 170, 228, 246, 258, 274, 293, 294
National average gains, 294
National mean score, 294
National Research Council, 146, 291
Neighborhood context, 266–268
Neoinstitutional theory, 15
Network augmentation, 95–97
Networked communities, 135
Neutral organization, 112
No Child Left Behind (NCLB), 7, 59, 137, 164, 241, 258, 266, 273, 278, 306
Nonprofit agencies, 236
Normative behavior, 16

O
Obama administration, 233, 243, 274
Occupational
  attainment, 14
  pathways, 99
  training, 194–197
Online
  civics curriculum, 261
  courses, 287
  games, 251
Open admissions, 185, 188–191, 300
Optimal matching, 115, 118–121, 123
Organizational differentiation, 99
Origin, 16–18, 29, 46, 69, 75, 212, 303, 304
Outcomes theory, 39

P
Paradigmatic statistical methods, 88
Parental
  choice, 77
  educational attainment, 309
  expectations, 174
Parenting roles, 16
Path-dependent process, 58, 61
Peer effects models, 91
Peer group interactions, 236
Perfectionist model, 182–199
Performance expectations, 236
Physical health, 268
Pluralistic society, 282, 284
Policy
  decisions, 54, 273
  development process, 54, 57, 60, 61, 78
  legacies, 56, 57, 61, 72, 77, 78, 305–306
Policymaking, 58, 59, 67, 68, 273–275

Political influences on education, 3
Political theory, 53, 60
Postindustrial culture, 11–31
Postsecondary
  attainment, 304
  education, 61, 308
  graduation rate, 304
  institutions, 166, 175
Poverty, 59, 63, 67, 227, 229, 231, 236, 245, 247, 266, 270, 279, 280, 291, 308
Prior achievement, 120–122, 172, 181, 199
Private enterprise, 297
Privatization, 274, 275
Productivity, 112, 114, 117, 132, 167–170, 248, 287, 297–299, 309
Promise neighborhoods initiative, 268
Public
  colleges, 296–301
  data, 241
  education, 53–79, 235–239, 241, 242, 257, 258, 265, 274
  opinion, 73, 274
  policy, 24, 128, 129, 170, 207, 267, 275, 304
  school re-segregation, 308
  schools, 54, 55, 60–64, 67, 68, 71, 72, 74, 75, 77, 114, 166, 190, 199, 238, 243, 244, 246, 257, 259, 264–269, 271, 277–279, 281, 305, 308
  school system, 72, 74, 267, 269, 271, 283
  universities, 297, 298

Q
Quality control measures, 299
Quantitative analysis, 90, 246, 271

R
Race, 4, 63, 64, 66, 68, 69, 75, 76, 122, 174, 175, 209, 212, 214, 216, 237, 243–245, 247, 274, 279, 283, 304, 305
Race to the Top (RTTT), 243, 274, 279
Racial divide, 54, 60–62, 76
Racial segregation, 76, 245, 266
Reality mining, 90, 102
Redesign networks, 88
Reform, 2, 4, 5, 7, 44, 53–59, 61–74, 77–79, 131, 141, 163, 165, 166, 169, 171, 185, 186, 199, 238, 239, 241–244, 251–255, 267, 271, 274, 275, 278, 285–295

Relational trust, 93, 165, 269
Religion, 6, 11, 24, 281–284
Religious faith, 283
Religious practice, 283
Remedial courses, 192–195, 197, 198
Research and development (R&D), 127–130, 132, 135, 137, 145, 154, 155, 159–161
Residential segregation, 265
Road networks, 99

S

School
    accountability, 306
    attendance, 5, 18, 208, 232, 241
    characteristics, 3, 174
    choice, 42, 71–72, 74, 269, 270
    desegregation, 61, 62, 64, 65, 68, 69, 73, 285, 286
    improvement, 4, 153, 166, 242, 244, 249, 278
    organization, 4, 90, 111, 170, 171, 173, 174, 278
    performance, 169–171, 213, 229, 242, 266, 268
    policy, 3, 277, 280
    productivity, 167
    reform, 1, 2, 4, 44, 55, 57, 58, 77–79, 131, 163, 238, 241–244, 271, 278, 287
    segregation, 65, 77, 305, 308
    truancy, 268
Schooled society, 11–31, 43
Schools of education, 238, 247, 248
Segregation, 63–67, 69, 76, 77, 113, 245, 265–271, 279, 280, 305–308
Self-esteem, 236, 237
Semester credit hours, 299
Sexual abstinence movement, 182, 184
Shadow education, 42–44
Siblings, 39, 40, 211
Six-year graduation rate, 299
Skill-based grouping, 114, 117
Skill development, 236, 237, 239
Social
    capital, 3, 89, 95, 96, 144, 168, 182, 194, 205, 269, 309
    class, 15, 18, 29, 42, 122, 229, 279, 282, 290, 291, 299, 306
    development, 22, 164, 233
    inequalities, 4, 78, 112
    inequality, 111, 303
    institutions, 1, 13, 14, 24, 30, 277, 280
    media, 87
    mobility, 11, 16–18, 31, 45, 163, 285, 303
    network, 2–4, 7, 87, 92, 93, 95–99, 101, 260
    networking, 260, 261
    networks, 2–4, 7, 92, 93, 96, 97, 99, 101
    norms, 113, 212, 215, 238, 268
    organization, 5, 128, 130, 135, 146, 163, 269
    organization of schools, 163
    phenomena, 88, 97, 102, 254
    psychology, 159, 235–239
    services, 236, 267
    status, 13, 14, 16–18, 29, 113
    vulnerability, 266–267
Societal context, 35, 42
Societal factors, 2
Socioeconomic
    background, 38, 267
    segregation, 265–271
    status (SES), 17, 38, 40, 44, 213, 291
Sociograms, 94
Sociological Abstracts, 277–279
Sociological investigation, 13, 28, 29
Sociological studies, 207, 278, 280
Sociology of Education, 1, 2, 7, 13, 29, 35–47, 53, 87–104, 111, 113, 163, 165, 169, 207, 251, 281–294
Standardization, 38, 42, 300
Standardized graduation rate, 300
Standardized graduation tests, 301
Standardized test(ing), 42, 168, 169, 172, 236, 241, 249, 278, 280, 301
Standardized test scores, 92
Standard regression models, 91
Standards-based reforms, 286
Standards movement, 165, 248
Statewide accountability system, 273
Statewide Longitudinal Data Systems, 167, 171
Static networks, 88
Status attainment, 11, 13, 16–18, 24, 40, 53, 89, 90, 94–96, 101, 181, 183, 185, 186, 205, 267
Stereotype threat, 159, 236, 237
Stereotyping, 237
Stochastic-based models, 93
Stratification, 11, 13, 14, 18, 29–31, 43, 44, 163, 176, 181–200, 303, 310
Structuring agents, 130, 135, 139, 145, 156, 158
Student
    ability, 6, 113, 268
    achievement, 46, 54, 91, 116, 117, 119, 120, 165, 167, 168, 171, 191, 271, 288, 292, 294

assessment data, 117, 166
background characteristics, 167, 174
motivation, 27, 129, 165, 169, 174, 176
outcomes, 2, 3, 241, 242, 266, 290
performance, 44, 116, 117, 119, 164–171, 279
test performance, 121
Student/counselor ratio, 189
Summer learning loss, 175, 232
Systemic change, 288
Systemwide reform, 287

T
Targeted instruction, 111
Tax revenue, 298
Teacher
accountability, 163, 164, 173
assessment and accountability, 5
autonomy, 115
career satisfaction, 176
certification, 175
characteristics, 174, 291
collegiality, 165
effectiveness, 5, 27, 113, 118–121, 130, 149, 163, 165–169, 171–177, 232, 234, 268, 278, 287, 289, 290
effects, 119–123, 167, 171–175, 274
expectations, 237
hiring, 176
performance, 5, 164, 165, 169, 171
professional development, 165
professionalism, 165–166
recruitment, 166
remediation, 163, 174, 185, 191–192, 194, 246
social supports, 217, 218, 238
Teacher–student relationships, 169, 175, 236, 269
Teach for America (TFA), 166, 175, 176
Teaching profession, 5, 166, 278
Teach to the test, 279
Test
scaling, 172
score data, 241, 242
score performance, 167, 170
scores, 5, 20, 92, 103, 120, 164, 166, 171, 172, 174, 215, 242, 244, 246–248, 250, 273, 274, 278, 279, 282
Test-based accountability, 286
Testing, 35, 37, 43, 131, 151, 165, 173, 246–248, 258, 274, 275, 278–280, 290, 304, 306

Theoretical models, 29, 56, 289
Theories of education, 35, 42–43, 47, 56
Theory building, 39
Tracking, 41, 42, 87, 99, 112–114, 117, 121, 123, 174, 199, 282
Training institutions, 175–176
Training programs, 166, 175, 236
Transactional data, 4, 102
Transactionalism, 87–104
Transition from school to work, 5
Tuition tax credits, 64, 71, 72
Twitter, 292

U
Unemployment, 207, 236, 267
Unequal learning opportunities, 111
Unequal mobility, 308–309
Universal propositions, 39
Urban
black families, 266, 267
ghetto, 69, 70
neighborhoods, 266, 267, 270, 283, 284
public schools, 265–271
school reform, 55, 271

V
Value-added
analysis, 119
methodology, 88, 120, 134, 144, 175, 247, 285, 289–291
models (VAM), 5, 119–121, 167, 171, 177
performance, 168
scores, 5, 20, 24, 41, 60, 92, 103, 116, 117, 119–121, 164–166, 168–174, 192, 193, 195, 215, 228, 242, 244, 246–248, 250, 273–275, 278, 279, 282, 293, 294
Variable-centric methods, 91
Vocabulary, 116, 117, 229, 231
Vocational courses, 22
Vouchers, 3, 54, 60, 61, 63–68, 71, 72, 74–78, 275, 278

W
Walton Family Foundation, 275
Warm ups, 192
Welfare, 55–59, 74, 207, 208, 267
Workplace norms, 167